TRANSNATIONAL CINEMA IN A GLOBAL NORTH

Contemporary Approaches to Film and Television Series

A complete listing of the books in this series can be found online at http://wsupress.wayne.edu

GENERAL EDITOR

BARRY KEITH GRANT
Brock University

ADVISORY EDITORS

PATRICIA B. ERENS
School of the Art
Institute of Chicago

LUCY FISCHER
University of Pittsburgh

PETER LEHMAN
Arizona State University

CAREN J. DEMING
University of Arizona

ROBERT J. BURGOYNE
Wayne State University

TOM GUNNING
University of Chicago

ANNA McCARTHY
New York University

PETER X. FENG
University of Delaware

TRANSNATIONAL CINEMA IN A GLOBAL NORTH

Nordic Cinema in Transition

Edited by
ANDREW NESTINGEN
and
TREVOR G. ELKINGTON

WAYNE STATE UNIVERSITY PRESS   DETROIT

Copyright © 2005 by Wayne State University Press,
Detroit, Michigan 48201. All rights are reserved.
No part of this book may be reproduced without formal permission.

09 08 07 06   5 4 3 2

Library of Congress Cataloging-in-Publication Data

Transnational cinema in a global north : Nordic cinema in transition / edited by
Andrew Nestingen and Trevor G. Elkington.
p. cm. — (Contemporary approaches to film and television series)
Includes index.
ISBN 0-8143-3243-9 (pbk. : alk. paper)
1. Motion pictures—Scandinavia. I. Nestingen, Andrew K. II. Elkington, Trevor G. (Trevor
Glen), 1970– III. Series.
PN1993.5.S2T73 2005
791.43'0948—dc22
2004021360

∞ The paper used in this publication meets the minimum requirements
of the American National Standard for Information Sciences—
Permanence of Paper for Printed Library Materials, ANSI Z39.48–1984.

Grateful acknowledgment is made to The Graduate School Fund for Excellence & Innovation (GSFEI) of the University of Washington Graduate School and to the University of Washington Department of Scandinavian Studies Sverre Arestad Scandinavian Research Fund for generous support of the publication of this volume.

For LILA and OLAF STORAASLI
and JONNA GRØNVER and STEEN MØLLER JENSEN

Contents

Acknowledgments ix

Introduction: Transnational Nordic Cinema 1
Trevor G. Elkington and Andrew Nestingen

I. Trends in Transitional Nordic Cinema

1. Costumes, Adolescence, and Dogma: Nordic Film and American Distribution 31
Trevor G. Elkington

2. "Immigrant Film" in Sweden at the Millennium 55
Rochelle Wright

3. Film according to Dogma: Ground Rules, Obstacles, and Liberations 73
Peter Schepelern

II. The State and Film Markets in Transnational Times

4. The Danish Way: Danish Film Culture in a European and Global Perspective 111
Ib Bondebjerg

5. Breaking the Borders: Danish Coproductions in the 1990s 141
Pil Gundelach Brandstrup and Eva Novrup Redvall

6. Art or Industry? Battles over Finnish Cinema during the 1990s 165
Mervi Pantti

7. From Epiphanic Culture to Circulation: The Dynamics of Globalization in Nordic Cinema 191
Mette Hjort

Contents

III. Auteurism and Genre in Transnational Context

8. Globalization and the Auteur: Ingmar Bergman Projected Internationally 221
   Linda Haverty Rugg

9. "I'm a Lumberjack and I'm Okay": Popular Film as Collective Therapy in Markku Pölönen's *A Summer by the River* 243
   Thomas A. DuBois

10. Learning from Genre: Genre Cycles in Modern Norwegian Cinema 261
    Gunnar Iversen

11. Aki Kaurismäki's Crossroads: National Cinema and the Road Movie 279
    Andrew Nestingen

12. In and Out of Reykjavik: Framing Iceland in the Global Daze 307
    Birgir Thor Møller

13. Hrafn Gunnlaugsson—The Viking Who Came in from the Cold? 341
    Bjørn Sørenssen

   Contributors 357
   Index 361

Acknowledgments

This book consists of many handprints, all of which have helped mold its final shape. Our sincere thanks go to the contributors for their professional and enthusiastic participation, as well as their patience. We wish to thank Mette Hjort in particular for her participation in the panel "Global North: Nordic Cinema and Globalization" at the Society for Cinema and Media Studies meeting in Minneapolis, 2003, where some of the ideas for the book were first presented. Many who didn't contribute an article played a crucial role in the publication of the book. Rune Christensen of University of California, Davis, translated two of the essays with speed and precision. Peter Leonard provided technological fixes on order, and at the last minute, on several occasions. Research assistance that contributed to the volume has been provided along the way by two graduate students in the Department of Scandinavian Studies at the University of Washington, Hailey Lanward and Mia Spangenberg, for which we extend many thanks. Linda Norkool and Dagmar Patterson provided help in preparing the manuscript at key moments. The chair of the Scandinavian Studies Department, Professor Terje Leiren, also contributed to the publication of the book through the Sverre Arestad Scandinavian Research Fund, as well as in other ways. The University of Washington Graduate School supported the project, for which we're grateful. Thanks are also due to Rasmus Thord at Memfis Film, Sweden, who arranged for the cover image from *Jalla! Jalla!* (Josef Fares, 2000). The Norwegian Film Institute also provided some of the images in the volume. Warm thanks for all of the help!

It's a special pleasure to note the readers who improved the volume, from the level of the sentence to the organization of the volume. Robin DuBlanc smoothed out many kinks through her careful and thoughtful copyediting. Tytti Soila, Gorham Kindem, an anonymous reader at Wayne State University Press, and series editor Barry Keith Grant offered careful, substantive, and rich suggestions. Their readings of the manuscript corrected errors, anticipated problems, and pointed toward changes that improved the final volume. The book is better for their criticism; we're grateful and wiser for their involvement in the

Acknowledgments

project. We also wish to thank our editors, Kristin Harpster Lawrence and, especially, Jane Hoehner, for their proactive support and generous encouragement of this project from its earliest moments.

Some of the work that appears here is published with the permission of Museum Tusculanum. Peter Schepelern's essay appears in Danish as "Filmen ifølge Dogme: Spilleregler, forhindringer og befrielser" in *Nationale Spejlinger* (Museum Tusculanums Forlag, 2003) edited by Anders Toftgaard and Ian Halvdan Hawkesworth. Trevor Elkington's essay "Costumes, Children, and Dogma: Nordic Film and American Distribution" from the present volume also appears in an alternate, Danish translation in *Nationale spejlinger*. We're grateful to the Museum Tusculanum for allowing the articles to be published in English here.

Finally, our sincerest thanks go to our students, colleagues, and friends whose comments, questions, and criticisms have made an immeasurable contribution.

Introduction:
Transnational Nordic Cinema

Trevor G. Elkington and Andrew Nestingen

Flip through the program of any international film festival and you'll see the logic of nation-based film categorization at work. Each film, accompanied by the requisite summary, cast list, and stills, carries its singular national designation: Brazil, France, Japan, Sweden. At first glance, the classificatory logic seems unassailable: the designation marks the film's clearly discernible nationality, just as every passport indicates a national citizenship. One expects the actors to speak Portuguese, French, Japanese, or Swedish, the setting to be in the nation-state in question, and the points of cultural reference to arise in relation to its culture. The film is ostensibly about that nation-state and reflects its typical attitudes and conflicts. *Tout court* the film feels French, Swedish, Japanese, and so on.[1] To be sure, some remarkable examples carry multiple national identities, and sometimes a film focuses on a subnational group; nevertheless one tends to assume that one can understand non-Hollywood films by assuming that they—like a citizen of any country—reflect something typical about a national culture. This assumption would seem to apply in particular to the popular conception of the Nordic countries. Relatively small in terms of geography and population, perched on the northern frontier of Europe, it is tempting to expect a sense of national singularity, even isolation, from the Nordic countries. But the practices of their film industries, embedded as they are in the economically, politically, and culturally transnational relationships of these countries, have proven to be far from separate or isolated in the decades abutting the millennium. Today, Denmark, Finland, Iceland, Norway, and Sweden are integral sites in increasingly globalized film markets. In examining Nordic cinema at the millennium, how can we explain the relationship between transnational networks of production and reception and the significance of national categories?

Film production and reception in the Nordic region draw from diverse sources. The economic, political, and cultural relationships underpinning cinematic production, distribution, exhibition, and consumption are increasingly transnational. Singular, clearly bounded national polities, economies, and cultures are no longer the default point of reference, if they ever truly were. Financing for Nordic cinema productions is often multinational; the cultural-political bodies that provide funding for cinema cannot be fitted neatly within the borders of a single nation-state; and the networks of production, distribution, and exhibition through which all films pass are transnational. Audience tastes vacillate among popular, nostalgic national films, Hollywood blockbusters, art films, and local adaptations of popular genres, among others. The cultural politics of national representation on-screen sometimes interrogate the assumptions, myths, and associations of national identities; they can also flatter and reinforce national assumptions. Critics and scholars increasingly avoid distinctions between high and low culture that formerly produced the national auteurs and national cinematic canons for which Nordic cinema is known. At a millennial juncture characterized by globalization, national cinema takes shape on a crisscrossed economic, political, and cultural terrain. It is reasonable and salutary to ask, then, what is the state of Nordic national cinemas?

It might be helpful to begin by looking at a film that illustrates many of these issues: Jan Troell's *Hamsun* (1997). The film's funding and production were thoroughly transnational; by contrast, its themes are deeply national. Indeed, it can well be seen as a Norwegian prestige film; yet the authenticity of its prestige is qualified by a hodgepodge cast of Norwegians, Swedes, and Danes, a choice that raises questions about the type of audience for which the film was made. Furthermore, while the film is an auteur film directed by Jan Troell, it is also a genre film that seeks to capitalize on the popularity of European heritage films among European and American audiences. *Hamsun* furnishes an example of the way Nordic cinemas are dealing with a transnational media environment. Whether films like *Hamsun* are seen as clever negotiations of present conditions or Europudding mishmashes is open for debate.

Introduction

Hamsun's funding came from sources in Denmark, Norway, Sweden, and Germany as well as regional underwriters such as the Nordic Film and Television Fund and the E.U.'s Eurimages.[2] The film was produced by the Danish company Nordisk FilmA/S and is therefore ostensibly Danish if categorized by its producer's home base. But as is typical of Nordic cinema presently, national distinctions begin to disintegrate when finance- and production-based definitions are qualified by observations about the narrative, cast, and crew. Directed by Troell, a Swede, based on a work by a Dane, Thorkild Hansen, about a central figure and event in Norwegian history, the film freely mixes Nordic distinctions in its topic and production. The cast is also a mix of Nordic nationalities. The Norwegian author Knut Hamsun is played by Max von Sydow, who speaks Swedish throughout the film. His wife, Marie, also Norwegian, is played by the Danish actress Ghita Nørby, who speaks Danish throughout the film. Their children, also Norwegians, are played by Norwegian actors who speak Norwegian.[3] While Scandinavian film workers have often collaborated, and their languages are similar, *Hamsun* is an extreme example of mixing, and it complicates the film's authenticity as the story of Knut Hamsun. (Imagine a biopic about Ernest Hemingway with Sean Connery playing the lead, Scottish accent fully intact.) Categorization as a national film on the basis of funding or production is clearly problematic in the case of *Hamsun*. The problem of categorization becomes even more obscure when financing, production, and casting are juxtaposed with the film's narrative themes.

The book on which the film is based, Hansen's *Processen mod Hamsun* (The Trial of Knut Hamsun), is a documentary fiction of Hamsun's later life. When originally published in 1978, Hansen's book created controversy through its questionable treatment of a highly sensitive topic, Knut Hamsun's Nazi sympathies.[4] Hamsun, author of key modern novels such as *Sult* (1890, *Hunger*) and *Pan* (1894) and commonly thought of as the father of modern Norwegian literature and a central figure in European modernism, won the Nobel Prize in 1920. During the Second World War, while Norway was under Nazi occupation (1941–45), Hamsun publicly sided with the Nazis, going so far as to give Joseph Goebbels his Nobel medal during a 1943 visit to Berlin, writing editorials calling on resistance fighters to put down their weapons, and finally writing a glowing obituary of Hitler. After the war,

Hamsun was charged with treason but declared mentally incompetent by the Norwegian courts to avoid jailing the octogenarian cultural luminary. Hamsun responded by publishing an acid yet undeniably brilliant apologia as his final book, the autobiography *Paa gjengrodde stier* (*On Overgrown Paths*). Hamsun defended his embrace of Nazism as a form of protest against Anglo-American commercial domination of northern Europe and the Americas, also endeavoring to persuade readers that he had opposed Nazi methods and never knew about Hitler's "Final Solution." The book complicated even further his legacy in Norwegian culture.[5] Questions about Hamsun's Nazism embarrassed Norway at home and abroad, and his legacy was swept under the rug. It was truly Hansen's *Processen mod Hamsun* that brought the issue into public discussion for the first time; Troell's film revived interest in the debate at the millennium. The cultural significance of Hamsun's life made the film important in Scandinavia, and it is surely appropriate to see the seriousness of its topic as making *Hamsun* a prestige film.

But in consideration of the funding, production, and casting of the film, we can ask, prestige for whom? If prestige supposes an attempt at seriousness and authenticity, what is one to make of the hybrid *Hamsun*? Intriguingly, *Hamsun* was marketed primarily toward European audiences, with a secondary audience in North America and elsewhere, which further muddies the issue. When the film debuted in the United States, it won generous praise from critics. Kevin Thomas of the *Los Angeles Times* called it "easily one of the year's finest films," in his review from November 21, 1997. Yet Thomas's review, and it was not unusual, inadvertently highlights the complicated cultural identity of the film: among American audiences, most had no idea who Hamsun was, or why his story was of such grave importance for Norway and the Nordic countries. Nearly every reviewer of the film felt compelled to explain Hamsun's career and his significance. As Thomas writes, the film "succeeds stunningly in making us understand how Norwegian novelist and poet Knut Hamsun, winner of the 1920 Nobel Prize for literature, came to be one of the few major European artists to support Hitler." While national categorization is present, it is mentioned seemingly only to locate the production and answer the question of why the film is not shot in English. A more prominent national erasure can been seen later in the same review, when Ghita Nørby is dubbed "grande dame of Norway's actresses." This surely must have come as a surprising new accolade to Nørby herself, given her generally acknowledged status as one of the finest actresses in the history of *Danish* film and given that she speaks Danish throughout the film.

While the debate surrounding the film's content and its stance on Hamsun's life was lively in Norway and the surrounding countries, American audiences by and large were more interested in the film as another example of European costume drama and were not nearly as concerned with the issues of history that the film raised for Nordic audiences. This phenomenon isolates a key contradiction in considering Nordic film in transnational circulation. Gaffes like Thomas's not only reveal ignorance about Scandinavia, they help illuminate the nonnational production, marketing, and reception of Nordic cinema. The difference between Nørby's Danish and the other languages spoken by the rest of the cast are obvious to any citizen of the Nordic countries and might be seen as compromising the putative authenticity of the film. Yet the fact that Thomas inadvertently gets the wrong nation in praising a national characteristic indicates just how little nation matters as a category in what is ostensibly a national prestige film. In other words, for better or worse, *Hamsun*'s relative international success despite ignorance of its historical and national particularities can be seen as proof of the growing tendency to see all Nordic film as nationally indistinct, a trend the film cleverly exploits. Indeed, the film's marketing as a European costume drama draws on the success of *Babette's Feast* (Gabriel Axel, 1987, *Babettes gæstebud*) and *Pelle the Conqueror* (Bille August, 1988, *Pelle Erobreren,* 1987) as well as the successes of the Merchant-Ivory films and their many imitators. The film is presented as a trace of the European "other," a peek into a history specifically not "ours"—that is, not the history associated with Hollywood—even if the particularity of that history is inconsequential. It is the image of history that matters. That *Hamsun* was based on the true story of a Norwegian novelist became a curiosity, grounds for explanation by film reviewers.[6]

Evidently, then, a film like *Hamsun,* and in general Nordic cinema today, must be understood at least in part in the context of a "Global Hollywood." If Toby Miller and his coauthors are correct when concluding in their book *Global Hollywood* that "yes, Hollywood is global in that it sells its wares in every nation, through a global system of copyright, promotion, and distribution" (2001, 216), then it is inevitable that this factor will shape the kinds of films being made elsewhere, as it becomes a question of which kinds of films are most profitable across markets. In response to market pressure exerted by studio-based Hollywood films—seen as predominantly American in their cultural tropes but in fact the product of multinational corporations using the lowest common denominator to reach a global audience—Nordic cinemas have adopted strategies to compete against Hollywood juggernauts like *Titanic* (James Cameron, 1997). *Hamsun* is an example of how Nordic films are made with both domestic markets and export in mind.

So what about domestic Nordic cinema, then? Is it changing in response to this global-local dialectic? In order to understand the current state of domestic markets, we first need to examine their size. They are diminutive. They cannot generate the profits to finance large-scale cinema production. At the same time, their size increases their cultural importance for domestic publics, who recognize national cinemas as distinctive in a media environment saturated with images and languages from elsewhere. Box office admissions give a good picture. During 2001, for example, total admissions by nation ranged from 1.5 million annually in Iceland to 18.1 in Sweden, with Norway and Denmark at 12.5 and 11.5 million and Finland at 6.3 million. The percentage of total admissions taken by domestic films ranged from 3 percent in Iceland to 30 percent in Denmark, with Finland, Norway, and Sweden at roughly 10, 15, and 25 percent respectively.[7] In short, annual box office returns for all domestic films in all the Nordic countries combined add up to approximately US$100 million (roughly what a smash-hit Hollywood blockbuster makes on its opening weekend in the United States).[8] The profits generated by Nordic films domestically in turn dictate the budgets available for production. As a consequence, budgets are small, ranging generally between US$2 million and US$4 million. One of the ways that production of these national cinemas has been ensured is through robust institutional funding schemes administered by national film institutes, which merit discussion that we shall turn to shortly. Small Nordic national cinemas work on a different terrain than Hollywood, to be sure, but one that also differs from the larger national cinemas in Europe, Asia, and South America. They cannot avoid the compelling argument made by Finnish critics and producers in the 1930s to justify lowering of the entertainment tax on domestic production: only films made domestically can speak in the language of the nation to the nation. Where else will Danish, Finnish, Icelandic, Norwegian, and Swedish moves be made, if not in these countries? (see

Koivunen 1995, 234). Today, cobbling together a variety of interests and targeting numerous markets are ways to deal with transnational media dynamics that have a profound effect on domestic cinema production.

As the assessment of their size indicates, Nordic films account for only about 20 percent of domestic ticket sales, with Hollywood taking most of the rest. Taking Denmark as an example, between the years 1986 and 1996, four of the top five most successful films were U.S.-based films: *Out of Africa* (Sydney Pollack, 1985),[9] *The Lion King* (Roger Allers and Rob Minkoff, 1994), *Dances with Wolves* (Kevin Costner, 1990), and *Pretty Woman* (Garry Marshall, 1990).[10] How can films compete for audience share at home?

Competing can mean appropriating Hollywood production values. The one Danish film in the Danish top five is international director Bille August's film *House of Spirits*. The film is set in Chile and stars an international cast, not one of whom speaks Danish in the film. The film is characterized by the clear effort to make it resemble its international competition while maintaining some difference, in the hope of finding not only a national audience but an international one as well. Even in films aimed solely at national markets, the adoption of Hollywood formulas is an apparent competitive strategy. In films like *Blinkende lygter* (Anders Thomas Jensen, 2000, *Flickering Lights*), one sees Quentin Tarantino; in a film like *Pizza King* (Ole Christian Madsen, 1999), the Martin Scorsese of *Mean Streets*; in *Jägerna* (Kjell Sundvall, 1996, *The Hunters*), the action film; in *Elling* (Petter Naess, 2001), the oddball buddy film; or in *Jalla! Jalla!* (Josef Fares, 2000), the star-crossed romantic comedy. Each contains elements that are anchored in its national settings; at the same time, differences in style, genre, or aesthetics have become demonstrably homogenized.

In emphasizing the way in which Nordic cinemas aimed at foreign and domestic audiences have become transnational, we should not overlook elements that remain insistently national and are a key part of maintaining cultural expression in domestic markets. The most significant element in this regard is language. While films shot in English, like *The House of Spirits, Dancer in the Dark* (Lars von Trier, 2000), or *Cold Fever* can transcend national limitations, most of the films released domestically are shot in the national languages. Likewise, culturally specific issues, figures, and sensibilities complicate the idea that all film of the Nordic region can be marketed to, or even understood by, global audiences. Much of the humor in a film like *Jalla! Jalla!* with its tale of lovers that transgress ethnic lines, is predicated upon the particular cultural climate of Sweden, the interaction of cultural groups, and the presence of ethnic and national minorities that, while also a part of other communities, nevertheless take on a unique character in Sweden. Similarly, certain films are made in reaction to these globalizing forces, turning to a mythologized national past as a way of avoiding the bewildering complexities of the present. Films that draw on specific national histories or literature, such as the Danish World War II occupation drama *De nøgne træer* (Morten Henriksen, 1991), based on the novel by Danish author Tage Skou-Hansen, are arguably culturally—and therefore one might assume nationally—specific films. Films worthy of mention in this connection, among many others, include the Finnish hit *Ambush* (Olli Saarela, 1999, *Rukajärven tie*), the Swedish hit *Under the Sun* (Colin Nutley, 1999, *Under solen*), and the Norwegian historical melodrama-comedy *The Greatest Thing* (Thomas Robsahm, 2001, *Det Største i verden*). While international audiences may enjoy the action, drama, or comedy of these films and understand the general context, the films' language, settings, and narrative themes will resonate most strongly with a national audience. A balanced view of the transformation of Nordic cinematic cultures must be maintained, and the continued significance and popularity of films made chiefly for domestic audiences must not be dismissed.

As the examples so far suggest, the globalization of cinema should not be implicitly understood as a threat to Nordic national cinemas. One way the role of transnational interconnection can be seen to have stimulated Nordic cinemas is by providing film workers opportunity to influence colleagues and audiences outside the region. Nordic film workers have figured significantly in Hollywood in the past and do so as much as ever today.[11] In the search for marketable cinema, the studio-based industry has increasingly looked outside its own sphere for talent and inspiration, leading to the "crossing over" of directors like Bille August, Ole Børnedal, Lasse Hallström, Renny Harlin, Harald Zwart, Erik Skjoldbjærg, and others. Even Lars von Trier, though still independent of the studio system, is largely seen and marketed as an international (not a Danish) director after the success of *Breaking the Waves* (1995) and *Dancer in the Dark*. Similarly, the Hollywood remake of films like Skjoldbjærg's *Insomnia* (1997), Børnedal's *Nattevagten* (1994, remade as *Nightwatch* in 1998 with Børnedal at the helm), and others shows an awareness of the major releases in the Nordic region. Despite a tendency to see Hollywood as monolithic and entirely American, the studio-based industry has moved toward a global model, both in its business practice and in its product, through mergers, partnerships, and the homogenization of product, all based on a global focus, which opens a space for contributions from outside the American sphere.[12] To be sure, most studio-based films carry the indelible stamp of American culture, albeit with carefully combed and audience-tested references, so as not to be incomprehensible to a majority of international audiences, as a film like *Armageddon* (Michael Bay, 1998) shows.[13] Nevertheless, the influence of a movement like Dogma 95, which generated respect and varying levels of interest from directors ranging from Mike Figgis to Steven Soderbergh should not be overlooked, as Trevor Elkington's and Peter Schepelern's essays (chapters 1 and 3) in the present volume demonstrate.

Thinking of the films of the Nordic countries as national texts, while useful for quick distinctions at film festivals and award ceremonies, is inaccurate and misleading when trying to understand the elements of any given film in times of globalization and cultural transition. How do you explain the financing of a film like *Hamsun* in relation to national cinema, with its pan-European sources? What do you do with a film like *Breaking the Waves*, which bears no visible Nordic markers other than the nationality of the Swede Stellan Skarsgård and the Norwegian/Sami Mikkel Gaup? What do you say about crossover directors like Renny Harlin (*Die Hard 2*, 1990; *Cliffhanger*, 1993) or Harald Zwart (*One Night at McCools*, 2001; *Agent Cody Banks*, 2003)? Their films, largely studio-based genre fare, match audiences' tastes inside and outside Finland and Norway largely regardless of their directors' nationality, and yet within their home nations the directors' national origins generate interest and relative pride. By what methodologies does one even try to make national distinctions? In terms of the ambiguity of national cinema in the first place? In relation to arguments about transnational difference and the increasing insignificance of nation? By relating the various strands of these phenomena to globalization and transnationalism?

So far we have assumed the significance of national cinema in assessing contemporary issues in Nordic cinema. In order to understand Nordic cinema in transition from a national frame to a global one, we also need to assess critically the history and significance of national cinema in relation to changes and continuities today. Why has national cinema proved so resilient in the Nordic countries? A tradition of production and audience taste, institutionalized support for national cinema, and critical and scholarly cinema discourse have created, sustained, and guided distinct national cinemas in the Nordic countries. While transnational and postmodern paradigms may cause us to respond with incredulity to historical narratives like those of nation and auteur as national genius, we cannot simply dismiss this history and the body of cinema associated with these concepts. It is worth examining the three chief institutional reasons that national cinema has become the norm: production, state support, and critical reception.

The "by us, for us" model, in which companies produced films in the national tongue, using funding from within national borders, marketed for specific national tastes, has dominated Nordic cinema history, particularly in the post–silent cinema era (Soila, Söderbergh Widding, and Iversen 1998, 2–4). To be sure, from the earliest days of film production, the importance of global influence is evident. International trends found their imitators in Nordic cinemas. For example, the Danish comedians Bi and Fy exhibit a clear debt to early American slapstick comedies. Likewise, the westerns and detective films made in Scandinavia during the silent film and studio era participate in the origins of genres that, while most commonly associated with the American film industry, were popular fare for most early production companies throughout Europe. Moreover, various early film figures such as Asta Nielsen, Benjamin Christensen, Greta Garbo, Carl Th. Dreyer, and others, worked across national lines with reasonable fluidity. Their films often found an international following; this is particularly true of filmmakers working during the silent and early sound era. Nevertheless, the continual production of cinema for domestic distribution by companies like Svensk Filmindustri, Fennada Filmi, and Nordisk Film, to name some of the longer-lived producers, speaks to a long history of domestic production. This trend toward domestic-oriented production solidified during and after World War I, as Hollywood, benefiting from the late entry of the United States into a conflict happening outside its boundaries, established its dominance over the global film trade as the European film industries attempted to rebuild. The coming of sound film confirmed Hollywood's positioning, as English became the de facto global tongue for film. Generally speaking, after World War I, through the coming of sound, and up to and in some instances past World War II, film companies in the Nordic nations condensed, reducing or eliminating their foreign interests, and turned inward, focusing upon their domestic audience by producing films in the national language to reflect national interests.

The international profile of national film gained new importance with the rise of the art film in the 1960s. Since then, national cinema has been sustained by the nation-state's investment in film as a form of cultural expression through national film institutes.[14] The rise of the art film made cinema a logical site of state support for the arts, part of the Scandinavian welfare state's efforts at cultivating cultural expression and edification of the national audience. To the present day, the task of these institutes remains to develop production of feature films, shorts, and documentaries, to aid in distribution and marketing of domestic film both at home and abroad, and to maintain national film archives.[15] Today, a feature film cannot be made without foundation support: approximately half the financing of every Nordic film that makes it onto domestic, not to mention foreign, screens, comes from the film institutes.[16] Politicians, businesspeople, and film professionals have offered different reasons for their significance, but their significance itself cannot be disputed. The present essays by Ib Bondebjerg, Pil Gundelach Brandstrup and Eva Novrup Redvall, Mervi Pantti, Mette Hjort, and Gunnar Iversen (chapters 4, 5, 6, 7, and 10) testify to the continued if changing significance of the film institutes.

Finally, the category of the national has been developed through an extensive bibliography concerning national cinema in each of the Nordic countries that codifies the origins, continuity, and identity of the cinema as a component of the national culture. The nationality of the cinema has been elaborated most fully in the Nordic countries through national filmographies and popular histories of the national cinema: *Svensk filmografi* (1977–, The Swedish Filmography) is currently available in nine volumes, reaching 1999; *Suomen kansallisfilmografia* (1989–, The Finnish National Filmography) currently appears in eleven volumes, reaching 1996, and Norwegian and Danish single-volume filmographies also exist.[17] These texts naturalize national cinema as a form of cultural expression. They also provide the framework for university-level instruction in Nordic national cinemas and guide popular criticism. Hence they figure not only in scholarly discussions but in popular understandings of Nordic cinemas as national cinemas. These scholarly forms of categorization also explain why film has been viewed as a part of the national culture.

One might note here that little research has been done to assess the effects of globalization on cinematic production, reception, and discourse in the Nordic region. In English, for example, most volumes available on cinema in the Nordic countries take the national category as a given. Peter Cowie's many publications on Scandinavian cinema are organized by nation or auteur, as are volumes like Qvist and von Bagh's *Guide to the Cinema of Sweden and Finland* (2000). Tytti Soila, Astrid Söderbergh Widding, and Gunnar Iversen's volume *Nordic National Cinemas* (1998) also takes the nation as a given, although its cultural studies analysis helpfully problematizes the usual overemphasis on the art film, providing a picture of the diversity of Nordic cinemas. The present volume, by contrast, challenges historically the national as a point of departure in the first place, seeking to identify an ongoing transition in Nordic cinema: from national to transnational and global cinema. While historical continuities with national cinema analyzed by others exist, our argument is that at the millennial juncture, the influence and nature of the transition requires a new turn in the research, which will furnish more nuanced accounts of Nordic cinema in times of transnationalism and globalization. We return to this point at the conclusion of this introduction.

Yet, in taking transnationalism and globalization into account, we should not overlook the continued salience of the national in conceptions of cinema in the Nordic region. One cannot simply deconstruct images of nationality on-screen or point out counternational articulations and summarily dismiss the category of national culture altogether. But on the other hand, despite the extent to which production and reception, institutional support, and critical and scholarly paradigms have created and maintained the category of national cinema, changes associated with revisionist studies of nation, critiques of modern social identities, and the vicissitudes of globalization challenge the category of national cinema. Three areas of inquiry are particularly significant: first, work elaborating the ambiguity of the category of national cinema; second, methodologically driven questioning of national culture and cinema in film studies; and third, pressing questions about nation in times of globalization and transnationalism. These lines of argument place the status of Nordic national cinemas in a critical light.

Introduction

A number of scholars have argued that the category of national cinema itself is based on untenable assumptions; while national cinema putatively encodes the homogeneity and temporal continuity of a national culture, it may be better understood as a site of conflict, heterogeneity, and change. In part this is because national cinema is a highly ambiguous notion, as Andrew Higson (1995) has pointed out: it has meant an economic category for assessing cinema as national industry; it has denominated audience taste, where the question is what kinds of films the nation likes most—not necessarily domestic ones; national cinema has also meant a national canon, where national cinema means the greats, for example, Sjöström, Stiller, Bergman, and Widerberg, but not the rural melodramas that were popular among Swedish audiences during the 1930s, 1940s, and 1950s; finally, Higson observes that national cinema can be defined thematically in terms of identity, by character, theme, iconography, and the like (4–5). In view of this conceptual ambiguity, "it is important to acknowledge the limitations of a concept of national cinema as a seamless totality that somehow accurately expresses, describes, and itemizes the salient concerns and features of a given national culture," as Hjort and MacKenzie write (2000, 4).

The increased influence of cultural studies methodologies in studying cinema has also caused the assumed validity of national cinema to come into question. Numerous studies attempt to prize visual culture from the national rubric, in order to fabricate alternative rubrics of difference. The title of a double issue of *Camera Obscura* (Halle and Willis 2000-1), "Marginality and Alterity in New European Cinemas," sums up these critical efforts; the issues include essays focusing on how counternational cinemas unmask, denaturalize, and challenge national cinemas.[18] Volumes such as *Nationalisms and Sexualities* (1992) by Parker et al. inaugurated theoretical concern with these questions. Cultural studies research has broadened this inquiry by studying transnationalism, gender, and sexuality, as is evident in such texts as Kaplan, Alarcón, and Moallem's *Between Woman and Nation* (1999) and Cruz-Malavé and Manalansan's *Queer Globalizations* (2002).[19] These studies assume the ambiguity of national culture, reading it against the grain to show the way articulations of difference implicitly criticize nation, creating distance between expressions of difference and what are held to be hegemonic national-identity formations. In contrast to the national filmographies and histories that presuppose national homogeneity in their critical framework, these studies bracket that assumption, attempting to read a field of difference encoded in any particular film.

Globalization and transnationalism—understood generally as a massive increase in planetwide interconnection through new networks of communication, transportation, and exchange and a subsequent transformation of institutional governance and cultural consciousness—also mean that cinema takes shape on a new terrain. The Nordic region bristles with transformations associated with globalization and transnationalism, and these alter its cinematic production.

Significant changes transformed everyday life in the Nordic nation-states at the end of the twentieth century. The Nordic lands have often appeared ethnically and culturally homogeneous, and this assumption has figured prominently in assessment of their cultural texts as well. While one can point to historical elements that belie this ostensible homogeneity, it is clear that during the four decades preceding the millennium, the Nordic nation-states became increasingly porous nodes of global circulation, and the assumption of cultural homogeneity became increasingly tenuous. The rise of the welfare state, the arrival of workers, refugees, and asylum seekers since the 1950s, and the full-scale European and global economic integration of the Nordic nation-states since the 1980s have made these places truly transnational.[20] We can no longer assume—if we ever could—the economic, political, and cultural homogeneity of the Nordic nations, as a brief survey of the economic-cultural terrain of the Nordic world at the turn of the millennium makes evident.

Economic transformation has been significant. The importance of manufacturing in Sweden has led to deterritorialization of the relationships of labor and capital, in line with European Union neoliberal policy and typical disintegrated, flexible production practices of the day (Ingebritsen 1998). Sweden and Denmark have endeavored to "globalize" the Øresund region, as Berg, Linde, and Löfgren have shown (2000). The Finnish economy balances on the mobile telephone giant Nokia's fortunes, and the national economy has been deregulated and restructured itself to become competitive globally (Castells and Himanen 2001, 2002). The other, traditionally peripheral, Nordic states—Norway and Iceland—are also fully dependent on global exchange. Norway sits on North Sea black gold, the coffers of its generous welfare system shaped by the geopolitics of Middle East oil dynamics. Iceland, for its part, has tied its microeconomy to a national genetic database, effectively packaging and marketing its national genetic heritage through licenses held exclusively by publicly owned deCODE genetics (Palsson and Hardardottir 2002). Economic globalization fuels these Nordic economies, and there are myriad consequences for national culture, but these economic changes also destroy the peripheral location and homogeneous national culture that provided these countries with much of their identity during the postwar period.

Global migration associated with decolonization is also reshaping ideas about the ethnic makeup of these nations. Geographical marginality no longer means homogeneity arising from relative isolation. The economic migrants that came to Sweden and Denmark in the 1950s and 1960s and the political refugees that came from the 1970s to the 1990s make these societies more plural than they've ever been (Pred 2000; Gullestad 2002). By 2003, approximately 20 percent of the Swedish population had a background outside the country, as did 10 percent of the Danish population. Newly emergent hybrid cultural forms contrast with the homogeneity associated with national romantic beliefs about cultural identity, which have dominated in these countries historically. Today, Nordic ethnic nationalism delineates self and other in complicated, sometimes racist ways. Allan Pred and Marianne Gullestad have shown the ways in which assumptions about ethnically homogeneous national identity in Sweden and Norway have transformed in multicultural societies. The Danish elections of fall 2001, in which a right-wing coalition including the anti-immigrant Danish People's Party won the parliamentary majority, showed that the seams of Danish society were splitting in its efforts to recast itself as multicultural. All of the Nordic countries have seen extreme-right parties enter the political arena. The Nordic countries have integrated themselves into global networks of migration for more than four decades, with complex social consequences.

The material changes related to globalization and transnationalism make *national* cinema appear increasingly problematic as an analytical category. "The point here is that the global culture linked with postmodernism . . . has brought us to a point where the traditional association between national spaces and cultural practices cannot be sustained: there no longer seems to be a clear relationship between cultural practices and localities" (Gikandi 2001, 638).[21] When the relations of production, distribution, and exhibition that figure in the life of any film text are not coterminous with a singular national space, people, or outlook, can we truly call cinema *national,* or is this a nominalist mode of categorization that figures in the marketing imperatives of contemporary global business?

This anthology looks to challenge and complicate the nation-based model for critical reception that is common to film studies focusing on the Nordic countries. Starting from the claim that each country is embedded in globally pervasive forms of cinematic production and reception and participates in a globalized film discourse, the following essays provide evidence of the transnational aspects of Nordic cinema. Areas of focus include production and aesthetics, drawing evidence from policy and regulation, production practice and history, formalistic shifts, regional aesthetic trends, and individual directors and texts. In doing this, the volume situates the Nordic region within a complex discussion of issues surrounding globalization, where diverse local actors are compelled to work as a bloc within an intertwined European production network, with concern for the demands of a potentially global audience. Further, the volume seeks to unravel the complicated relationship between Nordic film and the dominant Hollywood or studio-based film industry, complicating notions of "Hollywood hegemony." If in fact English has become the language of globalization, and researchers studying English-language texts have become "custodians of globalization in the university" (Gikandi 2001, 647), then the common tendency in studies of globalization to default to concerns prominent in the Anglo-American context might well be seen to support studio-based hegemony, by sustaining a focus on it. It may be that study of a non-English-speaking tradition that is nevertheless an established participant in the global economy of cinema might offer suggestive insights into local-global, or national-global, dialectics. That is to say, if global films are thought to speak English, and if globalization begins among first world nations, then a voice with a Nordic accent may speak volumes in this debate.

The chapters in this book are divided into three sections. In each, as well as across the collection, we have tried to move from the general to the specific, from macro- to microlevel. The first section, "Trends in Transitional Nordic Cinema," looks at significant developments in content, themes, and styles of contemporary film in the Nordic region. This opening section provides both a sense of some major issues and entrée into the collection for readers less familiar with the history of

Introduction

Nordic cinema. The three chapters in part 1 trace connections between circulations of images, people, and aesthetic trends, seeking to explain the way transnational circulation has catalyzed production dynamics that both speak to local audiences and participate in global cinema. In chapter 1, "Costumes, Adolescence, and Dogma: Nordic Film and American Distribution," Trevor G. Elkington studies the marketing of Nordic film transnationally, paying particular attention to how these films have performed in the United States (or Hollywood's backyard). Initially associated closely with art cinema, Nordic film in the 1980s came into the mainstream through the back-to-back Oscar successes of *Babette's Feast* and *Pelle the Conqueror*. These films contributed to the common belief that Nordic film equaled costume drama, a notion that remained an effective marketing strategy well into the 1990s. However, shifting audience tastes and artistic imperatives within the Nordic region, mirroring changing tastes in the United States and elsewhere, have decreased interest in the costume drama genre at home and abroad. Domestically, the appearance of more experimental and popular cinema such as Dogma 95, romantic comedies, and gangster films have led to a decline in producing the types of Nordic drama popular through the 1980s and 1990s.

Rochelle Wright traces another emerging trend in chapter 2, "'Immigrant Film' in Sweden at the Millennium." The essay identifies a new trend in Swedish filmmaking, in which directors move beyond traditional notions of culture and ethnicity, reflecting the increasingly heterogeneous nature of the Swedish population. Swedish films such as *Jalla! Jalla!* (Josef Fares, 2000), *All Hell Let Loose* (Susan Taslimi, 2002, *Hus i helvete*), and *Before the Storm* (Reza Parsa, 2000, *Före stormen*) mark a boom of films made by a new generation of Swedes of immigrant backgrounds. Looking at these films, the essay explores the manner in which established genre conventions are applied to substantially new subject matter. Wright also studies the ideological outlook of these significant films.

In the final chapter of the section, "Film according to Dogma: Ground Rules, Obstacles, and Liberations," Peter Schepelern places the Dogma 95 concept within a global context by discussing its origins, influences, and effect upon an international body of filmmakers. When Lars von Trier announced the birth of Dogma 95 at an international film conference celebrating one hundred years of film history, scholars and journalists didn't know if he was serious or if they were witness to yet another joke from the Danish enfant terrible. The first Dogma film,

Thomas Vinterberg's *The Celebration*, exploded onto the international scene three years later, and suddenly the film world realized the split nature of the project. Both deadly earnest and unabashedly tongue-in-cheek, Dogma 95 launched the commercial viability of digital video filmmaking and spawned a host of fellow travelers, imitators, and fans. In introducing these trends, part 1 raises a question part 2 seeks to discuss. What is the relation between these trends and present modes of cinematic production?

The second section, "The State and Film Markets in Transnational Times," studies the relationship between governments, policy-making institutions, and national and transnational film industries, markets, and publics. The section's focus on economic analysis seeks to explain how national cinemas have recast themselves to deal with the dynamics of globalization. First, Ib Bondebjerg's essay, "The Danish Way: Danish Film Culture in a European and Global Perspective," discusses the impact of the European Union and other transnational and global pressures on Denmark's efforts to support domestic media, including cinema. Danish film policy was transformed through legislative changes made in 1997. The changes can be characterized by their transnational approach to film and their broader acceptance, and development, of support mechanisms for both art film and mainstream film. The basic structures of the film policy are still in place, but the concept of film and its nationality have transformed in the light of European integration and globalization.

Some of the consequences of these changes for production are analyzed by Pil Gundelach Brandstrup and Eva Novrup Redvall in their discussion of the state of regional collaboration in chapter 5: "Breaking the Borders: Danish Coproductions in the 1990s." They demonstrate that while political initiatives regarding film in Denmark have been based on industrial and culture-building arguments, the producers making coproductions tend to have financial motivations, despite the creative and cultural problems that may arise from such transnational arrangements.

Mervi Pantti's essay, "Art or Industry? Battles over Finnish Cinema during the 1990s," takes up a similar object of analysis, tracing the transformation of concepts of national cinema in Finland during the late twentieth and early twenty-first centuries. State support of film production in Finland has been justified by cultural and industrial arguments. In the 1990s, however, a new triangular alliance between the

Introduction

industry, the state, and the market has emerged, and policy makers have faced pressures to prioritize films with the greatest commercial potential.

Mette Hjort completes the section with chapter 7, "From Epiphanic Culture to Circulation: The Dynamics of Globalization in Nordic Cinema." Hjort situates domestic production in a transnational context, looking at an initiative in the area of Nordic media policy—the creation of the Nordic Film and TV Fund (NFTF)—in terms of Nordic imaginaries and networks of circulation. The essay assesses the evolution of the NFTF's vision and impact from a form of reactive globalization linked to national interests and frameworks to an increasingly denationalized infrastructure for the production of images and, equally important, circulation of filmmaking professionals. She concludes that this shift in conception and function has allowed, increasingly, for the emergence of a hybridized Nordic cinematic culture with Nordic as well as international appeal.

This section, in relying heavily upon the state of Danish cinema, reflects a common truth about coproductions and film globalization in the Nordic region: Denmark has become a significant role model for the other nations of the region, and as the essays by Bondebjerg, Brandstrup and Redvall, and Hjort illustrate, Danish cinema has been the most successful national film industry in navigating the complexities of transnational partnerships and global marketing, as is evident in the unanticipated success of the Dogma 95 film project. Pantti's essay, in focusing on Finnish film, provides an illustrative counterexample of how the Danish model has been emulated as well as how dynamics have differed.

Part 3 of the book, "Auteurism and Genre in Transnational Context," surveys individual films and the work of specific directors to assess how globalization works on the microlevel in Nordic cinemas at home and abroad. The film work and the auteur—the concepts on which the section is premised and which have lain beneath Nordic national cinema—have been contested concepts for many theorists of poststructuralism and transnationalism. Nevertheless, the essays suggest that specific films, auteurism, and the influence of specific directors require attention, even if they need to be considered in relation to the hybridization of the film text and the transformation of the auteur as the exportable image of national cinema. Of course, since the years of Benjamin Christensen, Mauritz Stiller, and Victor Sjöström, and on through Dreyer, Bergman, Kaurismäki, and von Trier, the international success of certain directors has propelled Nordic film to wider attention. And yet, international success of a given director decenters both national and auteuristic distinctions; if Lars von Trier can find a global audience for a film like *Dancer in the Dark*, which narratively has very little to do with the Nordic region, it is helpful to look beyond the auteur concept to study the deterritorialized appeal of the films. The films are no longer nationally specific, and his success may or may not be tied to national origins; in this context, his success as an auteur becomes a paradoxical promotional vehicle for Danish film, even a publicity scheme.

The section's first essay, chapter 8 by Linda Haverty Rugg, elaborates and complicates this argument. Rugg studies the circulation of Ingmar Bergman's auteurship in "Globalization and the Auteur: Ingmar Bergman Projected Internationally." She looks at the various ways Bergman has been appropriated, appearing in the most unexpected places. From Woody Allen and Jean-Luc Godard to *Bill and Ted's Excellent Adventure* (Stephen Herek, 1989), Bergman's legacy remains both controversial and inevitable. The question then becomes, at what point does Bergman stop being Swedish and start being global?

In the next essay, Thomas A. DuBois focuses on cultural circulation in Finland. His "'I'm a Lumberjack and I'm Okay': Popular Film as Collective Therapy in Markku Pölönen's *A Summer by the River*" explores the boom in Finnish "popular cinema" through Markku Pölönen's immensely successful feel-good film *A Summer by the River*. Drawing on a constellation of ideas important in Finnish popular culture during the late twentieth century, Pölönen creates a nostalgic echo of Finland's stereotypical male culture: that of loggers in rural Finland. The film, argues DuBois, offers Finnish audiences a self-consciously overt but narratively appealing "therapy piece" that provides a feel-good tribute to male bonding and masculine ethos, drawing on Robert Bly. The film uses Bly to recuperate belief in a once-pervasive, well-meaning, but endearingly imperfect patriarchy, leavened and domesticated in hindsight to suit the tastes of an altered society, which challenges a perceived crisis in masculinity following gender wars and structural unemployment in Finland during the 1990s.

Gunnar Iversen also looks at how local pasts figure in present-day cinema in chapter 10, "Learning from Genre: Genre Cycles in Modern Norwegian Cinema," a study of Norwegian filmmaker Nils Gaup's career. Arguably the most internationally oriented director in Norway, Gaup nevertheless draws directly upon culturally and nationally specific sources as the inspiration for his filmmaking. Films such as *Pathfinder* (1987) draw upon the legends and culture of the indigenous Sami people. The essay argues for an understanding of Gaup's work at the intersection of global and local concerns.

In his essay "Aki Kaurismäki's Crossroads: National Cinema and the Road Movie," Andrew Nestingen complicates the categorization of Kaurismäki's road movies in national terms. Kaurismäki's road movies, he argues, use genre to create paradoxical routes to viewing pleasure, raising questions about the status of the image in ostensibly national culture. The significance of the image becomes evident when we study Kaurismäki's cinema in terms of genre. This compels us to rethink the categorization of his films as forms of national expression.

In the collection's penultimate essay "In and Out of Reykjavik: Framing Iceland in the Global Daze," Birgir Thor Møller discusses the most recent addition to the film industry in the Nordic region, discussing the origins of the Icelandic film industry in relation to the films of one of its initiators and most experimental innovators, Fridrik Thór Fridriksson. In a country with only 280,000 citizens that became urbanized only during the second half of the twentieth century, the relationship between cinematic images of urban life in the national capital, Reykjavik, and images of the natural world of rural Iceland is fraught with consequences for the shaping of Icelanders' self-understanding. The essay uses this conflict as a central motif in understanding Fridriksson's films as well as the other films from this increasingly prolific film tradition.

Concluding this section, Bjørn Sørenssen's chapter 13, "Hrafn Gunnlaugsson—The Viking Who Came in from the Cold?" discusses Gunnlaugsson's Viking trilogy via the evolution of their influences. Borrowing liberally from sources as varied as Sergio Leone, Akira Kurosawa, and the Icelandic sagas, the director nevertheless establishes his own subgenre: the "cod western" or "northern." The essay concludes by discussing the third film of the Viking trilogy, *The White Viking* (1991), in light of its stylistic deviations from the previous films, noting this film's history as an international coproduction and offering evidence of the globalizing pressures exhibited in a film that on the surface seems obsessed with its Icelandic roots.

At the end of this introduction, it may be fitting to ask one last question: why this volume, and why now? As discussed above, the Nordic countries are integrated participants in globalized commerce, and they are central and savvy players on the global scene in political, economic, and cultural terms. And yet, as relatively small countries, the pressures under which they operate are different than the concerns of the United States, England, Germany, China, or other large nations. Studies of globalization, for better or worse, have tended to focus either upon the large and wealthy or the large and impoverished among nation-states. But what are the conditions in nation-states that are at once small and yet relatively well off? With the fall of the Berlin Wall and the creation of a unified Germany coupled with sweeping changes in the Baltic region and among the Nordic countries (ranging from the collapse of the Soviet Union and the reintroduction of Baltic neighbors Russia, Lithuania, Latvia, and Estonia as trade partners, to European Union membership for Finland and Sweden, on to the increasing precariousness of the Scandinavian universal welfare state), it is past time for a consideration of the Nordic film industry as a part of an economically and politically transforming Europe.

Given the relative scarcity of books in English on film from this region, any contribution to its literature is crucial. But more to the point, as we have argued in this introduction and as the contributors to this volume demonstrate, the national model for discussing the history of film in the region, relying as it does upon an isolated approach to each national history and its auteurs, requires revision. Inevitably, some important topics have been omitted from this anthology. In particular, while several essays address issues of reception and audiences of Nordic films, whether domestically or transnationally, it is a subject that requires further research and study. Moreover, representations of alterity and marginality, particularly in terms of diasporic and queer cinemas, require discussion beyond the scope of this project.

Film production is changing at an exponential rate in the Nordic countries as we write. No company or nation can afford to work in isolation, and given the increasing ability of films to reach an international audience, the factors involved in the production and distribution of any given film are ever more geographically spread, yet increasingly intricate. As the industry changes, so must our methodologies for studying and reading these films. As the following essays demonstrate, Nordic film is in transition between national and globalized cinema

Introduction

cultures. The questions, arguments, and revisions that arise in this volume invite continued investigation to better understand the trajectory of Nordic cinema.

NOTES

1. We echo Andrew Higson's remarks at the beginning of his *Waving the Flag,* where he discusses the cultural definition of national cinema in Raymond Durgnat's *Mirror for England* (1995, 4). Intriguingly, Higson does not mention language in his account of national cinema, though surely for all national cinemas whose countries don't count English as a national language, it is a highly significant form of national expression.
2. Contributors to the film were, by nation: Denmark—Nordisk Film A/S, Det Danske Filminstitut, TV 2 Denmark; Norway—Norsk Filminstitutt, TV 2 Norway; Sweden—SVT Drama, Svensk Filmindustri, Svenska Filminstitutet; Germany—Merkur Film A/S, Bayerischer Rundfunk, Polyphon Film- und Fernseh GmbH. For further discussion of the Nordic Film and Television Fund, see Mette Hjort's chapter 7 in the present volume.
3. The decision to have the actors speak their native languages was based on a variety of factors, such as the cost of dubbing and a general lack of success for films dubbed from one Nordic language to another. The decision seemed to have little effect on the film's critical and financial success in the Nordic countries (Andersen 1997, 352).
4. For critical discussions of Hansen's work, see Stecher-Hansen 1997; and Behrendt 1995.
5. For discussions of this fascinating episode, see Sabo 1999; and Zagar 1999.
6. Similar examples abound in Nordic film. A good example is the 1994 road movie filmed in Tokyo and Iceland, *Cold Fever* (Fridriksson), which bears a strong Icelandic stamp yet cannot truly be categorized as national. On the international film circuit, the film won awards at the Festróia festival in Portugal and at the Seattle International Film Festival. Icelander Fridrik Thór Fridriksson and American Jim Stark wrote the film, and Fridriksson directed it. It combined financing from nine production companies, whose offices are located in Denmark, Germany, Iceland, Japan, and the United States. Six producers cooperated on the film, including Peter Albæk Jensen of the Danish Zentropa Productions, the Icelander Ari Kristinsson, and George Gund III, otherwise known as owner of the NHL's San Jose Sharks and the NBA's Cleveland Cavaliers. The film was made with a largely Icelandic production crew, although the main actors were Masatoshi Nagase and Lili Taylor. For further discussion of the film, see Møller's remarks in chapter 12 of this volume. Lars von Trier's films provide similar examples: his Dogma film *The Idiots* (1998, *Idioterne*), set outside Copenhagen, shot in Danish with a Danish cast and crew, and articulating a ruthless critique of a particularly Danish middle-class sensibility, was made with Danish, Dutch, French, German, Italian, Swedish, and U.S. financing as well as funding from the Nordic Film and Television Fund. The transnational on-screen character of his next film, *Dancer in the Dark* (2000)—ostensibly set in Washington State, U.S.A., but filmed largely in

Trollhättan, Sweden, with Björk playing a Czech and Catherine Deneuve playing "Kathy"—combined funding from twenty-three different institutions, private and public, located in eleven different countries. The erstwhile homes of the film's capital: Denmark, Finland, France, Germany, Iceland, Italy, the Netherlands, Norway, Sweden, the United Kingdom, and the United States.

7. Statistics are from the Nordic Film and Television Fund Web site, http://www.nftf.net
8. By point of comparison, *The Matrix Reloaded* (Andy and Larry Wachowski, 2003) grossed over $91 million on 3,603 screens in its first weekend in the United States alone; this does not include the non-U.S. revenues generated in what is being considered the first truly global, simultaneous film opening. By June 15, the film had grossed roughly $500 million worldwide (figures from Internet Movie Database, http://www.imdb.com).
9. Though *Out of Africa* is based on the novel of the same name by Danish author Karen Blixen, the production itself had very little to do with Denmark. It has a largely American cast and was directed by the American filmmaker Sydney Pollack, working with a largely American crew and American production funds.
10. Indeed, of the fifty top-grossing films in Denmark during the 1990s, only fifteen are Danish in classification (Bondebjerg, Andersen, and Schepelern 1997, 404). The same trends are evident in statistical assessments of the other Nordic cinemas. For example, among the five top-grossing films in Finland between 1972 and 2000, only one was Finnish, *Numbskull Emptybrook in the Army* (Ere Kokkonen, 1984, *Uuno Turhapuro armeijan leivissä*).
11. For a historical survey of Scandinavians in Hollywood, see Wollstein 1994.
12. See Miller et al. 2001 for a comprehensive account of how Hollywood globalization plays out in ways similar to other global industries.
13. Although exceptions do occur, such as when the comedy *Wayne's World* (with its abundance of untranslatable slang phrases like "I think I'm gonna hurl") was marketed internationally. See Segrave 1997 for further discussion of how Hollywood works, and doesn't work, on a global level.
14. By the term *art film,* we're referring to David Bordwell's definition (1979), where he discusses the art film in terms of the auteur, narrative linkage, narrative conflict, and institutional practices of distribution and exhibition. For a discussion of the art film in the United States, see Wilinksy 2001. For a discussion of the connection between the art film and the emergence of national film institutes in the Nordic countries, see Soila, Söderbergh Widding, and Iversen's discussion by nation (1998).
15. See the respective Nordic film institutes' Web sites for more detailed accounts of their roles: the Danish Film Institute (http://www.dfi.dk), the Finnish Film Foundation (http://www.ses.fi), the Icelandic Film Fund (http://www.iff.is), the Norwegian Film Fund (http://www.filmfondet.no), and the Swedish Film Institute (http://www.sfi.se). For a discussion of the history and current status of the institutes, see Soila, Söderbergh Widding, and Iversen 1998; Hjort and Bondebjerg 2001; and Pantti 2000.
16. Funding has traditionally been distributed via grant competitions, through a consultant system, or administered by the film institutes' automatic repayments of

Introduction

production costs to producers based on total ticket sales. During the late 1990s, the Nordic countries all reformulated their funding policies to address issues of popular cinema and transnational financing schemes.

17. The definitive history of Danish cinema is Schepelern 2001, but also see Bondebjerg, Andersen, and Schepelern 1997; the definitive scholarly history of Finnish cinema comprises three separate volumes, Uusitalo 1967 and Toiviainen 1975, 2002; the definitive Norwegian volumes are Braaten, Holst, and Kortner 1995 as well as Evensmo 1992; on the Swedish cinema see Furhammar 1991. Histories of the Nordic national cinemas also exist plentifully in English. Soila, Söderbergh Widding, and Iversen 1998 has appeared in Routledge's National Cinemas series. And the indefatigable Peter Cowie has written several national studies (1985, 1990, 1991, 1995, 1999).
18. Articles discuss subnational cinemas of various sorts, queer cinemas, diasporic cinemas, and counternational cinemas. The articles' analyses focus primarily on the image, not on financing, distribution, or audience taste.
19. For similar discussions in relation to cinema, see the following texts, among others: Radel 2001 and Ciecko 1998.
20. An especially helpful, because thorough, account of integration is provided by Einhorn and Logue 2003.
21. Gikandi's view is typical of scholars working in North America and publishing transnational studies research—see, for example, Appadurai 1996; Bhabha 1994; Chambers 1994; Cheah 1998; Gilroy 1993; Rowe 2000; and Spivak 1999. Others working in the same context have responded skeptically to "vilifications" of the nation, underscoring the salutary effects of the nation-state and national culture (Jusdanis 2001, 4). See, for example Hjort 1996, 2000; Kymlicka 1995; Jusdanis 2001; Miller 1995; Smith 1990; Tamir 1993; and Taylor 1991. In the Nordic context, the debate about globalization and nation has focused on questions of national identity and changes associated with globalization. On questions of migration and nation, see Gullestad 2002; Jonsson 1993, 1996, 2001; and Pred 2000. On the transformation of national identity, see Alasuutari and Ruuska 1999; Eriksen 1993; and Karkama 1998.

WORKS CITED

Alasuutari, Pertti, and Petri Ruuska. 1999. *Post-Patria: Globalisaation kulttuuri Suomessa*. Sitra 224. Tampere: Vastapaino.

Andersen, Jesper. 1997. "I lommerne på Europa: Internationaliseringen af dansk filmproduktion." In *Dansk film, 1972–1997,* ed. Ib Bondebjerg, Jesper Andersen, and Peter Schepelern, 332–65. Copenhagen: Munksgaard-Rosinante.

Appaduarai, Arjun. 1996. *Modernity at Large: Cultural Dimensions of Globalization*. Vol. 1 of *Public Worlds,* ed. Dilip Gaonkar and Benjamin Lee. Minneapolis: University of Minnesota Press.

Behrendt, Poul. 1995. *Djævlepagten: En historie om Thorkild Hansen*. 2 vols. Copenhagen: Gyldendal.

Berg, Per Olof Laursen, Anders Linde, and Orvar Löfgren, eds. 2000. *Invoking a Transational Metropolis: The Making of the Øresund Region*. Lund: Studentlitteratur.

Bhabha, Homi. 1994. *The Location of Culture*. New York: Routledge.
Bondebjerg, Ib, Jesper Andersen, and Peter Schepelern, eds. 1997. *Dansk film, 1972–97*. Copenhagen: Munksgaard-Rosinante.
Bordwell, David. 1979. "The Art Cinema as a Mode of Film Practice." *Film Criticism* 4, no. 1: 56–64.
Braaten, Lars Thomas, Jan Erik Holst, and Jan H. Kortner. 1995. *Filmen i Norge: Norske kinofilmer gjennom hundre aar.* Oslo: Ad notam Gyldendal.
Castells, Manuel, and Pekka Himanen. 2001. *Suomen tietoyhteiskuntamalli*. Trans. Jukka Kemppinen. Helsinki: WSOY.
———. 2002. *The Information Society and the Welfare State: The Finnish Example*. Oxford: Oxford University Press.
Chambers, Iain. 1994. *Migrancy, Culture, Identity*. London: Routledge.
Cheah, Pheng. 1998. "Introduction, Part II: The Cosmopolitical Today." In *Cosmopolitics: Thinking and Feeling beyond the Nation*, ed. Pheng Cheah and Bruce Robbins, 20–44. Minneapolis: University of Minnesota Press.
Ciecko, Anne. 1998. "Transgender, Transgenre, and the Transnational: Sally Potter's *Orlando*." *Velvet Light Trap* 41: 19–34.
Cowie, Peter. 1985. *Swedish Cinema: From Ingeborg Holm to Fanny and Alexander*. Stockholm: Swedish Institute.
———. 1990. *Finnish Cinema*. Rev. ed. Helsinki: VAPK.
———. 1991. *Scandinavian Cinema: A Survey of Films and Film-Makers in Denmark, Finland, Iceland, Norway, and Sweden*. London: Tantivity, on behalf of "Scandinavian Films"—Nordic Cinema/Cinéma Nordique.
———. 1995. *Icelandic Film*. Reykjavik: Icelandic Film Fund.
———. 1999. *Straight from the Heart: Modern Norwegian Cinema, 1971–1999*. Kristiansund: Kom Forlag.
Cruz-Malavé, Arnaldo, and Martin F. Manalansan IV, eds. 2002. *Queer Globalizations: Citizenship and the Afterlife of Colonialism*. New York: New York University Press.
Durgnat, Raymond. 1971. *A Mirror for England: British Movies from Austerity to Affluence*. London: Praeger.
Einhorn, Eric S., and John Logue. 2003. *Modern Welfare States: Scandinavian Politics and Policy in the Global Age*. 2nd ed. Westport, Conn.: Praeger.
Eriksen, Thomas Hylland. 1993. *Typisk norsk: Essays om kulturen in Norge*. Oslo: C. Huitfeldt Forlag A. S.
Evensmo, Sigurd. 1992. *Det store Tivoli: Film og kino i Norge*. Rev. ed. Oslo: Gyldendal Norsk Forlag.
Furhammar, Leif. 1991. *Filmen i Sverige: En historia i tio kapitel*. Höganäs: Wiken.
Gikandi, Simon. 2001. "Globalization and the Claims of Postcoloniality." *South Atlantic Quarterly* 100: 627–58.
Gilroy, Paul. 1993. *The Black Atlantic: Modernity and Double Consciousness*. Cambridge: Harvard University Press.
Gullestad, Marianne. 2002. *Det norske sett med nye øyne: Kristisk analyse av norskinnvandringsdebatt*. Oslo: Universitetsforlaget.
Halle, Randall, and Sharon Willis, eds. 2000–1. "Marginalities and Alterities in New European Cinema, Parts 1 and 2." Special issue, *Camera Obscura* 44 (15, no. 2); 46 (16, no. 1).

Introduction

Hamsun, Knut. 1890. *Sult.* Copenhagen: Gyldendal.
———. 1894. *Pan.* Copenhagen: Gyldendal.
Higson, Andrew. 1995. *Waving the Flag: Constructing a National Cinema in Britain.* Oxford: Clarendon.
Hjort, Mette. 1996. "Danish Cinema and the Politics of Recognition." In *Post-Theory: Reconstructing Film Studies,* ed. David Bordwell and Noel Carroll, 520–32. Madison: University of Wisconsin Press.
———. 2000. "Themes of Nation." In *Cinema and Nation,* ed. Mette Hjort and Scott MacKenzie, 103–18. New York: Routledge.
Hjort, Mette, and Ib Bondebjerg. 2001. *The Danish Directors: Dialogues on a National Cinema.* Bristol: Intellect.
Hjort, Mette, and Scott MacKenzie. 2000. Introduction to *Cinema and Nation,* ed. Mette Hjort and Scott MacKenzie, 1–16. New York: Routledge.
Ingebritsen, Christine. 1998. *The Nordic States and European Unity.* Ithaca, N.Y.: Cornell University Press.
Jonsson, Stefan. 1993. *De andra: Amerikanska kulturkrig och europeisk rasism.* Stockholm: Norstedts.
———. 1996. *Andra platser: En essä om kulturell identitet.* Stockholm: Norstedts.
———. 2001. *Världens centrum: En essä om globaliseringen.* Stockholm: Norstedts.
Jusdanis, Gregory. 2001. *The Necessary Nation.* Princeton, N.J.: Princeton University Press.
Kaplan, Caren, Norma Alarcón, and Minoo Moallem, eds. 1999. *Between Woman and Nation: Nationalisms, Transnational Feminisms, and the State.* Durham: Duke University Press.
Karkama, Pertti. 1998. *Kulttuuri ja demokratia: Kirjoituksia kulttuurin nykytilasta.* Tietolipas 161. Helsinki: Suomalaisen Kirjallisuuden Seura.
Koivunen, Anu. 1995. *Isänmaan moninaiset äidinkasvot: Sotavuosien suomalainen naisten elokuva sukupuoliteknologiana.* Turku: Suomen Elokuvatutkimuksen Seura.
Kymlicka, Will. 1995. *Multicultural Citizenship: A Liberal Theory of Minority Rights.* Oxford: Clarendon.
Miller, David. 1995. *On Nationality.* New York: Clarendon.
Miller, Toby, Nitin Govil, Richard Maxwell, and John McMurria. 2001. *Global Hollywood.* London: British Film Institute.
Palsson, Gisli, and Kristin E. Hardardottir. 2002. "For Whom the Cell Tolls: Debates about Biomedicine." *Current Anthropology* 43: 271–302.
Pantti, Mervi. 2000. *"Kansallinen elokuva pelastettava": Elokuvapoliittinen keskustelu kotimaisen elokuvan tukemisesta itsenäisyyden ajalla.* Helsinki: Suomalaisen Kirjallisuuden Seura.
Parker, Andrew, Mary Russo, Doris Sommer, and Patricia Yaeger, eds. 1992. *Nationalisms and Sexualities.* New York: Routledge.
Pred, Allan. 2000. *Even in Sweden: Racisms, Racialized Spaces, and the Popular Geographical Imagination.* Berkeley: University of California Press.
Qvist, Per Olov, and Peter von Bagh. 2000. *Guide to the Cinema of Sweden and Finland.* Westport, Conn.: Greenwood.
Radel, Nicholas. 2001. "The Transnational Ga(y)ze: Constructing the East European Object of Desire in Gay Film and Pornography after the Fall of the Wall." *Cinema*

Journal 41, no. 4: 40–62.
Rowe, John Carlos, ed. 2000. *Post-Nationalist American Studies*. Berkeley: University of California Press.
Sabo, Anne. 1999. "Knut Hamsun in *Paa gjengrodde stier*: Joker, Ubermensch, or Sagacious Madman?" *Scandinavian Studies* 71: 453–74.
Schepelern, Peter, ed. 2001. *100 års dansk film*. Copenhagen: Rosinante.
Segrave, Kerry. 1997. *American Films Abroad: Hollywood's Domination of the World's Movie Screens*. Jefferson, N.C.: McFarland.
Smith, Anthony. 1990. "Toward a Global Culture?" In *Global Culture: Nationalism, Globalization, and Modernity*, ed. Mike Featherstone, 171–92. Thousand Oaks, Calif.: Sage.
Soila, Tytti, Astrid Söderbergh Widding, and Gunnar Iversen. 1998. *Nordic National Cinemas*. New York: Routledge.
Spivak, Gayatri. 1999. *A Critique of Post-Colonial Reason*. Cambridge: Harvard University Press.
Stecher-Hansen, Marianne. 1997. *History Revisited: Fact and Fiction in the Documentary Works of Torkild Hansen*. Columbia, S.C.: Camden House.
Suomen kansallisfilmografia. 1990–. 11 vols. Ed. Kari Uusitalo and Sakar Toiviainen. Helsinki: Suomen Elokuva Arkisto.
Svensk filmografi. 1977–. 9 vols. Ed. Lars Åhlander. Stockholm: Svensk Filminstitutet.
Tamir, Yael. 1993. *Liberal Nationalism*. Princeton, N.J.: Princeton University Press.
Taylor, Charles. 1991. "The Politics of Recognition." In *Multiculturalism and "The Politics of Recognition*," ed. Amy Gutmann, 1–51. Princeton, N.J.: Princeton University Press.
Thomas, Kevin. 1997. "Provocative, Haunting Life of Hamsun." *Los Angeles Times*, November 21, 16.
Toiviainen, Sakari. 1975. *Uusi suomalainen elokuva: 60-luvusta nykypäivään*. Helsinki: Otava.
———. 2002. *Levottomat sukupolvet: Uusin suomalainen elokuva*. Helsinki: Suomalaisen Kirjallisuuden Seura.
Uusitalo, Kari. 1967. *Suomalaisen elokuvan vuosikymmenet; johdatus kotimaisen elokuvan ja elokuva-alan historiaan, 1896–1963*. Helsinki: Otava.
Wilinksy, Barbara. 2001. *Sure Seaters: The Emergence of Art House Cinema*. Minneapolis: University of Minnesota Press.
Wollstein, Hans J. 1994. *Strangers in Hollywood: The History of Scandinavian Actors in American Films from 1910 to World War II*. Metuchen, N.J.: Scarecrow.
Zagar, Monika. 1999. "The Rhetoric of Defense in Hamsun's *Paa gjengrodde Stier* (On Overgrown Paths)." *Edda* 3: 252–61.

PART I

Trends in Transitional Nordic Cinema

CHAPTER 1

Costumes, Adolescence, and Dogma: Nordic Film and American Distribution

Trevor G. Elkington

How can films from the Nordic region be marketed transnationally? At first glance, it would seem a difficult task. The relatively small populations speaking each national language and the lack of widespread familiarity with Nordic cultures and histories would appear to relegate Nordic film to an inconspicuous place in global markets. What is more, as for any small national film industry, the struggle to compete against the Hollywood studio system's global hegemony occurs not only outside national borders but within them as well; Hollywood's dominance inside the Scandinavian nation-states further hampers the commercial viability of an indigenous film industry. In an international market dominated by American film, in a global distribution system increasingly steered by studio interests, in a production network ever more internationalized (in which financing often traces a complicated connection to global megacorporations), it may be that there is simply no room left for films from the Nordic region.

Recognizing the precariousness of their national film industries, Nordic governments have adopted strategies to support and fund national and regional filmmaking institutions in the belief that film could be a powerful expression of national culture. But the problem of marketing remains. Once a film is made, it has to find an audience, and governmental initiatives cannot force people to watch movies they don't want to watch. Consider that of the top ten box office performers in Denmark between 1986 and 1996, only three were Danish: *The Crumbs* (Sven Methling, 1991, *Krummerne*), *Walter og Carlo—op på fars hat* (Per Holst, 1985), and *House of Spirits* (1993, *Åndernes hus*), which is arguably not "Danish," as it is Bille August's adaptation of

Isabelle Allende's Latin American novel, starring a multinational cast and filmed in English (Bondebjerg, Andersen, and Schepelern 1997, 404). The remaining films were all Hollywood films, with the exception of the Australian *Crocodile Dundee* (Peter Faiman, 1986). The case is much the same in Iceland, Norway, Sweden, and Finland, where nationally produced films must compete against Hollywood films with big budgets, big stars, and big special effects. Films shot in the national language, appealing to national cultural references and norms, are often overshadowed.

Marketing Nordic films becomes even more difficult when they move outside their national borders. Finding an identifiable profile for a film—and finding an international audience for it—is a difficult task for any filmmaker, given the sea of films produced each year. Many low-budget films from around the globe never find their way to Europe, similarly, one might wonder whether Nordic films simply become lost in the influx of films made available to global audiences.

An important question is why would global audiences be interested in films from the Nordic region? Setting aside the language barriers, one might simply wonder whether a Swedish film has anything of interest to offer a citizen of Hong Kong, Mexico, Australia, or the United States. And yet Nordic films do achieve export status. They do go abroad to film festivals, they do gain international distribution, and they do achieve international acclaim. So what, then, is the best strategy for marketing Nordic film abroad? And how might one best go about determining the status of Nordic films as global commodities? If we are to argue that Nordic film is globalized, then how do we measure its global presence? These are difficult questions to answer, relying as they do on concrete variables such as gross box office receipts, theatrical screenings, and international distribution deals, as well as on intangible variables such as the influence of one film or director on another, the spread of genres, and international audiences' subjective impressions of what Danish, Finnish, Icelandic, Norwegian, or Swedish film might mean, either separately or collectively. One way of measuring global presence is simply to look at marketing and distribution trends, to focus on which films are being shown in which theaters. Such an approach has the advantage of being able to concretely demonstrate which films were available to be seen at a specific historical moment. However, in doing so, certain complexities arise. Is it possible to speak of global trends? In casting a wide net, how many details might escape?

Looking at marketing trends for Nordic film globally requires certain caveats and restrictions. For the purposes of this essay, globalization will be measured by a consideration of the distribution of films in the United States. This restriction is imposed for three reasons. First, by looking at the distribution of foreign film in Hollywood's backyard, one implicitly illustrates the swirl of pressures exerted on Nordic film in the global market. As Toby Miller and his coauthors persuasively argue in *Global Hollywood,* Hollywood film is the dominant globalizing force in the film industry; they note in passing that "Hollywood owns between 40 percent and 90 percent of the movies shown in most parts of the world" (2001, 3) before going on to ask the key question, "Is Hollywood really giving the people of the world what they want?" (15). Arguably, if there is a market for non-Hollywood films within the United States, as I contend there is, then Hollywood must be overlooking at least some aspects of audience demand within its own country—and therefore, by extrapolation, globally. Nordic films fill a specific, though perhaps diminutive, corner of that vacuum.

Second, given the common anxiety that globalization equals Americanization, demonstrating the ability to market non-American fare within the United States itself reveals the possibility of a global model that resists the monopolistic intentions of the vertically integrated studio system with its global commercial network. That is to say, if Nordic films can compete against American films *within the United States,* at whatever relative proportions, then conceivably a global market does exist for Nordic film, as well as a globalized distribution and exhibition system that can resist the monopolies of multimedia entertainment conglomerates. Of course, more often than not, when reaching a broad level of distribution, most non-Hollywood films inevitably end up working with the studio system in some way, most often through foreign distribution deals.

Finally, the resistance of American audiences to foreign or subtitled films is an imprecise but nevertheless telling measure of the marketability of Nordic film worldwide—the logic here being that if Americans will watch it, perhaps anybody will. Of course, this assertion raises the issue of the availability of Nordic films across the globe. Presumably, the United States, because of its enormous market size, draws more films from the Nordic region than, say, Morocco does. This suggests a positive positioning for Nordic film: it is not simply that Hollywood fails to offer something and Nordic film steps in to fill part of that gap, but that films from the Nordic region, individually and collectively, have something to offer that is uniquely and innately their own. This appeal would be marketable regardless of Hollywood production. However one looks at the equation, the underlying argument remains that whatever is offered by Nordic films—culturally, artistically, or ideologically—may have global appeal if it can be successfully marketed in the United States.

Measuring global market presence is complex due to the bricolage of sources: statistics from Nordic and American sources, film histories, and a subjective impression about what kinds of films are generally being seen in the United States and what trends can be observed over the last fifteen years. As such, the discussion necessarily reveals a broad overview of issues. In discussing what films were marketed in the United States between, roughly, the years 1986 and 2003, it is crucial to note the different levels of exhibition—the marked differences as well as the demonstrable overlaps between the film festival circuit, the art house circuit, and mainstream theaters. European films are difficult to distribute to mainstream theaters, and the factors that play into regional distribution are beyond the scope of this essay. It is safe to say that what might be seen in the multiplexes on the populous East and West coasts is not the same as the offerings found in the Midwest or other less populated regions. That a film wins an Oscar, is reviewed in the *New York Times,* or is seen at an international film festival in San Francisco is far from a guarantee that it will have been seen in Omaha or Bozeman.

It should be noted that Nordic influence on the U.S. markets dates to the silent era, and the long history of trade negotiations, embargoes, and migrations of artisans and businesspeople fleeing war, political persecution, or other political factors must be taken into consideration. Moreover, the importance of world-recognized filmmakers such as Dreyer and Bergman, or more recently August, von Trier, Troell, or Kaurismäki, speaks to the global representation of Nordic film. But generally speaking, just as globalization has gained momentum in the contemporary moment, so has the presence of Nordic film commodities in the United States increased since the 1980s; in particular, there has been an expansion above and beyond the specific clustered followings of various film auteurs. This is a significant develop-

Costumes, Adolescence, and Dogma

Pelle (Pelle Hvenegaard) in the stable in Bille August's *Pelle the Conquerer* (1987)

ment, implying as it does the attractiveness of Nordic film in general, as opposed to the idiosyncratic cinematic vision of a particular filmmaker. What has changed, particularly in the mid-1980s, is the prevalence and profile of Nordic film in the United States. Over a few short years, the success of a few key films largely determined not only the conception of what constitutes Nordic film for the American moviegoing population but also what kinds of films were selected for distribution and which films enjoyed commercial success. In looking at the marketing trends starting in the 1980s, one trend with three facets emerges: the importance of genre films, specifically historical costume dramas, literary adaptations, and coming-of-age films. How these types of films came to represent Nordic filmmaking in its entirety, and how that trend slowly evolved into something else, can be traced back to a few key films.

COSTUMES AND ADOLESCENCE

What a surprise it was when, as though out of nowhere, two Danish films consecutively won Best Foreign Language Film Oscars. Gabriel Axel's *Babette's Feast* (1987, *Babettes gæstebud*) and Bille August's *Pelle the Conqueror* (1988, *Pelle Erobreren*, 1987) not only proved the region's filmmaking potential but in many ways reflected and perhaps determined what most Americans came to expect of European film at the time. Both films were popular among critics. Rita Kempley, in her review for the *Washington Post,* praised *Babette's Feast* for its performances and its superlative capturing of atmosphere and setting, writing, "This deceptively modest story, with its quiet colors and contemplative characters, actually teems with contrasts and subtle dynamics. . . . Axel and his fine cast interpret Dinesen's ironic original with great charm and gentle comedy." Roger Ebert (1989) called *Pelle the Conqueror* "a richness of events," citing August's directing and superb performances by Max von Sydow (Lasse) and Pelle Hvenegaard (Pelle). Still, critical success is far from a guarantee of financial success, as many directors can attest. The difference for these two films lay in their appeal to a growing niche market of baby boomers and yuppies, well-educated middle- to upper-class Americans seeking an alternative to the increasingly formulaic Hollywood product.

The two films' financial success was directly attributable to their having won Best Foreign Language Film Oscars. Being nominated for or even winning an Oscar is far from a reliable indication of a film's artistic value, of course, or of its eventual place in film history; some of the greatest or most influential films of all time received no attention when they were released, while the list of Oscar winners is filled with films completely, and often rightly, forgotten. But the Oscar does reliably indicate what Americans are watching, or at least have the opportunity to watch, at a given period of time. Simply stated, without the award, it is debatable whether either of these two films would have received attention from nationwide distributors, Orion Classics in the case of *Babette* and Miramax for *Pelle*. With these distributors behind them, both films played in first-run theaters in major cities across the United States, breaking out of the art house and film festival circuit into which previous films from Nordic countries were generally relegated. After winning the Oscar, *Babette's Feast* went on to a total gross of $4.4 million, while *Pelle the Conqueror* grossed $2.1 million after its Oscar, respectable numbers for a foreign film in the United States.[1]

It is entirely possible that these two films could have been a historical fluke, a bit of obscure Oscar trivia: which two Danish films won the Best Foreign Language Film Oscar back-to-back in the late 1980s? Despite their success, the films' common traits (such as European settings, high-quality production values, and strong directing and acting) proved to be no guarantee of international notice, as *Waltzing Regitze* (Kaspar Rostrup, 1989, *Dansen med Regitze,* Denmark²) demonstrated one year after *Pelle the Conqueror:* it was nominated for but failed to receive the Best Foreign Language Film Oscar. Likewise, Søren Kragh-Jacobsen's *Emma's Shadow* (1988, *Skyggen af Emma,* Denmark) received some attention but not an Oscar nomination, grossing only a fraction of the two Oscar winners' receipts in the United States. What then, was the secret of their success? What helped these two films vault the gap between little-seen foreign film and nationally distributed Oscar winner? More than anything, it may have been a question of timing.

Without detracting from the work of the filmmakers, it is evident that *Babette* and *Pelle* appeared at a moment when American audiences had a growing taste for literary adaptations and historical costume dramas, particularly those of foreign origin: what Andrew Higson (1993) refers to in his essay "Re-presenting the National Past" as "heritage films," with clear overtones of nation-building and historical and cultural expression implicit within that term. In 1986 Ismail Merchant and James Ivory released *A Room with a View,* a costume drama set in turn-of-the-century Florence, based on the novel by E. M. Forster. The success of this film, and its predecessor *The Bostonians* (1984), based on the Henry James novel, led to a long line of successful Merchant-Ivory literary adaptations and costume dramas such as *Maurice* (1987), *Howards End* (1992), and *The Remains of the Day* (1993); they also inspired or influenced similar films from other filmmakers, such as *Impromptu* (James Lapine, 1991), *Enchanted April* (Mike Newell, 1992), *The Age of Innocence* (Martin Scorsese, 1993), and *The Wings of the Dove* (Iain Softley, 1997). Noting the popularity of these films is not to suggest that they were directly responsible for the success of *Babette's Feast* or *Pelle the Conqueror;* indeed, many of these films came after the historical drama, a genre with deep roots in the region, had already gained momentum in the Nordic countries. Rather, both phenomena mark a larger trend of popularity and success among films with pre–World War II historical settings, extravagant costuming, foreign languages (or at least foreign accents), and, most often, literary sources. More specifically, these two films indicate what American audiences came to expect from European film in general and Nordic film in particular.

Again using Oscar attention as a market index, it is possible to demonstrate the growing popularity of European costume dramas, particularly films with a setting prior to World War II. Looking at the films nominated for Best Foreign Feature Film in the years between 1976 and 2000, a significant trend is clearly identifiable. Five European pre–World War II costume dramas were nominated for a Foreign Film Oscar between 1976 and 1986. That number nearly triples to fourteen in the years between 1988 (*Pelle the Conqueror*) and 2000. The significance of this development as a distinctly *European* trend is reflected in the relative stability of costume dramas, American or otherwise, nominated for the category of Best Feature Film. Before 1987 eleven pre–World War II films were nominated; after 1988 fourteen films were nominated.[3]

In the final analysis, while the blossoming of European historical costume dramas mirrors a general trend in global filmmaking, it also reflects a particular set of expectations by American audiences toward European film, specifically the type of film that *Babette* and *Pelle* most clearly exemplify: stately, historical, literary, and (while perhaps tragic at times) ultimately inspirational and uplifting. A short list of major releases from Nordic countries that fit this generic category reads like who's who of filmmakers as well as a canonical index of recent Nordic film history: *Hamsun* (Jan Troell, 1996, Denmark), *The Magnetist's Fifth Winter* (Morten Henriksen, 1999, *Magnetisørens femte vinter,* Denmark), *Barbara* (Niels Malmros, 1997, Denmark), *As White as in Snow* (Jan Troell, 2001, *Så vit som en snö,* Sweden), *Good Evening, Mr. Wallengberg* (Kjell Grede, 1990, *God afton, Herr Wallenberg,* Sweden), *Jerusalem* (Bille August, 1996, Sweden), *Best Intentions* (Bille August, 1992, *Den goda viljan,* Sweden), *Sofie* (Liv Ullmann, 1992, Denmark), *Kristin Lavransdatter* (Liv Ullmann, 1995, Germany/Norway), *Misery Harbour* (Nils Gaup, 1999, Canada/Denmark/Norway), *Pan* (Henning Carlsen, 1995, Norway), and *Zero Kelvin* (Hans Petter Moland, 1995, *Kjærlighetens kjøtere,* Norway), to name just a few. The intention is not to indicate anything about the relative qualities of any of these films, only to point out that each of them was exhibited in the United States, be it at a film festival, art house theater, or, in a few instances, a mainstream venue. With few exceptions, they take as their source a novel with a historical setting, reaffirming the perception of Nordic filmmaking as inextricably linked to this particular genre and consolidating the notion that Nordic filmmaking is the expression of Nordic culture, both historical and literary.

The same dynamic can be demonstrated for the coming-of-age genre. Long a staple in the Nordic region, the genre remains a perennial favorite among national audiences. Early examples, such as *Ditte, Child of Man* (Bjarne Henning-Jensen, 1946, *Ditte menneskebarn*, Denmark), paved the way for a rapid growth of the genre through the 1970s and point directly to later examples, such as *My Life as a Dog* (Lasse Hallström, 1985, *Mitt liv som hund*, Sweden), *Twist and Shout* (Bille August, 1984, *Tro, håb og kærlighed*, Denmark), and *Show Me Love* (Lukas Moodysson, 1998, *Fucking Åmål*, Sweden). While coming-of-age films from Nordic countries have not had the Oscar success that the costume drama genre has enjoyed, or the accompanying financial rewards, they remain a popular and ever-present selection at film festivals and art film theaters. In fact, one might think of *Pelle the Conqueror* as having achieved the trifecta of Nordic film genres: a coming-of-age film based on a novel set before World War II. As such, its success is not only indicative, it may have been inevitable.

Another significant example of this dynamic can be found in Nils Gaup's *Pathfinder* (1987, *Ofelas*, Norway). Set roughly in the year 1000 AD, the film follows the adventures of Aigin (Mikkel Gaup), a teenage Sami whose family is killed by a band of invading Tchudes, a legendary group in Sami folklore. Escaping the marauders, Aigin finds his way to a friendly Lapp village whose inhabitants, upon hearing his tale, fear that he will be followed by the Tchudes and flee to the coast. Aigin stays behind, avenging his family through a series of ruses and cunning stratagems. Though quasi-historical, the film is clearly based on folktale and an accurate sense of detail; as such, it roughly fits the category of adaptation (though from nonliterary sources) as well as the costume drama, though in this case it is snowshoes and fur capes that take the place of corsets or peasant tunics. More important, the film mixes the action-adventure genre with the coming-of-age film; part of Aigin's challenge is to overcome his adolescent ways and fully assume and appreciate his place within Sami society. This successful genre hybrid found critical and popular support and was nominated for a Best Foreign Language Film Oscar.

As a strategy for global distribution, following in the well-worn footsteps of other genre films, heritage films gamble on the possibility of appealing to the same audience that made the original films successful. However, they also run the risk of arriving after that audience has become tired of the genre altogether. Consider that in the Oscars for the years 2000 through 2002, only one foreign-language film set prior to World War II has been nominated each year: one a musical set in Victorian India (*Lagaan,* Ashutosh Gowariker, 2001), one set in ancient Imperial China (*Hero,* Zhang Yimou, 2002), and one a martial-arts film set in a mythical feudal China that can only loosely be considered historical (*Crouching Tiger, Hidden Dragon,* Ang Lee, 2000). If these kinds of historical settings dictate a shift in American audiences' appetites for the history of other countries, it does not bode well for Nordic costume dramas. It has always been the case that genres wax and wane in popularity; it is inevitable that the same would apply to Nordic film exports, be they historical costume dramas, coming-of-age films, or whatever genre might strike the fancy of global audiences next.

AMERICAN INDEPENDENT FILM AND CONTEMPORARY NORDIC FILMMAKERS

In the years following the Oscar successes and a general upswing in Nordic film in the United States, a problem was on the horizon for Nordic film, one that few directors, producers, or studios in Europe or America could have anticipated. As quickly as American tastes had swung toward the kind of films Nordic film industries were skilled at producing, they appeared to begin to swing once more. Again, defining the reasons that commercial trends develop and persist is something of an alchemy. However, one significant development must be taken into account: the rise of the American independent feature film.

In 1989 Steven Soderbergh debuted his first feature film, *sex, lies, and videotape,* at a then relatively unknown film festival at a ski resort in the mountains outside Salt Lake City, Utah. Critical response was encouraging, but more important was the word-of-mouth publicity among audience members, which led the film to sell out its festival run. When Miramax's Bob and Harvey Weinstein bought the film for a little over $1.1 million, few could anticipate its success. Miramax launched a brilliant advertising campaign playing up twenty-six-year-old Soderbergh's auteur mystique as well as the title, with its generous hint of scandal. The film grossed $24.7 million in the United States alone, an unprecedented return for an independent film. Soderbergh later won the Palme d'Or for *sex, lies, and videotape,* and Hollywood took notice. The next year, that little film festival in Park City, Utah, was flooded with studio executives and industry insiders looking for the next Soderbergh. The legend of Sundance and the archetype of the "indie wunderkind" were born.

Costumes, Adolescence, and Dogma

In significant ways, the explosive rise of American independent film in the 1990s is tied to two significant social factors. One, the strength of the American economy during the 1990s brought more and more people to theaters in general. However, ticket sales for less mainstream foreign and independent films expanded rapidly in a market saturated by Hollywood films that had changed little since the early 1980s, geared as they were toward big-budget action films or light comedies. Two, within the United States, the so-called Generation X, well educated but underemployed, had gradually increased its economic status with the growth of high-tech market sectors and other better-paying jobs. This social shift is clearly reflected in the success of Gen-X films such as Richard Linklater's *Slacker* (1991) or Kevin Smith's *Clerks* (1994).[4] The popularity of such films reflected a growing desire among ticket buyers of this generation to see films reflecting their own interests; the subsequent distribution of independent films such as Linklater's *Dazed and Confused* (1993), *Kicking and Screaming* (Noah Baumbach, 1995), *Chasing Amy* (Kevin Smith, 1997) as well as studio films like *Reality Bites* (Ben Stiller, 1994) demonstrates Hollywood's close attention.

Inevitably perhaps, many of these directors were drawn by the siren call of Hollywood money, but whereas the studio system generally tends to discourage experimentation and dampen the urge to take risks, the success of independent film as an industry had now proven that the experimentation embraced by this new generation of filmmakers had a significant and profitable following. The studio systems did not, of course, offer these directors carte blanche to take huge financial risks; nevertheless, the impact of the independent industry is demonstrated by pointing to the popularity of recent highly unconventional films affiliated with the studio system: *Magnolia* (Paul Thomas Anderson, 1999), *Being John Malkovich* (Spike Jonze, 2000), *American Beauty* (Sam Mendes, 1999), *Three Kings* (David O. Russell, 1999), and *Fight Club* (David Fincher, 1999). Likewise, the bigger budgets and higher gross profits of films like *Election* (Alexander Payne, 1999), made for $8.5 million with partial studio investment by Paramount, or *Rushmore* (Wes Anderson, 1998), made for $10 million with investment from Touchstone, a boutique branch of the Walt Disney conglomerate, demonstrate the increasing appetite among American audiences for less conventional, more experimental fare, as well as the increasing willingness among studios to back these types of films.

Generally speaking, all of these movies emphasize characterization and dialogue over the common studio specialties of action, setting, or glamour. The impact of the independent film boom on the larger film industry, and on the Hollywood studio system, is undeniable. Indeed, at the 2003 Academy Awards, all five Best Picture nominations were technically independent productions, demonstrating the general shift in audience taste as well as a clear change in which types of films the studios are now financing. As one critic noted in the *New York Times*'s coverage of the event, "This illustrates . . . the almost total abandonment of the field by the major Hollywood studios, opening the way for minimajors and independent distributors to seize control of the day" (Lyman 2003).

Unfortunately, this may be bad news for Nordic film. Whereas films like *Babette* and *Pelle* seemed fresh and new at the time of their release, films similar in style, such as *Hamsun* or *Barbara*, run the risk of seeming outdated to larger circles of American audiences. Critical reception of both films was positive, even admiring. Stephen Holden of the *New York Times* praised Max von Sydow's portrayal of Hamsun, calling it a "career-crowning performance" (1997). *Barbara* received similarly favorable reviews. However, neither matched the popular acclaim of the earlier Oscar winners. An audience does exist for these films, as both played to enthusiastic festival and art house audiences. But the shift back to those venues is in itself indicative of a change in American tastes.

Fortunately, away from these more traditional films with their larger budgets, a change of aesthetic is occurring among filmmakers in the Nordic region, particularly among the younger generation currently being produced by film schools. It is a change that reflects a similar shift among American filmmakers. Given America's dominance over global film distribution, it is perhaps to be expected that international audiences develop a taste for the films Hollywood spends so much money ensuring they see. A film like *Pulp Fiction* (Quentin Tarantino, 1994) has as large a following internationally as it does domestically. Likewise, just as successful or unique films and directors inspire imitation within the American film industry, they also influence the international industry.

The influence of American independent films on many recent Nordic films is clear. Niels Arden Oplev's *Portland* (1996, Denmark), clearly recalls Gus van Sant's *Drugstore Cowboy* (1989). The numerous

Costumes, Adolescence, and Dogma

American imitations of Martin Scorsese's seminal film *Mean Streets* (1973)[5] are echoed in a film like *Pizza King* (Ole Christian Madsen, 1999, Denmark), which follows a group of young immigrants through Copenhagen's criminal underworld. The undeniably Tarantinoesque flavor of Nicolas Winding Refn's films *Pusher* (1996, Denmark) and *Bleeder* (1999, Denmark) and other films like *In China They Eat Dogs* (Lasse Spang Olson, 1999, *I Kina spiser de hunde*, Denmark), *Flickering Lights* (Anders Thomas Jensen, 2000, *Blinkende lygter*, Denmark), or *Bad Luck Love* (Olli Saarela, 2000, Finland), does not lessen their appeal, nor did it impede their domestic success.[6] Even gratifyingly unique films like *Bye Bye Blue Bird* (Katrin Ottarsdóttir, 1999, Denmark) or *Eggs* (Bent Hamer, 1995, Norway)—with its quirky characters and vibrant dialogue—or *Let's Get Lost* (Jonas Elmer, 1997, Denmark) and *101 Reykjavik* (Baltazar Kormákur, 2000, Iceland), with their loose slacker charm, owe a debt to Jim Jarmusch's *Stranger Than Paradise* (1984) or any number of Hal Hartley films (*The Unbelievable Truth* [1990], *Trust* [1991]). Likewise, the Norwegian director Erik Skjoldbjærg's noir thriller, *Insomnia* (1997, Norway) was not only remade starring Al Pacino, directed by Christopher Nolan (*Memento*, 2000), and distributed by Warner Brothers, the film was also issued in DVD form as part of the prestigious Criterion Collection, a label more commonly associated with elaborate re-releases of film classics like *Beauty and the Beast* (Jean Cocteau, 1946, *Belle et la Bête*) or *The Passion of Joan of Arc* (Carl Th. Dreyer, 1928, *La passion de Jeanne d'Arc*). The recent Finnish film *The River* (Jarmo Lampela, 2001, *Joki*, Finland) bears the clear markings of indie legend Robert Altman's freewheeling, kaleidoscopic narratives like *Nashville* (1975) or *Short Cuts* (1993). One fitting example of the transnational potential of Nordic film is in Lukas Moodysson's *Together* (2000, *Tilsammans*, Sweden), which grossed over $1 million at the American box office. The film garnered enthusiastic reviews: Roger Ebert noted its "gentle, observant humor" (2001b), and Kenneth Turan of the *Los Angeles Times* called it "relaxed, intimate, wonderfully clear-eyed and altogether charming" (2001). These reviews came despite the film's seemingly inherently "Swedish" story about a small-scale commune of the type strongly associated with 1970s-era Scandinavian socialism.

The point is not to dismiss recent Nordic films as unoriginal or to suggest that any one of the films mentioned intentionally imitates another, more successful film, though obviously imitation occurs. Nor is it my intention to argue that all contemporary Nordic film is an echo of Hollywood or American film production. Rather, I wish to underscore the significance of transnational exchange, to demonstrate that neither film production nor distribution develops within a hermetically sealed national, or even regional, culture. Nordic film cannot be dismissed for playing to Hollywood's worst traits; on the contrary, there is a clear discourse between the best of new generations of American and Nordic filmmakers. And to the region's collective credit, there have been relatively few attempts to imitate the worst excesses of the "blockbuster aesthetic." Indeed, as Søren Kragh-Jacobsen once said in a slightly different context, "In that area we can't beat the Americans anyway, so we Europeans should head in another direction" (Iversen n.d.). Clearly, the growing demand for an alternate film aesthetic was met by and shaped through American independent film, and that success has permeated transnational filmmaking culture. If a film of a particular genre or style does well critically or financially, it becomes that much easier for a similar film to be made and find distribution, regardless of its national origin. In the increasingly internationalized film industry, it is inevitable that a significant filmmaking trend in the United States will be reflected in the product of other nations, and the Nordic region is no exception. What is perhaps less readily predictable is that the influence flows both ways: not only from the United States to northern Europe but also from northern Europe to the United States.

As an example, in June 1997 the Toronto International Film Festival Group, an organization that runs the well-known film festival of the same name as well as a yearlong program of foreign and independent film, organized a festival titled "Northern Encounters," which included retrospectives of Lars von Trier, Carl Dreyer, Aki Kaurismäki, and Fridrik Thór Fridriksson as well as numerous other films from the Nordic countries. The festival featured a sampling of the so-called Danish New Wave with three films, *The Eighteens* (Anders Rønnow-Klarlund, 1997, *Den attende,* Denmark), *Portland,* and *Hamsun*. Likewise, in 1998 the Washington Commission for the Humanities organized its first Scandinavian Film Festival, a film program that traveled from Seattle to Portland and elsewhere, featuring Jonas Elmer's quirky comedy *Let's Get Lost* as well as the more traditional *Hamsun.*

The appeal of these and similar festivals comes in part from their clearly non-Hollywood programming. Don Irvine of Toronto's *Globe and Mail* titled his 1997 review of the Toronto festival "Cold Relief from

Hollywood," evoking both the arctic setting of several of the films as well as the general understanding of Nordic film as a refreshing alternative to more typical programming choices. Clearly, an awareness of the region's less mainstream offerings has been growing in North America. Ole Bornedal's serial-killer thriller *Nightwatch* (1994, *Nattevagten*, Denmark), while not distributed widely in America in its Danish version, did inspire a remake, helmed by Bornedal and starring Ewan McGregor. Bille August directed the Hollywood adaptations of Isabelle Allende's novel *House of Spirits* and Peter Høeg's *Smilla's Sense of Snow* (1997). While none of these films were wildly successful among critics or at the box office, they did indicate a willingness by American distributors to take on films by Nordic directors; moreover, these films demonstrate a willingness among Nordic directors to work in genres that appeal to the American audience. Even more significant, all these films and festivals predate both the premier of Thomas Vinterberg's *The Celebration* and the influence of the Dogma 95 concept. At the same moment that changing tastes among American audiences threatened to undermine the appeal of traditional Nordic film exports, a new generation of filmmakers appeared and spoke to that changing taste successfully.

DOGMA 95 AND TRANSNATIONAL IMPACT

When Lars von Trier announced the Dogma 95 project at "Le cinéma vers son deuxième siècle," a 1995 Paris conference gathered to celebrate the first century of film and discuss film's future, even American critics took notice. Von Trier strode onto the stage, announced the Dogma cri de coeur, and threw red leaflets with the Dogma Manifesto and Vow of Chastity into the puzzled crowd; his actions could not help but awaken a certain curiosity. He was already known internationally, primarily for the success of his films at the Cannes Film Festival. *The Element of Crime* (1984) won the Technical Grand Prize and was nominated for the Palme d'Or; *Europa* (1991) won the Technical Grand Prize, the Jury Prize, and Best Artistic Contribution as well as a Palme d'Or nomination. In the intervening three years between the announcement of Dogma and the first film, von Trier made his major American breakthrough with *Breaking the Waves* (1996), a film that evoked a deeply split critical reaction. Roger Ebert (n.d.) admiringly called it "emotionally and spiritually challenging" as well as "bold, angry and defiant," noting how rarely such movies are made, while in his review for the *Los Angeles Times,* Kenneth Turan called it "skillful and provocative filmmaking sent on a fool's errand . . . the flimsy illusion of profundity more than the real thing itself" (1996). Critics and audiences seemed completely baffled by the film's apparently straight-faced endorsement of sacrifice through sexual depravity, and many seemed entirely ignorant of any potential irony in the final moment of Bess's divine ascension amid peals of heavenly bells. While only a moderate success at the box office, grossing $4 million in U.S. ticket sales, the film ensured that anything with which von Trier was associated would awaken awareness and controversy. So when the first Dogma film reached American theaters, an audience stood ready to receive it, though perhaps not with unquestioning hearts.

Any skepticism about the Dogma project or Lars von Trier's association with it was completely erased with the opening of Thomas Vinterberg's *The Celebration* (1998, *Festen,* Denmark). Critics loved it. The film's premiere in New York inspired a long article in the *New York Times* on the Dogma project, including an interview with Vinterberg. The newspaper's review of the film was full of praise not only for its audacity but also for the beauty and poignancy of its story. Janet Maslin, well known for her discriminating tastes, called the film "a virtuoso feat" (1998). Distributed by October Films, at the time an up-and-coming independent distributor, which subsequently became a major independent ministudio, the film played in most major cities across the United States, grossing $1.6 million by February 1999 and enjoying vigorous video sales after its theatrical release.

While box office receipts were impressive, and the film was praised for its sense of Aristotelian unity and grand tragedy, most significant was the impact of Dogma's main concepts: that film could be technically simple and restrained, and yet still be effective. *Dogma* and *chastity* quickly became buzzwords among film fans and industry representatives alike. Ironically, for many American critics and filmmakers, the revolutionary zeal of the Dogma project became inextricably tied to a production detail that was not explicitly part of the Dogma project: the use of digital video as a filmmaking technology. In a single film, Vinterberg's *The Celebration* proved the viability of feature-length digital filmmaking, simultaneously reinvigorating interest in Scandinavian cinema among U.S. audiences and filmmakers. Von Trier may have been the more well-known director, but it was Vinterberg's film, without question, that launched the innumerable Dogma and Dogma-esque imitators.

In an article for *Res Magazine*, a journal devoted to "the Future of Filmmaking" and specifically digital technology, John Turk writes: "Filmmakers looking to make the switch from film to DV [digital video] seemed to be waiting for a form of proof that would validate DV as a viable filmmaking medium. Along came Thomas Vinterberg's *The Celebration* and suddenly the conversation about format switched to a conversation about substance—not in methodology, but in content" (1999, 14). The implication is simple: Vinterberg's film proved to the world that a film could be shot on digital video, a format more commonly associated with surveillance cameras and home video, and that such a film could be both a commercial and an artistic success.

Yet the technology often became inseparable from the Dogma ideology in general. In an interview for the same magazine, Mike Figgis (*Leaving Las Vegas*, 1995) clearly echoes the Dogma rhetoric in discussing his film *TimeCode* (2000): "Film has become such a prostituted art form—it's been to bed with far too many people and we know that. In the crudest terms, we don't feel like we're getting a virgin anymore. So one has to reinvent a kind of *chastity* for the cinema, one that allows you to enter the relationship with cinema in a fresh way" (Willis 2000a, 33; emphasis added). Figgis's film, shot on digital video under constraints quite similar to the Dogma Vow of Chastity, shares more than technology with the Dogma project; the director's entire purpose seems one of revolution and renewal. Vinterberg once called *The Celebration* and Dogma 95 his "attempt to undress film, to reach the 'naked film'" ("Dogme95 FAQ" n.d.). Likewise, Søren Kragh-Jacobsen praised the project for "its liberation from the way a director can be raped by technology, the fact that you can be tyrannized by all the expensive gear" (Iversen n.d.). While it should be noted that Kragh-Jacobsen agreed to be a member of the project only after being assured that he could shoot on film stock, nevertheless the tenor of Dogma 95's rhetoric, with talk of tyranny, revolution, and liberation, clearly spilled over into the dialogue surrounding DV technology itself. With the premiere of *The Celebration* and the substantial media buzz that surrounded the Dogma project in general, the cinematic validity of digital video became synonymous with a revolutionary stance against Hollywood. Digital video was to be the democratic technology that filmmakers had longed for, the tool that would allow anyone with the adequate time and inspiration to make film art.

The distribution and reception of von Trier's Dogma film, *The Idiots* (1998, *Idioterne*), was impaired by a conflict between the director and the American film-rating system over its explicit sex scenes and depiction of erect penises. In order to receive anything other than an X rating, the offending scenes would have to be cut; von Trier insisted that the film be released uncut, with offending scenes masked by black bars as a testament to its censorship. The resulting imbroglio delayed the release of *The Idiots* for over a year, during which time Kragh-Jacobsen's far less provocative film, *Mifune* (1999, *Mifunes sidste sang*), was released to praise and attention. Winning the Silver Bear at the Berlin Film Festival, *Mifune* was well received by audiences, grossing $2.3 million in the United States, and by critics, who noted its "naturalness, freshness and warmth that is often so transporting it's magical" (Stack n.d.). Eventually *The Idiots* was released, with von Trier's black bars firmly in place. But by then the impact of Dogma 95 had already been felt, and the list of converts to the Dogma church of digital video was long and by now, perhaps, commonplace. Art house renegade Harmony Korine, screenwriter of the controversial *Kids* (Larry Clark, 1995) and director of *Gummo* (1997), premiered his Dogma film *julien donkey-boy* (1999), a film that violated the Vow of Chastity in many direct ways but nonetheless demonstrated that at least the spirit of Dogma could be translated to the United States.

Dogma would have earned its place in American film history even had it inspired no imitators and been responsible for only the four Danish films of the original project (the fourth was Kristian Levring's *The King Is Alive*, which debuted in 2000). But providing as it did the first proof of a new technology for filmmaking, one that was easy to work with, cheap enough to be widely accessible, and now artistically acceptable, Vinterberg and company's use of digital video inspired numerous films by American filmmakers. Miguel Arteta's film *Chuck & Buck* (2000) was one of the first to appear; it was immediately compared to the Dogma films for its style and aesthetic immediacy. Arteta specifically chose digital video on the strength of *The Celebration*, noting, "We were sold totally after seeing that film," before going on to make the common connection between DV and a sense of emotional truth: "We knew digital would work for *Chuck & Buck* because it's a very intimate, character-driven story" (Willis 2000b, 44).

Likewise, when Jennifer Jason Leigh and Alan Cumming decided to shoot their digital film, *The Anniversary Party* (2001), the very nature of the project sounded like a Dogma film. They gathered their closest Hollywood friends, a glamorous ensemble including Gwyneth Paltrow, Parker Posey, Kevin Kline, and Phoebe Cates as well as Cumming and Leigh themselves; found an available mansion in the Hollywood hills; and shot for three weeks. Based on a script that follows a party over nearly a twenty-four-hour period, complete with revelations, accusations, resolutions, and reconciliations, the film's immediate parallels to *The Celebration* are obvious. Leigh admits getting the idea for the film after finishing work on Kristian Levring's *The King Is Alive*. Codirector Cumming states of the experience: "I think more people should make more films like this—about people talking. We should go back to films that are about things, about language and not just about car chases or people shooting each other. . . . I think we should go back to telling stories by telling language" (Willis 2001, 41). Interestingly, Cumming does not praise the medium for its fabled intimacy, noting that "we tried as hard as we could to disguise the fact that we shot on DV in the finished film—it's still an intensely ugly medium" (39), but one wonders if this is a question of the medium's lacking intimacy or its all too intimate ability to reveal the film's stars for the ordinary people that they are. For an ensemble of Hollywood actors, the possibility of being less than beautiful at all times must be disturbing.

More significant in its impact on American filmmaking was Dogma's proof that making a film could be both technologically and financially accessible. For a beginning filmmaker, working with a limited budget and often with other beginners, the freedom to make mistakes that do not sink the project budget is most attractive. Even Cumming notes that "on video, if you fuck up, it's no big deal. You just get on with it" (Bailey 2001, 14).

More to the point, the kinds of films made available by the flexibility of digital video are quite different in nature than those made available by traditional film technology, a fact anticipated by the success of *The Blair Witch Project* (Daniel Myrick and Eduardo Sànchez, 1998) and exploited to its fullest by von Trier's fabled one hundred cameras in *Dancer in the Dark* (2000). Even Spike Lee, who at Cannes in 1999 proclaimed his distrust of digital technology, stating, "I don't even cut on Avid [a digital editing system]" (Kaufman 1999, 6), had changed his tune by 2000, praising the technology for its flexibility during his production of his film and digital hybrid, *Bamboozled* (2000). For Lee and others, these projects would quite literally have not been possible had it not been for the breakthrough of digital video, a breakthrough that must be directly credited to the success of Vinterberg's *The Celebration* and the rest of the Dogma films. Lee best sums it up in speaking of *Bamboozled*: "*The Celebration* was the film that showed me that this could be done" (Goldstein 2000, 49).

With the success of *The Celebration* and *Mifune*, and to a lesser extent due to the notoriety of *The Idiots*, Dogma certification has become a visa to American shores, regardless of national origins. Lone Scherfig's romantic comedy *Italian for Beginners* (2001, *Italiensk for begyndere*, Denmark) received positive reviews in the American press. Stephen Holden in the *New York Times* called it "a movie that looks like a John Cassavetes film but ends up emitting the benign feel-good vibrations of a movie like *Enchanted April*" (2001). Levring's *The King Is Alive*, in many ways the most artistically challenging and rewarding of all the Dogma films, has elicited mixed reviews. Roger Ebert noted how the film stuck in his thoughts: "Ungainly, ill-formed, howling and desperate, it was there, and endured" (2001a). On the other hand, the *Los Angeles Times* called it "stylish and gritty" (Thomas 2001) but felt it lacked impact. Audience response has likewise been mixed, and the film has not enjoyed the financial success of the previous Dogma films, perhaps because of its quite explicitly artistic use of the video image. Susanne Bier's *Open Hearts* (2002, *Elsker dig for evigt*, Denmark) and Ole Christian Madsen's *Kira's Reason: A Love Story* (2001, *En kærlighedshistorie*, Denmark) were both released commercially in the United States to positive reviews and moderate box office gross.

Mads Egmont Christensen argues in his essay "Dogma and Marketing" that the international marketability of Dogma films was hurt by what he calls the "hit-and-run strategy" used to sell Kragh-Jacobsen's *Mifune* at the Berlin Film Festival. He notes that the buzz generated internally by the film, along with the previous success of *The Celebration*, led to a bidding war among distributors at the festival. But as he writes, "Everybody—sellers and buyers alike—made the mistake of confusing the internal marketing elements and the specific arguments which needed to be applied in the sale between the agent and the distributor, with the potential of the external marketing. It was in other words impossible for the distributors locally to recreate the sensation that they had experienced at the market in Berlin, and have that work for their audiences" (2000). Consequently, the films that followed, such as *The King Is Alive* and *Truly Human* (Åke Sandgren, 2001, *Et rigtigt menneske*, Denmark), may have been hampered internationally by distributors operating on the principle "once bitten, twice shy." On the other hand, both *The King Is Alive* and *Truly Human* are experimental in style and narrative; the Dogma films that have tended to perform best in the United States have been those with the most implicitly humanistic and accessible content, such as *The Celebration* and *Italian for Beginners*.

But even the fact that the recent Dogma films received notice on the level of the *New York Times* and the *Los Angeles Times* indicates the breadth of Dogma's significance; prior to *The Celebration,* Dogma films would have been limited to art house and festival circuits—if they had been distributed in the United States at all. And more to the point, reviews in the mainstream press speak to Dogma's lasting influence on a transnational and potentially global level. As it stands, Dogma 95 has become the cinematic equivalent of open-source coding. Similar to Linux, it provides a format for universal application and as such, invites revision, improvement, and realignment according to the particular demands of the application. Regardless of whether the various directors inspired by its impulse recognize their debt to its ideas, the useful impact of Dogma 95 continues to shape a certain niche of international filmmaking. Of course, the American film audience is a fickle beast, as any foreign filmmaker can attest, and whether the current attention being paid to Dogma films and their imitators will in time pass remains to be seen. Perhaps it is enough to enjoy for the moment the attention it has brought to the filmmaking efforts of the Nordic corner of the globe.

Examining popular trends to see which Nordic films perform well and which are ignored in the United States overlooks the larger, much more complicated picture of the Nordic film industries within their respective nations. Films from Nordic countries that find any type of an audience in the United States are only a fraction of actual films produced within the five nations annually; consequently, studying the transnational marketing trends of this wealth of films by focusing on films that make it "over there" is a bit like trying to understand an elephant, or even a mouse, through a microscope. We focus on one small detail at a time, but in consequence may never come to see the larger animal. On the other hand, the fact that only a fraction of the films available for distribution actually are distributed in North America indirectly points to the significance of these trends. American audiences in general seem to choose the familiar: the costume drama, the coming-of-age film, and now the Dogma film. Consequently, they tend to ignore films that fall outside those expectations. Yet as each genre gives way to formula and potential audience alienation, so the stage is set, one hopes, for a new trend, when a fresh and unexpected cinematic vision comes along to push audiences and filmmakers in another direction.

NOTES

1. Gross receipts information as reported on the Internet Movie Database (http://www.imdb.com).
2. For the purposes of this essay, nationality is assigned according to the film's production company or the primary funding source, as specified on the Internet Movie Database (http://www.imdb.com). While necessary, such a system inevitably oversimplifies the complexities of coproduction.(See chapter 5 for a discussion of transnational coproduction.)
3. The numbers do not, however, reflect the significant general upswing in historical dramas as initiated by films outside Oscar contention, films that include a significant number of the Merchant-Ivory imitators.
4. Shot for $23,000 using friends for actors and borrowed locations for settings, *Slacker* grossed over $1.2 million in the United States alone. Seizing on the precedent set by *Slacker, Clerks* was shot for $27,000 on location in the convenience store where Smith once worked. It was distributed by Miramax, later to become the major independent film distributor, and grossed over $3.1 million in the United States.
5. *Laws of Gravity* (Nick Gomez, 1992), *Amongst Friends* (Rob Weiss, 1993), *Menace II Society* (Hughes Brothers, 1994), among others.
6. Refn was educated in the United States at the American Academy of Dramatic Arts before returning to Denmark to pursue his filmmaking career. At the time of writing, *Flickering Lights* has just been given a commercial DVD release and is available in the major video chains such as Blockbuster and Hollywood Video. On the cover, Jensen is referred to as a cross between "Tarantino and the Coen Brothers," a clear indication not only of the apparent influence of these filmmakers but also of the distributors' awareness that this type of neopulp noir fare has a potential transnational audience. The box also prominently touts Iben Hjejle's appearance in the film, even though her role calls for relatively little on-screen time, attempting to capitalize on any name recognition from her role in *High Fidelity* (Stephen Frears, 2000).

WORKS CITED

Bailey, Andy. 2001. "Party Crashers." *IFC Rant* (May–June): 12–14.
Bondebjerg, Ib, Jesper Andersen, and Peter Schepelern, eds. 1997. *Dansk film, 1972–97.* Copenhagen: Munksgaard/Rosinante.
Christensen, Mads Egmont. 2000. "Dogma and Marketing." *p.o.v.* 10 (December). http://imv.au.dk/publikationer/pov/Issue_10/POV_10cnt.html
"Dogme95 FAQ." n.d. *Dogme95.* http://www.dogme95.dk
Ebert, Roger. 1989. Review of *Pelle the Conqueror. Chicago Sun-Times.* http://www.suntimes.com
———. 2001a. Review of *The King Is Alive. Chicago Sun-Times,* May 18. http://www.suntimes.com
———. 2001b. Review of *Together. Chicago Sun-Times,* September 14. http://www.suntimes.com
———. n.d. Review of *Breaking the Waves. Chicago Sun-Times.* http://www.suntimes.com
Flickering Lights (Blinkende lygter). 2003. Directed by Anders Thomas Jensen. 109 min. Vanguard Cinema. DVD.
Goldstein, Steve. 2000. "By Any Means Necessary: Spike Lee on Video's Viability." *Res Magazine* 3, no. 4: 49.
Higson, Andrew. 1993. "Re-presenting the National Past: Nostalgia and Pastiche in the Heritage Film." In *Fires Were Started: British Cinema and Thatcherism,* ed. Lester Friedman, 109–29. Minneapolis: University of Minnesota Press.
Holden, Stephen. 1997. "From His Olympian Heights, Deaf to the Alarm Below." *New York Times,* August 6.
———. 2001. "Finding Right Spark for a Guy with a Problem." *New York Times,* October 2.
Irvine, Don. 1997. "Cold Relief from Hollywood." *Toronto Globe and Mail,* June 15.
Iversen, Ebbe. n.d. "Shrugging Off Technical Tyranny." *Dogme95.* http://www.dogme-95.dk
Kaufman, Anthony. 1999. "1999 Cannes Film Festival." *Res Magazine* 2, no. 3: 6.
Kempley, Rita. 1988. Review of *Babette's Feast. Washington Post,* April 8.
Lyman, Rick. 2003. "*Chicago* Tops Oscar Nominees: Miramax Lifted into the Front Ranks among Studios." *New York Times,* February 12.
Maslin, Janet. 1998. "A Family Making Orphanhood Look Good." *New York Times,* October 7.
Miller, Toby, et al. 2001. *Global Hollywood.* London: British Film Institute.
Stack, Peter. n.d. "Back to the Farm." *San Francisco Chronicle.* http://www.sfchronicle.com
Thomas, Kenneth. 2001. "*The King Is Alive* Travels Stylish but Barren Territory." *Los Angeles Times,* May 11.
Turan, Kenneth. 1996. "*Waves* Is a Stylized Look at Love, Loss." *Los Angeles Times,* November 20.
———. 2001. "Happy *Together* Looks Kindly on Messy Lives in a Commune." *Los Angeles Times,* September 7.
Turk, John. 1999. "DV PAL Filmmaking from Start to Finish: A Case Study." *Res Magazine* 3, no. 1: 14–25.

Willis, Holly. 2000a. "Mike Figgis Redefines the Screen in *Time Code 2000*." *Res Magazine* 3, no. 1: 32–35.
———. 2000b. "Obsession for Men." *Res Magazine* 3, no. 3: 42–45.
———. 2001. "Party Crashers." *Res Magazine* 4, no. 3: 36–41.

CHAPTER 2

"Immigrant Film" in Sweden at the Millennium

Rochelle Wright

Around the millennium, the notion of "immigrant film" received a great deal of media attention in Sweden, prompted in particular by the virtually simultaneous debuts in fall 2000 of three directors with roots in Lebanon or Iran: Josef Fares, with *Jalla! Jalla!* Reza Bagher, with *Wings of Glass* (*Vingar av glas*) and Reza Parsa, with *Before the Storm* (*Före stormen*).[1] Since all three directors also scripted or coscripted their films, artistic control over the material resides primarily with these individuals. Though the films themselves are quite dissimilar, ranging from comedy to family drama to political thriller, they all delineate a personal view of Swedish society that incorporates the experiences of characters who, like their creators, are immigrants from the Middle East. *Jalla! Jalla!* and *Wings of Glass* in particular highlight differing cultural expectations with regard to gender roles and loyalty or solidarity within the family. Another director born in Iran, Susan Taslimi, explores this issue in greater depth and from several different perspectives in her first feature, *All Hell Let Loose* (*Hus i helvete*), released two years later in 2002.

Despite the dramatic emergence of these directors with comparable backgrounds and analogous thematic concerns, "immigrant film" per se is hardly a new phenomenon. Directors and scriptwriters with a non-Swedish heritage are by no means unique to the current millennium, and minority groups have been portrayed in Swedish film since at least the 1920s. This particular confluence of "ethnic" subject matter does nevertheless display certain distinctive features that emerge more clearly when placed in historical context, with regard to both the film medium itself and the ongoing evolution in Swedish society and social attitudes that it reflects.

Before about 1950 the population of Sweden was largely homogenous. Only a few ethnic minorities had significant numbers within the country's borders, most notably the Sami, the Finns, and the Jews. In the postwar period, this situation has undergone a radical transformation. Today at least 1 million individuals, more than one-eighth of all residents, have a non-Swedish heritage; more than 150 different nationalities are represented. In other words, during a relatively short time, the last fifty years or so, Sweden has become a multiethnic and multicultural nation.

This profound demographic shift has been studied extensively by historians, sociologists, and ethnologists. With regard to cinematic representations, two broad issues are of particular interest: first, the manner in which films from the 1930s, 1940s, and 1950s provide insight into contemporary perceptions of established minority groups, and second, how the depiction of various immigrant subcultures in more recent films mirrors and comments on social change.[2]

Until about 1960 ethnic stereotyping was extremely common in Swedish film. The 1930s are associated with the so-called *pilsnerfilm* (literally, "light-beer movie"), a genre that has its roots in the *folklustspel* (folk comedy) of stage tradition, though more sophisticated screen comedy also flourished. A common feature is the conventionally "happy" ending intended to please the audience by rewarding virtuous characters and punishing villains—or indeed anyone who threatens the status quo. With startling frequency the designated outsider figure is a Jew, inevitably portrayed as a Shylock out to take monetary advantage of ethnic Swedes.

Though Swedish anti-Semitism was seldom of the virulent variety found on the Continent, there is no doubt that it increased and flourished in the 1930s and that this development is correlated to the many negative portrayals in film. Jewish figures embody an anti-Semitic stereotype that had international currency but is placed in an entirely Swedish context. Though individuals are seldom verbally identified as Jewish, there are numerous specific ethnic markers differentiating them from a posited Swedish norm: dark, curly hair; a large, hooked nose; flamboyant gestures and body language; a strong accent; or a typically Jewish name. Cinematic Jews of the 1930s are pawnbrokers, moneylenders, or engaged in questionable financial speculations. Though occasionally figures of ridicule, they are usually portrayed as a threat, the elimination of which is frequently essential to the film's resolution. In Gustaf Molander's 1933 hit, *Dear Relatives* (*Kära släkten*), for instance, the assembled clan unites to forcibly remove the Jewish character, while in Weyler Hildebrand's *Shanty Town* (*Söderkåkar*), from 1932, the equivalent figure is humiliated by a version of tarring and feathering.

However offensive to a viewer of today, these portrayals were not, by and large, deliberately intended to be malicious. Rather, the Jewish characters are stock figures functioning within predictable narrative formulas and were apparently accepted as such. Contemporary reviews almost never comment disapprovingly on negative caricatures, and many of the films incorporating an anti-Semitic motif were extremely popular, with viewer statistics of 750,000 to 1 million.

In the 1940s and 1950s the most popular film genre, in several instances attracting audiences of 1.5 or 2 million, was the rural melodrama, which promoted nostalgic longing for a traditional culture that by then had largely disappeared. A common menace to this agrarian idyll comes from another negatively depicted outsider category, an indigenous pariah group, the *tattare* (or *resande*—travelers—as they called themselves).[3] Tattare are vilified to an even greater degree than Jewish characters had been a decade or two earlier, depicted as utterly beyond the pale of civilized society: the men are thieves, swindlers, and violent drunkards, while women are sexually provocative. Structurally, however, the narratives tend to follow a similar pattern: order is restored at the film's conclusion when tattare are removed from the scene, and the obligatory stalwart young Swedish couple takes over the family farm.

Two other ethnic groups are also represented with some frequency in Swedish films from the 1930s to the 1950s, the Sami and the Finns, but here there is greater variation. Wilderness melodramas often focus on conflict between the reindeer-herding Sami and Swedish settlers: disputes over land ownership and access that resemble those between Indians and ranchers in the American western. By no means are all individual Sami characters portrayed negatively, but frequently the group as a whole is depicted as primitive or opposed to technological progress. Heathen Lapps practicing black magic are always condemned. Other, more ethnographically oriented films employ a quasi-documentary style to draw attention to colorful, exotic Sami traditions and customs that set them apart from the rest of the Swedish population. In the rural melodrama, particularly if localized to so-called *finnskogar* ("Finn forests," areas settled centuries earlier by immigrants from across the Baltic), Finnish characters, like tattare, may be villains or social outcasts, but films set in Finland during World War II reflect Swedish support for the Finnish cause.

Most stereotypical images of outsider figures or minority groups in Swedish films before about 1960 convey an "us against them" ideology. Less-than-flattering clichés about ethnic subcultures are employed to create a common sense of national or ethnic identity; the distinctive, and of course positive, qualities of "Swedishness" are highlighted when their perceived opposite is manifest. This polarization is clearly intended to reinforce a positive self-image among members of the dominant culture (and to attract large audiences to movie theaters), but a viewer of today is likely to construe it as promoting prejudice, complacency, and smug self-satisfaction.

Positive counterbalances may nevertheless be found in a handful of films that comment directly on contemporary reality or the recent historical past. During World War II, for instance, anti-Semitic caricatures disappear; instead, cinematic dramas such as Anders Henrikson's *Dangerous Ways* (1942, *Farliga vägar*) and Gustaf Molander's *The Invisible Wall* (1944, *Den osynliga muren*) overtly encourage audience sympathy for refugees who are the victims of Nazi persecution. In the mid-1950s revisionist films like Hampe Faustman's *Our Lord and the Tattare* (1954, *Gud fader och tattaren*) and Gunnar Hellström's *Simon the Sinner* (1954, *Simon Syndaren*) convey a more sympathetic view of individual tattare figures by portraying them as psychologically vulnerable and as victims of social ostracism. The shift away from negative stereotyping may in part reflect a gradual change in social attitudes toward the groups in question, but it does not necessarily reflect their actual historical situation. As is the case with all films designed primarily to entertain, the image of non-Swedish ethnic minorities is largely determined by the fictional construct itself, its ideological underpinnings, and the type of narrative patterns it employs.

The 1960s are a transitional period with regard to ethnic subject matter. Postwar immigrant groups do not yet appear, but we find the first analytical consideration of Swedish anti-Semitism in Erland Josephson's television play *Benjamin* (1960), directed by Hans Abramson as well as two insightful, sympathetic, and psychologically convincing cinematic depictions of Jewish Holocaust survivors in Gunnar

Höglund's *Obsession* (1964, *Kungsleden*) and Jörn Donner's *Rooftree* (1967, *Tvärbalk*). Johan Bergenstråhle's documentary-style *A Baltic Tragedy* (1970, *Baltutlämningen*), based on P. O. Enquist's acclaimed novel *The Legionnaires* (*Legionärerna*), focuses on another would-be refugee group attempting to flee to Sweden in the immediate aftermath of World War II. In these examples Swedish filmmakers tackle difficult, painful subject matter in a serious and artistically sophisticated manner. But in contrast to the extraordinary popularity of certain earlier films, these drew embarrassingly small crowds. It appears that the Swedish audience, like the moviegoing public elsewhere, preferred being entertained to being challenged.

Two English-language films of Ingmar Bergman produced during the 1970s—*The Touch* (1971) and *The Serpent's Egg* (1977)—have Jewish protagonists. These films are not among Bergman's most artistically successful, but *Fanny and Alexander* (1982, *Fanny och Alexander*), his last film, offers a far more nuanced consideration of issues of Jewish identity and is widely acknowledged as a masterpiece. Here, the Jewish character Isak Jacobi appears in three separate contexts: in the "small world" of the Ekdahl family; in the "great world" outside, especially with regard to his dealings with the bishop and his sister; and in his own home and shop, with his own nephews. His behavior is clearly differentiated in each of these situations and is determined by the manner in which he adjusts and accommodates himself to the norms and expectations of the particular circumstances. While Isak is not fully integrated into Swedish society and may be the object of intense, visceral anti-Semitism, as the attitude of the bishop and his sister demonstrates, he is loved and appreciated within the Ekdahl family. Using both his wits and what appear to be magical powers, he succeeds in rescuing the children, Fanny and Alexander, from the bishop's clutches. Thus the Jewish outsider triumphs over the emblem of Christian patriarchal authority. Most important, Isak and the other Jewish characters are identified with the life-affirming, positive values of the imagination, of artistic creation, and of magic and mystery, a complex of motifs that had fascinated and preoccupied Bergman for much of his career.

The so-called new Swedes, postwar immigrants to Sweden, began appearing in film narratives in the 1970s. In contrast to the negative stereotyping so prevalent in earlier decades, films from the 1970s and 1980s examine the circumstances of various immigrant subgroups largely from their own point of view, revealing both how they define themselves vis-à-vis the dominant culture and how they perceive its attitudes toward them. Authenticity and verisimilitude are promoted by the use of actors (some of them nonprofessional) who belong to the immigrant group under consideration and speak their native language on camera.

A number of scriptwriters and/or directors of these films have immigrant backgrounds or personal ties to those who do. Johan Bergenståhle's *Foreigners* (1972, *Jag heter Stelios*), focusing on Greek immigrants, was based on a partially autobiographical novel by Theodor Kallifatides, who also wrote the script. Barbara Karabuda, director of *Black-skull* (1981, *Svartskallen*), a television film about a Turkish boy trying to adapt to life in Sweden, is married to the film's Turkish cinematographer, Günes Karabuda, and has lived in Turkey.[4] Agneta Fagerström-Olsson, director and scriptwriter of *Seppan* (1986), grew up in the multicultural environment portrayed in the film.[5] Carlo Barsotti, who came to Sweden from Italy as an adult, draws in part on his own emotional responses to a different culture in *A Paradise without Billiards* (1991, *Ett paradis utan biljard*).

The new ethnic minorities represented in Swedish film since 1970 include many groups that are numerically most prominent in the Sweden of today. Emphasis in these narratives tends to be on newcomers, the problems they encounter, and their attempts to adjust. The us-against-them constellation of earlier decades is now reversed, resulting in a generally sympathetic depiction of immigrants and their situation, while ethnic Swedes are frequently construed as a negative Other, and Swedish prejudice and ignorance may be castigated. There is often an implicit didacticism with regard to the Swedish audience, which is encouraged to reject ethnocentric attitudes and become more sensitive to and accepting of diversity.

The success of this laudable if at times heavy-handed effort at education and reform is at best debatable. Whereas earlier entertainment films that incorporated negative ethnic stereotyping often drew large audiences, few of these earnest, reality-based narratives attracted more than a few thousand viewers on their initial theatrical release—though many were subsequently shown on television. A few films, moreover, reached a larger cross-section of the public with a more lighthearted approach, notably Dusan Makavejev's *Montenegro* (1981), which parodies preconceived notions about the unrestrained sexuality and dubious hygiene of "primitive" immigrant groups, and Suzanne Osten's *Just You and Me* (1994, *Bara du och jag*), where the Swedish-born female protagonist of half-African heritage pokes fun at ethnic stereotypes by donning a Josephine Baker outfit, complete with a skirt made of bananas.

In several films of the early 1990s older, more established ethnic groups, in particular Jews, also receive cinematic reconsideration. Anti-Semitism is examined from various perspectives and in several historical contexts: Stockholm in the 1920s in Åke Sandberg's *The Slingshot* (1993, *Kådisbellan*), central Europe in the final months of World War II in Kjell Grede's *Good Evening, Mr. Wallenberg* (1990, *God afton, herr Wallenberg*), and contemporary Sweden in Suzanne Osten's *Speak! It's So Dark* (1992, *Tala! det är så mörkt*). In Susanne Bier's *Freud Leaving Home* (1991, *Freud flyttar hemifrån*), which incorporates a great deal of traditional Jewish humor, a present-day Swedish-Jewish family illustrates various and divergent responses to a common Jewish heritage, from ultra-Orthodox to completely assimilated.[6] Several of these films won prizes and/or reached relatively large audiences. *The Slingshot* was even a modest hit internationally.

That some individual directors and scriptwriters involved in these film projects have a personal connection to Judaism helps explain the choice of subject matter, but the prominence of Jewish motifs may also be related to the representative or emblematic nature of the Jewish Other. Unlike the much larger non-Swedish minority groups of the postwar immigration wave, Jews have experienced prejudice not only in Sweden but throughout Europe for centuries, even millennia. Their fate in Germany and occupied Europe during the Third Reich illustrates the ultimate consequences of ethnic hatred, a lesson that can be applied both to present-day Swedish circumstances and to ongoing ethnic strife in various international contexts.

Since the mid-1990s, however, the focus on Jewish individuals and circumstances has receded and a new category has emerged: films set in urban areas with large immigrant populations. Examples are Daniel Fridell's *Cry* (1995, *30:e november*), a Romeo and Juliet story in which immigrants and skinheads substitute for Capulets and Montagues; David Flamholc's *Night Bus 807* (1997, *Nattbuss 807*), which downplays interethnic romance but features a similarly violent ending; and Peter Lindmark's *9 millimeter* (1997), for which the model clearly is the American gangster film. These films make some attempt to convey the social reality of immigrant ghettos but generally lack both psychological depth and narrative complexity.

In recent decades, of course, television has largely taken over the mass entertainment function of film. With regard to ethnic subject matter two series, each in four one-hour segments, have been particularly influential: *Hammarkullen, or See You in Kaliningrad (Hammarkullen, eller Vi ses i Kalinengrad)*, directed by Agneta Fagerström-Olsson and broadcast in 1997, and Geir Hansteen Jørgensen's *The New Country (Det nya landet)*, shown on television in spring 2000 and within a few months cut to feature length and released in movie theaters. *Hammarkullen*, set in the suburb of that name in the city of Göteborg, where representatives of many different subcultures coexist with varying degrees of integration, deftly interweaves and develops numerous separate stories, some of which concern questions of ethnic and cultural identity. *The New Country* addresses similar issues from a quite different perspective. In this road movie, two refugees seeking political asylum—Massoud, a middle-aged man from Iran (Michalis Koutsogiannakis) and Ali, a much younger one from Senegal (Mike Almayehu)—go on the lam with a former Miss Sweden (Lia Boysen). During the course of their travels, as they gain more exposure to the country and its people and greater insight into themselves, each undergoes a shift in attitude regarding the opportunities Sweden offers. All three protagonists are psychologically convincing and remain sympathetic even when their behavior is anything but admirable. This series has probably done more to foster understanding of the plight of refugees, or immigrants in general, than any of the aforementioned films.

The films that in 2000 prompted so much media discussion of "immigrant film"—*Jalla! Jalla! Wings of Glass*, and *Before the Storm*—represent, along with *All Hell Let Loose*, yet another new development in their foregrounding of immigrants from the Middle East. All except *Before the Storm* also examine gender issues, which previously had not been a major focus of ethnic representations regardless of the group portrayed. *Wings of Glass* and *All Hell Let Loose*, furthermore, do so from a largely female perspective and feature female protagonists, a notable departure from the male bias otherwise common in films about recent immigrants (and for that matter in film in general).

Jalla! Jalla! directed and scripted by Josef Fares, is both a romantic comedy that concludes with two pairings that cross ethnic barriers and a buddy film in which ethnic background is irrelevant to friendship. The two young men, Roro (played by Josef's brother Fares Fares)—a skinny, dark-haired Lebanese who speaks with an accent—and Måns (Torkel Petersson)—a muscle-bound, fair-skinned Swede with a shaved head—work together for the park district of a small Swedish town. They share an easy camaraderie and trust that belie the obvious visual and aural markers, which would customarily identify Måns as a Swedish skinhead and Roro as the svartskalle who is his potential victim. But such is not the case, and the film narrative undercuts this stereotype in numerous ways by positioning Måns as naïve, vulnerable, and uninformed, whereas Roro in most regards is confident and self-assured.

Visiting Roro's home, Måns encounters traditions and food with which he is not familiar. When he is at a loss, Roro intervenes to explain, a reversal of the pattern seen in earlier films where immigrants must turn to others to gain access to mainstream society. Måns's shaved head is mocked by Roro's grandmother, who considers it a handicap that makes the Swede less attractive on the marriage market. Though Grandma is anything but physically imposing, she is forthcoming and feisty, and Måns, a soft-spoken mumbler under the best of circumstances, is at a further disadvantage because he does not understand Arabic and must rely on Roro to translate. Similarly, at the flea market where Roro's father sells his wares, the young men watch his technique as he works a Swedish customer, with Roro serving as liaison between cultural spheres and codes of conduct.[7] Throughout it is Måns who is uncertain, Roro who is capable of mediating and interpreting.

Måns's self-image is also jeopardized because his masculinity is in question in more obvious ways as well. Much of the film narrative revolves around his sexual dysfunction and increasingly comical or bizarre attempts to cure it, all of which cast him in a slightly ludicrous light. Further contradicting the stereotype of the strong, silent male, Måns not only reveals his problem to Roro and turns to him for advice, he also confides in complete strangers: a family he encounters at an outdoor café and, even more improbably, the policeman who interviews him after his arrest. (That Måns acts out his anger and frustration by smashing his furniture only underscores his feelings of, well, impotence.) The film also associates a particular style of testosterone-induced posturing and aggression with certain breeds of dog and their owners. Tellingly, when Måns is unwittingly roped into dog-sitting, the animal escapes and he suffers the consequences. In short, Måns's hapless behavior gainsays his hypermasculine appearance in every way. Though the narrative does not belabor the point, it thus suggests that stereotypes may be unreliable or deceptive.

In contrast to Måns's difficulties, Roro and his Swedish girlfriend, Lisa (Tuva Novotny), have an emotionally and, it would seem, physically satisfying relationship. The obstacle to their match is not her parents, whose idyllic house in the country is as iconographically Swedish as a painting by Carl Larsson, but the well-intended effort of Roro's extended Lebanese family, unaware of Lisa's existence, to marry him off to Yasmin (Laleh Pourkarim), a member of their own group. Predictably, after a series of complications, this effort is thwarted in the end when Roro publicly declares his love for Lisa and elopes with his father's blessing. The bride, in turn, escapes her controlling brother, the cardboard villain of the piece, to find true happiness with Måns. The film's message is that love and friendship trump cultural difference.

An undercurrent or subtext throughout the film hints at conflicts that never develop or that simply do not exist. Lisa's father pays no attention to Roro's ethnic heritage and facilitates the couple's union. Divergent backgrounds have no fundamental impact on the friendship between Måns and Roro. The park district work team also includes a completely silent African, whose bemused expressions provide unspoken commentary on the main action (and whose efforts to tame and protect his giant Afro add gentle visual humor). The smoothly functioning cooperation among the three young men serves as a striking emblem of an integrated, multicultural (and perhaps somewhat idealized) society.

Through Yasmin, the film also touches on the difficult situation of young women from Middle Eastern backgrounds whose options, even in Sweden, are limited by family pressure and prevailing cultural norms. This motif is not, however, central to the narrative, which depicts romantic and sexual quandaries primarily from a male perspective. Interestingly, both Lisa and Yasmin are largely passive characters, waiting to be rescued by their male counterparts rather than taking action to achieve their goals. Thus although the narrative plays on ethnic stereotypes to call into question conventional standards of masculinity, overall it reveals a conventional perspective on appropriate male and female roles.

"Immigrant Film" in Sweden at the Millennium

In *Wings of Glass,* directed and coscripted by Reza Bagher, the romantic attachment between a Swede and a young woman of Iranian heritage is less central to the narrative than the generational conflict within her family and her own struggle for self-definition as she straddles two cultures. In the opening scene the Swedish-born protagonist, Nasli Kasheni (Sara Sommerfeld), appears for a job interview after having given her name as Sara Lundström over the phone. When challenged, she claims this white lie was necessary if she hoped to be granted an interview at all. But even among her Swedish friends Nasli is known as Sara, and much of her energy is devoted to trying to fit in among them by acting like any ordinary Swedish eighteen-year-old: smoking, drinking, staying out late, dressing provocatively, and acquiring a tattoo. Yet she remains uncertain of her own identity. When her closest girlfriend, a tall blonde, reacts with shock to the possibility that she might be Muslim, Nasli comments wryly, "Vete fan vad jag är" (Who the hell knows what I am).

Nasli's widowed father, Abbas (Said Oveissi), feels obligated by a long-ago promise to his wife to provide for Nasli and her older sister, Mahin (Aminah Al Fakir), by arranging comfortable marriages for them. Nasli reacts furiously to Abbas's announcement that he has identified potential suitors for his daughters, a response neither Abbas nor Mahin understands. (It is later revealed that Abbas has chosen Mahin's partner knowing that she is already in love with him, a circumstance that places both Abbas's exercise of parental control and Mahin's seeming passivity in a somewhat different light.) Subsequently, though Nasli is happy to work in her cousin Hamid's video store, she rejects his romantic attentions.[8] Frustrated by what he perceives as Nasli's indifference to him, Hamid (Rafael Edholm) later tries to rape her. When Abbas, who is economically dependent on Hamid, does not unhesitatingly support Nasli, she angrily breaks with her father. After several violent arguments, however, the two are tentatively reconciled. Abbas appears willing to accept Nasli's Swedish boyfriend, Johan (Alexander Skarsgård), who has gone out of his way to win over the older man. With her father's support Nasli earns a motorcycle license, symbol of her longing for freedom. Encouraged by Johan, Nasli also begins coming to grips with her culture of origin. She resumes her Iranian name among Swedish friends and even utters a few words of her heritage language.

The film avoids obvious clichés and a simplistic view of the Muslim attitude toward women by making Abbas a largely sympathetic figure. Though he is the product of a culture that asserts patriarchal control over female members of the household, he genuinely loves his daughters and wants to do well by them. He has made significant sacrifices on their behalf, not least with regard to his career: in Iran he was a famous actor performing on the national stage, whereas in Sweden his only audience is a group of preschoolers who complain loudly about his faulty Swedish and refuse to sit still for the show. As a single parent Abbas has borne a double burden. Several scenes reveal that within the home he has assumed the traditionally female role in the absence of his deceased wife. A more culturally consistent pattern would be for him to expect his daughters, who after all are adults, to take over all domestic chores, yet neither Nasli nor her more compliant and traditional sister are assigned or have assumed primary responsibility for such tasks. The fact that Abbas cooks, vacuums, and cuts out coupons makes it more difficult for the viewer to regard him solely as a patriarchal tyrant.

Most significant, despite the family's dependency and a personal financial obligation to Hamid, Abbas eventually believes Nasli's version of events and does not protest when she informs him she intends to press charges against her would-be rapist. Whether or not Abbas's reaction is believable in the context of this particular subculture, the nuanced portrayal of both father and daughter makes it possible for the Swedish audience to view Nasli's rebellion, her struggle to achieve autonomy, as typical of most teenagers' rejection of parental authority and search for a coherent identity rather than as motivated solely by cultural and ethnic differences.

Both *Jalla! Jalla!* and *Wings of Glass* are clearly aimed at young people, though they played well with audiences of all ages; *Jalla! Jalla!* was seen by more than 700,000 Swedes, a number that rivals the audience size for the most popular films of the pretelevision period.[9] Both films were also critically acclaimed; *Wings of Glass* won a Guldbagge, a Golden Bug, Sweden's Oscar, as the year's best film. In both instances, much of the credit goes to skillful scripts and direction and engaging performances by all the principal players, but the broad appeal of these films may also be correlated to their upbeat message that integration is possible and ethnic differences can be bridged in the multicultural Sweden of today. This premise may be an oversimplification of contemporary reality, one that sidesteps very real social, economic, and cultural gaps, but it provides a hopeful and emotionally satisfying happy ending.

"Immigrant Film" in Sweden at the Millennium

Like *Wings of Glass*, Susan Taslimi's *All Hell Let Loose,* which she both scripted and directed, focuses on an angry, rebellious daughter who chafes under patriarchal restraints. In this family drama, however, the conflict is far more volatile and lacks the optimistic resolution of either Bagher's film or *Jalla! Jalla!* As *All Hell Let Loose* opens, Minoo (Melinda Kinnamon), a young woman in her twenties, is returning from America to her Iranian family in Sweden to attend her sister's wedding. It is gradually revealed that several years earlier Minoo had been thrown out by her father, Serbandi (Hassan Brijany), after having an abortion. Still feeling himself disgraced by her behavior, he does not welcome her return. Unbeknownst to the family, while abroad Minoo has worked as a stripper, perhaps appearing in low-budget pornographic films as well. Whether she did so in desperation or in deliberate defiance is not revealed.

Now that Minoo is back, Serbandi tries desperately to reestablish complete control by determining what she wears, where she goes, and whom she sees, an effort that Minoo finds various strategies to circumvent. Minoo is not, furthermore, the only woman in the family who resists patriarchal authority. Her sister, Gita (Melize Karlge), maintains the pretence of playing by the household rules but is in fact already sexually involved with her fiancé. Nana, their mother (Caroline Rauf), is openly contemptuous of her husband and eager to act on her attraction to a Swedish sewing machine repairman who makes house calls. And Serbandi's mother (Bibbi Azizi), who knows even less Swedish than the grandmother in *Jalla! Jalla!* invokes the privilege of age to speak her mind, often to quasi-scatological effect and not infrequently directing the invective at her son.

The harder Serbandi strives to assert his dominance, the less actual control he is able to seize and the more frantic he becomes. On Gita's wedding day, despite the protests of the bride and the efforts of Nana to intervene, he punishes Minoo for disobedience by locking her in a bedroom, but she manages to escape and exact her revenge. A traditional Middle Eastern belly dancer is slated to perform at the wedding festivities. Wearing a blonde wig and a black leather bikini, Minoo steps in instead and does a striptease. Serbandi, very drunk, experiences a complete meltdown, denouncing not only Minoo but also his wife and the bride in such a way that it is he, rather than they, who is most humiliated. As the guests depart in embarrassment, Grandma suggests that since Minoo has finally arrived they can all sit down to eat.

The final scene of *Jalla! Jalla!* also shows the grandmother and other family members surveying the remains of a ruined wedding feast, but in that film the "correct" pairings had been affirmed. In *All Hell Let Loose,* though Gita and her new husband appear to be a love match, the wedding itself is almost secondary and the physical devastation in its aftermath represents emotional wreckage within the family. No one wins. Serbandi's authority will never recover, but by challenging him publicly in such a provocative manner Minoo has also made her own situation untenable.

Taslimi's film was released in 2002, a year of widespread media attention in Sweden to the predicament of girls from Muslim countries whose male relatives expect unquestioning obedience and submission. Most infamously in the case of Fadime Sahindal, differing standards of acceptable female behavior had led to murder within the immigrant community. Whereas *Jalla! Jalla!* and *Wings of Glass* offer the reassurance that integration is possible and cultural differences can be resolved, *All Hell Let Loose* suggests the potential for violence underlying such conflicts. Though the film ultimately illustrates the breakdown of patriarchal authority, it does so without providing a positive alternative.

Before the Storm, directed and coscripted by Reza Parsa, resembles *All Hell Let Loose* in that it offers no easy solutions to the dilemmas it raises, but in other respects it contrasts starkly with the other recent films under discussion. The story lines of *Jalla! Jalla! Wings of Glass,* and *All Hell Let Loose* all highlight the intersection of immigrant subcultures with mainstream or majority society, stressing in particular various ways the generation now reaching adulthood negotiates cultural difference. Put another way, though by and large they avoid ethnic stereotyping, all three films overtly concern the immigrant experience per se. *Before the Storm* does not.

The complex plot interweaves two narrative strands, one centering on Ali (Per Graffman), a middle-aged man from a nameless land in the Middle East, the other on Leo (Emil Odepark), a Swedish seventh-grader who is relentlessly bullied at school. Ali came to Sweden eighteen years earlier and appears fully assimilated; he works as a taxi driver, has married a Swede, and is a loving father to two adolescent daughters. Unbeknownst to his family or anyone else, however, he was formerly an antigovernment guerrilla leader who fled the country when a mission went tragically wrong. Now a courier from his homeland tracks him down and blackmails him: unless he assassinates a Swedish industrialist who provides military aid to the repressive regime, the wife he left behind and the son he never knew will be brutally murdered.

While facing this agonizing moral dilemma, Ali befriends Leo, who is in his younger daughter's class, urging him not to give in to the humiliating demands of his tormentor, Danne, but to assert himself. Misunderstanding the advice, Leo surreptitiously borrows a pistol from his mother, a police officer, lures Danne into the forest, and shoots him.

By establishing a tie between personal suffering and political oppression, the film challenges the audience to consider the underlying motivations for violence and to ask if there are circumstances in which it may be justified. The ethical dilemmas posed are not black and white: the decision to manufacture launching pads for missiles that will murder innocent civilians may be reprehensible from a broader political or human rights perspective, but it saves factory jobs in Sweden, including that of Leo's father, prompting a family celebration.

At the last possible moment Ali spares the factory owner, extracting a promise from him to sell no more weapons abroad. Thanks to a miscommunication, Ali's family back home is released anyway. Danne survives and the conscience-stricken Leo turns himself in. But the film's conclusion offers little hope or moral resolution: the final montage reveals that the capitalist entrepreneur signs a contract after all and that Ali's family is blown to bits in the continuing guerrilla warfare. Throughout the narrative, Ali's immigrant status, ethnic identity, and position within Swedish society are of secondary importance. Neither does the film focus on ethnic conflict in the international arena, but rather on Ali's moral quandary and the impossibility of erasing the past or determining the course of future events.

Though powerful, gripping, and brilliantly acted, *Before the Storm* did not attain the broad popularity of *Jalla! Jalla!* or *Wings of Glass*. In retrospect it seems that critics also, though mostly complimentary, underestimated the film's achievement. One who is better qualified than most did not. Ingmar Bergman, who by his own account sees every Swedish film produced, proclaimed *Before the Storm* "den bästa svenska film som har gjorts på senaste år"(the best Swedish film of recent years) ("Bergman," Björkman 2002b, 139). Whether or not one agrees with that assessment, by moving beyond specifically ethnic constellations Parsa further expands the definition of "immigrant film," perhaps to the point of making such a designation meaningless.

This brings us once again to the question of what differentiates these works of the new millennium from their predecessors. As previously noted, the fact that the directors are immigrants who depict members of their own ethnic group is scarcely groundbreaking. To varying degrees, Fares, Bagher, Parsa, and Taslimi also employ established genre conventions and narrative patterns.[10] The appearance of their debut feature films within a very short time frame nevertheless caused critics and audiences to examine them collectively and take note of subject matter and themes they had in common. Just as several films from the early 1990s that explore Jewish subject matter are the product of a particular generation examining its roots, these more recent films represent the coming-of-age of another group. Fares, born in Lebanon, and Bagher and Parsa, native to Iran, came to Sweden as children or teenagers in response to the volatile political situation in their homelands. All received formal training in film at Scandinavian institutions and gained experience making shorts before writing and directing full-length features. Taslimi, who immigrated as an adult, first established herself as an actor (she had a role in Parsa's short, *The Limit* [1995, *Gränsen*]) and then turned to directing. Summarizing this movement into the cultural mainstream, critic Helena Lindblad comments, "Den generation berättare med invandrarbakgrund som den litterära världen länge önskat sig, hamnade hos filmen istället" (The generation of storytellers from immigrant backgrounds that the literary world had long yearned for ended up making films instead) (2002, 32–33).

Most important, however, is that the films themselves present immigrants as a self-evident part of Swedish society. Fares, Bagher, Parsa, and Taslimi hope to counteract stereotypes, not by moralizing or by casting members of minority groups as victims but by portraying the Swedish reality they themselves know, where immigrants are individuals rather than merely representatives of particular subcultures. All of them, furthermore, forcefully resist being ghettoized as immigrant directors. Their goal is simply to make good films, defined by Parsa as "konstnärligt viktiga, personliga filmer som även kan underhålla och beröra en vanlig publik" (artistically significant, personal films that also can entertain and move the general public).[11] This attempt to bridge the gap between art film and popular entertainment suggests the true scope of their efforts.

"Immigrant Film" in Sweden at the Millennium

NOTES

1. The title *Jalla! Jalla!* is a salutation or exhortation to get a move on. Throughout this essay, English-language release titles are employed in italics, as listed on the Internet Movie Database (http://www.imdb.com). All other "nonrelease" title translations are my own and follow the Swedish title in parentheses.
2. For more detail on films that premiered between 1930 and 1995, see Wright 1998.
3. Though they did not, in actuality, share a clearly defined ethnic heritage, *tattare* were widely regarded as descended from gypsies and were often assigned traits associated with that group.
4. *Svartskallen* is a widely used epithet for (dark-haired) immigrants or those of immigrant heritage.
5. The film's title is the nickname of the area where the story is set.
6. As a coproduction with the Danish Film Institute, the film was also released in Denmark under the title *Freud flytter hjemmefra;* the director, Susanne Bier, and female lead, Scandinavian film star Ghita Nørby, are also Danish, once again illustrating the complexities of distinguishing a film's national origins.
7. Though Roro's father—played by Jan Fares, the real-life father of the director and lead actor—appears unassimilated, the film demonstrates repeatedly that he uses this pose to his own advantage. Feigning gullibility and lack of technological sophistication, the father sits back and watches while a Swedish vacuum cleaner salesman cleans the entire apartment.
8. First cousins are not considered appropriate candidates for marriage by most present-day Swedes. Abbas's preference for a close family member not only illustrates differing cultural norms, it also underscores the sense of security he finds only within his immediate circle.
9. Viewer statistics are compiled by Svenska Filminstitutet.
10. See in particular Koskinen 2002.
11. All four directors, along with Peter Birro, who scripted *Hammarkullen* and *Det nya landet,* have been interviewed in print and on television on the topic of "immigrant film." The quotation is from *Mosaik,* "Vem skapar bilden?" (Parsa 2001). Parsa has also commented obliquely on the implicitly discriminatory overtones of such "immigrant" terminology by noting, "Den dag man sätter invandrarregissöretiketten på exempelvis Colin Nutley, är man hjärtligt välkommen att också sätta den på mig (The day people label Colin Nutley, for instance, an immigrant director, they're quite welcome to call me one, too) (Björkman 2002a, 126). Nutley, an Englishman, has lived and made films in Sweden for well over a decade and is frequently lauded for his insight into Swedish mentality. As Parsa observes, he is never identified as an immigrant director.

WORKS CITED

Björkman, Stig. 2002a. "'Det enda man kan och ska gå efter är sin hjärna och sitt hjärta. Mest hjärta.' Reza Parsa i samtal med Stig Björkman." In *Fucking film,* ed. Stig

Björkman, Helena Lindblad, and Fredrik Sahlin, 121–36. Stockholm: Alfabeta.
———. 2002b. "'Jag ser allt': Ingmar Bergman i samtal med Stig Björkman." In *Fucking film,* ed. Stig Björkman, Helena Lindblad, and Fredrik Sahlin, 137–44. Stockholm: Alfabeta.
Koskinen, Maaret. 2002. "Konsten att förena gammalt och nytt: Form och berättande i *Jalla! Jalla!*" In *Fucking film,* ed. Stig Björkman, Helena Lindblad, and Fredrik Sahlin, 99–110. Stockholm: Alfabeta.
Lindblad, Helena. 2002. "Det nya filmlandet." In *Fucking film,* ed. Stig Björkman, Helena Lindblad, and Fredrik Sahlin, 27–34. Stockholm: Alfabeta.
Parsa, Reza. 2001. Interview in "Vem skapar bilden?" *Mosaik,* Swedish TV 2, March 22.
Wright, Rochelle. 1998. *The Visible Wall: Jews and Other Ethnic Outsiders in Swedish Film.* Carbondale: Southern Illinois University Press; Uppsala: Centre for Multi-ethnic Research.

Film according to Dogma: Ground Rules, Obstacles, and Liberations

Peter Schepelern
Translated by Rune Christensen

People took notice when, in the spring of 1995, Lars von Trier presented Dogma 95, a manifesto that—referring back to the French New Wave's admirable but ultimately insufficient effort around 1960—went on the offensive against certain tendencies in contemporary film. Dogma 95 proclaimed a "rescue mission" against the predictable dramaturgy, superficial action, and technological cosmetics that are so prevalent in the Hollywood-dominated repertoire of theaters all over the Western world.

The so-called Vow of Chastity announced the Dogma artists' ten commandments, a set of aesthetic rules that suggest alternative methods for film production:

1. Shooting must be done on location. Props and sets must not be brought in (if a particular prop is necessary for the story, a location must be chosen where this prop is to be found).
2. The sound must never be produced apart from the images or vice versa. (Music must not be used unless it occurs where the scene is being shot.)
3. The camera must be hand-held. Any movement or immobility attainable in the hand is permitted. (The film must not take place where the camera is standing; shooting must take place where the film takes place.)
4. The film must be in color. Special lighting is not acceptable. (If there is too little light for exposure the scene must be cut or a single lamp be attached to the camera.)
5. Optical work and filters are forbidden.

6. The film must not contain superficial action. (Murders, weapons, etc. must not occur.)
7. Temporal and geographical alienation are forbidden. (That is to say that the film takes place here and now.)
8. Genre movies are not acceptable.
9. The film format must be Academy 35 mm.
10. The director must not be credited. (Dogma95)

Restricted access to cinematic technology sought to ensure that technical obstacles would obstruct the production process at a number of crucial junctures. The commandment that the film should be recorded in 35 mm Academy format was soon modified to require only 35 mm *distribution*. The reason for this was that the creative possibilities of the new digital video (DV) camera first became apparent in the period after the Manifesto was written (the beginning of 1995) and before the shooting of the first Dogma film (in the summer of 1997). And the somewhat curious last commandment that the director must not be credited appears, more than anything else, to be a self-ironic joke, yet it underlines a fundamental point in Dogma: to fight the conceptual notion of "the artist." "I am no longer an artist. I swear to refrain from creating a 'work,' as I regard the instant as more important than the whole," reads the Vow of Chastity's final oath (Dogma95). The artist as grand auteur should disappear into anonymity, and the spontaneous moment should be prioritized over the calculated plan. What counts is inspiration here and now, not subsequent deliberations during post-production.

The main purpose of the rules was to create a countermovement against (primarily American) mainstream film's adoration of genre clichés and special effects as well as its tireless dance around the golden calf. The list of commandments was a jeering attack on the Hollywood mastodon à la David versus Goliath or, more accurately perhaps, the mouse and the elephant. In the Dogma film one should not hide behind technical illusions ("To Dogma 95 the movie is not illusion!") but instead fight "the film of illusion," understood as "a technological surge that results in the elevation of cosmetics to God." Now the truth had to appear: "My supreme goal is to force the truth out of my characters and settings. I swear to do so by all means available and at the cost of any good taste and any aesthetic considerations" (Dogma95).

Film according to Dogma

As seen in Jesper Jargil's documentary *De lutrede* (2002, *The Purified*), the Dogma text, dated March 13, 1995 and signed by von Trier and Thomas Vinterberg, was presented by von Trier, printed on a fire-red pamphlet with the Manifesto on one side and the Vow of Chastity on the other, to the audience of a conference at the Odéon Théâtre de l'Europe in Paris commemorating the hundredth anniversary of cinema on March 20, 1995 (Frodon, Nicolas, and Toubiana 1995). It was received as a jeering provocation, an ironic comment of von Trieresque dimension. But the joke was that it was serious.

ACCORDING TO THE RULES

In the text of the Dogma Manifesto there are two tendencies present that have little relation to one another. The first concerns the ability to express oneself through and despite restrictive ground rules (see the Vow of Chastity, but also the Manifesto's demand for "discipline") and despite multiple limitations—like a directorial Robinson Crusoe, the filmmaker has to make do with what is there. Second, the director is obligated to work against aesthetic refinement by reducing the aesthetic concerns—in fact, *without* aesthetics whatsoever (see the demand that the Dogma artist must resist the many possibilities of advanced film technology as well as "all aesthetics"). Both of these tendencies reflect cultural and film-historical traditions.

Naturally, the film medium has always had its ground rules. They appear in the form of the technical obstructions and limitations under which the medium operates—for example, at one time silence was an inevitable and limiting obstacle. But there are also *aesthetic* ground rules: that is, conventions regarding the expressive possibilities of film language, the characteristics of genre, and the structures of dramaturgy. Such rules are dictated not out of necessity but by consensus. There is, for example, nothing that prevents making a western in which all the cowboys love to play piano, but such films are not made because it goes against consensus. However, from time to time films are made that break with consensus and consequently expand norms.

Von Trier did this himself in *The Kingdom* (1994, *Riget*) when he successfully transgressed the 180-degree rule and other commonly accepted rules regarding editing. As early as *Epidemic* (1987), von Trier played with enigmatic metalevels (the film contained a film within a film and revolved around the preparation of a screenplay) akin to the literary tradition of stylistic eccentricities and bizarre systems: a tradition whose most important godfathers are Joyce, Nabokov, Borges, and the peculiar Raymond Roussel (who interested von Trier's coscreenwriter in the early films, Niels Vørsel), followed by authors like Arno Schmidt, John Barth, Walter Abish, Martin Amis, Svend Åge Madsen and, especially, the members of the literary fraternity OuLiPo, established in 1960, whose chief figures Raymond Queneau, Georges Perec, and Italo Calvino worked with creative obstacles and inspirational rules, their so-called *contraintes*. Queneau created formalistic virtuosities such as *Exercices de style* (1947, *Exercises in Style*), which tells the same minor event in ninety-nine different ways, and in *La disparition* (1969, *A Void*), Perec manages the feat of writing an entire novel without using the letter "e" (except in the author's name). The movement refers to Stravinsky's edict that "the more constraints one imposes, the more one frees oneself of the chains that shackle the spirit . . . the arbitrariness of the constraint only serves to obtain precision of execution" (Oulipo 2002). As Stravinsky writes elsewhere, "the desire we feel to let order conquer chaos, to liberate our project's straight line from the confusion of possibility and the ideas' murkiness, necessitates the demand for dogmatism" (Stravinsky 1942). In this context, one also has to keep in mind that art, from the Renaissance to the romantics, develops under numerous formalistic demands: for example, metric forms (sonnets, terzains, quatrains) and musical forms (sonatas, fugues, rondos), which are also systems of ground rules that generally have been a source of inspiration. Naturally, there have also been artistic developments that went against convention, as was the case with the entire transition from romanticism to modernism, but at the same time new ways of expression often revolve around establishing new and more individualistic ground rules.

The parallels in cinematic history to these self-enforced limitations are films that operate under particular rules; innumerable films operate within diverse voluntary boundaries—for example, the use of "real time" in Alfred Hitchcock's *Rope* (1948), the use of subjective camera throughout an entire film like Robert Montgomery's *Lady in the Lake* (1946), the sophistry of New Wave directors like Alain Resnais, Jean-Luc Godard, and Jacques Demy—not to mention the perhaps greatest complex of bizarre ground rules of cinema history, the entire labyrinthine system of Peter Greenaway's enigmatic rebuses and intertextual puzzle pictures in films like *The Draughtsman's Contract* (1982) and *Drowning by Numbers* (1988). One must also include—as a direct inspiration for von Trier—Jørgen Leth's productions, for example, *Det perfekte menneske* (1967, *The Perfect Human*) and *Livet i Danmark* (1971, *Life in Denmark*), with its ironic formalism (see von Trier and Leth's coproduction *The Five Obstructions*, [2001, *De fem benspænd*]; von Trier and Leth 2001).

And then there is von Trier himself, who has had many approaches to his dogmatic crusade. There are ground rules, particularly internal ones, to be found in the earlier films, and there have been several previous more or less cryptic manifestos (see Johansen and Kimergaard 1991). There is *Epidemic*'s sarcastic embrace of amateur filmmaking, *The Kingdom*'s striking break with the basic grammar of film editing (and in many ways the *The Kingdom* has to be viewed as the work that instigates the Dogma idea); there is the handheld camera of *Breaking the Waves*, which turned it into a unique big-budget avant-garde film. Not to mention the bizarre ground rules of the theater production *Verdensuret* (1996, *The World Clock*), and his work-in-(not so much)-progress *Dimension*, for which von Trier has shot two minutes of film per year, starting in 1992. The project is scheduled to shoot for thirty years total. Von Trier has explored the possibilities of artistic ingenuity according to all the rules of the game. Essentially, the only novel aspect of the Vow of Chastity is that it represents a publicized institutionalization of the ground rules as creative principles for the film world in general. It should be noted that the constraints of the Vow of Chastity, to a large extent, are targeted at von Trier himself, a self-flagellating "Kill Your Darlings"-therapy (see Schepelern 2003): "The provocation is always initially inwardly directed, and then it becomes other-directed as a side effect," says von Trier (Hjort and Bondebjerg 2001, 221), just as he has also said, "All of these rules are designed for me to relinquish control. It has always been very technically important for me, how a film's colors look. It is a great relief to have a rule that says: 'This is color film, you can't do anything with it.' If you look at all the rules, they have been more or less constructed in a way so that I do not do what I have done for a long time" (Roman 2001, 50). It is an agonizing process that also stimulates: "In all actuality, it's a kind of masochistic play with pain for me," he says in *The Purified*. Thus it is also in relation to von Trier that the rules create the greatest sacrifice (see Monggaard 2000, 100)—the director's anonymity, for example, is all the more telling when applied to von Trier, who in the opening of

Breaking the Waves covers the entire frame with his name in the largest print possible, than it is when applied to Kristian Levring (*The King Is Alive*, 2000), who is accustomed to the anonymous presentation of his work from his professional background in the world of advertising.

THE IMPOVERISHED ART

The film medium has a tradition of opulence and grandiosity (in one word: Hollywood!), but the history of cinema also circumscribes tendencies toward the modest and humble, corresponding to the Vow of Chastity's rejection of superfluous technology as well as its final oath of forsaking aesthetics. Examples of great classic ascetics include Carl Th. Dreyer's *The Passion of Joan of Arc* (1928, *La passion de Jeanne d'Arc*) and Robert Bresson's *A Man Escaped* (1959, *Un condamné à mort s'est échappé*) as well as Ingmar Bergman's interim-period movies like *Winter Light* (1962, *Nattvardsgästerna*) and *Persona* (1966) that almost entirely forsake entertainment and technological gluttony.

This also goes for the most influential manifestos of cinema history that typically—like Dogma 95—condemn the superficial, commercial, and false, illustrating an idealistic quest for truth. As an example, there are concrete rules about the film production in a number of Dziga Vertov's many manifestos from the 1920s, when he—with his documentary-style film journals *Kino-Pravda* (1922–25) and his main achievement, *The Man with the Movie Camera* (1929, *Tjelovek s kinoaparatom*)—was one of the leading figures in the wave of revolutionary Russian silent movies. In a number of short and energetic texts, he wrote off the cinematic drama as bourgeois and ancient and pointed instead to the type of political nonnarrative propaganda film that he himself made: "The film drama is opium for the people. Death to the screen's immortal kings and queens! The ordinary mortal people, recorded at their usual workplace shall live! . . . Death to the staging of everyday life: film us unexpectedly like we are" (Vertov 1973, 44), reads his 1926 "Preliminary Instructions to the Kinoglaz Circle." In that text he promotes "quick means of transport, film of high sensitivity to light, nimble handheld cameras, as well as just as portable lighting equipment" (48).

After the war Italian neorealism reacted against the glamour of Hollywood (and also against the "the era of the white telephones" in Italian film) and chose amateur actors, real locations, and a close-to-reality dramaturgy that originated in the banalities of everyday life. This was presented in scriptwriter Cesare Zavattinis's manifesto, "Some Ideas on the Cinema" (1952) and turned into praxis in main works like Vittorio de Sica's *The Bicycle Thief* (1948, *Ladri di biciclette*) and *Umberto D* (1951), both movies with a screenplay by Zavattini. With neorealism, cinema has moved "from an illusionary and equivocal evasion, to an unlimited trust in things, facts and people" (Zavattini 1966, 217). Zavattini stresses that "cinema should never turn back. It should accept unconditionally, what is contemporary. Today, today, today" (224). The answer to achieving this aim lies in liberation from technique and money: "Technique and capitalist method however, have imposed collaboration on the cinema. . . . It is obvious that when films cost sixpence and everybody can have a camera, the cinema would become a creative medium as flexible and as free as any other" (227).

That takes us to the young Frenchmen, who in 1959–60 emerged as "la nouvelle vague." The New Wave—with François Truffaut, Jean-Luc Godard, and Claude Chabrol as the main figures—never created a manifesto, although they were somewhat inspired by Alexandre Astruc's "The Birth of a New Avant-Garde: La caméra-stylo" (originally published in 1948) that argues for making film "the most extensive and clearest language there is" (1968, 22), as well as Truffaut's sarcastic review of the established cinema's weaknesses in the article "A Certain Tendency in French Cinema" (1954). But the New Wave's praxis was, in itself, a statement of purpose and intent—to break with the literary and conformist tradition of quality within the film medium and create spontaneous, less presumptuous films that entirely ignore conventions of editing and traditional dramaturgy.

Even though the New Wave directors eventually went in different directions, they started out as a kind of brotherhood of autodidactic film fans: that is, the directors from the circle around the journal *Cahiers du cinéma* (Truffaut, Godard, Chabrol, Jacques Rivette, and Eric Rohmer). From the beginning, there was a friendly atmosphere and a certain collective spirit. They celebrated the auteur ideology of artistic individuality, but they also collaborated. This can be witnessed in the movement's main work, Godard's *Breathless* (1960, *A bout de souffle*), based on a synopsis by Truffaut, with Chabrol functioning as a kind of assistant. It was filmed on authentic locations without any staging and partially with a handheld camera.

There were simultaneous New Wave movements in many film

nations; in West Germany, a group of young directors emerged and prophesied new times to come in the so-called Oberhausen Manifesto from 1962. Ironically, it was not these twenty-six directors (including Alexander Kluge and Edgar Reitz) who realized the ideas but instead the more obvious talents of the 1970s—Rainer Werner Fassbinder, Werner Herzog, and Wim Wenders: "This new film requires new freedoms. Freedom from the usual conventions of film-making. Freedom from commercial influences. Freedom from the dominance of interest groups. . . . The old film is dead. We believe in the new film" ("Oberhausen Manifesto" 1983, 5).

An indicative development that in many ways anticipates Dogma 95 is Godard's gradual deconstruction of film language and his break with commercial production and distribution. After the breakthrough years of the New Wave, Godard's films from the mid-1960s on became extremely fragmented and radically removed from mainstream film. *La chinoise* (1967) was accompanied by a short manifesto that announced a fight against Hollywood and the commercial film by creating—"both economically and aesthetically, that is, on two fronts—a national, free, brotherly, comradely, and friendly film art" (Godard 1998, 303). With *The Joy of Knowledge* (1968, *Le gai savoir*), about two people who read various texts aloud in a radio studio, he dismantled the narrative tradition in an anything but joyful way. From this low point, which coincided with the revolutionary events in Paris of May 1968, Godard left the commercial film universe and started—with people like his good friend Jean-Pierre Gorin—the Groupe Dziga Vertov, which produced his next films: *British Sounds, Pravda,* and *Vent d'est* (all 1969). Paying tribute to the Russian model as well as Brecht's political and anti-illusionary *Verfremdungs*-theater, the group presented deliberately antiaesthetic movies in a grainy 16 mm format, full of political proclamations. Furthermore, as an objection to auteur-individualism, the films were made collectively and anonymously (although the attention the films received was due mostly to the fact that Godard was behind them). Godard later returned to normally distributed 35 mm features, but with little commercial success.

Less radical—and consequently more influential, maybe—is John Cassavetes, who occupies a central position within anticommercial and antiaesthetic cinema with works like *Husbands* (1970) and *A Woman under the Influence* (1974), in which the poor aesthetics and the jerky camera movements forcibly put the actors at the center. This considerable cinematic chastity, which rejects outside effects, continued with directors like Mike Leigh, Ken Loach, Terence Davies, and Hal Hartley.

In modern cultural history, the 1960s in general hosted an outbreak of antiaesthetic initiatives. Within painted art, a group of young Italian artists started the so-called *arte povera*, which, like so many other movements of the time (for example, minimalism, concept art, and pop art)—aimed to undermine the classical concept of art. Arte povera rejected pompous and luxurious art and approached a "poor art" that used cheap materials like sand, ash, straw, wax, lead, rubble, and old newspapers. The deceased Piero Manzoni is considered a pioneer of this movement, and his controversial *Merda d'artista* (1961) is a can of the artist's own feces, the ultimate worthless material (see Celant 1991). The artists demonstratively avoided painting; instead, they collected things in collages and engaged in happenings. It is art that will not appear as a work—it is simply compressed newspaper (Michelangelo Pistoletto), rocks with rotting vegetables (Giovanni Anselmo), pebbles (Piero Gilardi), scrubbing brushes (Pino Pascali), sheets (Luciano Fabro), old bags and pieces of clothes (Jannis Kounellis), small mounds of rubble and straw (Mario Merz). As expressed by the movement's main spokesman, the critic Germano Celant, who was in charge of the organized exhibitions in Genoa (1967), Torino (1970), and Munich (1971), the movement looked for "de-culturalization, regression, primitivism, and submission, toward pre-logical, pre-iconographic states, toward elementary and spontaneous politics, a tendency toward the basic elements of nature (earth, water, snow, minerals, warmth, animals) and life (body, memory, thought) and behavior (family, spontaneous action, class struggle, violence, environment)" (Celant 1969, 227, reprinted in Harrison and Wood 1992, 887). Arte povera was anticommercial all the way, as exemplified by its "worthless" materials and its artist who "denounces his role as an artist, intellectual, painter or writer and rediscovers how to comprehend, to feel, to breathe, to walk, to understand, to make oneself a human being."

A related initiative within theater of the 1960s was the Polish artist Jerzy Grotowski's theater laboratory in Wroclaw. He articulated his method in the 1965 manifesto, *Towards a Poor Theatre,* which had a lasting international influence on the development of the avant-garde theater. In Grotowski's theater, influenced by Stanislavsky, Brecht, and Artaud, "we consider the personal and scenic technique of the actor as the core of theatre art. . . . By gradually eliminating whatever proved superfluous, we found that theatre can exist without make-up, without autonomic costume and scenography, without a separate performance area (stage), without lighting and sound effects, etc." (Grotowski 1975, 15, 19). The only thing that could not be left out was "the actor-spectator relationship of perceptual, direct, 'live' communion" (19).

Grotowski rejects the "rich" theater: "No matter how much theatre expands and exploits it mechanical resources, it will remain technologically inferior to film and television. Consequently, I propose poverty in theatre. . . . The acceptance of the poverty of theatre, stripped of all that is not essential to it, revealed to us not only the backbone of the medium, but also the deep riches which lie in the very nature of the art-form (Grotowski 1975, 19, 21). And perhaps the actors benefit the most: "The actor is reborn—not only as an actor but also as a man—and with him, I am reborn" (25). Grotowski's thoughts heavily influenced the ideas of his assistant, the Italian-born Eugenio Barba, about an ascetic theater, realized with the Odin Theater (in Denmark since 1966).

BACK TO LUMIÉRE

By most standards, Dogma 95 is related to its predecessors. Generally speaking, it appears as antiestablishment, an initiative against bourgeois and luxurious art, against the role of the artist as a concept. Instead, it looks toward reality, toward truth that has no illusions, toward the unpretentious, humble, and humanistic.

Dogma has not set a political agenda, but when notions like "the decadent filmmaker" and "the individual film" are attacked, the language as such—perhaps as a parody?—points back to the ideological debates of the 1970s, also emphasized by the semimilitaristic word selection: "It is no accident that the phrase avant-garde has military connotation: Discipline is the answer . . . we must put our films into uniform, because the individual film will be decadent by definition!" (Dogma95). One hears von Trier's ironic salute to the political environment that he experienced in the 1970s, which his own Dogma movie *The Idiots* (1998, *Idioterne*) specifically addresses.

A *dogma* is a religious command that one should not question but merely follow—as has always been the case with religions' and other irrational ideologies' method: "To create dogmas is to limit the spirit, the dogma is nothing but an explicit ban against thinking," according to the German philosopher Ludwig Feuerbach, who was a salient figure in the rationalistic struggle of the 1800s against the irrationality of Christianity (1960, 254). This aspect casts a somewhat spiteful shadow over Dogma 95, as there seems to be a direct conflict between the dogmatic and the innovative.

Dogma 95 stands out as a type of cinematic fundamentalism, a back-to-nature movement, back to Lumière's cinematic innocence. It is about liberation through relinquishment. About peeling away the film's superfluous tricks and effects to reach the "poor" film: "I think the need to go back to basics, which the rules are a response to, is more urgent now than ever before," says von Trier (Hjort and Bondebjerg, 2001, 222). It is about turning your back on technology and (re)discovering the human being. But one philosophical weakness is the fact that the logical but also paradoxical consequence of the Vow of Chastity is to also get rid of the camera. If you want to exterminate all the technological effects of the film, why save the most dominant? The camera itself is the one element that is most against nature's order! And what about the actors? Why do the settings have to be real and contain authentic material, when the actors can be inauthentic—that is, be actors? It seems there is no explanation for that, but then again, dogmas are dogmas exactly because we should not question them.

It seems obvious that if you continue the cinematic exploration of a "true" reality, then you would necessarily have to give up the actors and—like Vertov—the entire fiction. But then you would only have moved into documentarism à la the French cinema vérité, Frederick Wiseman's *direct cinema,* or the TV series *An American Family* (Craig Gilbert, 1973), where the camera followed a Californian family's life through seven months—a documentary that paved the way for the more recent eruption of reality TV. *The Idiots* is clearly indebted to this type of authentic reporting, a kind of sociological documentary focused on human behavior (with its occasional interviews, the film appears like a documentary-pastiche). The film's cinematography looks much like the handheld and entirely antiaesthetic video recordings of the pornographer Ed Powers's home-video sex films, with lighting and camera visibly present.

But the point of Dogma 95 is exactly that the movement does not aim toward documentarism, where the method would appear not at all invigorating but rather conventional. (It should be mentioned that von Trier in 2001 actually presented another manifesto and nine points for a Dogma documentary, called *Dogumentary* (see Christensen 2001; Dabelsteen 2002 and *Converging with Angels* 2002). Dogma presents a challenge to fictional film, creating a dialectic between fiction and the pursuit of truth. Essentially, it is the same tendency that can be witnessed in neorealism and other approaches to realism over the history of cinema (for example, theoretical proponents of realism like André Bazin and Siegfried Kracauer, who also sought to expel the art of illusion for a truthful portrayal of reality while maintaining the framework of fiction). But even though the Dogma text—like the "poor" artist initiatives—demands aesthetic cleansing and an ascetic production apparatus that implies a low budget (though that is not explicitly stated), it is obvious that the Dogma movement is also an invitation to join in a game with fun rules. Just as it is fun to play children's games where there are a number of obstacles, like Twister or pin the tail on the donkey, it is fun to witness what happens when directors must work without elements of customary film technology. It corresponds to having a vacation in a re-created Iron Age village: try to make do without the technology of the last thousand years and see how you do! It also compares to the TV show *Survivor*, which stages a basic human drama by denying the contestants access to fundamental technical accessories. A typical symptom of Western culture, the idea of survival as entertainment probably would not make sense in a famine-stricken third world country.

Dogma 95 started as a movement with the 1995 Manifesto; original members included von Trier and Vinterberg, Søren Kragh-Jacobsen, and Kristian Levring as well as the documentary filmmaker Anne Wivel, who soon left the group. The production companies were Zentropa (von Trier's company) and Nimbus (Vinterberg's company), now both situated in the so-called Film City established by von Trier in 1999 in Avedøre, outside Copenhagen. The initial Dogma project—the production of five films with a budget of $125,000 each (an amount that was exceeded in many cases)—had originally received a promise of financial support directly from the Danish cultural minister, Jytte Hilden; this shortcut around the usual governmental bureaucracy surrounding public film financing met resistance within the Danish Film Institute. And in the meantime, Jytte Hilden had been replaced as cultural minister for unrelated reasons and the ministry no longer considered itself obligated by her promise. The project was then saved by DR (Danish state television) via producer Svend Abrahamsen and chief executive Bjørn Erichsen, who stepped in and provided the financial support in return for exclusive TV rights.

In this connection, it should be mentioned that the Dogma movies not only represented a technological and productive simplification but also a considerable liberation from the usual administrative system, which marked a unique artistic freedom for the directors. Essentially, they managed to assure financing for the movies without having submitted a single script, as none had been written at the time when the contract was negotiated. The films were made without any approval from consultants, dramatists, producers, or investors. However, this was not the case for the next set of Danish Dogma movies, which all followed the correct route through the bureaucracy of the Film Institute.

On April 1, 1998, the members of the Danish Dogma fraternity, who had kept in touch through e-mail during the years their different projects were developed, finally formulated two certificates, testifying that Dogma 1: *The Celebration (Festen)* and Dogma 2: *The Idiots (Idioterne)* had been "produced in compliance with the rules set forth in the Dogma 95 manifesto." In 1999 Dogma 3: *Mifune (Mifunes sidste sang)* appeared, in 2000 Dogma 4: *The King Is Alive* and *Italian for Beginners (Italiensk for begyndere)*, in 2001 *Truly Human (Et rigtigt menneske)* and *Kira's Reason: A Love Story (En kærlighedshistorie)*, in 2002 *Open Hearts (Elsker dig for evigt)*, and in 2003 *Old, New, Borrowed, and Blue (Se til venstre, der er en svensker)*. The films have all been released without crediting the director, but according to reliable sources, the directors are as follows: Thomas Vinterberg, Lars von Trier, Søren Kragh-Jacobsen, Kristian Levring, Lone Scherfig, Åke Sandgren, Ole Christian Madsen, Susanne Bier, and Natasha Arthy.

The Dogma phenomenon became known very quickly on the international film scene, and the Dogma movies received a lot of attention from the very beginning. The first two Dogma movies were part of the program at the film festival in Cannes, where *The Celebration* received the Jury's Special Award; even though it did not receive any awards, *The Idiots* generated a lot of exposure. *Mifune* received two Silver Bears and two other awards in Berlin. Later on, *The King Is Alive* was selected for the series *Un certain regard* in Cannes without receiving any awards; *Italian for Beginners* won the Silver Bear and two other awards, the Audience Award among them, in Berlin. The expression *Dogma* was soon adopted into everyday language, and the films' connection to a collective movement—their branding, so to speak—made them more visible on the international market and consequently easier to promote.

A LONG NIGHT'S JOURNEY TOWARD DAY

Thomas Vinterberg's *The Celebration* became an international breakthrough for Danish cinema, for Dogma, and for Vinterberg. He had already created high expectations with the shorts *Sidste ongang* (1997, *Last Round*), his graduation film from the Danish Film Institute, and *Drengen der gik baglæns* (1994, *The Boy Who Walked Backwards*), as well as the feature film *De største helte* (1997, *The Greatest Heroes*). The intense and powerful story of *The Celebration* was an instant hit.

The expatriate Christian (Ulrich Thomsen) returns home for his father's (Henning Moritzen) sixtieth birthday. In a speech during the extravagant dinner, Christian tells how his father sexually abused him and his twin sister, who had recently committed suicide. In spite of verbal and physical protests from the other guests, Christian continues his revelations, and when his other sister (Paprika Steen) finds a note from the deceased twin, there can no longer be any doubt. The next morning, his father apologizes, and Christian can continue with his life.

The story, which is told like an Aristotelian drama with stringent compliance to the unity of time, place, and action (with the stately manor Skjoldenæsholm as its setting), has a somewhat mysterious origin that seems to confirm that all movie productions have a secret. Vinterberg has been quoted as saying "that most of [the story] came from my imagination" (Roman 2001, 79), which may be a modified version of the truth, since the story closely follows a supposedly authentic case aired on a radio show on DR (*Koplevs Krydsfelt*, March 28, 1996), in which a young man related the story as his own. Incongruities in the narrative of the anonymous young man created some doubt as to the authenticity of his story, and later it was revealed (in Lisbeth Jessen's radio montage *After "The Celebration,"* DR January 23, 2002, see Thorsen 2002) that the young man invented the whole thing: there was no celebration, there was no speech, and there was no incest.

The script, written by Vinterberg and Mogens Rukov, who has gained status as some kind of "Dogma doctor" (also highlighted by his role as a strict Dogma judge in Jargil's *The Purified*), could have easily been made into classic theatrical film art. It is no surprise that it was adapted to the stage in 2000 by the dramatist Bo hr. Hansen, and it has since been produced in many countries with great success—particularly in Germany. Vinterberg's film presents this family drama—which relates closely to a theater tradition from August Strindberg and Henrik Ibsen to Eugene O'Neill, Edward Albee, and Lars Norén—as a flexible cinematic flow, constituted by the searching and interrogating camera that does not give up, an incessant tool for reaching the truth in accordance with the Vow of Chastity from Dogma 95—though there is a certain irony in the fact that the story the film was based on turned out to be a lie. In this way, the cinematography matches the project of the story, just like the theatrical form opens everything up for the actors. They are allowed to "act out" to an extent that the ordinary film-shooting procedures normally deny.

While *The Idiots* in many ways remains the quintessential and most radical Dogma film (unsurprisingly, since Dogma was von Trier's idea to begin with), *The Celebration* was the ideal first release for the movement. With its mainstream accessibility and traditional tenor, it showed the world that the Dogma method did not concern only an avant-garde and experimental form—the method could create results that managed to attract a relatively large audience.

A crucial element of the Dogma method is the development of a new attitude toward filming. Since the video camera does not require film, the filmmakers tend to shoot a lot of material—often more than one hundred hours and far more than what they need. They shoot not only many takes of the same scene but also improvised and alternative takes, just to see what comes out of it. The final version of *The Celebration* as well as the later *Italian for Beginners* and *Kira's Reason* have entire subplots and characters cut out. It was implied in von Trier's original idea that the Dogma camera should not frame reality—that is, arrange it within an aesthetic framework—but instead point toward it (see Schepelern 2000b, 233). This also applies to the approach to the material, which is not limited by the boundaries of the script but allows for different versions and even different films (as coming DVD editions might reveal).

ANARCHISTS IN SØLLERØD

Dogma 95 has a retrospective connection to the French New Wave movement that was the inspiration of the Manifesto. Indeed, von Trier originally contacted Vinterberg with an offer to participate in the start of a "new" new wave (see Kelly 2000, 137) to replace the "old" New Wave, where "the goal was correct but the means were not! The New Wave proved to be a ripple that washed ashore and turned to muck" (Dogma95).

One of the New Wave's favorite approaches was to focus on a group whose members adopt a laid-back, improvised lifestyle that goes beyond bourgeois norms: this applies to the American antihero in Godard's *Breathless* and to the triangle in *Band of Outsiders* (1964, *Bande à part*) and *A Woman Is a Woman* (1961, *Un femme est une femme*); with increasing political awareness, it goes for *Pierrot le fou* (1965). With Truffaut, it applies to the short *Les mistons* (1957), the sulky schoolboys in *The 400 Blows* (1959, *Les quatre cents coups*), and the triangle in *Jules and Jim* (1961, *Jules et Jim*). It applies with Chabrol to the young people in *The Cousins* (1959, *Les cousins*) and *The Good Girls* (1960, *Les bonnes femmes*). *The Idiots* ties itself to this tradition with its story of an anarchistic group of loafers who play and have fun; and—as a reference to this film-historical connection—the film actually received positive comments from Godard himself (quoted in Monggaard 1998).

The plot revolves around the emotionally disturbed Karen (Bodil Jørgensen), who meets up with a group of young people (Jens Albinus, Nikolaj Lie Kaas, Anne Louise Hassing, Louise Mieritz, Troels Lyby) who are staying in an empty Søllerød villa over the summer in order to engage in a sociopsychological experiment. The group has agreed to a pact that requires them to act as developmentally disabled people in public, or, as they describe it, "to spass" (*at spasse*) in front of the rest of the world—in places like a restaurant, a public pool, a factory, a bar—to try to reach their "inner idiots."

The Idiots stands out as the quintessential Dogma movie because the technical and aesthetic rules are framed by a plot that also concerns an experiment with ground rules, about dealing with a challenging test: Does the teacher dare to "spass" in front of the art class he teaches? Does the housewife dare to "spass" when she returns home to her family? Does von Trier dare to "spass" with the cinematic language? The group is searching for a primordial state, the inner idiot, just like von Trier is looking for a primordial film art. Transgressing the bourgeois norms—including those prohibiting nakedness and sexual orgies—is matched by the transgression of the cinematic consensus of film art.

The Idiots can be viewed as an expression of von Trier in his humanistic phase. After the demonic fall of cynical or powerless men in the Europe trilogy—*The Element of Crime* (1984, *Forbrydelsens element*), *Epidemic* (1988), and *Zentropa* (1991, *Europa*)—it is now, with *Breaking the Waves* (1996), *The Idiots,* and the musical *Dancer in the Dark* (2000), emotional and warm women who have to soften our hearts. *The Idiots* celebrates the romantic conception that children, idiots, and, especially, sensitive women have particularly easy access to human primordial feeling. As a counterweight to this slightly pathetic theme, there is a witty and comical aspect that ridicules the hypocritical and snobby bourgeoisie. Perhaps the film is most appealing through its formal daring, the energy, and the audacity of the whole project.

Von Trier thinks of *The Idiots* as "the truest and the most sublime [film] I have made" (1998, 277). "It is wonderful that the Dogma rules have thrown aesthetics away" (236)—but he also remarks that aesthetics follow along anyway, almost by themselves. This paradoxical situation also goes for control.

In a press release for *The Idiots* (see Øvig Knudsen 1998), von Trier described Dogma 95 and *The Idiots* as an initiative to let go of control. Of course, control is a crucial factor in von Trier's universe. But actually, the movie—with its apparently open and improvised scenes filmed in a style à la a bad home movie—is just as formalistic as *Zentropa*, where everything was shot according to elaborately designed plans. An ego of the caliber that encompasses von Trier's control mania inevitably follows the director wherever he goes. Where else would it live?! The film's screenplay was ready from the first day of shooting. The improvisations that took place were largely left out of the final product, and 90 percent of the filming was done by von Trier himself. Also, Dogma's stern commands come from von Trier himself. So, it seems like control is firmly established, even though the director credits himself as ". . . . ."

The documentary filmmaker Jesper Jargil followed the filming of *The Idiots,* which resulted in the documentary *The Humiliated* (1998, *De ydmygede);* along with *The Exhibited* (2000, *De udstillede),* about von Trier and Morten Arnfred's theater experiment *Verdensuret* (The World Clock), and *The Purified* (2002, *De lutrede),* about the Dogma brothers' self-examining discussions, it creates a trilogy of the Dogma movement with the common title *Troværdighedens rige* (The Kingdom of Credibility)—a grand cinematic achievement about Dogma and the mysteries of artistic creation.

REVISITING THE OLD FARM

Von Trier surmised in his diary from *The Idiots* that Søren Kragh-Jacobsen probably would be the one who would have most trouble "accepting the whole project" (1998, 160), and when *Mifune* appeared, it was obvious—although it did not veer away from the Dogma rules—that it was a Søren Kragh-Jacobsen film.

Mifune, written by Kragh-Jacobsen, Mogens Rukov, and Anders Thomas Jensen, is only Kragh-Jacobsen's second film for an adult audience, and it is closely related to the first one, *Isfugle* (1983, Kingfishers). In the interim period, he made some of the best Danish children's movies—*Rubber Tarzan* (1981, *Gummi Tarzan*), *Emma's Shadow* (1988, *Skyggen af Emma*), and *The Boys from Saint Petri* (1991, *Drengene fra Sankt Petri*). *Mifune's* two brothers, the city slicker (Anders W. Berthelsen) and his mentally challenged brother (Jesper Asholt), correspond with modifications to the odd couple in *Isfugle*. *Isfugle* is a beautiful movie that—together with films like Malmros's Århus trilogy (with *Kundskabens træ* [1981, The Tree of Knowledge] as the main achievement), Bille August's *Honey Moon* (1978, *Honning måne*), and Morten Arnfred's *Me and Charly* (1978, *Mig og Charly*) and *Johnny Larsen* (1979)—makes up the core of the sensitive humanistic art film that has been a defining feature of Danish cinema since the 1970s. These films all portrayed sorry, fragile Danes struck by the uneventful occurrences of everyday life, but they were conscientiously filmed in soft colors and characterized by solid acting. Contemporary times call for more vitality, which we get in *Mifune*.

Curiously, as far as plot goes, the film contains some of the same elements as *The Celebration* and *The Idiots*. In *Mifune*, we also find a lost son (Anders W. Berthelsen), and the plot revolves around his return to the farm where he grew up, where various skeletons are hiding in the closets; here we even have a "real" idiot (Jesper Asholt) as well as a redemptive woman (Iben Hjejle)—all of which becomes a recipe to cure a possessed man. Luckily, some equality has been achieved, as she also has her traumas that have to be cured: I redeem you if you redeem me. That is the stuff that makes up good melodrama. And *Mifune* is fearless melodrama that does not hold back (even though genre is against the rules). The film's main location, on the island of Lolland, represents in many ways a perverse caricature of the idealized Danish farm immortalized in the books of Morten Korch

(1876–1954). Korch was a popular writer whose novels, which were set in the Danish countryside, were turned into a number of successful films. For many, his books represent all that is worst in popular taste. Interestingly enough, von Trier was executive producer for a tongue-in-cheek TV series based on these sentimental stories (*Morten Korch*, 1999–2000). But although Kragh-Jacobsen satirizes country farm romanticism, he ultimately ends up celebrating the old song of the city as stressful, false, and cheap—a place where the orgasms are intense but also impersonal.

It is interesting to see how the Dogma method can lead to a film of the classical tradition. Essentially, Dogma 95 does not state that the images have to be shaky; the handheld camera can be held by a person who does not have the shakes. That is how the images are in *Mifune*, which unlike the others was recorded in traditional 35 mm, beautiful and classical. Dogma is visible only in occasional shots with too much contrast as the lack of lighting plays in. But the film works, as if Dogma has made Søren Kragh-Jacobsen sweep some of the neatness away. The diabolical is given a voice, and true emotions shine through.

INTERACTIVE NEW YEAR'S

While the fourth Dogma brother, Kristian Levring, was putting the last touches on his Dogma film, *The King Is Alive*, the four directors worked together on a production that combined the Dogma rules with a new collective experiment. The cooperative aspect in itself was already present in Dogma and in the Manifesto's warning that "the individual film will be decadent by definition."

D day (2000, *D dag*) is four Dogma films (outside the official list) that were recorded and directed live as four uninterrupted takes. The four filmmakers each directed—from a central control room—one actor with a film crew on a tour through the center of Copenhagen in the hour before the millennium celebrations.

The actors' performances, which rely heavily on improvisation, were based on a rough-draft screenplay and one rehearsal. Every character represents one thread that becomes intertwined into a common story about a bank robbery. Thomas Vinterberg followed the neurotic detonation expert Niels-Henning (Nikolaj Kopernikus); Lars von Trier followed the vindictive housewife Lise (Charlotte Sachs Bostrup), who participates in the heist to expose her husband's (Stellan Skarsgård) infidelity; Søren Kragh-Jacobsen followed the banker Boris (Dejan Cukic), whose insistent friend (Jesper Asholdt) ends up with all the money; and Kristian Levring followed Niels-Henning's buddy Carl (Bjarne Henriksen), who has to send his girlfriend away and calm down a suicidal person. The four films, of seventy minutes each, were then released the next day—January 1, 2000—during prime time on the four Danish television stations (supplemented by another three channels that showed shots from the control room as well as all four films in a split-screen frame). The idea was that the viewers could create their own film with their remotes, editing their own plot from the four strains of action.

The history of fiction has witnessed many earlier examples of this type of complementary narrative, where a story is presented from several different perspectives. The decisive leap to the audience's interactive participation comes with the German production *Mörderische Entscheidung* (1991, Murderous Decisions)—a colorful drama by Oliver Hirschbiegel in the form of two parallel TV films that follow the male and female lead respectively. It was televised simultaneously on ARD and ZDF, so that viewers could shift between the two parallel plots: *Umschalten erwünscht* ("channel hopping encouraged") read the subtitle. A variation of this narrative technique—and a project that closely resembles *D Day*—is Mike Figgis's *Timecode* (2000), which tells its story through four different parallel plots that are viewed simultaneously in a four-way split screen. The viewer's attention is then controlled by the sound, as the dialogue can be heard only in one place at a time (see Roman 2001, 136)

In other media, there are earlier examples, like John Kirzanc's Canadian play *Tamara* (1984), in which five to six different parallel plots are played out in as many localities within a grand mansion, and the viewer then has to choose which plot to follow. There is also von Trier's own theater experiment *Verdensuret* (1996, The World Clock), where the audience can choose between fifty-three different characters' lives, over fifty performances of three hours each, and in nineteen different locations. The characters go through changes that are laid out in a big manual and guided by lamps that turn on and off according to computer impulses controlled by a link to the movements of a colony of ants in New Mexico! (Jesper Jargil's footage from the performance is the background for the documentary *The Exhibited*, 2000). It is this characteristic—also known from computer games—of multiplayer interactivity that von Trier and the other Dogma brothers try to use as a means of cinematic expression in *D Day*.

D Day was received as an experiment that was more interesting than successful. The problem with letting the audience choose a plot is that you can only choose one thing at the expense of something else, and you cannot know beforehand what you're selecting—or what you're not selecting. You do not know what is important and what is not. If *Hamlet* were narrated in this fashion, you could potentially end up missing the ghost scene and instead waste your time watching Ophelia polish her nails.

Of course, you can defend the method with the fact that the fictional in this way comes to represent real life, as we also make choices in real life that cannot be altered. Maybe they can be regretted, but time cannot be turned back and repeated. That is reality for you—but perhaps that is why art needs to do something different. It is a considerable appeal of fiction that it gives you the opportunity to experience events marked by coherence and meaning, liberated from reality's trivialities, empty waiting, and mistaken decisions. There is a difference between the choices in real life and the choices of art.

On one hand, *D Day* is a somewhat disappointing project in interactivity as an aesthetic method, but on the other hand, it is an exciting experiment in new ways of production—approximately four and a half hours of low-budget film, assisted by new logistic, administrative, and technical methods, were produced live in seventy minutes. In December 2001 an edited version (by Valdis Oskarsdóttir) was released under the title, *D dag—den færdige film* (D Day—The Completed Film).

THE KING, THE QUEEN, AND THE HUMAN

The disappointing *D Day* could be taken as a sign of the Dogma movement fading out after the first three surprisingly successful releases. Yet the name still carried enough commercial value for a series of Danish pornographic films to be released under the collective title *Dogma* (without the approval of the Dogma brothers). Even though chastity, for all too apparent reasons, is very limited in these films, they are—as much pornography is—most likely produced in accordance with the majority of the Dogma rules. One of the films was even titled *Festen* (1999, The Celebration) and had a cover in the same style as the movie poster for Vinterberg's *The Celebration*. There are no similarities in plot between the two films, but one of the actors from the porno series, Lasse Helmer Sørensen, alias Porno Lasse, actually had an authentic Dogma experience as a hard-core stand-in for the group sex scene of *The Idiots* (see von Trier 1998, 248).

In the spring of 2000, the fourth Dogma brother finally presented his film in Cannes. *The King Is Alive* (cowritten by Anders Thomas Jensen) is a story about a group of people who have gotten lost with their bus in the Namibian desert and practice Shakespeare's *King Lear* while they wait for rescue or death. Before this project, Kristian Levring, who knew von Trier from the Danish Film School, where he was trained as an editor, had had an international career in advertising (except for one insignificant feature film, *Et skud fra hjertet* [1986, A Shot from the Heart], which has thematic similarities to his Dogma movie with its desert setting). *The King Is Alive* is produced in English and displays symptoms of a certain Dogma-related decadence. It is less spontaneous than the other Dogma movies and seems more like an étude in Dogma technique. With reference to Volker Schlöndorff's *Voyager* (1991), based on Max Frisch's novel, it has the characteristics of an intellectualized disaster film. But the performances, by actors like Jennifer Jason Leigh, Bruce Davison, and David Bradley, are intense, and so is the beauty of the dramatic African setting, which also seems to bypass the rule about forsaking "everything aesthetic."

After *The King Is Alive*, the next round of Danish Dogma films began, starting with Lone Scherfig's *Italian for Beginners* (Dogma 12, 2000), Åke Sandgren's *Truly Human* (Dogma 18, 2001), and Ole Christian Madsen's *Kira's Reason* (Dogma 21, 2001). The fourth film in this second wave should have been by Henrik Ruben Genz, known for his children's movie *Theis and Nico* (1998, *Bror, min bror*), but he withdrew; instead Natasha Arthy's *Old, New, Borrowed, and Blue* (Dogma 32, 2003) became the next one.

Italian for Beginners, which was released in December 2000, became another triumph for Danish cinema and the Dogma concept. Lone Scherfig, who during 1999–2000 had made thirteen episodes of Zentropa's television series *Morten Korch*, became the first active Dogma sister, and after winning the Silver Bear in Berlin (February 2001), there was no doubt that she was also the Dogma queen. *Italian for Beginners* is Dogma—but with modifications. In this film, Dogma comes to church (the Dogma certificate hangs on the wall of the priest's office), but you cannot overlook the fact that the film—more than any of the earlier Dogma films—has broken the Vow of Chastity's eighth commandment: "Genre movies are not acceptable." Without a doubt, the film is a romantic comedy, and it is precisely the genre-related organization of the romantic connections between the six somewhat odd and traumatized main characters that is the film's strength. The new priest and widow (Anders W. Berthelsen) and the clumsy assistant at the bakery (Anette Støvelbæk), the impotent hotel receptionist (Peter Gantzler) and the Italian waitress (Sara Indrio Jensen), the aggressive cafeteria manager (Lars Kaalund) and the emotional hairdresser (Ann Eleonora Jørgensen): each adds a distinct voice to the film's ensemble performance.

The film, written by the director but incorporating the actors' own ideas, excels with its tragicomical elegance and character interaction. It is a feel-good movie about how six people find happiness and love despite the intrigues and banal trivialities of everyday life—culminating in the grand finale in Venice where all the right characters come together. The combination of modern realism and stylized romantic intrigue—with about three funerals and the prospect of just as many weddings—succeeds to perfection, just as the Dogma technique again proves to be a shortcut to a simplified production process, flowing narration, and brilliant acting. But at the same time, it is obvious that the movie, in spite of its low budget and Dogma rules, is unmistakably mainstream, to which the film's huge commercial success in Denmark also testifies. Groundbreaking avant-garde cinema simply does not sell 820,000 tickets in a country of only 5.3 million.

The Swede Åke Sandgren, who went to the Danish Film School with von Trier, has—apart from a couple of Swedish movies—made three children's movies in Denmark: the short film *Johannes' hemmelighed* (1985, Johannes's Secret), where Jesus, in the shape of a girl, takes a boy on an adventuresome journey; *The Miracle in Valby* (1989, *Miraklet i Valby*), about a group of kids traveling back in time to the Middle Ages; and the latest, *Beyond* (2000, *Dykkerne*), about a group of teenagers who discover an old Nazi submarine. All the films are effectively narrated adventures with symbolic elements. The Dogma film *Truly Human* (2001), written by the director, could be placed in a similar category, as an imaginary allegory about a mysterious youth (Nikolaj Lie Kaas in another "idiot" role) who crops up—as a mix between Jesus, Kaspar Hauser, and Pinocchio—with naïve goodness in the middle of civilization and is received with disbelief and fear but also curiosity and desire. The young man, who is a little girl's materialized imaginary big brother, is placed in a refugee housing facility where he is pursued sexually, accused of being a pedophile, and attacked. *Truly Human* is a politically correct film that focuses on Danes and their relation to "aliens." Even though it fizzles out in the end and gives a somewhat weak moral lesson about parents who are too obsessed with their careers and neglect their kids, a series of touching, comical, and magical moments between the evil world and the good person are quite successful.

Ole Christian Madsen's first feature film, *Pizza King* (1999), was produced under Dogmalike conditions; and both that and the television production *Edderkoppen* (2000, The Spider)—an example of elaborately updated film noir formalism—used improvisation. The Dogma movie *Kira's Reason* (2001) is about the pain of love, about a painful relationship. Kira (Stine Stengade) is married to the entrepreneur, Mads (Lars Mikkelsen), and she is the mother of two little boys. She has been through depression and psychosis and now returns home to the family. There are obvious references to Cassavetes's *A Woman under the Influence* (1974), one of the main inspirational figures for Dogma, especially in the scene where the woman is greeted by a surprise party upon her return from the mental institution. In both cases, it becomes clear that a surprise party is not exactly what the fragile woman needs right now. One can also detect a connection to *The Celebration*—perhaps through Mogens Rukov's contribution to the script. *Kira's Reason* also portrays festive celebrations with a somber subtext as well as plenty of family trauma—sibling jealousy, a father's neglect, and infant death. The film is a chamber play told with great confidence, and the acting is impressive and convincingly framed by the camera's often extreme close-ups. What is most touching are the small painful moments, such as when one of the guests at a dinner party (Claus Strandberg, with a face marked by years of experience) leans over toward the awkwardly hyper hostess (Kira) and discreetly asks her: "Are you nuts?"

Before Natasha Arthy's film was finished, the third wave of Danish Dogma movies began. First came Susanne Bier's *Open Hearts* (Dogma 28) in 2002. In 2004, Annette K. Olesen released Dogma 34, *In Your Hands* (*Forbrydelser*), a prison drama written by Kim Fupz Aakeson; other forthcoming Dogma directors at the time of writing include Icelandic Dagur Kári, who gained a reputation for himself with

Film according to Dogma

Lost Weekend (1999), his graduation film from the Danish Film School, and Charlotte Sachs Bostrup, who acted in *D Day* and who has directed a number of commercial youth films. The decision as to who gets to make the Danish Dogma movies is typically made by producers from Zentropa and Nimbus Film in cooperation with DR.

Before *Open Hearts*, Susanne Bier had made six regularly produced features. Her Dogma film, with a screenplay by Anders Thomas Jensen, is a romantic melodrama about a relationship struck by a coincidental disaster that—painfully and ironically—becomes the occasion for another romantic relationship. Two young people, the geography student Joachim (Nikolaj Lie Kaas) and the cook Cecilie (Sonja Richter), have just decided to get married when he steps out in front of a car. He survives, but he is paralyzed from the neck down. His reaction is to reject Cecilie even though she wants to continue their relationship. The doctor Niels (Mads Mikkelsen), whose wife, Marie (Paprika Steen), drove the car but was not to blame for the accident, takes care of the devastated Cecilie. When Joachim steadfastly continues to reject Cecilie, she begins a relationship with Niels, who has problems at home with his teenage daughter, Stine.

Open Hearts is a kind of secularized *Breaking the Waves*. Great love is confronted with the ultimate test, but in mundane reality there are no redemptive miracles or ringing bells. Here it does not help to sacrifice oneself. In a development resembling the stages that the psychologist Kübler-Ross has defined for people faced with death, Joachim finds a way out of his anger and reaches an acceptance of his fate, and in the end, all the characters can continue their lives on the terms that exist.

The film's theme revolves around a heart-wrenching accident that turns everything upside down, but not so much that the world doesn't ultimately continue in its familiar tracks, a scenario that is also suggestive of Dogma's status within contemporary Danish cinema. Despite the Dogma movement's revolutionary potential, Danish film is moving toward—or returning to—a certain normality, or business as usual. A couple of months before *Open Hearts* was released, two other Danish movies with a similar style and thematic came out. Annette K. Olesen's *Minor Mishaps* (*Små ulykker*) and Jesper W. Nielsen's *Okay* (both 2002 and both with a script by Kim Fupz Aakeson) are not Dogma movies, but they pursue the same authentic style (*Minor Mishaps* was inspired by Mike Leigh's Dogma-related method), and the theme of the quintessential Danish middle-class family struck by disaster is the same. *Open Hearts* does not really move beyond the somewhat repetitious portrayal of the ups and downs of the Danish family, but the acting is still superb.

Natasha Arthy's 2003 Danish Dogma movie, *Old, New, Borrowed, and Blue*, continues this trend. The film's screenplay is by Kim Fupz Aakeson, who also wrote Arthy's debut movie, *Mirakel* (2000, Miracle). *Old, New, Borrowed, and Blue* tells the story of Katrine (Sidse Babett Knudsen), who is getting married. Her big sister, Mette (Lotte Andersen), is in a psychiatric hospital due to a depression over a boyfriend who suddenly left her two years earlier and went to Africa. This boyfriend, Thomsen (Björn Kjellman), resurfaces at Katrine's house before the wedding. It turns out that he also had a fling with her before he left for Africa, and in the middle of all the wedding preparations, it occurs to Katrine that it is the charming and impulsive, but unfortunately also HIV-positive, Thomsen that she loves.

The film follows the trail of the other Danish Dogma movies with its relatively large number of characters and the almost obligatory "idiot," in this case, the mentally ill sister. But more profoundly, it continues the "normalization" of Dogma that seems to be taking place. Like the two previous female directors, Arthy presents a feel-good movie that appeals especially to women, appealing to the desire for relationships and family life exposed through engaging performances and moving stories from everyday life. And there is no doubt that Arthy delivers. Her film is moving and funny, warm and bittersweet. But it is also fairly conventional. Dogma, as mentioned before, rejects genre, as a genre always comes with its own implicit set of rules. Especially toward the end, *Old, New, Borrowed, and Blue* approaches the model for romantic comedy. What starts out as a story where the characters have freedom to move in many directions ends up succumbing to clichés—from comical crosscuts between the bachelor and bachelorette parties to the farcical disaster of the church wedding.

Overall, the later Danish Dogma movies have surprised skeptics because of the method's continuing success. Focusing on characters and narrative is still a frugal approach that makes the actors' performances stand out with high intensity. But it also seems clear that this movement, which started as a radical challenge to the mainstream, has now been incorporated into the mainstream. It began with *Italian for Beginners* and continues with *Open Hearts* and *Old, New, Borrowed, and Blue*—not really revolutionary film art, but (and exactly for that reason) capable of attracting large audiences to the theaters.

Film according to Dogma

DOGMA FOR BEGINNERS

Internationally, interest in Dogma has been overwhelming—seminars, books, TV programs. A number of international directors have made Dogma films—at the present moment, twenty non-Danish Dogma films have been released. The first were Jean-Marc Barr's *Lovers* (Dogma 5) and Harmony Korine's *Julien Donkey-Boy* (Dogma 6), both from 1999. Barr, who regularly performs in von Trier's productions (with the lead role in *Zentropa* and smaller roles in *Breaking the Waves, Dancer in the Dark, Dogville,* and the incomplete *Dimension*), debuted as a director with *Lovers* without much recognition. It is a small love story from Paris—simple, everyday realism with an authentic look, filmed by Barr himself—about a romantic relationship between a young French girl who works in a bookstore and a young Bosnian painter who ends up getting arrested as an illegal immigrant.

Harmony Korine, one of the more controversial characters within avant-garde cinema, created quite an uproar as a scriptwriter for Larry Clark's *Kids* (1995), with its overly sensationalized portrayal of the sex lives of very young teenagers in the United States. Korine had his directorial debut with the infamous *Gummo* (1997), which wallows in life's unbearable ugliness among poor people in Ohio. His third film, the Dogma film *Julien Donkey-Boy,* is a similarly alternative feature that continues the portrayal of marginalized and grotesque characters in the underworld of American rural areas, focusing on a schizophrenic young man and his sister, with Werner Herzog as the despotic head of the family. The film clearly breaks the Dogma rules, among other things by using double exposure, voice-over, slow motion, and a montage of still shots: "Optical work and filters are forbidden."

Other international Dogma films are registered by the Dogma secretariat at Nimbus Film (see Dogma95). Daniel H. Byun's South Korean *Interview* (2000, *Intyebyo*). The film does not explicitly mention that it is registered as Dogma 7 (originally Dogma 7 referred to a scheduled German film, *Broken Cookies,* that Udo Kier should have directed; the film was never realized). *Interview* is a long-winded story about making a documentary about love. It is full of metaelements like scenes of filming (for example, by Tarkovsky's grave in Paris), interview situations, and video recordings (including one that uses forbidden background music). Furthermore, there is José Luis Marques's Argentinean *Fuckland* (Dogma 8, 2000)—a spy satire about a young Argentinean's visit to the Falkland Islands, where he seduces a young English girl, and the American *Chetzemoka's Curse* (Dogma 10, 2000), made by Rick Schmidt. Schmidt's film is a cinema vérité–like portrayal of people in a small town in Washington, constructed around six real-life stories told directly to the camera. Antonio Domenici's Italian *Diapason* (Dogma 11, 2001) has two parallel narratives—one about an aging filmmaker who wants to persuade a female star to act in his film and the other about a group of brutal criminals who terrorize the Roman nights. Martin Rengel's Swiss *Joy Ride* (Dogma 14, 2001) is a rather boring *wahre Geschichte* about some young men's random murder of a young woman (even though murder is explicitly against Dogma rule no. 6). Rich Martini's American "no-budget" *Camera* (Dogma 15, 2000) contains a series of pathetically narrated small stories about a camera in the hands of different people. For example, we witness a jealous husband's surveillance of his wife, a woman's farewell speech to her lover, and a suicide jump from the Golden Gate Bridge. The film has cameo appearances by Oliver Stone and Jack Nicholson. Shaun Monson's American *Bad Actors* (Dogma 16, 2000) was shot over a weekend as an improvisation about a group of would-be actors' work under the direction of an older alcoholic actress, played by Cissy Wellman, the daughter of the classic Hollywood director William Wellman. Leif Tilden's American *Reunion* (Dogma 17, 2001) depicts a group of high school students who meet up twenty years later, à la Lawrence Kasdan's *The Big Chill* (1983); a similar theme is used in Juan Pinzás's Spanish *Once upon Another Time* (Dogma 22, 2001, *Era outra vez*), about the reunion of a group of old school friends. The same director also made the wedding story *Días de voda* (Dogma 30, 2002). Dogma 19 is Mona J. Hoel's Norwegian *Cabin Fever* (2000, *Når nettene blir lange*), about a family crisis during the Christmas holiday, a kind of *Celebration* in a ski cabin. Steve Sobel and Vladimir Gyorski's American *Resin* (Dogma 23, 2001) follows a young American convicted of petty crimes who is sentenced to at least twenty-five years of prison due to the Californian "three strikes" law. Additionally, there is Vincent Lannoo's Belgian *Strass* (Dogma 20, 2001), which goes behind the scenes of a theater school; Andrew Gillis's American *Security, Colorado* (Dogma 24, 2001), which portrays a young woman's doubts about art and love; and Michael Sorenson's American *Converging with Angels* (Dogma 25, 2002)—a very long film about a male prostitute who takes care of a woman in trouble. Matthew Biancaniello's short *The Breadbasket* (Dogma 29, 2002) is about an actor's struggle with obesity. A symptomatic scene of this film has the main character running up a steep trail toward the Hollywood sign—a witty allegorical representation of Dogma as a tough diet directed at Hollywood's overbearing bulk.

In addition, there is Vladan Zdravkovic's Swedish *Babylon* (Dogma 9), which has a number on the list but has not been finished; while James Merendino's American *Amerikana* (Dogma 13)—a road movie about two friends on a trip from South Dakota to Los Angeles—was produced in 2001 but has not yet been released.

Generally, the non-Danish Dogma movies are of limited quality, and Dogma's influence outside Denmark will become truly interesting only if "important" foreign directors let themselves get involved with the Dogma project. Both Claude Chabrol (see Zander n.d.) and Roman Polanski (quoted in Monggaard 1999) have expressed a certain arrogance toward the method, while Spielberg (see Harbison 1999), Mike Figgis ("In a sense, I have created my own dogma," Roman 2001, 139), Jim Jarmusch (see Roman 2001, 164), Gus van Sant (see Roman 2001, 173), and Wim Wenders (see the documentary *FreeDogma* 2000; Roman 2001, 184) have shown some interest, but so far without anything materializing.

It is worth noticing that Dogma in Denmark is a method used by highly qualified directors, while Dogma outside Denmark has been adopted by a more diffuse group of low-budget directors. In many cases, the Dogma films appear to be debut releases, which explains why the Dogma wave outside Denmark has turned mostly to muck. Undoubtedly, Dogma can be a useful cleansing process for the mainstream director who needs to return to some sort of originality, but it is probably not such a good idea to suggest Dogma for beginners.

THE AVEDØRE TREATMENT

How much did Dogma achieve with its project? Did we get closer to the truth? Did we extinguish aesthetics?

Within aesthetics, it has almost become a dogma that a break with the established notion of aesthetics does not mean that one places oneself outside aesthetics, but only that one makes aesthetics more elastic and expansive. Attacks on aesthetics, from Marcel Duchamp's pissoir art to Andy Warhol's soup cans, did not lead to the downfall of art—instead, the art institution incorporated these initiatives into its conceptual space. Likewise, Dogma's deceitful attack on the aesthetics of cinema—understood as perfectionist-polished formalism—has not caused a rupture of aesthetics as we know it. It has only meant that some good work has been made in a lively style that ultimately lies within the conventionalized opportunities of the cinematic medium. For Dogma is not extreme avant-garde. Perhaps it is not even avant-garde at all. Ultimately, one cannot escape style and aesthetics. Handheld camera and real settings without artificial lighting is no less of a style than formalistic ideas of color manipulation and special effects. Aesthetics is inevitably tied to art no matter what precautions—or ground rules—you follow.

Surprisingly, Dogma 95 has managed to get both the world of film and audiences to accept a quasi-religious and ironic set of rules as an invigorating artistic method. Certainly, there are low-budget movies that on the surface do not look much different than the Dogma films (except that some are black and white)—for example, in Denmark, Jonas Elmer's *Let's Get Lost* (1997), Nicolas Winding Refn's *Pusher* (1996), and latest, Tómas Gislason's *P.O.V.* (2002). Internationally, there are alternative camera-conscious works like Patrick Duncan's *84 Charlie Mopic* (1988), Remy Belvau, André Bonzel, and Benoit Pooelvoorde's Belgian *Man Bites Dog* (1992, *C'est arrivé près de chez vous*), Kevin Smith's *Clerks* (1994), and, most recently, stunts like Daniel Myrick and Eduardo Sanchez's *The Blair Witch Project* (1999). There are also mainstream movies like Joel Schumacher's *Tigerland* (2000), Steven Soderbergh's *Traffic* (2000), which the director calls his "49 million dollar handheld Dogma film" (Roman 2001, 13), and his later film *Full Frontal* (2002)—a digital video low-budget film realized with Soderbergh's own ten commandments to the actors. Overall, there is no doubt that the attention given to Dogma internationally has been encouraging and stimulating for the whole independent film environment.

Even though the notion of Dogma as a method of truth—in spite of all assurances of the opposite—probably is an illusion, the Avedøre treatment of cinematic abstinence has proven to pay off. While Dogma has not been a radical development in the evolution of film language and probably did not produce a more impressive "ripple" than the New Wave's, at least it has become an inciting approach that is especially stimulating for its actors.

The paradoxical liberation that the Dogma rules brought to the whole film process has proven to be highly beneficial for actors—perhaps most evident in *The Celebration* and *The Idiots* but also prevalent in more conventional films like *Mifune* and *Italian for Beginners*. Dogma gives freshness and intensity to the production process, which also seems to have stimulated a new and more spontaneous style for Danish film in general, as can be witnessed in Jonas Elmer's *Mona's World* (2001, *Monas verden*), Gert Fredholm's *One-Hand Clapping* (2001, *At klappe med en hånd*), Jesper W. Nielsen's *Okay* (2002), and Annette K. Olesen's *Minor Mishaps*. For von Trier, Dogma was part of a development, starting with *Breaking the Waves* and *The Kingdom*, wherein he approached a humanistic element—primarily—by getting closer to the actors. With Dogma he has forced himself farther down this road, and it is worth noticing that he continues in this direction. *Dancer in the Dark*—even though it was no Dogma film—maintains the closeness to one dominating main character, and *Dogville* from 2004—a minimalist alternative that refers back to Brecht's *Verfremdungs* theater—is an attempt to cleanse film of almost everything but the plot and the actors.

In conclusion, Dogma has managed to get filmmakers to reject technological intoxication and—by focusing more on the actors—discover a human aspect as well as artistic freedom. Whether Dogma can, on an international level, stimulate a film art that—without losing its appeal to the audience—offers an alternative to the mainstream film is an open question. But for now, a handful of Danish movies has shown the way.

WORKS CONSULTED

Addonizio, Antonio, et al., eds. 1999. *Il Dogma della Libertà: Conversazioni con Lars von Trier*. Palermo: Edizioni della battaglia/L'Atalante.

Astruc, Alexandre. 1968. "The Birth of a New Avant-Garde: La caméra-stylo." In *The New Wave*, ed. Peter Graham. New York: Doubleday. Originally published as "Naissance d'une nouvelle avant-garde: La Caméra-Stylo," *L'écran français* 144 (March 1948).

Björkman, Stig. 1999. *Trier om von Trier. Samtal med Stig Björkman*. Stockholm: Alfabeta.

Celant, Germano. 1969. *Art Povera: Conceptual, Actual, or Impossible Art?* London: Studio Vista.

———. 1991. *Piero Manzoni*. Milan: Arnoldo Mondadori Arte.

Christensen, Claus. 2000. "Festen der forsvandt." *Weekendavisen*, May 5.

———. 2001. "Documentary Gets the Dogma Treatment." *Film* 19 (November).

Christov-Bakargiev, Carolyn, ed. 1999. *Arte Povera*. London: Phaidon.

Dabelsteen, Per. 2002. "Nyt dogme: Triers rene dokumentar." *Politiken*, October 30.

Dixon, Wheeler Winston. 1997. *The Films of Jean-Luc Godard*. Albany: State University of New York Press.

Dogma95. http://www.Dogma95.dk
Feuerbach, Ludwig. 1960. *Pierre Bayle: Ein Beitrag zur Geschichte der Philosophie und Menschheit* (1838). In *Sämtliche Werke*, vol. 5. Stuttgart: Frommann Verlag.
Frodon, Jean-Michel, Marc Nicolas, and Serge Toubiana, eds. 1995. *Le cinéma vers son deuxième siècle: Colloque international*. Paris: Le Monde.
Godard, Jean-Luc. 1998. *Jean-Luc Godard par Jean-Luc Godard*, vol. 1: *1950–1984*. Paris: Cahiers du cinéma.
Grotowski, Jerzy. 1975. *Towards a Poor Theatre*. London: Methuen.
Hallberg, Jana, and Alexander Wewerka, eds. 2001. *Dogma95: Zwischen Kontrolle und Chaos*. Berlin: Alexander Verlag Berlin.
Harbison, Georgia, and Jeffrey Ressner. 1999. "Putting on the Dogma." *Time*, October 11.
Harrison, Charles, and Paul Wood, eds. 1992. *Art in Theory, 1900–1990*. Oxford: Blackwell.
Hjort, Mette. 2001. "Dogma 95: A Small Nation's Response to Globalization." *Politologiske studier* 4, no. 3 (September). Copenhagen: Institut for Statskundskab, Copenhagens Universitet.
Hjort, Mette, and Ib Bondebjerg, eds. 2001. *The Danish Directors. Dialogues on a Contemporary National Cinema*. Bristol: Intellect.
Hjort, Mette, and Scott MacKenzie, eds. 2003. *Purity and Provocation: Dogma 95*. London: British Film Institute.
The Idiots. 1998. Press book. Copenhagen: Zentropa.
Jacobson, Karen, ed. 2001. *Zero to Infinity: Arte Povera, 1962–1972*. Exhibit catalogue. Minneapolis: Walker Art Center.
Jerslev, Anne. 2002. "Dogma 95, Lars von Trier's *The Idiots*, and the 'Idiot Project.'" In *Realism and "Reality" in Film and Media*, ed. Anne Jerslev. *Northern Lights—Film and Media Studies Yearbook 2002*. Copenhagen: Museum Tusculanum.
Johansen, Troels Degn, and Lars Bo Kimergaard, eds. 1991. *Lars von Trier: Sekvens Filmvidenskabelig årbog 1991*. Copenhagen: University of Copenhagen.
Kelly, Richard. 2000. *The Name of This Book Is Dogma95*. London: Faber and Faber.
Lumholdt, Jan, ed. 2003. *Lars von Trier—Interviews*. Jackson: University of Mississippi Press.
MacKenzie, Scott. 2000. "Direct Dogma: Film Manifestos and the *Fin de Siècle*." *p.o.v.* 10 (December).
Matthews, Harry, and Alastair Brotchie, eds. 1998. *Oulipo Compendium*. London: Atlas.
Monggaard Christensen, Christian. 1998. "Ud i intetheden." *Information*, July 17.
———. 1999. "Film: En polak kom forbi—Polanski i København." *Information*, November 19.
———. 2000. "Danske Dogmar." In *Film and Fin de Siècle: Essays om 90'ernes film*, ed. Peter Christensen and Bo Tao Michaëlis. Copenhagen: Gyldendal.
Motte, Warren F., ed. 1986. *Oulipo: A Primer of Potential Literature*. Lincoln: University of Nebraska Press.
Müller, Marion. 2000. *Vexierbilder: Die Filmwelten des Lars von Trier*. St. Augustin: Gardez!-Verlag.
"Oberhausen Manifesto." 1983. In *Cinema in the Federal Republic of Germany*, ed. Hans Günther Pflaum and Hans Helmut Prinzler. Bonn: Inter Nationes. Original Ger-

man in *Dogma95: Zwischen Kontrolle und Chaos,* ed. Jana Hallberg and Alexander Wewerka (Berlin: Alexander Verlag Berlin, 2001).
Oulipo. 2002. http://www.nous.org.uk/oulipo.html
Øvig Knudsen, Peter. 1998. "The Man Who Would Give Up Control." In *The Idiots* press book. Copenhagen: Zentropa.
Porcelli, Tina. 2001. *Lars von Trier e Dogma.* Milan: Il castoro cinema.
Raskin, Richard, ed. 2000. "Aspects of Dogma." *p.o.v.* 10 (December).
Roman, Shari. 2001. *Digital Babylon: Hollywood, Indiewood, and Dogma 95.* Hollywood: IFILM.
Rukov, Mogens. 2002. *Festen og andre skandaler.* Ed. Claus Christensen. Copenhagen: Lindhardt og Ringhof.
Schepelern, Peter. 1999. "Filmen ifølge Dogma: Spilleregler, forhindringer og befrielser." *Dansk film* 1 (May): 12–16.
———. 2000a. "Ånden i myretuen." *Film* 7 (February): 6–9.
———. 2000b. *Lars von Triers film: Tvang og befrielse.* Copenhagen: Rosinante.
———. 2003. "'Kill Your Darlings': Lars von Trier and the Origins of Dogma 95." In *Purity and Provocation: Dogma 95,* ed. Mette Hjort and Scott MacKenzie. London: British Film Institute.
Schepelern, Peter et al., eds. 2001. *100 års dansk film.* Copenhagen: Rosinante.
Sesslen, Georg. 2001. "Dogma." In *Dogma95: Zwischen Kontrolle und Chaos,* ed. Jana Hallberg and Alexander Wewerka. Berlin: Alexander Verlag Berlin. Danish original: "Oprør i blindgyden," *Kritik* 140 (1999).
Stevenson, Jack. 2002. *Lars von Trier.* London: British Film Institute.
Stravinsky, Igor. 1942. *Poétique musicale sous forme de six leçons.* Cambridge: Harvard University Press.
Sudmann, Andreas. 2001. *Dogma 95: Die Abkehr vom Zwang des Möglichen.* Hannover: Offizin.
Thorsen, Nils. 2002. "Afsløring: En hvilken som helst lighed med historier, haendelser og personer, nulevende eller døde, er helt tilfaeldig og utilsigtet." *Politiken,* November 24.
Truffaut, François. 1954. "Une certaine tendance du cinéma français." *Cahiers du cinéma* 31 (January).
Turner, Jane, ed. 1996. "Arte Povera." In *The Dictionary of Art,* vol. 2. London: Macmillan.
Vertov, Dziga. 1973. "Vorläufige Instruktion an die Zirkel des 'Kinoglaz.'" In *Schriften zum Film.* München: Carl Hanser.
Vinterberg, Thomas, and Mogens Rukov. 1998. *Festen.* Copenhagen: Per Kofod.
von Trier, Lars. 1998. *Dogma 2: Idioterne. Manuskript og dagbog.* Copenhagen: Gyldendal.
von Trier, Lars, and Jørgen Leth. 2001. "The Five Obstructions." *Film* 19 (November): 26–27.
von Trier, Lars, and Thomas Vinterberg. 2000. *Dogma 95.* In *Lars von Triers film: Tvang og befrielse,* ed. Peter Schepelern, 222–23. Copenhagen: Rosinante. English translation in Raskin 2000; Kelly 2000.
Wuss, Peter. 2002. "Analyzing the Reality Effect in Dogma Films." *Journal of Moving*

Image Studies 1, no. 2 (Spring). http://www.uca.edu/org/ccsmi/jounal2/ ESSAY_-Wuss.htm

Zander, Peter. n.d. "Die zehn Verbote." http://morgenpost.berlin1.de/archiv1999/990422/feuilleton/story110515.html

Zavattini, Cesare. 1966. "Some Ideas on the Cinema." In *Film: A Montage of Theories*, ed. Richard Dyer MacCann. New York: Dutton. Originally published as "Alcune idee sul cinema," *Revista del cinema italiano* (December 1952).

DOGMA FILMOGRAPHY

Revised list of films registered with the Dogmasekretariat: http://www.Dogma95.dk

Dogma 1: *Festen* (*The Celebration*). 1998. Denmark, Thomas Vinterberg, Nimbus Film.

Dogma 2: *Idioterne* (*The Idiots*). 1998. Denmark, Lars von Trier, Zentropa Entertainments.

Dogma 3: *Mifunes sidste sang* (*Mifune*). 1999. Denmark, Søren Kragh-Jacobsen, Nimbus Film.

Dogma 4: *The King Is Alive*. 2000. Denmark, Kristian Levring, Zentropa Entertainments.

Dogma 5: *Lovers*. 1999. France, Jean-Marc Barr, TF1 International.

Dogma 6: *Julien Donkey-Boy*. 1999. U.S.A., Harmony Korine, Independent Pictures.

Dogma 7: *Interview*. 2000. South Korea, Daniel H. Byun, Cine 2000 Production.

Dogma 8: *Fuckland*. 2000. Argentina, José Luis Marques, Atomic Films.

Dogma 9: *Babylon*. (Uncompleted.) Sweden, Vladan Zdravkovic, AF&P, MH Company.

Dogma 10: *Chetzemoka's Curse*. 2000. U.S.A., Rick Schmidt, FW Productions.

Dogma 11: *Diapason*. 2001. Italian, Antonio Domenici, Flying Movies.

Dogma 12: *Italiensk for begyndere* (*Italian for Beginners*). 2000. Denmark, Lone Scherfig, Zentropa Entertainments.

Dogma 13: *Amerikana*. 2001. U.S.A., James Merendino, Cologne Gemini Filmproduktion and Zentropa Entertainments. (Undistributed.)

Dogma 14: *Joy Ride*. 2001. Switzerland, Martin Rengel, Abrakadabra Films.

Dogma 15: *Camera*. 2000. U.S.A., Rich Martini, Rich Martini.

Dogma 16: *Bad Actors*. 2000. U.S.A., Shaun Monson, Nicole Visram.

Dogma 17: *Reunion*. 2001. U.S.A., Leif Tilden, Kimberly Shane O'Hara and Eric M. Klein.

Dogma 18: *Et rigtigt menneske* (*Truly Human*). 2001. Denmark, Åke Sandgren, Zentropa Entertainments.

Dogma 19: *Når nettene blir lange* (*Cabin Fever*). 2000. Norway, Mona J. Hoel, Freedom from Fear A/S.

Dogma 20: *Strass*. 2001. Belgium, Vincent Lannoo, Dadowsky Film.

Dogma 21: *En Kærlighedshistorie* (*Kira's Reason: A Love Story*). 2001. Denmark, Ole Christian Madsen, Nimbus Film.

Dogma 22: *Era outra vez* (*Once upon Another Time*). 2000. Spain, Juan Pinzás, Atlántico Films.

Dogma 23: *Resin*. 2001. U.S.A., Vladimir Gyorski and Steve Sobel, Organic Film.

Dogma 24: *Security, Colorado*. 2001. U.S.A., Andrew Gillis, Grammar Redeo.

Dogma 25: *Converging with Angels*. 2002. U.S.A., Michael Sorenson, Artistry and Rhythm Filmworks.
Dogma 26: *The Sparkle Room*. (Uncompleted.) U.S.A., Alex McAulay, Voltage USA.
Dogma 27: *Come Now*. (Uncompleted.) U.S.A.
Dogma 28: *Elsker dig for evigt* (*Open Hearts*). 2002. Denmark, Susanne Bier, Zentropa Entertainments.
Dogma 29: *The Breadbasket*. 2002. U.S.A., Matthew Biancaniello, My Way or the Highway Films. (Short film.)
Dogma 30: *Días de voda*. Spain, Juan Pinzas, Atlantic Films.
Dogma 31: *El Desenlace*. (In production.) Spain, Juan Pinzas, Atlantic Films.
Dogma 32: *Se til venstre, der er en svensker* (*Old, New, Borrowed, and Blue*). 2003. Denmark, Natasha Arthy, Nimbus Film.
Dogma 33: *Residencia*. 2003. Chile, Artemio Espinosa Mc, Nuevo Extremo Cine TV Digital.
Dogma 34: *Forbrydelser*. 2004. Denmark, Annette K. Olesen, Zentropa Entertainments.
Dogma 35: *Cosí x Caso*. 2004. Italy, Cristiano Ceriello, Cinema Distribuzione.com.

DOGMA-RELATED FILMOGRAPHY

Lars from 1–10. 1998. U.S.A., Sophie Fiennes.
De ydmygede (*The Humiliated*). 1998. Denmark, Jesper Jargil.
FreeDogma. 2000. France, Roger Narbonne.
De lutrede (*The Purified*). 2000. Denmark, Jesper Jargil.
The Name of This Film Is Dogma95. 2000. England, Saul Metzstein.
De udstillede (*The Exhibited*). 2000. Denmark, Jesper Jargil.

PART II

The State and Film Markets in Transnational Times

CHAPTER 4

The Danish Way: Danish Film Culture in a European and Global Perspective

Ib Bondebjerg

With the coming of the 1990s, Danish film experienced unprecedented international popularity. While films such as *Babette's Feast* (Gabriel Axel, 1987, *Babettes gæstebud*) and *Pelle the Conqueror* (Bille August, 1988, *Pelle Erobreren*, 1987) had drawn attention to Danish film, largely through their Oscar successes in the late 1980s, the success of these films cannot account for the international profile attained by directors like Lars von Trier, film movements like Dogma 95, or individual films like *Breaking the Waves*. Indeed, the international success, both commercially and aesthetically, of Danish film in the 1990s mirrored a similar blossoming within national borders, as Danish films fared better against their foreign competition, most significantly against Hollywood mainstream productions. What lies behind the burgeoning success of Danish film, nationally and internationally? On the one hand, changes in the national policies surrounding film support opened the door for films that radically differ from their ancestors in Danish film. On the other, a new generation of filmmakers, primarily educated at the Danish Film School or abroad, found ways to combine the artistic and experimental with the mainstream, seeking inspiration inside and outside national borders. The Danish New Wave of the 1990s presents an important case study for the interconnection of international commerce, national public policy, and individual aesthetics.

In 1997, a new law concerning public support for cinema in Denmark was passed. This was the third major film law since the initial Danish film law was passed in 1964. The original legislation celebrated film as art, not just entertainment, for the first time. The second and more important law, from 1972, created the first Danish Film Institute (DFI), securing the basic public funding structures for Danish film culture. The 1997 law created a new unified body for all forms of publicly supported film in Denmark, a new institution that would continue to be called the Danish Film Institute but would integrate the three earlier institutions of Danish film culture: the Danish Film Board, established in 1938, which focused on public funding and distribution of documentary films and films for educational and informational purposes; the Danish Film Museum, established in 1941 and charged with raising critical awareness about cinema, circulating information about film, and collecting and preserving the national film heritage; and the Danish Film Institute, which from 1972 to 1997 was the institutional arbiter of public support for feature films.

The 1997 law, and the reorganization mandated by it, marked a major change in Danish film policy and film culture. It was the culmination of a long historical development in which a nationally oriented, market-driven film culture was (1) replaced by a more *defensive, national art film–support strategy* (as the previous market-driven film culture ran into deep crisis during the 1960s); and (2) later (from the mid-1980s on as the art film policy passed into a crisis phase) was replaced by adherence to a film policy that was increasingly *proactive, internationally oriented, and pluralistic* in relation to mainstream and art film. The international breakthrough for the new Danish wave at the millennium thus results from a long tradition of strong fundamental support for art films and the institutions that fund and support them. One of the most important institutions outside the Danish Film Institute is the independent Danish Film School, established in 1966, which since the 1980s in particular has successfully trained creative screenwriters, photographers, directors, and also some of the most important producers of the 1990s generation. However, the international breakthrough of Danish film in the 1990s is also a consequence of another shift in legislation that occurred in 1989, when it became clear that Denmark could not survive as a film nation on just art films: there was a continuing need to ensure mechanisms for a renewal of mainstream cinema as well.

The 1997 law that created the new Danish Film Institute also created the instruments to professionalize the national support system and to retool old institutions that were not geared to meet the challenges of an ever more global cinema culture. The new DFI developed a structure that addressed all aspects of filmmaking: from screenplay, preproduction and development, to production and distribution, through marketing—both nationally and internationally—and finally to the broader cultural dissemination of information about Danish film and film in general. The structure of the new DFI was designed to match the production system in the private cinema sector; the DFI's institutional mechanics now follow each film from initial conceptualization to final archiving of the film as a part of the historical heritage. The expertise and professional level of the funding policy and strategies were strongly boosted to match the private sector and the complexity of modern internationalized film production and distribution. Existing support mechanisms were further developed and new mechanisms were created to cover a much broader scope of film types.

The initial vision for the new organization, and its accompanying five-year plan, outlined a clear, proactive, pluralistic support strategy. Consequently, the DFI was able to convince the parliament to increase the annual budget to DKr 450 million (US$70 million) annually, a sum that made it possible to go from an average of ten to fifteen films a year to twenty to twenty-five. The increase in funding allowed a freer hand in underwriting the work of a new talented generation that now did not have to wait to make their first films but could produce more often and thus take more chances. To be sure, the breakthrough of Danish film that began in the late 1990s was not the result only of public film policies and new strategies but also the result of a happy meeting between an abundant quantity and quality of talent and new funding mechanisms and increased support. It is necessary to recognize that film cultures like this take decades to build, and the roots of contemporary Danish film go back to the 1960s and the first development of a new modern film culture.

THE CLASSICAL, NATIONAL MAINSTREAM CULTURE

The historical periods of Danish film culture in general correlate with those of international cinema. However, the gradual establishment of a public film policy and this policy's influence on the general public's reception of film—as an art form or as entertainment—have changed perceptions of film dramatically over time. If we leave out the silent period, the first period of sound film, *the classical film culture* (1930–60), can be characterized as a mainstream culture to which cinema was supplied by a basically private sector film business, grounded in a national star system supporting typically Danish film genres. Basically, film was not recognized as an important new art form; rather, it was generally considered a pastime or entertainment, reflected in the fact that film was taxed as entertainment and did not receive the exemptions enjoyed by the other arts—for example, literature. However, early in the history of Danish cinema, public institutions were created to secure an artistic and educational alternative to mainstream, entertainment-oriented film. Some of the money from the tax on mainstream film (40 percent) and cinema tickets was recirculated to support film production. In 1938, legislators passed a law creating the Filmraadet (Film Council) and a Filmfond (Film Fund) (in existence from 1938 to 1964). The Filmraadet served mainly as an advisory board to governmental cinema policy makers. The Filmfond supported films of special cultural value and documentaries. The law in 1938 also established the *Statens Film Central* (National Film Board, 1938–97). This and Dansk Kulturfilm (Danish Culture Films, 1932–95) were the main public institutions for production and distribution of films of special cultural and educational value, in practice meaning mostly documentaries. Generally speaking, the state was suspicious of cinema as mainstream culture; support for feature films was rarely given—and then only granted retroactively for films dealing with important social problems.

Film production in the classical period was dominated by a Danish version of the American studio system, with four dominating production companies, each with its unique profile (see Engberg 1990; Dinnesen and Kau 1983; Schepelern 2001; Bondebjerg forthcoming). The oldest company, Nordic Film, had the most pluralistic and artistic profile, including some of the new realistic directors of the 1940s and 1950s like Bjarne and Astrid Henning-Jensen and Ole Palsbo. Through the 1950s, under the hand of the master of popular cinema, Erik Balling, the company clearly changed the quality of mainstream cinema. Palladium, the other big company with a broad, pluralistic profile, produced Carl Dreyer's films, among others, as well as films by important, serious-minded new directors like Johan Jacobsen. ASA (started in 1937) quickly developed into the dominant company for popular film series of the period. ASA was the home of the two most productive mainstream directors in the classical Danish film culture, Lau Lauritzen and Alice O'Fredericks, who made films in such dominant genres as the Danish heritage film, based on Danish author Morten Korch's popular novels, romantic comedies, and family comedies. However, ASA also occasionally produced more serious social melodramas. The last of the four big companies, Saga, although not established until 1946, became an increasingly important company through the late 1940s and early 1950s, producing some of the few Danish crime films as well as several important realistic dramas. However, the company very soon developed into the primary producer of pure comedy production, based on the box office draw of the greatest farce talent in Danish cinema, Dirch Passer.

Danish film in this period was thus basically a privately driven, mainstream film culture. It was primarily a domestic cinema with very little export, even to the other Scandinavian countries, and with very little transnational coproduction. During most of the classical period there was a clear tendency toward a division of labor between national film production and the import of European (mostly British, German, French, and Italian) and American films: Danish films particularly dominated in genres that came in series, like the heritage film and the variety of popular comedies, whereas the more violent genres (like crime films and thrillers) and the more serious melodramatic forms were scarce and mainly represented by American and European films. Tellingly, the Danish film culture of the 1930s has often been characterized as a period where the sun always seemed to shine (Jørholt 2001) and where popular music and song were merged with a strongly nostalgic, nationalistic mood in comedy after comedy. Influence from American cinema was, of course, inevitable, and both the early American musical and screwball comedies did influence Danish film genres, but the more inward-looking nature of the national film profile is clear, particularly when compared, for instance, to Danish film in the silent era, when Danish film culture and production were more international and outward looking.

The German occupation from 1940 to 1945 changed this to some degree: the Germans banned films from allied countries, creating a challenge to Danish film culture in the sense that genres that had not previously held a strong position in national production began to blossom. An internationalization and professionalization of Danish film genres and film language took place, and in the mainstream film culture, a broader generic mix developed—with, for example, the development of Danish traditions of film noir (see Bondebjerg 2003), genuine crime film, and more elegant romantic comedy, inspired by American screwball comedy via the leading artistic director from this period, Johan Jacobsen (see Bondebjerg 1996). At the same time, a stronger and more varied melodramatic tradition and a stronger sense of realism developed, inspired by (among other things) first, French poetic realism and later, Italian neorealism. Again, new directors such as Johan Jacobsen, Ole Palsbo, Bjarne Henning-Jensen, and Bodil Ipsen led the way. The period 1940–60 thus also saw the development of a more artistic, internationally European- and American-inspired Danish film that was later to be developed as the Danish contribution to the European New Wave film after 1960 (see Bondebjerg 2000).

However, the period after 1950, when Danish society gradually transformed from a more traditional rural society to a modern urban welfare state, was also a period dominated by two of the most popular mainstream film series ever made in Denmark. On the one hand, we have the popular melodramatic heritage series based on the novels of Morten Korch, with *The Red Horses* (Alice O'Fredericks, 1950, *De røde heste,* ASA), a film seen by 2.4 million Danes that year (still the most widely seen film in Danish film history) and followed by seventeen other films in the same series between 1950 and 1976. The film series vibrates with strong national and nostalgic elements, celebrating a rural Denmark on the verge of disappearing but also to some extent mediating between the old historical world and a new modernity (see Bondebjerg forthcoming; Soila, Söderbergh Widding, and Iversen 1998; Troelsen 1980). On the other hand, we have the *Far til fire* series, with the first film from 1953, *Father of Four* (Alice O'Fredericks, *Far til fire,* ASA) followed by eight more films between 1953 and 1971. The films deal with a more modern type of urban family, reflecting both changes and tradition in the dominant family structure at that time. These two film series, combined with the more modern series *The Olsen Gang* (Erik Balling, *Olsen-banden,* Nordisk) with thirteen films between 1968 and 1981 (a film series that combines international genre-parody with a deep understanding of national Danish cultural stereotypes), are the ultimate Danish mainstream films (see Bondebjerg forthcoming; Soila, Söderbergh Widding, and Iversen 1998).

It is very telling that even in the 1990s, the Korch tradition continues to play a role, as Lars von Trier's production company made a long-running series for Danish TV2 based on the Korch novels: even in the era of Danish cinema's international breakthrough, mainstream cinema continues to have a role to play in these modernized remakes, just as their recirculation on TV, video, and DVD have given new life to the original films. At the same time, the accumulated figures for the top twenty films after 1976 (the first year with systematic figures for individual films in Danish film statistics) show that of the top twenty Danish-only films between 1976 and 1996, seven are *Olsen-banden* films, and even one of the old *Far til fire* films makes it to number nine on the list. The films are popular enough that even on the list for all films, we find no fewer than six of the same films, with *The Olsen Gang Sees Red* (Erik Balling, 1976, *Olsen-banden ser rødt*) as number one and *The Olsen Gang Outta Sight* (Erik Balling, 1977, *Olsen-banden deruda*) as number three. The films from the classical or early modern national mainstream culture thus easily compete with American films in popularity, and on the total list of all films between 1972 and 1996, we find Danish-only films (ten), American films (nine), and one British James Bond film (see top twenty lists in Bondebjerg, Andersen, and Schepelern 1997, 403–6).

THE FIRST MODERN BREAKTHROUGH IN DANISH CINEMA: NEW WAVE AND PUBLIC CULTURAL POLICY

The strong dominant mainstream culture of the classical and early modern period ran into a severe crisis with the rise of television as the preeminent audiovisual medium after 1960. The number of cinema tickets sold annually dropped more than 30 percent (from 43,921,000 in 1960 to 23,856,000 in 1970), and the number of cinemas also decreased dramatically between 1960 and 1972 (see Bondebjerg 1997, 204–6; Engberg 1990). Apart from mainstream genres like *Olsen-banden* and the new erotic comedies that appeared after the loosening of pornography laws, many of the established national mainstream genres stagnated and failed to make enough profit for established companies to expand. This is marked symbolically by the fall of the most successful mainstream company (ASA) of the classical film era, sold in 1964 to Sven and Lene Grønlykke, who transformed the company into a more art film–oriented company reflecting Danish New Wave cinema. The other major mainstream company, Saga, survived until 1976; additionally, Merry Film, a company established in the late 1950s, closed in 1972, followed by the biggest fall of them all, the venerable and most well-established company, Palladium, which, after having survived for a few years on light erotic comedies, closed in the early 1970s.

The crisis of mainstream cinema and the subsequent development of a new Danish art film by the New Wave generation of the 1960s was the basis for the first move toward a new public film policy in 1964. For the first time, film was accepted among intellectuals and made part of the very active cultural policies of the new welfare state in the 1960s. Film shifted in designation from entertainment to culture and art in the public mentality and in cultural politics. The cinematic culture of this period developed public efforts to support film as a threatened art form in the age of modern mass media and television. From 1964 to 1981, during which time the decline of the cinema sector intensified and the public cultural film policy was developed, the private mainstream sector declined in quality and almost entirely disappeared, and the once-strong Danish genre films were threatened, as was the established national star system. The last real audience success made without public support was Erik Balling's long-running *Olsenbanden* series (thirteen films from 1968 to 1981, with a follow-up in 1998). The last film in the initial series (made in 1981) was until recently the last film made outside the public support system. Since then, only very few Danish films, whether considered mainstream or art films, commercially successful or not, have been made without some form of public support and funding.

Thus, the first elements in the Danish model of film-support policy and filmmaking were developed contemporaneously with the birth of a modern welfare state and its broad cultural policy. Film policy began to be seen as part of the wider formation of a modern national culture. The new policies had at least two basic elements: *the defense of autonomous, artistic production* from the effects of commercial market forces and a public effort to secure *democratic pluralism* through dissemination of cultural variety in the face of the homogenization threatened by concentration and globalization. Danish film policy in the first law from 1964—and even more strongly expressed in the law of 1972—stressed support for *film as art* or *film as enlightenment and information*. The impact of the new European art film was clear, and it changed the public notion of film. What is more, new Danish directors emerged as artists. With *Hunger* (1966, *Sult*), Henning Carlsen put Danish film on the international agenda for the first time since Dreyer; along with him, Palle Kjærulff-Schmidt, Lene and Sven Grønlykke, and others, it was evident that a new point of departure was in place for a modern national film culture (Bondebjerg 2000). However, this new

Danish wave of art films did not generally succeed at the box office. Accompanied by the decline of mainstream cinema, the crisis continued. Many of the new midsized and smaller companies that developed after the decline of the Danish studios began to show signs of instability.

The law from 1964 was a first step in the direction of a fully established public support system for films, but the step was far from sufficient. The entertainment tax on films was removed, but a new 15 percent fee on tickets was introduced instead, a kind of cinema tax. The money from this new ticket fee was used in two ways. First of all, the money from foreign films was given to the new and stronger Filmfond, an institution established with the 1964 law to support art film production, the new Danish Film School, the Film Museum, and not least the National Film Board for documentaries, which was also strengthened. On top of the support for more artistic feature films, a Short Film Council was also established, with the aim of developing a more independent, experimental documentary film (see Krarup and Nørrested 1986; Nørrested and Alsted 1987). All in all, the law was a boost for art film. But the new possibilities for vertical integration simultaneously strengthened the private sector and thus the mainstream film culture, and this mainstream film support was further developed with an automatic support for successful films: the 15 percent ticket fee for Danish films was automatically transferred to the production company. The 1964 law thus established a double mechanism that was later to be developed more systematically with the 1972 law: on the one hand, art film support was established; on the other hand, some support for the private sector and mainstream film was maintained. This double principle of regulating the market was explicitly expressed in comments on the law: "It was necessary for the production of valuable art films also in general to improve the conditions of the film industry. If there are no production facilities in this country, no art films will be produced" (*En kulturpolitisk redegørelse* 1969, 119).

THE BIRTH OF A SUCCESSFUL MODERN PUBLIC FILM POLICY, 1972–90

The mechanisms established with the 1964 law, however, soon proved to be weak and inadequate: support of neither mainstream film culture nor of the art film seemed to make a real difference. The national cinema crisis continued. The new law from 1972, which in Danish cultural circles is often called "the world's best film law," provided a fundamental correction in both structural and economic terms. First, the cinema sector was completely liberalized and deregulated, and all fees and taxes were removed. This significantly increased private sector potentials and gave a stronger incentive for investment and for concentration and integration of production and distribution. Moreover, it opened opportunities for foreign investment. Second, the Danish Film Institute was established with a permanent annual budget for different forms of film support. The basic new mechanism was the development of an organization that could allocate support for primarily art films. Independent consultants were appointed, three for feature films and three for documentaries; each consultant controlled an individual budget with which he or she could support both script development and production. The artistic evaluation was thus placed in the hands of individuals, whose appointments were, for obvious reasons, limited to a three- to five-year term. Outside this support for art film production, another system for more experimental and grassroots-oriented forms of production was created through the so-called Workshop, later called Det Danske Filmværksted (the Danish Film Workshop). Another important development added to the law in 1982 was the establishment of a special fund for children's and youth films, which were given their own consultant and a budget of at least 25 percent of the total budget for film support. Other areas that received support in the new law were art film distribution and the establishment of the Danish Film Studio, an independent body under the Danish Film Institute with its own board. The intention behind this independent studio was to secure production facilities for smaller and medium-sized production companies that might otherwise have difficulties on the free market.

Even though the new law did to some extent develop a double strategy of supporting both art film culture and the more general film culture, the ideological core of the law remained, as stated in the law, "support for film art in Denmark." The additional support mechanisms were not central to the law and not backed by strong economic mechanisms. At the same time, it is important to note that public support was definitely identified primarily as a *national culture issue:* Danish films were meant to support and express a specific Danish national identity and culture. This film policy aimed at the defense and development of artistic film and documentary film as national culture, whereas mainstream-oriented film culture was supposed to be taken care of by market forces both nationally and internationally. In 1972, Denmark had just entered the European Community, but cultural policy was not seen in a broader international perspective, and the globalization and coproduction of the late 1990s was not anticipated.

The development of this film policy was a logical and understandable move at the time, and the definition of a Danish film as a film with a Danish director and producer, with a Danish theme and story, and with Danish actors speaking Danish was not seen as a problem in this early period. But in the long run, this support system, decisively bent toward art film and with a clearly national orientation, became problematic and increasingly motivated by a defensive attitude in the administration of policy. If not already evident, this attitude became obvious in 1984, when Lars von Trier made his first film, *The Element of Crime*, which contradicted the definition of a national film and which had to be allowed a special exemption from the rules in order to receive support. Following this incident, the definition of a Danish film was gradually liberalized during the 1980s, and in 1989 the key definitions were changed through new legislation. A Danish film is now defined as in some way contributing to the development of the quality and diversity of Danish film culture. During the 1980s, Danish film culture thus opened itself more directly to European and global film culture. To be succinct, Danish film culture left its defensive national orientation, a move that is clearly one of the reasons for its international success in the 1990s.

Along with the shift in the definition of national film, a number of other influential changes occurred. One thing the 1972 law had done was to liberalize the distribution and cinema sector, allowing vertical integration, meaning that production companies could also control cinema chains. This was done explicitly to strengthen the decaying private cinema sector. In the 1980s, however, it became obvious that genre films and other forms of popularly oriented, private sector films could no longer function unless incentives were given from the public sector. In the early 1980s, the situation was such that almost no films could be made without some form of public support. The privately owned, market-driven mainstream industry was in fact extinct. Therefore, an important but controversial change was the introduction in 1989 of the so-called 50/50 support system, which meant that support could be given to a film with both quality and a large audience potential on an automatic basis, provided 50 percent of the budget had been acquired privately. The 50/50 system was created as a popular supplement to the consultant-driven art film support mechanisms and was meant to counterbalance elitist tendencies in film support. This new support principle was also based on a broadening of the official aim of film policy, which was further broadened in the new film law of 1997: whereas the 1972 law only talked about support for film as art, the new laws defined public support as support for film as *art,* for film *culture* in general, and for *cinema.*

The ideological changes in modern Danish film culture after 1972 are thus very clear, both in terms of what the law says and the actual tendencies in the production and development of films. The Danish model seeks a balance between art film and mainstream film: the art film's purely aesthetic definition of quality (in the previous system, technically determined by independent film consultants who personally decided which films to support) has been supplemented by a more market-driven and audience-oriented definition of quality. At the same time, a defensive national strategy and concept of Danish films was transformed into a more open, internationally oriented concept of filmmaking.

THE GLOBALIZED MULTIMEDIA CULTURE AFTER 1990

The Danish system as it had developed by the end of the 1980s was in principle a well-balanced system, furnishing public support for both mainstream and art films, with special focus on films for children and youth and with elements of support for a broad mixture of documentary and experimental film forms. It was still fundamentally a nationally oriented system in its basic construction, but at the same time it was developing a stronger, more versatile strategy, allowing not only Nordic coproductions but also European coproductions. Since 1990, the full impact of the new system for film support has become apparent, as the move toward Nordic/European coproductions and a globalization of Danish film culture has occurred. The new and united Danish Film Institute, as established in 1997, moved toward a more open, proactive, and internationalized strategy and a more diverse, strategic pluralism in both support mechanisms and the general structure and vision of its cinema policy. Danish film culture of the 1990s could therefore be seen, in a more internationalized context, as a publicly supported return to a balance between some of the qualities of the art film tradition, typically dominant in Europe since the 1960s, and the more mainstream orientation of the classical film culture, typically dominant in the U.S. film sector.

New systems of support have also been developed to open more doors (the Short Film Fund, the Film/TV Fund, support for computer games and interactive, digital films, and so on), there is more money and support for the development of screenplays and even preproduction and development, and there is a stronger emphasis on distribution and marketing. Additionally, the star system is returning in Danish film culture, cultivated by mechanisms in the European system and festival circuit that support young European stars. Many of the best Danish actors in the classical film culture had not just national but international star quality; however, they never crossed borders. The crossover success of a young generation of Danish film stars (Iben Hjejle and Ulrich Thomsen, for instance) is hence novel and may prove a stimulus and benefit to Danish film culture. The same goes for the new generation of directors and producers: there is a definite change in the concept of genres in the Danish New Wave, a broader acceptance of mainstream genres and international inspiration; there is also less tension between the concept of film as art and self-aware popular film made for large audiences; and hostility toward the big dominant other—Hollywood—has also diminished. We are dealing with a new generation that is accustomed to a more global world of media and mixing of cultures and genres, continuing the trends established by the older generation, represented by, among others, Gabriel Axel and Bille August, who—together with Lars von Trier—paved the way for a broader globalization of Danish cinema. Furthermore, it has clearly been a successful strategy to turn the weakness of a small nation into a global brand: the introduction of low budgets and especially the Dogma 95 film concepts (see Hjort and MacKenzie 2003) turned economic restrictions into artistic strength. The works of Lars von Trier and Thomas Vinterberg combined art film success with a very precise and provocative marketing strategy. Dogma 95 is now internationally as important as the European New Wave of the 1960s.

At the policy level, this transformation is evident in the law of 1997, wherein the support for film culture and new types of audiovisual products is clear. According to the legislation, "the purpose of this law is to support film art, film culture and cinema culture in Denmark." At the same time, it is stated that film means all forms of moving images except television production. The exclusion of television is because television production in Denmark is already publicly supported through the two main public service channels, Denmark's Radio (DR) and Danish TV2. But in fact one of the new elements in film policy after 1997 has been the establishment of a completely new funding mechanism for films that break down the film/TV distinction. Furthermore, new genres of interactive documentary and experimental multimedia productions, as well as new support for computer games through the Film Institute, suggest that media convergence will begin to erase borders between traditional media, just as globalization is diminishing the significance of national borders (see *Film* 2003).

The new vision for Danish film culture in this globalized multimedia culture was expressed clearly in a document titled *Overordnede støttepolitiske retningslinjer* (General Principles of Support), published by the Film Board of the DFI on April 29, 1999:

> The DFI's support policy has both a film artistic and film cultural aim. The support mechanisms must ensure the production of an artistic plurality of Danish film genres that reflects and develops cultural identity, Danish culture and language, and at the same time puts Danish film on the international map. The support must ensure strong production of feature films, documentaries, short films, and new media. The national film policy must emphasize the Nordic and European dimension because film today is, more than ever, transnational. The film policy shall contribute to the development of a well-functioning Danish film culture as the basis for reaching artistic and cultural aims. This means establishing and supporting a strong film market and infrastructures for production, distribution, marketing, and exhibition, where public funding and private market forces work together to the mutual benefit of both sectors. (author's translation)

If we look at the support instruments established recently (2003), we see a rather large diversity in public support mechanisms, with many new instruments developed after 1990:

The consultant system (film law, §6) remains fundamentally a continuation of the system from 1972, with three consultants for feature films, three for documentary films, and two consultants for youth films and children's films. The consultant system is the core component in public support and is guided by aesthetic criteria. Although not specifically mentioned in the law, the consultant system is intended to support both quality films with smaller market potential and those with larger market potential.

The 60/40 system is a renewal of the old 50/50 system that counterbalances the art film orientation of the consultant system. This mechanism aims to cultivate films that can "contribute to promote film art and film culture and are judged potentially to be films that can attract a larger audience" (film law, §12; author's translation). The 60/40 system applies only to feature films but may be extended to documentary films in the future.

The workshop system is designed to sustain and support film and multimedia products that can "promote professional and experimental film and talent development" (film law, §2, par. 6).

The Short Film Fund (Dansk Novellefilm) was established in 1992 as an autonomous institution based on cofinancing between the DFI, DR, and TV2; it is organized through an executive board representing the three partners. The Short Film Fund has made a significant contribution to the development of new talents in Danish cinema during the 1990s. Two films produced through the fund have won an Oscar—*Election Night* (Anders Thomas Jensen, 1997, *Valgaften*) and *This Charming Man* (Martin Strange-Hansen, 2002, *Der er en yndig mand*). This fund has been terminated and replaced by a new Talent Fund.

The Talent Film Fund (Talentudviklingspuljen) was established in 2003 with an annual budget of DKr 25 million. It is directed by a board that includes one representative from TV2, one from DR, two from the DFI, and one independent film consultant. The fund aims to develop film language and narrative forms and to stimulate the dynamism and diversity of Danish film culture.

Screenplay, development, and preproduction support must also be mentioned, for it is an integral part of the whole system and receives large allocations in the increased budget. The emphasis on screenplays and development has had a direct impact on quality and professionalization in the new Danish cinema. It has furthermore allowed companies to produce films without excessive time pressure, nurturing proper development at all stages of film production.

Regional funding and financial incentives have become important, as efforts have been made to establish new centers for film production in Århus, the second largest city in Denmark, as well as in Odense, the third largest. Money from local firms, European Union regional funds, and the DFI play an important role here.

Support mechanisms for film culture in general provide a framework aimed at stimulating and sustaining the marketing and distribution of cinema, an area that the DFI has sought to professionalize much more. This fund provides support for art film, for renewal of local cinemas, and for training and educating film professionals. These support mechanisms all aim at strengthening film culture both as a mainstream phenomenon and as art.

The important changes in Danish film culture since 1990 are the structural changes in the funding of national cinema, the amazing upturn in audience figures for Danish cinema both at home and abroad, and the increase in the global "brand value" of Danish cinema (closely related to Lars von Trier and the Dogma-film phenomenon, in particular). If we make a three-way comparison between the structure of the film production sector in Denmark in the late 1990s, the classical film culture, and the production structure of the modern film culture between 1960 and 1990, the tendency appears to be toward a more centralized and professionalized production sector centered around a few big, internationalized companies, with some dominant middle-sized companies; in contrast to the 1960–90 period, the small yet unstable film companies that dominated then are now disappearing (see table 4.1). This trend indicates, together with market share figures for Danish film abroad and at home, that the film policy has succeeded in creating a new and better balance between mainstream and art film, between market and public sector.

The increase of film production from around ten to fifteen films before 1997 to twenty to twenty-five films after 1997 is reflected in the market share of Danish films between 1995 and 2002. The latest figures indicate a market share of approximately 30 percent and a reduction in American dominance. In contrast, European films command a small market share, so in a general sense it is fair to say that Danish film culture is a Danish-American hybrid. Danish films do extremely well, together with American films, but European films do not enjoy success at the box office (see table 4.2).

The same fact is clearly reflected in the top twenty films shown in Denmark in the same period (1995–2001; see table 4.3). Of course, *Titanic* beats everything in that period, but it is astonishing that Dogma

Table 4.1
Danish film production, 1995–2001, listed by film companies

Production company	Total productions	Percentage of total productions
Large companies	62	55
Zentropa	22	19.5
Egmont (total)	20	17.7
Per Holst	13	11.5
Nordisk	7	6.2
Nimbus	8	7.1
Grasten	6	5.3
Metronome	6	5.3
Middle-sized companies	21	18.5
M & M	5	4.4
Thura	5	4.4
Balboa & Balboa 2	4	3.5
Angel/Arena	4	3.5
Græsted Film & Fjernsyn	3	2.7
Small companies	30	26.5

Sources: Bondebjerg 2003, calculations based on the list of films produced each year in Schepelern et al. 2001; and data on films from 2001–2 at www.dfi.dk.

Table 4.2
Danish audience market share of films, 1995–2001, measured by origin

	1995	1996	1997	1998	1999	2000	2001
United States	81	67	66	78	59	73	59
Europe	7	15	13	9	15	8	9
Denmark	8	17	19	13	26	18	28
Others	3	0	2	0	0	1	4

Source: Bondebjerg 2003, based on *Fact and Figures* 2001 and 2002, issued by DFI. Also see data at www.dfi.dk.

films like *Italian for Beginners* (Scherfig, 2000, *Italiensk for begyndere*), in third place, and one of Susanne Bier's low-budget modern romantic comedies, *The One and Only* (1999, *Den eneste ene*), in second place, can beat high-budget American and English films like *Harry Potter, Golden Eye,* and *Independence Day*. These figures indicate that the line between art films from small nations and high-budget mainstream films has shifted in the present film culture. The figures furthermore indicate that even in a globalized media culture, the national European film cultures can do rather well in their own market, whereas they still have difficulties on a more global scale. The tendency of Danish directors to make foreign-language films and to try out high-budget international coproductions is, however, the other side of the success of national low-budget and Dogma films.

The other side of the coin in this "double rule" (the tendency, as in Denmark, for the domestic market to be dominated by homegrown and American films) is the almost complete absence of films from a number of important European nations among the list of most popular films—even if we extend the list to the top fifty or one hundred. Between 1995 and 2001, sixty-eight French films were shown in Danish cinemas, but the majority sold fewer than 10,000 tickets; only twenty-two Italian films made it to Denmark, and among them only two sold more than 100,000 tickets. German and Spanish films were almost invisible (Bondebjerg 2003). Results indicating the impact of ten years of European programs of cinema support have yet to be published. Recent figures for Scandinavian films on both the European and American market may show some new trends, however, and Denmark has proved to be the dominant nation so far. But the figures remain small, and there is a long way to go before a globalization of the national European cinema is realized (see table 4.4).

European film culture remains very much divided by national lines, although one aim of European Union policy is to create a common audiovisual sector and market that preserves the diversity of European cinema. Danish film culture in the late 1990s to a large degree has moved toward a more global and international profile, and Denmark has received a relatively large percentage of the European Union funding. In 2001, according to the Danish Media Desk, 90 percent of all Danish applications found E.U. support, receiving about DKr 11 million; in addition, large sums have been invested in Danish-European and even Danish-American coproductions. However, international coproduction was

Table 4.3
Top twenty films released in Denmark, 1995–2001, by ticket sales

Title	Year	Origin	Company	Director	Tickets
Titanic	1998	USA	Paramount	Cameron	1,362,510
The One and Only (Den eneste ene)	1999	DK	Metronome	Bier	843,149
Italian for Beginners (Italiensk for begyndere)	2000	DK	Zentropa	Scherfig	818,835
Tarzan	1999	USA	Disney	Lima	634,269
Harry Potter	2001	USA	Warner	Columbus	629,419
The Olsen Gang's Last Stab (Olsen-bandens sidste stik)	2001	DK	Nordisk	Hedegaard	628,801
Anja and Viktor (Anja og Viktor)	2001	DK	Grasten	Sachs Bostrup	571,660
Golden Eye	1996	USA	MGM	Campbell	545,604
Star Wars: Episode I	1999	USA	Lucas Film	Lucas	542,974
Love at First Hic' (Kærlighed ved første hik)	1999	DK	Grasten	Villum Jensen	521,339
The Full Monty	1997	UK	20th Century	Cattano	466,378
Independence Day	1996	USA	20th Century	Emmerich	464,358
Just a Girl (Kun en pige)	1995	DK	Grasten	P. Schrøder	456,718
Toy Story II	2000	USA	Pixar	Lassiter	451,186
Flickering Lights (Blinkende lygter)	2000	DK	M & M	T. Jensen	435,726
Hunchback of Notre Dame	1996	USA	Disney	Wise	430,948
Mulan	1998	USA	Disney	Bancroft	428,194
Smilla's Sense of Snow (Frøken Smillas fornemmelse for sne)	1997	DK/EU	Eichinger	B. August	411,654
The World Is Not Enough	1999	UK/USA	EON, MGM, UA, et al.	Apted	411,010
The Celebration (Festen)	1998	DK	Nimbus	Vinterberg	403,611

Source: Bondebjerg 2003, based on calculations of basic statistical data on all films shown in Denmark between 1995 and 2001. See data at www.dfi.dk.

Table 4.4
Top 20 Scandinavian films released in EU and USA, 1996–2000, by ticket sales

Title	Year	Origin	Tickets
Breaking the Waves	1996	K/S/FR/N	4,120,303
Dancer in the Dark	2000	DK/FR/DE/NL	3,500,216
The Celebration (Festen)	1998	DK	2,750,424
Show Me Love (Fucking Åmål)	1998	S	1,923,920
Pippi Longstocking (Pipi Longströmp)	1997	S/CA/DE	1,757,450
The Olsen Gang's Last Stab (Olsen-bandens sidste stik)	1998	DK	1,087,610
Mifune (Mifunes sidste sang)	1999	DK/S	937,455
The Hunters (Jägarna)	1996	S	929,977
Pippi on the South Seas (Pipi i Söderhavet)	1999	S/DE	883,726
The One and Only (Den eneste ene)	1999	DK	877,151
Health Spa (Hälsoresan)	1999	S	867,628
Together (Tilsammans)	2000	S/DK/IT	849,134
The Idiots (Idioterne)	1998	DK	797,377
Adam & Eva	1997	S	786,388
Jerusalem	1996	S/DK/N/SF	768,799
Under the Sun (Under solen)	1998	S	742,068
Solan, Ludvig and Gurin	1998	N	677,456
Svensson, Svensson	1997	S	523,451
Hamilton	1998	S/N	523,386
In Bed with Santa (Tomten är far)	1999	S	519,284

Source: Bondebjerg 2003, based on Film 16 (2001): 38.
Abbreviations:
CA Canada
DE Germany
DK Denmark
FR France
IT Italy
N Norway
NL Netherlands
S Sweden
SF Suomi/Finland

only one element in Danish film culture of the 1990s. Perhaps the biggest factor in the recent success of Danish cinema is the diversity of forms and support structures, which are also clearly visible when we examine trends in genres and aesthetic forms in the new Danish cinema.

BETWEEN NATIONAL AND GLOBAL CINEMA: GENRES AND AESTHETIC TRENDS IN NEW DANISH CINEMA, 1990–2003

In 1987, Gabriel Axel's *Babette's Feast* (*Babettes gæstebud*) won the Oscar for Best Foreign Film. Axel was the first Danish director to win the award. The Oscar symbolized a transformation under way in Danish cinema culture, which became further evident during the 1990s. When Bille August repeated the triumph in 1988 with *Pelle the Conquerer (Pelle Erobreren),* making it a "double" (the Palme d'Or in Cannes followed by the Oscar for Best Foreign Film), the victory seemed less symbolic; rather, a clear indication of the real globalization of Danish cinema. It is worth noting that 1988 also inaugurated the first larger European project for coproduction, Eurimages, aimed at making high-budget European films that could compete with Hollywood, and that 1990 saw the launch of the more systematic Nordic equivalent, the Nordic Film and TV Fund. The liberalization of the more defensive national film policy that took place after 1989 hence ran parallel to both European and Nordic trends supporting the internationalization of small as well as large national European countries (on this point, see also Hjort and Bondebjerg 2001, 16–20; Andersen 1997). The two films that won an Oscar both indicate a strategy of globalization that has been characteristic of Danish cinema during the last decades. Both films draw from an established national and international literary heritage that is cinematically transformed into a universal epic but that maintains a specific national or Nordic dimension and modality in narrative structure and aesthetics. For Bille August in particular, these successes paved the way for a more direct "Hollywoodization" of some of his later films, which were based on international best sellers.

A closer examination of Danish cinema's first strategy of globalization, which aims at a more pan-Nordic, pan-European, and global audience and is normally based on coproduction and much larger budgets than the average Danish film, reveals at least three subtendencies. One tendency is toward direct *Hollywoodization,* which means that Danish directors shoot Hollywood-style mainstream films, adding a European,

Nordic tone to them. The main examples here are Bille August's *House of Spirits* (1993), based on Isabel Allende's international best seller and shot in English with an international cast, and his international thriller *Smilla's Sense of Snow* (1997), based on Peter Høeg's international bestselling novel. These films endeavor to combine elements of psychological realism, August's artistic trademark in his national and Nordic productions, with American dramaturgy and genre models, but do not fully succeed. Finally, August's *Les misérables* (1998) is based on the oft-filmed novel by Victor Hugo. Perhaps an indication of the dangers in this strategy is August's subsequent return to his Nordic roots in psychological realism.

The second important strategy in the globalization of Danish cinema is the *European coproduction,* in which a film is made by a Danish director and a Danish major-producer but normally features a European/international cast and English dialogue. This type of film is essentially an art film production but carries obvious elements of the classical genre film, by which it often seeks to reach a larger audience than a normal European art film production. The most obvious examples here are Lars von Trier's *Breaking the Waves* (1996), which is an original and in many ways aesthetically innovative erotic melodrama (with handheld cinemascope!) and his *Dancer in the Dark* (2000), a musical with a brilliant and new magically aesthetic touch by von Trier, combining elements of American and European tradition. In Danish film, von Trier is the key representative of the European art film tradition, although his first films—*The Element of Crime* (1984), *Epidemic* (1988), and *Europa* (1991)—did not reach a large global audience. The breakthrough for a new European art film with larger audience potential came with the bigger coproduced films that combine art film and genre elements. Thomas Vinterberg (*It's All about Love,* 2003) and Lone Scherfig (*Wilbur Wants to Kill Himself,* 2002) have also confirmed this international move toward a new European art film, often with some influence and inspiration from American film.

The third subtendency of globalization in Danish cinema is the already mentioned *Nordic literary heritage film* (see also Hjort 2003c). As a national film convention, this type of film has a long tradition in Denmark as well as in other countries—not least the English heritage film based on the classical literary tradition of Britain (see Higson 1996, 2000). Although the tradition is firmly embedded in the national literary canon, it is not of national interest only; on the contrary, it was through such films that Denmark's international breakthrough occurred in the work of Gabriel Axel and Bille August. The success of such films draws on the authority of the literary canon from which these films emerged; they filmatized texts that were already international best sellers but also carried the imprimatur of European culture and history, which appeals to a large American and international audience. These films do not have a large international cast, however, relying instead on a national cast—although in some cases, as in Axel's *Babette's Feast*, one big international star (Stephane Audran) is featured. *Babette's Feast* precisely combined Karen Blixen/Isak Dinesen's international reputation, the qualities of a carefully staged heritage film, and some star quality.

Qualitatively better examples of this Nordic national heritage tradition are Bille August's films *Pelle the Conquerer* and *The Best Intentions* (1992, based on Ingmar Bergman's memoirs) as well as *Jerusalem*. August's films exemplify the Nordic art film tradition, with its strong psychological dimension. The narration in *The Best Intentions*, for instance, is based on a number of carefully selected tense psychological and social situations that form a thematically complex image of the social psychology of family life in Sweden at the fin de siècle. It thematizes the difference of life in the city and in the country, but most of all it presents a thematic network of pictures dealing with the psychology of the two main characters, who are caught in a battle between two different ways of living: the mild, loving world of Anna versus the severe, conscience-stricken mind of Henrik. The visual style stresses the conflict: very long shots and slow narrative speed, symbolic use of silence, mise-en-scène that places characters in situations of interaction, and the clear symbolic use of a montage alternation between closed indoor spaces and open landscapes, with special attention to light/shadow and colors. The narration and visual style invites the viewer to identify with individuals mostly on the levels of everyday time and memory time. It is a special kind of psychological realism.

August's Nordic psychological realism is one of the important Nordic art film forms next to von Trier's European art film tradition, and in many ways August and von Trier stand out as two different prototypes in contemporary Danish cinema: August's Nordic films are reality driven in the first place and story driven in the second, whereas von Trier's earlier films are image or form driven and often guided by self-imposed rules and restrictions that emphasize a search for nonconventional effects (see Schepelern 2000, 2003). In contrast to August, for whom the authenticity of the image and psychological and emotional empathy are important, von Trier has clearly stated, "When I decide on a theme, this is just an excuse for making images. The first thing I look at when I pick the time and the location is whether I can construct the images and visual effects I am looking for" (Von Trier, in Drouzy 1991). Von Trier has since developed into a much more emotional, story-driven narrator interested in genres and classical narration.

The literary heritage film is also important for other directors, like Morten Henriksen, which is particularly evident in his last production, *The Magnetist's Fifth Winter* (1999, *Magnetisørens femte vinter*), based on P. O. Enquist's Swedish novel; the film illustrates the strength and importance of the literary heritage film tradition. In this tradition we also find Nils Malmros's *Barbara* (1997), which was seen by some 400,000 in 1997. One of the latest examples of this tradition is Ole Bornedal's film *I Am Dina* (2002, *Jeg er Dina*) based on Herbjørg Wasmo's Nordic best seller, featuring Gerard Depardieu amid a Nordic cast.

This tradition is not just Nordic but also a purely national genre. Anders Refn's fine film *Black Harvest* (1993, *Sort høst*), based on a novel by Gustav Wied, is a period film about the landed aristocracy at the fin de siècle. It features an "upstairs-downstairs" motif that presents a broad social and psychological portrait of Danish history and culture. It is also an aesthetically strong film, with its use of the cinemascope format. As an important national genre, this type of film often reaches a large audience, also—and perhaps especially—when it is based on newer best sellers or classics; examples include Peter Schrøder's *Lost Spring* (1993, *Det forsømte forår*) and *Just a Girl* (1995, *Kun en pige*). The latter is based on a novel by one of Denmark's most widely read female best-selling authors (Lise Nørgaard) and was seen by some 500,000 viewers in its theater release and by twice as many on television. Hans Kristensen's traditional but immensely popular film, *The Twopenny Dance* (1999, *Klinkevals*), based on another best seller written by a woman, is another example. The adaptation of Danish and Nordic literary classics to film is an important element in contemporary Danish mainstream cinema, even considered solely on the level of national box office.

The internationalization of Danish cinema through Hollywoodization is not the only, and perhaps not even the most important, strategy of globalization. New Danish cinema has to a great degree embraced a return to the basics of European art film and realism in a new mixture of generic mainstream forms and art film forms. This trend is associated chiefly with the global success of Dogma 95, which can well be seen as a low-budget strategy for filmmaking in a global age when new technologies have made low-budget filmmaking aesthetically more appealing and accessible. As Mette Hjort has recently argued (2003a), Dogma 95 can be seen as a cinematic political act, the response of a small nation to globalization, which differentiates it completely from the coproduction strategies and the big budgets. Mette Hjort defines Dogma 95 as a "non-nationalist response to globalization" establishing an explicit contrast with the Nordic heritage tradition. Hjort goes on to argue: "Whereas the heritage films belonging to a tradition of 'quality' film-making foreground *national* or *transnational belonging* . . . Dogma 95 . . . is an attempt to resist the dynamics of an intensified localism fuelled by globalism by focusing attention, not on heritage and ethnicity, but on the very definition of cinematic art and on the conditions of that art's production" (38). In the Dogma 95 manifesto, artistic arguments are welded with economic logic, the combination of which has furnished Danish and international Dogma filmmakers with the freedom to make unusual films and experiments without having to involve a lot of coproduction bureaucracy and potential artistic compromises. In many ways Dogma 95 and ancillary low-budget filmmaking practices have been the most important and original Danish contribution to new strategies for small national cinemas in times of globalization. And, as Hjort has shown in another article (2003b), the globalization of the Dogma 95 concept and the publicity and debate around it have been clever artistic and very cheap branding strategies as well, contributing to, among other things, the growth of the Internet as a useful site for building transnational networks and spreading ideas.

The network that has facilitated this strategy for the globalization of film art is, however, also supported by the rise of an increasingly diverse global cinema festival circuit and numerous documentary films related to and documenting the Dogma 95 concept. Hjort offers a striking statistical account of the Danish Dogma films and their festival appearances (2003b, 137): Thomas Vinterberg's *Celebration* did not merely win a prize in Cannes, the film also participated in no fewer than seventy festivals, winning prizes in several of them; Lars von Trier's *Idiots* appeared at forty-two festivals; and Søren Kragh-Jacobsen's *Mifune* appeared at thirty-eight; the latter number also approximates total festival screenings for Lone Scherfig's *Italian for Beginners*, Åke Sandgren's *Truly Human* (2001, *En rigtigt menneske*), and Ole Christian Madsen's *Kira's Reason* (2001, *En kærlighedshistorie*). Globalization clearly includes the widening of an art film festival network, which, coupled with the commercial and artistic success of these films, has contributed to increased viability of films that were formerly considered marginal in terms of market potential and audience reach. As already indicated, some of the Dogma 95 films compete quite well with the big American blockbusters on a national level. Dogma 95 has proved that big is not always beautiful and that coproduction, big budgets, and commercial marketing are not always the only avenues to global success.

The diversity of Danish directors, strategies, and tendencies during the 1990s is striking, and it is probably one of the reasons for the recent success and creativity of Danish cinema. There is not just one answer to globalization but many; national mainstream and genre films remain significant, as does the production of national art films. Stretching between the global, the national, and the local is important. One of the finest representatives of modern Danish art film and the strong realist tradition is Nils Malmros, who made his first feature film in 1968. He is in many ways the prototype for the national Danish auteur (see Hjort and Bondebjerg 2001, 137; Jørholt 1997). His films are extremely Danish and even regional, almost all of them set around the large provincial town Århus in Jutland; at the same time, they are somehow universal. Malmros is not as internationally widely known as he ought to be, but he is a seminal figure in the modern Danish art film, and his films are widely viewed and well known in Denmark.

A young rising director like Nicolas Winding Refn, on the other hand, is clearly very inspired by new American independent cinema, as exemplified in his Danish films *Pusher* (1993) and *Bleeder* (1999), as well as in his latest "American" film, *Fear X* (2003). He has developed a completely international production profile, but he remains influenced by both European art film and American independent movies. Ole Bornedal, who launched the new American-inspired genre film in Denmark with his *Nattevagten* (1994, *Nightwatch*) has said, rather provocatively, about his film and the new generation of directors and

The Danish Way

their interest in American-inspired genre film:

> There had been two big box office successes before *Nightwatch*. One was *House of the Spirits*, which was the film that our parents and grandparents went to see.... The other film, *Waltzing Regitze*, was classic Danish film art at its best. It effectively conveyed a fine story that simply appealed to a wide audience. *Nightwatch's* impact was somewhat different. It was in many ways more modern and appealed to a younger generation. *Nightwatch* made use of a contemporary cinematic language while mobilizing the classic thriller genre, and it was driven uniquely by a strong sense of narrative desire.... It pursued certain entertainment values almost shamelessly. I don't think the film is a great work of art, but it did help to legitimate the idea that even European film art can make good use of generic stories. (quoted in Hjort and Bondebjerg 2001, 233–34)

The use of basically American film language and generic formulas are not novel, to be sure. In fact, with *Cop* (1976, *Strømer*) and the later TV series *Once a Cop* ... (1987, *Engang Strømer* ...), Anders Refn had already introduced more direct action–genre language into Danish film culture during the 1970s. Nevertheless, the New Wave of the 1990s has done this on a broader basis. Today Danish film and televisual culture is much more international in its generic formulas and aesthetics than in the modern and classical film periods.

The open globalization of Danish film culture and film language is a clear feature of the 1990s, yet the national and local dimensions also remain strong. Among the not so internationally known directors from the youngest generation, for instance, Lotte Svendsen and Jonas Elmer (see portrait and interview in Hjort and Bondebjerg 2001), both of whom clearly remain within the local-national framework, with mostly European inspirations. Lotte Svendsen's films combine inspirations from one of the big national directors and creative renewers of the Danish social comedy, Erik Clausen. But as Svendsen herself remarks in an interview (Hjort and Bondebjerg 2001), she is also strongly inspired by the European art film, first of all Mike Leigh's social realism but also Emir Kusturica's farcical, surrealistic symbolism in films like *Underground* (1995).

In conclusion, the new Danish cinema of the 1990s and its present national success and international acclaim have resulted from two chief sources. First, it has been stimulated by a successful public support system, which has a long tradition but has proved flexible enough to adapt itself to the new global challenges faced by cinema. Second, a generation of directors and producers who combine art and business, and art and the mainstream, in new ways has changed the profile of Danish cinema from a more or less art film–dominated national tradition to a more open European and international tradition. An important consequence of this is the resurrection of a new qualitative mainstream genre tradition—and hence a new breakthrough to a larger audience. This breakthrough to a larger audience, the fact that cinema is now all over the media all the time, is also related to the fact that a new star system has developed, supporting the national and international establishment of this mainstream culture. But mainstream tendencies are not dominant; on the contrary, the strength of Danish cinema culture right now is the pluralism and diversity of its many tendencies and generations, the coexistence of both national and international art film traditions and national and international mainstream genre tendencies.

WORKS CITED

Andersen, Jesper. 1997. "I lommerne på Europa." In *Dansk film, 1972–97*, ed. Ib Bondebjerg, Jesper Andersen, and Peter Schepelern, 332–66. Copenhagen: Munksgaard/Rosinante.

Bondebjerg, Ib. 1996. "Film Comedy, Modernization, and Gender Roles: Aspects of Romantic Comedy in Danish Cinema." In *A Century of Cinema*, ed. Tybjerg Casper and Peter Schepelern. Sekvens. Filmvidenskabelig årbog. Copenhagen: University of Copenhagen.

———. 1997. "Fra biograf til hjemmevideo." In *Dansk mediehistorie*, Vol. 3: *1960–1995*, ed. Ib Bondebjerg and Klaus Bruhn Jensen, 200–44. Copenhagen: Samleren.

———. 2000. "Film and Modernity: Realism and the Aesthetic of Scandinavian New Wave Cinema." In *Moving Images, Culture, and the Mind*, ed. Ib Bondebjerg, 117–33. Luton: University of Luton Press.

———. 2003. "Filmen i mediekulturen." In *Dansk mediehistorie*, vol. 4: *1995–2000*, ed. Klaus Bruhn Jensen, 175–96. Copenhagen: Samfundslitteratur.

———. Forthcoming. *Filmen og det moderne: Filmgenrer og filmkultur i Danmark, 1940–1972*. Copenhagen: Gyldendal.

Bondebjerg, Ib, Jesper Andersen, and Peter Schepelern, eds. 1997. *Dansk film, 1972–97*. Copenhagen: Munksgaaard/Rosinante.

Dinnesen, Niels Jørgen, and Edwin Kau. 1983. *Filmen i Danmark*. Copenhagen: Akademisk forlag.

Drouzy, Martin. 1991. "Biografisk skitse." In *Filmvidenskabelig Årbog, 1991*. Copenhagen: University of Copenhagen.

Engberg, Marguerite. 1990. *Danish Films through the Years*. Copenhagen: Det Danske Filminstitut.
Film. 2003. Theme on Interactive film (in Danish). No. 28 (April–May). Copenhagen: Danish Film Institute.
Facts and Figures. 2001–2. Annual statistic reports from the DFI, http://www.dfi.dk
Higson, Andrew. 1996. "The Heritage Film and British Cinema." In *Dissolving Views*, ed. Andrew Higson. London: Cassell.
———. 2000. "National Cinema(s), International Markets, and Cross Cultural Identities." In *Moving Images, Culture, and the Mind*, ed. Ib Bondebjerg, 205–14. Luton: Luton University Press.
Hjort, Mette. 2003a. "Dogma 95: A Small Nation's Response to Globalisation." In *Purity and Provocation: Dogma 95*, ed. Mette Hjort and Scott MacKenzie, 31–47. London: British Film Institute.
———. 2003b. "The Globalisation of Dogma: The Dynamics of Meta Culture and Counter-Publicity." In *Purity and Provocation: Dogma 95*, ed. Mette Hjort and Scott MacKenzie, 133–58. London: British Film Institute.
———. 2003c. "Tak for musikken spillemand: Heritage film på dansk. In *Nationale spejlinger*, ed. Anders Toftgaard and Ian Hawkesworth, 139–67. Copenhagen: Museum Tusculanums Forlag.
Hjort, Mette, and Ib Bondebjerg. 2001. *The Danish Directors: Dialogues on a National Cinema*. Bristol: Intellect.
Hjort, Mette, and Scott MacKenzie, eds. 2003. *Purity and Provocation: Dogma 95*. London: British Film Institute.
Jørholt, Eva. 1997. "Erfaringens filmiske prisme: Nils Malmros' filmkunst." In *Danske film, 1972–97*, ed. Ib Bondebjerg, Jesper Andersen, and Peter Schepelern, 242–63. Copenhagen: Munksgaard/Rosinante.
———. 2001. "1930–39: Sol over Danmark." In *100 års dansk film*, ed. Peter Schepelern et al., 90–120. Copenhagen: Rosinante.
Krarup, Helge, and Carl Nørrested. 1986. *Eksperimentalfilm i Danmark*. Copenhagen: Borgen.
En kulturpolitisk redegørelse. 1969. Betaenkning, 517. Copenhagen: Folketinget.
Nørrested, Carl, and Christian Alsted. 1987. *Kortfilmen og staten*. Copenhagen: Forlaget Eventus.
Schepelern, Peter. 2000. *Lars von Triers film: Tvang og befrielse*. Copenhagen: Rosinante.
———. 2003. "'Kill Your Darlings': Lars von Trier and the Origins of Dogma 95." In *Purity and Provocation: Dogma 95*, ed. Mette Hjort and Scott MacKenzie. London: British Film Institute.
Schepelern, Peter et al., eds. 2001. *100 års dansk film*. Copenhagen: Rosinante.
Soila, Tytti, Astrid Söderbergh Widding, and Gunnar Iversen. 1998. *Nordic National Cinemas*. London: Routledge.
Troelsen, Anders, ed. 1980. *Levende billeder af Danmark*. Copenhagen: Forlaget Medusa.

CHAPTER 5

Breaking the Borders: Danish Coproductions in the 1990s

Pil Gundelach Brandstrup and Eva Novrup Redvall

Following the international triumphs in the late 1980s of Gabriel Axel's *Babette's Feast* (1987, *Babettes Gæstebud*) and Bille August's *Pelle the Conqueror* (1988, *Pelle Erobreren*, 1987), Lars von Trier and Dogma 95 attracted international attention to Danish cinema in the 1990s, proving that Danish films were able to travel and had an appeal outside the borders of Denmark. However, the international recognition of Oscars and Palms is by no means the only important way Danish cinema crossed borders during the 1990s. One of the most salient and significant changes of Danish cinema in the 1990s was the exploding rise in the number of transnational coproductions. While nine majors (films primarily Danish, with foreign economic collaboration) and ten minors (films primarily foreign, with Danish economic participation) were produced in the period 1980–89, sixty-one Danish majors and forty-six minors were made in the following ten years—a rise of more than 600 percent. As examined in several other studies (for example, Hjort and MacKenzie 2000), the notion of national cinema has been challenged by globalization during the last couple of decades, and this rise in the number of coproductions is one reason why it is increasingly difficult to define Danish cinema. Exchange of creative and technical personnel is growing, and films more frequently seek locations abroad and/or contain languages other than Danish. Moreover, the many collaborations across borders complicate the traditional perception of what constitutes a Danish film and what it should look like. International coproduction can be seen as a characteristic example of the influence of internationalizing and globalizing mechanisms on Danish film production and output.

Over the last two decades, it has become politically necessary to reflect on the changes in the international film scene. Entering the 1990s, the Danish Film Institute (DFI) loosened the requirements for films to be considered Danish in order to oblige newly established funding schemes such as Eurimages and the Nordic Film and TV Fund; after 1989 a film no longer had to be staged in Danish, and this political liberalization of the definition of Danish film has been key in the rise in coproductions. Other reasons for the coproduction boom are increased budgets and the reduced percentage of state funding, which have forced the film industry to seek financing outside Denmark, as it is impossible for this risk-laden business to mobilize enough private financing within the country. This chapter focuses on Danish coproductions in the 1990s, in particular with regard to the tight bonds between the Danish film industry and the film industries of other Nordic countries. After a short historical outline of Danish coproductions before the 1990s, we offer an analysis of the reasons for the rise in the number of Danish coproductions by looking at the political, economic, cultural, and creative arguments for coproducing. Transnational coproduction as a mode of producing and financing is not used for any one particular type of film, but in examining the output of the many Danish coproductions of the period, a number of tendencies appear regarding setting, actors, language, locations, and budget. In the following, we present a way of categorizing the films while at the same time considering the impact of the coproduction mode on the films themselves as well as on Danish cinema as a whole.

DANISH COPRODUCTIONS BEFORE THE 1990s

Historically, European countries have always coproduced on a bilateral basis, but never as intensively as in the 1990s. In the silent era, collaboration across national borders was relatively uncomplicated, and many Danish film companies (most remarkably Nordisk Film Kompagni) produced silent films together with a wide range of European countries. However, the introduction of sound put these collaborations under pressure, and since then the vast majority of Danish coproductions have been made with neighboring Nordic countries. The most notable exceptions are the few American productions in the 1950s through the 1970s and Gabriel Axel and Henning Carlsen's attempts at international coproduction with France in the 1960s, followed by their big productions of *Babette's Feast* and *The Wolf at the Door* (1986, *Oviri*), respectively, in the 1980s.[1] Gabriel Axel's adaptation of Karen Blixen's classic won an Oscar for Best Foreign Language Film, while Henning Carlsen's historical drama with an English-speaking Donald Sutherland as the French painter Paul Gauguin (who for many years lived in Denmark) received mixed reviews in Denmark but performed satisfactorily internationally.

Early Scandinavian collaboration was especially based on "traveling plots," meaning the filmmakers borrowed plots from each other for remakes. Henning Carlsen's Danish-Swedish-Norwegian *Hunger (Sult)* from 1966 is considered by many to be the first "true" coproduction because the Scandinavian collaboration clearly manifests itself on the screen. The film is also one of the rare examples of a successful coproduction, despite its transnational mix of cast and crew. The scriptwriter, the cinematographer, and director Carlsen were Danish. The author of the classic novel *Hunger* was Norwegian Knut Hamsun, and the two main actors were both Swedish, resulting in a somewhat absurd mix (at least to a Scandinavian audience) insofar as a Swede portrays a Norwegian reflecting in Swedish on the harsh nature of life in Oslo. Nonetheless, the film was hailed as an artistic triumph in all the Scandinavian countries, convincing many local filmmakers that audiences would accept creative casting and evident collaboration on screen as long as the film is of high quality. However, Henning Carlsen's next expensive Scandinavian collaboration, *We Are All Demons* (1969, *Klabautermanden*), illustrated that coproducing wasn't necessarily a safe recipe for success. Based on a novel by the Danish-Norwegian author Aksel Sandemose and with a cast of Danish, Swedish, and Norwegian actors, the film aimed for all Scandinavian markets, but was modestly received in all countries by both critics and audiences.

In fact, Scandinavian coproduction did not result in a success on the scale of *Hunger* until Bille August made *Pelle the Conqueror* in 1988. August's adaptation of the classic novel by Danish author Martin Andersen Nexø, with Max von Sydow in the adult lead as the Swedish father to the Danish-speaking boy Pelle, won both the Golden Palm in Cannes and an Oscar for Best Foreign Language Film. The film was even awarded the prize as the best film of the year in both Denmark and Sweden, exemplifying some of the confusion in regard to a film's nationality that sometimes arises from coproducing. This type of close collaboration among Denmark, Sweden, and Norway is based on the cultural affinities and linguistic similarities of the three countries. A closer look at Danish coproductions of the 1990s shows that this Scandinavian base was central both to the overall rise in coproductions and to how audiences could detect increasing cross-cultural collaborations on screen.

But why coproduce at all? The reasons for the rather sudden and significant rise in the number of coproductions include historically specific reasons—such as motivating, inspiring film successes and new lucrative funding schemes—as well as more "universally valid" arguments such as economic necessity and a search for bigger markets. Many of the arguments for coproducing are not new. In the 1920s and from the 1950s and on, some European countries have had tight collaborative bonds. Then, as today, film producers could see the obvious advantages of sharing the financial risk related to filmmaking among several parties, of expanding their markets, and of trying to establish distribution alliances abroad.

The different arguments supporting coproduction, the historically specific as well as the universally valid ones, are tightly intertwined but fall into three major categories: the political, the economic, and the cultural/creative. While the political arguments incorporate both trade and cultural-political perspectives, the economic and cultural/creative arguments should be considered in relation to both the films per se and the industry as a whole.[2]

POLITICAL ARGUMENTS

Politically, three principal arguments for furthering coproduction have dominated the discourse: (1) a protectionist argument with an intention of trying to create counteralliances against the United States to protect the national film industry; (2) an "industry-furthering" argument supporting the national film industry through alliances; and (3) a "culture-building" argument with the purpose of emphasizing a shared cultural identity through coproductions.

The first two arguments arise from reaction to the overwhelming influence of the American film and media industry on European film supply and consumption. The intention behind the protectionist initiatives has usually been to protect the European film scene from being dominated by American films.[3] The "industry-furthering" initiatives have mainly been a matter of professionalizing and specializing the European film industry to create big-budget films to compete with American blockbusters and to expand European cooperation, distribution circuits, and markets. Through these trade political initiatives, it is hoped to cultivate a big European "domestic market" making it less difficult for large European companies to maneuver between the various cultural-political objectives and audience preferences in European countries. In *Europa Europa,* Martin Dale maintains that the key question in Europe's film future is "how to make films which will successfully cross borders—that are accessible to many people in many countries" (1992, 2).

The third argument is founded in Europe's linguistic and cultural barriers. Apparently, the populations of European countries can agree on watching American films. However, the vast majority of European films do not easily cross borders. There has been a political desire to attract the European public's attention to Europe's cultural particularities as well as to its shared history and background, and audiovisual products have been considered a possible means of so doing.

In the context of a discussion of the Danish government's enhanced investment in film in 1998, the director of the Danish Film Institute, Henning Camre, commented on the European perspective:

> The truth is that it is on this cultural and industrial field that the battle of civilization is fought today. Film and other audiovisual products are not any type of product. They communicate ideas of values and lifestyle, ethical dilemmas, behavioral and cultural models, and artistic heritage. And in a Europe trying to cooperate within, these pictures represent cultural unity as well as variety and thus make up a crucial cultural grounding for Danish as well as European identity. (1998, 32; authors' translation)

Elsebeth Gerner Nielsen, then minister of culture, underscored the idea of cinema as an important cultural factor:

> When supporting film, you are simultaneously promoting a very broad cultural effect. Film and TV keep on influencing the way we understand the world. At the same time, film is the basis of the development of other electronic media. Danish film can therefore more effectively than any other medium contribute to the preservation and development of Danish culture and identity. (1998; authors' translation)

The enhanced state support of cinema reflected not only a wish for the improvement of the supply and quality of Danish film but also the understanding of film as a medium, bringing together Danes in an experience of sharing a national culture and identity.

Danish Film Politics

At the end of the 1980s, several political changes reflecting aspects of rising globalization were preparing the way for a boost in transnational coproduction. On a European level, Eurimages and the Media programs emerged, in a Nordic framework the Nordic Film and TV Fund (NFTF) was established, and nationally, the Danish film law was changed in order to serve these transnational initiatives.

Because of its small domestic market, the Danish film industry is dependent on state funding. The subsidy comes from a desire to secure a varied film output and is distributed through an independent institution: the Danish Film Institute. The DFI subsidizes only Danish film, but in the film law of 1989, the requirements for a film to be considered Danish were loosened. In addition to the establishment of a twofold funding scheme subsidizing both art films and more commercial projects, the most significant change—on the production side—of the film law was a liberalization of the definition of a Danish film. Whereas a Danish film before 1989 had to be made in Danish and with a considerable amount of artistic and technical personnel coming from Denmark (the film law of 1982, §23), it now had to either be made in Danish *or* contain a special Danish artistic or technical effort contributing to the promotion of film art and film culture in Denmark. The novel and more flexible definition of what constitutes a Danish film made it easier for Danish producers to collaborate with foreign partners and still be subsidized by the DFI. At the same time, the DFI earmarked money for transnational funding schemes such as the NFTF and Eurimages, and in 1991, Denmark became the second country in Europe to institutionalize the pan-European idea by establishing the Danish Media Desk to advise the film industry on the European possibilities for coproducing within Europe. The political openness toward these new ways of financing has been of great importance in increasing the number of coproductions.

European Film Politics

Two important European funding programs were established in the late 1980s: Eurimages, within the framework of the European Council, and the Media programs, in the context of the European Union. Whereas

Eurimages's primary purpose is to subsidize coproduction between its member countries from both a cultural and economic point of view,[4] the Media programs support in-service training of film personnel and distribution across national borders from an an exclusively economic perspective. Being a part of these European projects was indeed lucrative to the Danish film industry in the 1990s. While contributing approximately DKr 16.4 million, nineteen Danish majors received more than EUR 8 million (approximately DKr 60 million) from Eurimages, and, paying 1.7 percent of Media's budget, the Danish film industry received more than four times that contribution in the 1990s.[5]

Parallel with this economic benefit, another important aspect has been Media's international in-service courses such as the European Audio-Visual Entrepreneurs (EAVE) and Atelier du Cinéma Européens (ACE). EAVE and ACE both introduce producers to aspects of international filmmaking in general and in relation to a specific project. In the 1990s, more than 115 Danish film and media professionals attended these courses and established important networks.

Nordic Cooperation

Without a doubt, European audiovisual programs had a big impact on the rise in Danish coproductions. However, the most important political initiative to Danish coproductions as well as Nordic film production in general was the establishment of the Nordic Film and TV Fund in 1989. Based on collaboration among fifteen partners, including the Nordic Council of Ministers, the Nordic film institutes, and several Nordic TV networks, the purpose of the NFTF is to promote the production and distribution of audiovisual projects in Nordic countries. In order to obtain support from the NFTF, a film has to be guaranteed theatrical distribution in a minimum of two Nordic countries and have a broadcast agreement with at least one of the fund's TV partners, but the fund has no requirements as to pan-Nordic themes, national quotas, or the composition of the films' artistic or technical staff.[6] This means that in practice, other than its role in increasing the transnational distribution of Nordic films, the NFTF does not directly further the shared cultural identity of Nordic countries.

However, with the rise in the number of coproductions in the 1990s, the objective of furthering audiovisual cooperation in Scandinavia has been achieved. Of the sixty-one Danish majors, forty-three received funding from the NFTF, participating in the top-up financing—meaning the last part of the budget, which can be difficult to secure. According to Svend Abrahamsen, chairman of the NFTF and previous chief of coproduction at the largest Danish national broadcaster, DR, Lars von Trier's *The Kingdom* (1994, *Riget*) and the Dogma films, for instance, would not have been made without financial support from the NFTF.[7]

Transnational funds and programs have undoubtedly affected the boom in coproductions. It naturally took a few years for the political changes in 1989 to have an impact on the mode of production and for the films to reach the screen, but as early as 1991, the changes were evident. The financing figures of the funded Danish films bear witness to the fact that the possibilities of foreign financial support have been widely used.

ECONOMIC ARGUMENTS

The political effort to increase and improve audiovisual collaboration across borders has resulted in new sources of financing for the Danish film industry. The average percentage of state funding of a Danish film's budget dropped significantly throughout the 1980s and 1990s, from 51–61 percent in 1985–89 to 47 percent in 1992–97 (Bondebjerg, Andersen, and Schepelern, 1997, 421–32; *Facts and Figures* 1998). This is partly due to increased budgets and partly because of the DFI's choice of dividing the funds among an increasing number of films.[8]

With a budget of DKr 42.7 million, *Breaking the Waves* (Lars von Trier, 1996) was the most expensive production in the 1990s, and except for the years 1990 and 1995, each year's most expensive film has been a transnational coproduction. From the mid-1990s, a budget exceeding roughly DKr 14.5 million has necessitated foreign funds. The result has been a significant internationalization of the financing of Danish films, where 21 percent of the films' budgets in 1992–97 came from abroad (Stenderup 1998, 10). This foreign financing has come primarily from funding schemes such as Eurimages and the NFTF, but regional funding schemes in Sweden, such as Film i Väst, and Germany, like FilmFörderung Hamburg, have also contributed to a significant number of films.

Economic need due to a small domestic market and the scarcity of private investors has indeed been a motivating factor leading to an increase in the number of coproductions, and a number of productions in particular have had an economic rather than a creative incentive. In these entirely economically motivated coproductions, often called "switch projects" or "dealings," the producers/companies participate in each other's projects to meet the requirements of qualifying for international funds despite a lack of obvious creative or practical reasons to cooperate. Most often these barter deals between two producers result in films that are targeted at the major producer's domestic market, and therefore do not contribute to the politically stimulated creation of shared European or Nordic stories/identities or in the transnational distribution of films.

However, there can also be economic reasons for avoiding the mode of coproduction. In many cases, coproducing increases the costs of a film considerably due to the expenses of extensive funding applications, translation of scripts and contracts, traveling, completion guarantees, and so on. In addition to this, demanding requirements for instance, in relation to the composition of the artistic and technical staff—are sometimes attached to foreign money.[9] However, the high percentage of foreign financing indicates that Danish producers in the 1990s considered the trouble worthwhile.

CULTURAL AND CREATIVE ARGUMENTS

Through transnational funding schemes, cultural-political initiatives have set the scene for creative collaboration across borders. Enhanced state support for cinema reflected not only a wish to improve the supply and quality of Danish film, but also an effort to promote the understanding of film as a medium, bringing together Danes in a shared national culture and identity.

However, the "culture-building" and creative aspects of coproduction are seldom the reason for film producers' and directors' wish to collaborate on a transnational basis. For creative reasons, such as the choice of director or the nature of the story, some projects provide opportunity for coproducing, but our interviews with a number of Danish producers indicate that the primary motives are rarely creative or cultural. In many cases, creative bonds arise during a production, but the direct incentive for Danish coproductions in the 1990s was economic, motivated by the political funding initiatives. Without a doubt, several of the international collaborations and extensive productions have been inspiring to Danish film professionals. However, the mix of coproducers and requirements from various funding sources may create artistic problems for the films, and often the multinational cast and crew complicate work on the set. But as proven by the director-producer-executive producer team at Zentropa (Lars von Trier, Vibeke Windeløv, and Peter Aalbæk Jensen), it is possible to maintain creative control over coproductions, despite complex financing, while avoiding projects ending up as films without identity or integrity due to several investors wishing to intervene in the production.

The cultural and linguistic affinities within the Scandinavian countries naturally makes collaboration across borders simpler, and there are a some examples of tight creative bonds between Denmark and Sweden, such as Bille August's collaboration with Ingmar Bergman on *Best Intentions* (1992, *Den goda viljan*) or Danish director Susanne Bier's collaboration with Swedish scriptwriter Jonas Gardell on *Like It Never Was Before* (1995, *Pensionat Oskar*) and *Once in a Lifetime* (2000, *Hånden på hjertet*). In terms of the practical aspects of transnational filmmaking, the majority of directors and producers mostly see possibilities in learning from foreign working methods, though problems may also arise from different approaches even on a Scandinavian level—as, for instance, pointed out by the Danish director Morten Arnfred, who found noticeable differences in the working methods of Danish and Swedish crews when making the Danish major *Night Vision* (*Spor i mørket*) in 1997 (Hjort and Bondebjerg 2001, 162). The Danish producer Lise Lense-Møller also experienced language-related problems during the shooting of *The Magnetist's Fifth Winter* (Morten Henriksen, 1999, *Magnetisørens femte vinter*) due to the mix of Norwegians, Swedes, Danes, Icelanders, and Faeroese in the crew.

As is evident in the following analysis of the Danish coproductions of the 1990s, the notion of coproduction in some cases denotes a cultural and creative collaboration, while in other cases it primarily denotes a purely financial collaboration, making it impossible to determine whether the final film is a transnational coproduction or a strictly nationally financed film.

DANISH COPRODUCTIONS OF THE 1990s

As mentioned above, the number of coproductions rose significantly in the 1990s. It naturally took a few years for the political changes of 1989 to have an impact on the production form, but as early as 1991, the

Table 5.1
Number of coproductions in the 1990s

	1990	1991	1992	1993	1994	1995	1996	1997	1998	1999	Total
Majors	1	6	3	5	6	4	10	8	12	6	61
Minors	1	7	9	6	5	4	1	7	2	4	46
Total	2	13	12	11	11	8	11	15	14	10	107

Source: Based on statistical material from the Danish Film Institute, *Facts and Figures* 1991–2000.

changes were evident (see table 5.1). Though the number of coproduced films per year varies somewhat, there were all together many more coproductions made in the 1990s than in any other decade in Danish film.[10]

Tables 5.2 and 5.3 show how Sweden has been the preferred coproduction partner, being involved in 84 percent of the Danish majors and producing more than half of the Danish minors. Denmark's other Nordic neighbor, Norway, takes a strong second place.[11]

The Danish coproductions of the 1990s share some common traits when it comes to budget, choice of actors, setting, locations, language, and so on. Choices in cast and language are especially interesting because these are the features that reveal most clearly to the audience that a film has been coproduced. At the same time, it is a very tangible expression of the internationalization of Danish cinema.

The majority of the films fall into the drama genre. However, when considered in terms of the coproducing countries, the size of the budget, the language spoken, and the setting of the stories (historical vs. contemporary), the films fall into four major categories: the big-budget international film, the historical Nordic film, the contemporary Nordic film, and the cofinanced national film. Though these four broad categories are more rigid than the films themselves (and as a result, one could argue that some films fit into more than one), the categories are useful for examining the major trends of the Danish coproductions in the 1990s.

Big-Budget International Coproductions

The opportunity to find substantial financing abroad through coproducing has made it possible for the Danish film industry to make films

Table 5.2
Participation from other countries in Danish majors

Sweden	Norway	Germany	Finland	France	Iceland	Italy	Holland	England	US
51	28	12	6	6	6	4	4	3	3

Source: Facts and Figures 1991–2000.
Note: Countries involved in only one major: Costa Rica, the Faeroe Islands, Greenland, Poland, Portugal, and Russia.

Table 5.3
Origin of major production company of Danish minors

Sweden	Norway	Iceland	Germany	England	Finland	France	India	Poland
25	10	4	2	1	1	1	1	1

Source: Facts and Figures 1991–2000.

with bigger budgets. These films are usually shot in English, have co-producing partners outside of the Nordic countries, and as a result try to appeal to a large, international market.

The most remarkable productions made on big budgets (on a Danish scale, that is) and aimed at an international (art cinema) market are Lars von Trier's *Europa* (1991; DKr 22 million), *Breaking the Waves* (1996; DKr 43 million), and *Dancer in the Dark* (2000; DKr 98.7 million). In matters of production, von Trier's films have been suited for coproduction with their foreign locations, multinational casts, and use of the English language. The worldwide success of his films show that the stories have relevance to people of many nationalities.[12] Von Trier was the only director making international films on this scale in Denmark in the 1990s. Another Danish director, Bille August, made his expensive productions, *House of the Spirits* (1993, *Åndernes hus*) and *Smilla's Sense of Snow* (1997, *Frøken Smillas fornemmelse for sne*), outside the country as German majors with some financial support from Denmark. Having obvious bankable elements such as famous stars, best-seller story lines, high production value, and impressive special effects, the films are hard to distinguish from regular Hollywood films.

On a smaller scale, a few other Danish majors in English were made, all of which had obvious reasons for being made in English, as the stories were set outside of Denmark. The films of Lars von Trier were situated in Cairo, central Europe, Scotland, and the United States, while other stories took place in Poland (*The Island on Bird Street,* Søren Kragh-Jacobsen, 1997, *Øen i Fuglegaden*), Costa Rica (*A Scent of Paradise,* Peter Ringgaard, 1997, *Et hjørne af paradis*), and partially in Russia (*The Russian Singer,* Morten Arnfred, 1993, *Den russiske sangerinde*). The foreign locations made the choice of English seem natural to a Danish audience, but even with a logical blend of languages, English-language majors—with the exception of von Trier's—have had a hard time at the Danish box office.

From the outset, the national audience seems to have had less interest in Danish films made in non-Nordic languages, and the rare, illogical combinations of Danish stories shot in English were poorly received by critics and audiences alike. One could choose to accept the seemingly odd choice of language in Gabriel Axel's ambitious adaptation of Saxo's story of Hamlet, *The Prince of Jutland* (1996, *Prinsen af Jylland*) because of famous actors like Helen Mirren and Gabriel Byrne and the historical distance to the mythical story. But it seems absurd when English actors pronounce local names and places with an accent and Danish actors speak English in Copenhagen during World War II in *A Day in October* (Kenneth Madsen, 1991, *En dag i oktober*).

All in all, few Danish big-budget international coproductions were made in the 1990s, and only von Trier and August successfully found an audience domestically and internationally. However, following the international success of the Dogma films and popular national films, a remarkable number of other directors have made English-language big-budget films premiering in 2002–3, such as Ole Bornedal with *I am Dina* (2002, *Dina*), Lone Scherfig with *Wilbur Wants to Kill Himself* (2002, *Wilbur begår selvmord*), Thomas Vinterberg with *It's All about Love* (2003), Søren Kragh-Jacobsen with *Skagerrak* (2003), and Nicolas Winding Refn with *Fear X* (2003). However, these ambitious productions have generally found a much smaller national audience than expected, despite the recent national success of the directors.[13]

The significant number of Danish directors wanting to shoot films in English provoked a discussion in 2000 about the principles of the DFI financing foreign-language Danish films, since the expensive productions drain the funding for films telling Danish stories in Danish and targeted primarily at the national audience. This dilemma of the relationship between nurturing the national film culture and becoming a player on the international film scene will be salient for Danish film in the years to come.[14]

Historical Nordic Coproductions

Except for von Trier's films, the coproductions with budgets exceeding DKr 25 million were mostly historical dramas cofinanced with other Nordic countries and based on a literary source or on the life of a well-known person. The films normally mixed popular actors from the Scandinavian countries to tell stories that all countries could connect with. In most cases, some kind of input from the coproducing Scandinavian countries can therefore be spotted on the screen.[15]

Historically, the successful *Hunger* set an example for this type of coproduction, adapting a literary classic, set in historical time, and casting a mix of Scandinavian actors. Films from the 1990s using this recipe include the Danish majors *Hamsun* (Jan Troell, 1996, DKr 34.4 million), *Barbara* (Niels Malmros, 1997, DKr 34 million), and *The Magnetist's Fifth Winter* (DKr 32 million). Most historical Nordic coproductions have cast native-speaking actors to avoid problems of comprehension and questions of authenticity. In his two Swedish majors, *Best Intentions* and *Jerusalem* (1996), Bille August chose an all-Swedish cast instead of using some Danish actors in the Swedish story. Bo Widerberg made the same choice in his Danish major *All Things Fair* (1996, *Lærerinden*), which consequently did not have anything Danish on the screen but did have a primarily Danish crew behind the camera. As a result, this officially Danish film performed much better in Sweden than in Denmark (475,620 vs. 75,045 tickets sold), since the Swedes were familiar with the director, the two leading stars, the locations, and, not least, the language.

Hamsun is one of the few examples of a film that has successfully cast actors against their natural language. The film, which is directed by the Swede Jan Troell, tells the story of the last years in the life of the Norwegian author Knut Hamsun. The internationally acclaimed Swedish actor Max von Sydow was chosen to play the title role, and the well-known Danish actress Ghita Nørby was cast as his Norwegian wife. Each spoke his or her respective language, while their three children spoke Norwegian. In spite of this unnatural use of languages, the film won both critical and popular acclaim. However, there have been many complaints about other creative casting decisions, such as when in the Danish *Barbara*, the lead role was played in Norwegian by Anneke von der Lippe, or when actress Sofie Gråbøl in *Two Green Feathers* (1995, *Pan*) was the only Danish-speaking character in the Norwegian surroundings of Henning Carlsen's adaptation of Knut Hamsun's novel.

In the case of *The Magnetist's Fifth Winter*, it was decided early on that all actors (a mix of Swedes, Norwegians, and Danes) should speak their mother tongue to support the authenticity of the acting. The Swedish novel by Per Olov Enquist was based on the life of the Austrian magnetist Franz Anton Mesmer, but producer Lise Lense-Møller and director Morten Henriksen relocated the story from Austria to Sweden. Furthermore, by changing the magnetist's nationality to Danish, a number of obvious language problems were avoided. This means that while the town citizens speak Swedish or Norwegian, determined by the nationality of the actor (though held in one language within a family), the Danish actor Ole Lemmeke, playing the foreign magnetist, was able to speak Danish in a predominantly Swedish cast.[16]

There are several reasons for coproducing the historical Nordic stories. First of all, the films are typically more expensive than the average Danish film due to sets and costumes, which forces the producers to find foreign financing. Second, a mix of languages seems to be more acceptable in the historically set stories,[17] providing the producer and the director the opportunity of trying to attract the interest of audiences from several countries by casting a combination of national stars. The best seller or historical person on which the stories are based is normally also known within Scandinavia and thereby serves as a bankable element to attract several audiences as well as a sort of market survey, indicating that the plot can travel across borders. Furthermore, producers are more willing to risk money on material that is already popular, since scripts based on these existing sources are easier to present to potential coproducing partners. Of course, the perfect situation would be source material with inherent elements from several countries to make the Nordic collaboration appear natural on-screen.

These films are not tight creative and cultural collaborations; rather, the primary reason for these coproductions has been to raise the money needed to tell the historical stories and at the same time try to reach a bigger market by working together with Nordic partners. Most films have seemed natural to coproduce because of the source material, but of the resulting films only a few have been able to attract audiences outside the country of the major producer.

Contemporary Nordic Coproductions

Parallel with the production of expensive historical films, a series of cheaper Nordic films (normally less than DKr 15 million) telling contemporary stories were made. These films were typically based on original scripts and contained locations or characters/actors from other Nordic countries. Several of these films had stories entirely or partially situated in Sweden, such as *Bad Seed* (Carsten Fromberg, 1996, *Ondt Blod*) and *The Greatest Heroes* (Thomas Vinterberg, 1996, *De største helte*); in Iceland with *Wildside* (Simon Staho, 1998, *Vildspor*); in the Faeroe Islands (*Bye Bye Blue Bird,* Katrin Ottarsdottir, 1999); and in Greenland (*Heart of Light,* Jakob Grønlykke, 1998, *Lysets hjerte*), making it natural to find a coproducer in the country. The titles mentioned here date from 1996 on, and in general the late 1990s marked a shift from historical dramas toward more genre-inspired contemporary Danish cinema.

In a few cases, this geographical motivation extended beyond the Nordic countries. For instance, Danish characters traveled to Portugal (*Family Matters,* Susanne Bier, 1993, *Det blir i familien*) and Italy (*Katja's Adventure,* Lars Hesselholdt, 1999, *Falkehjerte*), but some of these traveling stories were criticized as being a mere excuse for achieving foreign funding. Some thought that *Family Matters* might as well have taken place in a remote part of Denmark, and film critics questioned whether the Danish-Swedish coproduction *The Big Dipper* (Birger Larsen, 1992, *Karlsvognen*) would have been a better film had the single mother in the story simply moved to another place in Denmark instead of moving to Sweden.

Some of these coproductions might have been to some extent artificially designed to contain elements from more countries to meet the demands of international funds. In this regard, adding a foreign character seems less complicated than changing the locations of the story, and quite a few Scandinavian characters have appeared in Danish majors, since the similarities in language make them rather easy to incorporate in contemporary stories. The primary exchange of actors has been between Denmark and Sweden. Swedish actors appear in bigger or smaller parts in Danish majors such as *Sophie* (Liv Ullmann, 1992,

Sofie), *The Great Day on the Beach* (Stellan Olsson, 1991, *Den store badedag*), *Credo* (Susanne Bier, 1997, *Sekten*), *The Man Who Would Live Forever* (Torben Skjødt Jensen, 1999, *Manden som ikke ville dø*), *I Wonder Who's Kissing You Now* (Henning Carlsen, 1998), *Gone with the Fish* (Lotte Svendsen, 1999, *Bornholms stemme*), and perhaps most memorably in *The Kingdom*, where Ernst-Hugo Järegård got to curse Denmark in Swedish from the roof of the state hospital in Copenhagen. In most cases, the Scandinavian visitors have spoken Danish with an accent to avoid dubbing or subtitling. This sometimes created peculiar situations, as when two Swedish actors speak to each other in Danish with Swedish accents in *Family Matters*.

As with the historical films, the motivation for coproducing the contemporary stories has primarily been to find additional financing and to attract interest in the film in other Nordic countries. Though, to a certain degree, actors have worked across borders, the outcome hasn't been the desired creation of inter-Nordic film stars, and often the mix of actors and languages has arguably disturbed the domestic audience more than it has helped sell the film in other countries.

Cofinanced National Productions

Where some of the Danish coproductions stand out as clear transnational productions with a mix of actors, language, and/or locations, others bear no mark of foreign participation on the screen. These cofinanced rather than coproduced films fall into a variety of genres and are usually cheaper productions that rarely premiere outside of Denmark. In some instances, there has been collaboration behind the camera, but the vast majority of these films are purely the result of cofinancing.

Producers sometimes agree to switch projects, investing in each other's national productions to be able to apply for international funding. Among the Danish majors cofinanced with Sweden, but with no sign of transnational collaboration, are *Body Switch* (Jørn Faurschou, 1995, *Farligt venskab*), *On Our Own* (Lone Scherfig, 1998, *Når mor kommer hjem*), *Baby Doom* (Peter Gren Larsen, 1998), and *The Twopenny Dance* (Hans Kristensen, 1999, *Klinkevals*). Germany has been involved in *Night Vision, Albert* (Jørn Faurschou, 1998), and *The Olsen Gang's Last Show* (Tom Hedegaard, 1998, *Olsen Bandens sidste stik*).[18]

Some Danish minors have significant Danish participation in front of or behind the camera, as when Danish directors like Bille August

(*The Best Intentions* and *Jerusalem*), Susanne Bier (*Freud Leaving Home*, 1990, *Freud flytter hjemmefra* and *Like It Never Was Before*), and Rumle Hamlerich (*Black Lucia*, 1992, *Sort Lucia*) have made films in Sweden. While some minors use Danish actors like Sofie Gråbøl in *The Isle of Darkness* (Trygve Allister Diesen, 1997, *Mørkets ø*) or Nicolaj Coster Waldau in *Misery Harbour* (Nils Gaup, 1999), others have no visible Danish input or technical personnel, such as Lukas Moodyson's *Show Me Love* (1999, *Fucking Åmål*) or the Norwegian comedy *Junk Mail* (Pål Sletaune, 1997).

The genre of animation is unique with regard to coproductions. Some animated films like *Hans Christian Andersen and the Long Shadow* (Jannik Hastrup, 1998, *H. C. Andersen og den skæve skygge*) are based on national stories, but most films have international potential from the outset due to the absence of actors and lifelike locations. The films' visual environment travels well, and the films are easily dubbed. With the exception of one film (*The Snooks*, Jørgen Vestergaard, 1992, *Snøvsen*), all Danish animation films of the 1990s were coproduced, but interestingly—as with the live-action films—they did much better in their national markets than abroad even though they were dubbed.[19]

The 1990s: A Decade of Coproduction

Successes among the Danish coproductions in the 1990s have been rare, though some of the historical Nordic films like *Hamsun*, *Barbara*, and *The Magnetist's Fifth Winter* have achieved artistic acknowledgment, and von Trier has managed to maintain his unique style in spite of the extensive coproduction apparatus and the many often conflicting interests of investors in his films. The performances at the box office of the historical Nordic films have varied; however, none of them performed remotely close to that of the most popular national films. Part of the explanation is of course the overall quality of the films or the fact that the drama genre traditionally does not have the same appeal as other genres (for example, the comedy and thriller). Another important reason may very well be that the films, in trying to contain a little something for everyone, have ended up with a less distinct profile for audiences in different countries. The Danish audience has preferred Danish productions to be in Danish all through the decade, which might indicate that cofinancing on a long-term basis is the best solution unless intercultural political ambitions get in the way.

"SCANDINAVIAZATION" BEFORE INTERNATIONALIZATION

In general, the 1990s was a fruitful decade for Danish cinema, with new ideas in terms of film policy, the production and marketing of film, and a pluralistic film output of both popular local comedies and genre-inspired films from a new generation of filmmakers as well as films with the ability to interest audiences abroad, like those of Lars von Trier and his Dogma brotherhood. This breadth of Danish cinema was much indebted to the dualistic political approach to Danish film, supporting both artistic *and* commercial films on a national *as well as* an international scale. The significant rise in the number of coproductions can be seen as partly a result of this new strategy, and the coproductions have marked the film output of the 1990s, especially through the emergence of expensive Nordic and international films. However, the larger budgets only occasionally resulted in critical praise and bigger audiences, and one can argue that the coproduction mode had greater impact on the industry and the quantity of films than on the quality of the films produced and thereby on the audience.

Except for Lars von Trier's films, the coproductions have generally performed disappointingly at the box office, while the much cheaper and national-appearing (not to mention effectively branded) Dogma films, such as *The Celebration* and *The Idiots*, have had success both domestically and internationally. Coproduction is not a magical answer to all problems, but it can be the best or sole solution for individual films. Judging from the many coproductions that never found an audience outside their domestic market, it is becoming increasingly clear that cofinancing and codistribution might be the best way to successfully cross borders in the near future.[20]

From an economic point of view, coproduction has obvious advantages, and transnational funding schemes have been lucrative for Danish films. The European educational programs and the making of transnational films have contributed to qualifying Danish film professionals and creating important networks. In terms of quantity, the political intent to promote European and Nordic collaboration has resulted in several coproductions of great importance to the industry. However, in terms of quality, many of the films have not been very well received, and the audience seems to prefer national films.

From a "culture-building" standpoint, it is hard to say what influence, if any, the coproductions might have had on creating a European or Nordic feeling of identity and belonging, since such fundamental reflections are difficult to measure and normally happen over a long period of time. But one can conclude that cultural and creative reasons only seldom have been the incentive for coproducing. Economic arguments have carried greater weight, but in fact there have been few examples of the much-criticized "Europudding" or "Nordic puddings" that carry a confusion of cultural compromises and thereby lack an inherent, particular identity.

On top of the financial support from transnational funds, foreign film institutes, and production and distribution companies, Danish films have collected considerable support from regional funds, especially in Sweden and Germany, often with the stipulation that the money be spent in the region to further its industry and trade. As a result, a number of Danish films have been shot in the Swedish studios and landscapes of Trollhättan,[21] and from a trade political point of view, it is regrettable when Danish productions "leave" the country. The increasing mobility of Danish film productions as a result of foreign financial support can be seen as an example of the diminished significance of national borders on the film industry. Furthermore, when other European countries have region-based trade-oriented funding schemes, Denmark may be forced to follow suit to keep productions within the country. The founding of a Danish trade-oriented film fund was widely discussed in the 1990s but never established, and the few existing Danish regional funds still have only moderate means at their disposal.

The statistics for transnational collaboration in the 1990s appear impressive, but in reality Danish coproductions have primarily been in collaboration with the nearest neighbors and with Scandinavia as a base. One might speak of a *scandinaviazation* rather than an internationalization of the films. With the founding of the Nordic Film and TV Fund, collaboration between Nordic countries was systematized, and in regard to Eurimages's requirement of a minimum of two coproducing countries, it seemed obvious to turn to the most familiar neighboring markets.

However, as a whole, increased cross-national cooperation has broadened horizons and given Danish filmmaking an appreciable boost. Danish filmmakers have, so to speak, attended a sort of *coproduction school* in the 1990s, acquiring important knowledge of international work methods, financing mechanisms, market premises, and audience preferences. Directors and producers alike have gained the knowledge and confidence necessary to try their hands at larger productions abroad, as illustrated by the many English-language premieres in 2002–3. In that way, the decade was a transitional phase, preparing for the leap into larger international films through primarily Nordic coproductions.

The increasing number of coproductions naturally makes it harder to clearly define what signifies a Danish film or Danish cinema as a whole, since the borders are, in a figurative sense, disintegrating, and the films' nationality becomes a legal term rather than an inherent cultural identity. In light of the much-discussed internationalization straining small national film cultures, the 1990s represented a growth period for Danish cinema, as it earned both national and international recognition. As mentioned above, this recognition is the result of the interplay of many different aspects, of which coproduction is only one—but the one that most clearly shows the international ambitions and the many ways in which Danish films, visibly and invisibly, broke the borders in the 1990s.

NOTES

1. The 1950s saw the production of U.S.-Danish action B films by Sidney Pink, such as *Reptilicus* (1961). With the legalization of porn in 1969, a number of soft-core porn films were coproduced, especially with the United States, on Danish grounds, such as *The Birthday Party* (1971, *Liderlige Lisbeth*) and *The Sinful Dwarf* (1974, *Dværgen*). Gabriel Axel pioneered international coproduction with France in the episode film *Amour* (1970), having one of the three stories on the nature of love played in French. Henning Carlsen shot *A Happy Divorce* (*En lykkelig skilsmisse*) with French actors in France in 1975.
2. Part of the information in the following is based on interviews with a number of significant people in the film industry. Among them are the producers Per Holst, Erik Crone, Lise Lense-Møller, and Ulrik Bolt Jørgensen as well as representatives from the Scandinavian Film Institutes, Eurimages, and the Nordic Film and TV Fund.
3. The protectionist approach existed in a very limited number of areas in the 1990s, for example, through support to a small selection of art cinema theaters. However, the protectionist idea comes into play indirectly through trade and cultural-political initiatives with the purpose of promoting the European film and media industry and a European identity.
4. Until January 1, 1998, a minimum of three members had to be involved in a production in order to obtain support; the requirement was reduced to two members

and a distribution agreement with a third member.
5. Based on information from the Danish Media Desk and Eurimages.
6. Before 1994, the fund required coproduction between at least two Nordic countries.
7. The fund's requirements of foreign theatrical distribution and broadcasting have also contributed to earlier (at the preproduction stage) commitment from the broadcasters.
8. In 1980–84 the average Danish film budget was DKr 4.2 million, compared to 1995–99, when this had risen to DKr 12.3 million.
9. For example, in Sweden in the 1990s there were quotas for artistic participation, set at a minimum of 20 percent Swedish. Von Trier's *Europa* (1991) is an example of illogical maneuvers to fulfill quotas. The production company Zentropa flew in extras from France to fulfill demands attached to the French money (Andersen 1997, 347).
10. The number of minors may be even higher, as minors not receiving state funding do not necessarily figure in the statistics from the DFI. There is, however, no reason to believe that these films would change the geographical distribution significantly.
11. The total number of table 5.2 is not identical with the number of Danish majors, as there can be more minor countries involved in one production.
12. Interestingly, even a "national" Dogma film like *The Idiots* (Lars von Trier, 1998, *Idioterne*), which seems 100 percent Danish on the screen, found several international coproducers (in Germany, France, Italy, the Netherlands, and Sweden) due to von Trier's fame in the art cinema circuit—and probably also due to the production company Zentropa's impressive number of subsidiary companies outside of Denmark.
13. The Dogma films *The Celebration* (1998, *Festen*) by Thomas Vinterberg and *Mifune* (1999, *Mifunes sidste sang*) by Søren Kragh-Jacobsen found a large national audience, and Lone Scherfig's Dogma comedy *Italian for Beginners* (2000, *Italiensk for begyndere*) ended up being one of the best-selling films of the previous years at the Danish box office, with 818,835 admissions. Ole Bornedal made a name for himself with the highly popular thriller *Nightwatch* (1994, *Nattevagten*, remade by Bornedal in the United States in 1998), and Nicolas Winding Refn's debut *Pusher* (1996) and the related *Bleeder* (1999) gave him a reputation as one of the exciting names of a new generation in Denmark as well as abroad.
14. The DFI and the Ministry of Cultural Affairs have tried to deal with this issue in the agreement for the film political objective of 2003–6, stating that of the eighty to one hundred films to be produced in the period, sixty-five to eighty are to be in Danish, while fifteen to twenty-five are to be foreign-language, international coproductions with Danish participation.
15. Due to fewer coproductions with Finland and Iceland and the differences in language, the input on-screen has primarily been Norwegian and Swedish, and the majority of coproductions are predominantly Scandinavian rather than Nordic.
16. Historically, the mix of Swedish and Norwegian can be explained by the many Norwegian settlements in the Swedish town Umeå at the time of the story.
17. That linguistic authenticity is less important to historical films is, for instance,

mentioned by former director of the DFI Bo Christensen in connection with a case study of the large-scale children's film *Eye of the Eagle* (Peter Flinth, 1997, *Ørnens øje*) (Finney 1998, 90). One of the reasons for this is probably the Scandinavian countries' shared language and past as one country: the distance of history contributing to blurring the distinctions of nation, at least in the minds of the audience.

18. Some producers also invest in foreign productions expected to do well in their territory, which explains the German money in the thirteenth and last film about the unlucky criminal gang Olsen Banden, whose endeavors in the films from 1968 to 1981 had a fair amount of success in the German market.
19. The Danish hits *Amazon Jack* (Flemming Quist Møller, 1993, *Jungledyret Hugo*) and *Amazon Jack Is Back* (Flemming Quist Møller, 1996, *Jungledyret Hugo—den store filmhelt*) sold 362,298 and 237,518 tickets in Denmark, but only 15,860 and 70,794 in Sweden.
20. That the focus in the NFTF in 1994 shifted from coproductions per se to distribution agreements across the Nordic borders clearly illustrates the wish that Nordic films be watched outside of the domestic market; too many Nordic coproductions in the 1990s never found an audience outside their native country. As proven by the Nordic coproduction year 1991–92—with a joint effort at the Cannes film festival, where five films were launched as "the largest Nordic coproduction project ever"—coproduction is of no use if the films are not followed up by concentrated distribution efforts.
21. The Swedish Film i Väst fund gives grants on the condition that 1.5 times the amount is spent in the region. The shooting of *Dancer in the Dark* in Trollhättan, Trollywood in colloquial language should have contributed DKr 10–15 million in profits to the region (Rosenkrands 2000, 25–27).

WORKS CITED

Andersen, Jesper. 1997. "I lommerne på Europa: Internationaliseringen af dansk filmproduktion." In *Dansk film, 1972–97*, ed. Ib Bondebjerg, Jesper Andersen, and Peter Schepelern, 332–65. Copenhagen: Munksgaard/Rosinante.
Bondebjerg, Ib, Jesper Andersen, and Peter Schepelern, eds. 1997. *Dansk film, 1972–97*. Copenhagen: Munksgaard/Rosinante.
Camre, Henning. 1998. "En ny æra i dansk film." *Dansk film* 4, no. 9: 32–33.
Dale, Martin. 1992. *Europa Europa: Developing the European Film Industry*. Paris: Academie Carat.
Facts and Figures. 1991–2000. Copenhagen: Danish Film Institute.
Finney, Angus. 1998. *A Snapshot of Nordic Cinema*. Oslo: Nordic Film and TV Fund.
Hjort, Mette, and Ib Bondebjerg. 2001. *The Danish Directors*. Portland: Intellect.
Hjort, Mette, and Scott MacKenzie. 2000. *Cinema and Nation*. London: Routledge.
Nielsen, Elsebeth Gerner. 1998. Press release, August 25.
Rosenkrands, Jacob. 2000. "Fremskredne planer om et dansk Hollywood på Fyn." *Ugebrevet mandag morgen* October 23, 25–28.
Stenderup, Thomas. 1998. "Tørre tal." *Dansk film* 2, no. 9: 8–13.

CHAPTER 6

Art or Industry?
Battles over Finnish Cinema during the 1990s

Mervi Pantti

Film is both culture and an industry in its own right. Yet it seems that in the eyes of governmental bodies film is a peculiar hybrid, for it is not considered to be either culture or industry. It is not really culture, which has traditionally been supported by the state. Money invested in cinema is not used for building monuments or facilities; rather every cent is spent on actual content. Hence attaining the same type of understanding and support that is given to older, more traditional forms of culture is a difficult task for cinema. Yet neither is cinema really an industry, in the sense that once you have a ready prototype, and maybe even big investments from the state, you are essentially guaranteed market-based profits. When speaking of cinema as industry, the prototype is always an integral part of the finished product; therefore the risks are always great—especially in a small market area like Finland. Cinema is an art form that also has inseparable industrial elements. Consequently, cinema should be seen as a site of possibility, where relatively small-scale investment by the state can create effects that are not economically insignificant, and which can have profound cultural importance. (Astala 2003)

In the first 2003 issue of *SESinfo,* a publication of the Finnish Film Foundation (Suomen elokuvasäätiö), the foundation's chief of production, Erkki Astala, expresses his consternation about the Finnish government's inability to understand the twofold nature of cinema: as both art and industry. His comments identify a key aspect of the film industry in Finland and more widely in the Nordic countries. Nordic cinema has not turned out to be a profitable branch of the nation-state's industrial tree, although many films have won awards at international film festivals, and individual films have earned sizable profits in the highly competitive international arena. As a result, Nordic cinema requires sustained state support in order to survive. In the name of national culture and the vitality of the cinema, this has become a widely accepted fact, albeit underwritten by varying financial contributions in different contexts. An indication of the necessity of state support can be seen in the relation between production cost and audience size. In Finland, for example, only a few films cover their production expenses with box office receipts. A film needs approximately 100,000 viewers simply to cover its production costs; scaled by size, if released in the United States this would mean a film would need to reach an audience of 5 million viewers—or make US$50 million in box office receipts—to cover production costs. Since the 1960s, few Finnish films had crossed this magical line until the recent Finnish film boom, which began in 1999. In that year, four domestic films attracted more than 200,000 viewers.

The development of the film industry in Finland, as in other Nordic countries, has been difficult and uncertain, with problems usually attributed to small national markets and U.S. domination. The variety of contradictory and sometimes highly controversial views on how national support for the cinema should be organized, and what types of film should receive support, has also hampered the stabilization of Nordic national cinemas. The history of Finnish cinema during the last forty years reflects these problems; this history can be seen as having a wavelike motion, with national cinema flowing through peaks from one trough to another. By the late 1960s the Finnish New Wave had come about, and the government had taken its first steps toward funding cinema: state film prizes were established to support national films, with the aim of cultivating an artistically more ambitious and economically more secure Finnish cinema. These hopes were crushed by 1974, when only two films were made in Finland, both of them popular comedies. At the same time, dreams of reaching a harmonious consensus on state funding for national cinema collapsed when the state committee for cinema appointed in 1970 became mired in disagreement, and political conflicts between cultural and business interests made further work impossible.

As a consequence of these struggles, the Finnish Film Foundation, which had been established in 1969, was reorganized and taken under government control. In 1977 the foundation began to function under parliamentary oversight, which in practice meant that the government would nominate the foundation's members and in so doing consider both political contingencies and cinema organizations' interests, attempting to maintain equal representation of both. Since then, the Finnish Film Foundation has been the only organization to receive state appropriations for the support of cinema production. Although political conflicts continued to figure in the foundation's activities throughout the 1980s, the reorganization of the foundation assured the rise of Finnish film production from its nadir in the 1970s to its present numbers—approximately ten feature films annually. The foundation enjoyed a large increase in support during the 1980s, as appropriations granted to the foundation quadrupled from roughly Fmk 10 million in 1980 to more than Fmk 40 million by 1990. However, the recession and bank crisis that Finland underwent during the early 1990s diminished funding; film subsidies were continually cut back through the mid-1990s, leading Finnish cinema into another crisis. In addition to decreasing subsidies, audiences also decreased in size. The national media blamed the Finnish Film Foundation for destroying Finnish cinema with wrongheaded production policies. It was not until Jouni Mykkänen took over as managing director in 1995 that production politics were stabilized and the heated discussion of cinema politics cooled down.

The purpose of this chapter is to look at the factors that contributed to the birth of the much-celebrated boom in Finnish film at the turn of the millennium. I will concentrate in particular on changes in the political discourse of Finnish cinema during the 1990s. The balance between art and industry, national and international, has always been at the center of Finnish cinema's political discourse. The conventionally stable factor in these debates has been the assumption that Finnish cinema is chiefly a constituent element of national identity, a crucial anchor point for national culture. By contrast, discussions about economic growth and international distribution are two new elements that were introduced into discussions of Finnish cinema during the 1990s. These issues have become prominent at the same time that state funding of cinema has been criticized for other reasons. Complaints heard from participants working in the field of cinema over unfair politics and insufficient governmental subsidies have also received regular attention in the media. These criticisms reprise those of an earlier era, the studio era of Finnish cinema, 1920–60, when the fight against parsimonious government was also prominent; during that period, the big production companies attributed the lack of state support to an "attitude problem." During the last few decades the Finnish Film Foundation has taken the same line of argument in its calls for increased funding from the state.

STATE AND CINEMA IN FINLAND

"There is no art form which is self-sufficient. Therefore it is only natural that the state should subsidize the cinema" (*Suomen kinolehti* 1938, 258).

In Finland, as in the Nordic context, it has been "natural" for the state to subsidize film production—but only since the 1960s and never in a volume that would fully satisfy the film industry or film-policy decision makers. However, since the arrival of television and the collapse of the studio system in the early 1960s, production subsidy has been nothing less than a lifeline for national cinema.

State intervention in the cultural field is usually justified from one of two distinct points of departure. On the one hand, the rationale can be *cultural*, in which case the nation's image, identity, and values are concerned. Especially significant factors are then ones that can be seen as sustaining national values and cultural traditions, elements that are significant for national identity. This point of departure for state intervention is often connected with the notion that culture cannot be left at the mercy of market forces, because doing so would ultimately lead to lower-quality cultural products and hence the deterioration of national identity. The other starting point sanctioning state intervention is an *economic* one. The economic grounds for state intervention are often connected with either internal or external threats—for example, a recession in the national cultural industry or the perceived dominance of foreign cultural products in the domestic market. During the last few years in western Europe, the economic starting point has increasingly been yoked to hopes of economic growth—that is, helping culture not merely to survive but to flourish economically—as states have begun to accept arguments about the benefits of domestic cultural industries that are internationally competitive and are hence a source of job creation, for example. As a result, states have taken measures to ensure that some of the capital spent on funding the cultural industry sector stays within the nation-state and the companies in question based within the state's borders. In Denmark, for example, "national"

Art or Industry?

films made in English—which may prove competitive with Hollywood cinema in domestic and international distribution—can receive state subsidies (see chapters 4 and 5).

Finnish cinema policy has been shaped by the art/industry controversy since the 1920s, when film producers began fighting against the taxation of cinema, which they thought was unreasonable. At the time, cinema was primarily categorized as entertainment, much like the itinerant circuses of the day, and was thus heavily taxed. Between this early period and the present, one can identify three periods of film policy (1917–60, 1961–76, 1977–), which are categorized according to the state's changing attitude toward cinema, whether neglectful, exploitative, or supportive (Pantti 2000). Over the course of these periods the film industry's main argument for state funding has remained largely unchanged, namely, that cinema figures significantly in the expression of national identity and is thus worthy of support. However, the contemporary era of art/industry controversy must be seen in a new macroeconomic context in comparison with previous eras, especially the second one, during which the subsidy of domestic film production became a part of the welfare state's general cultural policy, and cinema was finally accepted among the established arts. During the second period, 1961–76, the crucial question was what kind of film was to be subsidized. The state subsidized only cinema that was deemed to be at an "artistically high level" (*Valtioneuvoston päätös valtion elokuvapalkintojen jakamisesta* 1962, § 3). This policy led to the emergence of a division between art and nonart cinema, which ultimately led to a split between state-subsidized art film and popular cinema that catered to the public's taste. This art/industry division should also be understood in relation to an ideological shift that occurred among the Western capitalist states during the 1970s, which resulted in a movement away from planned economies and welfare politics toward market-oriented policy. This ideological movement has had a clear impact on cultural institutions and organizations supporting the national arts. As Jim McGuigan has observed, the public sector is now expected to function in a pseudo-capitalistic way (1996, 63).

This new context has not meant that state financial support has diminished in significance, or even become questionable, even if film production relying heavily on state support has been strongly criticized in European cinema discourse during the 1990s. Instead, this new context has altered the rationale for state support, as the ideological separation between art and industry has lost some of its importance since the 1980s. Indeed, it seems that the emergent trend reprises some of the arguments made during the 1920s and 1930s—namely, that cinema is a good investment for the national economy. This view of economic gain is emphasized in the *Objectives for the National Cinema* program of the Finnish Film Foundation: "The economic importance of the audiovisual sector is constantly increasing. Worldwide, most jobs will be created in this sector. The European audiovisual market has been one of the fastest-growing sectors during the last few years. Growth is expected to continue, and the money consumers spend on audiovisual products is predicted to double during the next five years" (*Suomalaisen elokuvan tavoiteohjelma* 1999).

A key element in statements of European cultural policy during the 1990s was the prediction that culture and art in general would increase in direct economic value. Culture is now thought to bring along many economic advantages: companies, jobs, and—in cooperation with the tourist industry—travel income. In order to cultivate culture's direct economic value, it is argued, culture needs to be marketed more effectively, to be properly "commodified." This new era of cultural policy can be clearly seen in a Finnish Ministry of Education report from the early 1990s, which argues vigorously against the conventional art concept and the distinctions that it instantiates. In this conventional model, high art furnishes the standard, and the cultural policy of the welfare state is judged, guided, and enacted from above by a cadre of technocrats who view things from the standpoint of high culture. This policy loses its effectiveness in a new era of cultural policy, according to the report: "The cultural oppositions which previously guided one's perception and thinking are losing their importance. It is harder and harder to find justification or grounds for thinking only of oppositions such as high culture/popular culture, art/entertainment, national/international, center/periphery, rural/urban, etc." (*Kupoli* 1992, 29–30).

This criticism is especially concerned with citizens' personal choices and lifestyles, which were thought to have received short shrift in earlier forms of cultural policy that valued the "general good" more highly. In the 1992 report, the state is seen primarily as an organizer and financial provider; it significantly aims at abolishing the power of the state to make evaluative judgments about "cultural worth." Like the arguments made before the 1960s, this argument also maintains that subsidies from the state should be greater and more widely used.

However, there is something new and contradictory in comparison with earlier arguments. An implication of these new policy statements is the notion that the "dependency culture" of the arts must be diminished, which can occur by strengthening the notion that culture is a for-profit industry. Hence, "traditional culture and art institutions have a lot to learn from the economic sector and its marketing departments" (*Kupoli* 1992, 15).

It is intriguing that this discourse of art as a dependency culture has wrapped its tentacles around governmental cultural policy and cinema policy. In the early 1990s, cinema policy as guided by the managing director of the Finnish Film Foundation, Marianne Möller, articulated as one of its goals the strengthening of domestic production companies' position and the Europeanization of film production. This policy can be seen as an attack on the politics of cinema subsidy and ostensible dependency: "A functioning industry cannot cling to a subsidy system like a toddler to its mother's skirt. If a film does not reach viewers in its domestic arena, it is hardly a consolation that it has been a success in some festival far away. We cannot use festival achievements as our only argument when we need more money for production" (Möller 1995). With statements like this, Möller did not win undivided popularity in the film sector, but her views clearly had a "state function." That is, her rhetoric closely resembles that of the Ministry of Trade and Industry, which discusses the drawbacks of a state support system for the arts, maintaining that "healthy, long-term, innovative, and competitive business cannot be created under the control of a subsidy system" (Eriksson 1994, 43).

FINNISH FILM PRODUCTION DURING THE 1990s

The promotion of domestic film production and its distribution has been delegated to the Finnish Film Foundation, which at the present time receives an annual appropriation of about EUR 10 million; with this budget it must finance film, television, and video production and distribution, promote film culture, and support the export of Finnish film. The sum is used to subsidize about ten feature films and thirty-five shorts and documentaries. The Finnish Film Foundation is an independent foundation guided by the Ministry of Education's cultural policy sector. The Ministry of Education nominates members to the foundation's board of trustees, the board of trustees nominates the managing director of the foundation, and the managing director nominates the other members of the board and oversees their tasks. There is currently a law on promoting the cinema that dictates the parameters of the foundation's financial support (2000).

Film subsidies granted by the foundation are awarded on a discretionary basis, which in practice means that each project is evaluated according to established criteria. At the same time, automatic support is also distributed, but it is given on economic grounds related to the box office success of any given film. In the foundation, two people determine the funding for feature films: as stated in the Web pages of the Finnish Film Foundation, head of production Erkki Astala is responsible for films that "primarily strive for quality as independent films," and production adviser Olli Soinio works with films that "aim to find a wide national audience" (http://www.ses.fi). This division of labor shows that Finnish production is split more clearly than ever into two production genres, "artistic" and "popular."

In addition to the public financial support from the film foundation, the other pillar of funding for national cinema is television sales. The Finnish Film Foundation and the public service broadcasting company YLE signed a contract in 1984 governing presale of domestic films supported by the foundation, guaranteeing that films that had received support would appear on national television. In the early 1990s, the major commercial television company MTV3 signed a similar contract. During the 1990s coproductions with television companies also became more common. Although television has undoubtedly diminished the audience figures for the national cinema in theaters, it has also increased the audience overall; films that do not have success in theaters may reach hundreds of thousands of viewers when shown on television.

The simultaneous role of the Finnish Film Foundation as a promoter and a guide for Finnish film cannot be overemphasized; no film project can be realized without production support from the foundation. The foundation gives money for *scriptwriting* (a maximum of EUR 8,500 per film); for *development*—for example, for planning shooting and production (a maximum of EUR 100,000); for *support of preproduction* (a maximum of 70 percent of production expenses, or a maximum of EUR 700,000); and for *marketing and distribution purposes* (a maximum of EUR 70,000). In addition to these forms of subsidy, the foundation can grant *postproduction support*. To be eligible for this sup-

Table 6.1
Financing of Finnish films, 2001 (budget total EUR 14 million)

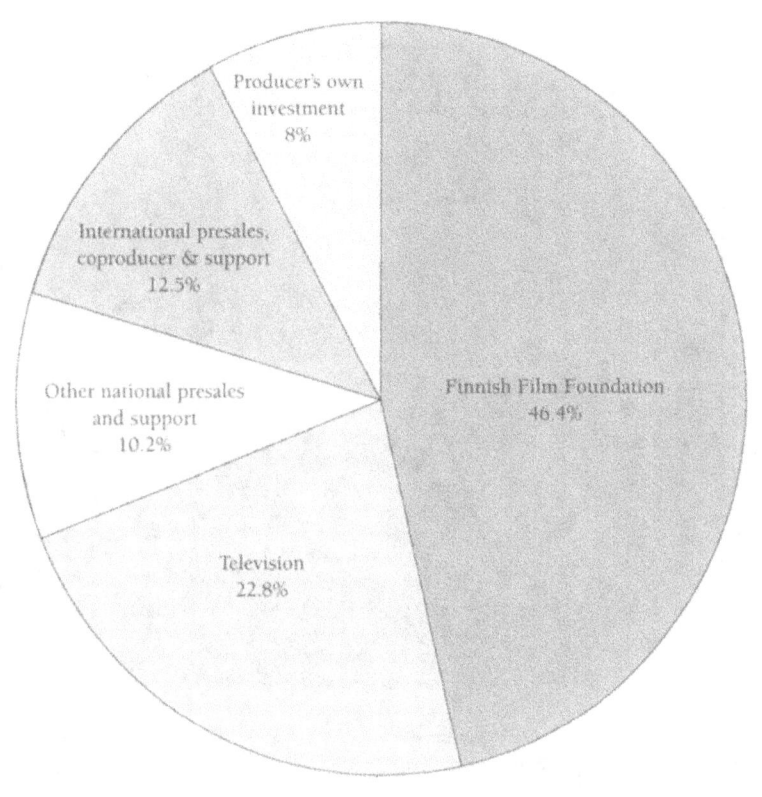

Source: Erkki Astala, Finnish Film Foundation.

port (EUR 3.50 per ticket sold), films must reach an audience of at least 45,000 viewers during their first year of domestic exhibition. This support is capped at 350,000; if the foundation has granted the film pre-production support, the two subsidies together cannot exceed EUR 700,000.

The reorganization of the Finnish Film Foundation at the end of the 1970s had a stabilizing effect on Finnish film production. National film production has, since the rearrangement, remained more or less at

Table 6.2
Domestic films in Finland, 1991–2002

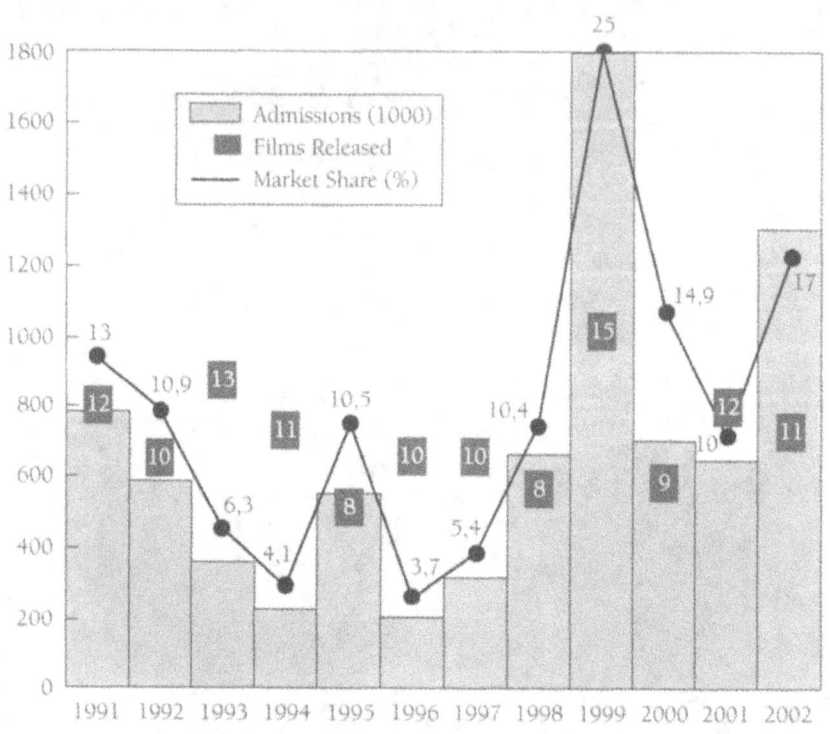

Source: Erkki Astala, Finnish Film Foundation.

the same level of production (approximately ten films per year). The number is fairly high considering Finland's population of 5 million. Moreover, one must remember that films imported from the United States increasingly dominate the market. The stabilization of production has not had any direct, instant effect on the number of viewers, however. Indeed, audience numbers decreased consistently from the late 1970s until the mid-1990s, when an all-time low was reached. The year 1994, generally described as a catastrophic one for Finnish cinema, saw domestic film's share of total viewers drop to 4 percent; in raw numbers, domestic film attracted only 200,000 viewers in 1994. By

Art or Industry?

contrast, in 1999 it accounted for 25 percent of all theater visits, which translated to 1.8 million viewers in total. In that year, four of the ten films with the highest number of viewers were Finnish: Olli Saarela's *Ambush (Rukajärven tie)*, Aleksi Mäkelä's *Wild Ones (Häjyt)*, Raimo Niemi's *Tommy and the Wildcat (Poika ja ilves)*, and Timo Koivusalo's *The Swan and the Wanderer (Kulkuri ja joutsen)*.

Stabilizing the number of films produced has not translated into a stabilization of production companies, however; this issue has been pivotal in cinema policy discussions. There are currently thirty domestic production companies concentrating on feature films. They all share a few characteristics: they are small (employing two to six people), they do not have significant financial resources at their disposal, their production of films is not regular, and they cannot bear large financial risks. Some ten of these companies can produce films consistently, which in practice means one film annually. Currently, the average production expense for a Finnish feature is around EUR 1 million. To illustrate the current state of production in Finland, it is helpful to compare the Finnish situation to the Danish one. Denmark, whose population and economy are roughly the same size as Finland's, produces more than twenty films annually, and these include films with budgets exceeding EUR 10 million. The financing of these films is made possible by foreign investment: Danish cinema is to a significant degree supported by film distributors and television companies of the big European states (see chapter 5). The foreign funding of Finnish films, at 12 percent, is still very modest compared to the other Nordic countries.

The domestic film industry, if it is defined in a traditional way, including production, distribution, and exhibition sectors, no longer exists in Finland. For example, in the crucial distribution sector, all the big companies are foreign. Hence it is more of a rule than an exception that outside the United States the film industry concept refers to a twofold system (Moran 1996, 7). Typically, the first element of this twofold system is an integration of the distribution and exhibition sectors, which is defined by its private economic interests. Domestic distribution and exhibition are hence closely connected with the big production companies in Hollywood (even when locally owned). The second element of the system is the state-supported national production sector. The distribution of Finnish films changed greatly in the 1990s; previously, films were distributed only by the Finnish Finnkino, but today all the biggest international distributors (FS-Filmi, UIP, Columbia Tristar Egmont, Buena Vista, and Sandrew Metronome) compete for the distribution rights of domestic films.

Although the system of vertical integration was never as important in Finland as it was in the United States, the major Finnish studios—or the "three majors," Suomen Elokuvateollisuus, Suomi-Filmi, and Fennada-Filmi—controlled the film trade in Finland before the 1960s. Structural change in Finnish film production dates to the late 1950s and early 1960s, when, in connection with the ideal of the European auteur-film, small director-led companies replaced the pro-

Table 6.3
Finnish feature film producers, 1996–2002

Company	Films
MRP MATILA 7 RÖHR PRODUCTIONS	6
DADA-FILMI / FENNADA-FILMI	5
ERE KOKKONEN OY	5
KINOPRODUCTION LTD.	5
SOLAR FILMS	5
ARTISTA FILMI	4
KINOTAR	4
MARIANNA FILMS	4
SPUTNIK	4
BLIND SPOT PICTURES	2
FANTASIAFILMI	2
FILMINOR	2
GNUFILMS	2
JÖRN DONNER PRODUCTIONS	2
KINOTAURUS	2
LASIHELMI FILMI	2
REPPUFILMI	2
VILLEALFA FILMPRODUCTIONS	2

Source: Erkki Astala, Finnish Film Foundation.

ducer-led studios, which had been based on a model dependent upon division of labor and segmented production. A movement away from the industrial model of production toward a cultural one took place. Unlike in Sweden, where Svensk Filmindustri (SF) has remained the largest film company for more than seventy-five years, in Finland the three majors of the studio era either went out of business or their production volume dropped to the same level as the small companies that emerged during the 1960s. Today, three types of production companies operate in Finland: production-led companies or "production houses" (for example, Matila and Röhr Productions and Solar Films); director-led companies, which produce films only by one particular director (for example, Artista Film and Villealfa Film Productions); and a middle ground between these two types of companies, which is covered by production companies committed to certain directors but not exclusively (for example, Kinotar).

Production companies and others in the film sector have unanimously agreed on one thing since the 1920s: the state does not offer sufficient support for national films. Even after recent restructuring of subsidy distribution, the slow growth of state contributions to the cinema industry has dominated discussion of film policy and issues related to it. Production companies, filmmakers, and members of the Finnish Film Foundation are particularly incensed about funding for comparative reasons: the other Nordic countries' cinema industries receive twice as much state funding. Erkki Astala and Jouni Mykkänen have in numerous interviews referred to the "Danish model," which has managed to sustain its success of the late 1980s by increasing the amount of public funding appropriated for the national cinema. The Finnish Film Foundation's *Objectives for the National Cinema* program, 2003–5, highlights the difference by calling for an increase in state funding that would bring state support up to the level of other Nordic countries (EUR 25 million). The program argues that an increase is necessary to sustain the boom in Finnish cinema that began in the late 1990s and to create a new "industrial era" to replace the one lost in the 1950s.

THE FINNISH FILM BOOM

While more funding is needed, the change that occurred in the late 1990s should not be overlooked. Titles of 1996 editorials in the maga-

Table 6.4
Film production in Nordic countries, 2001

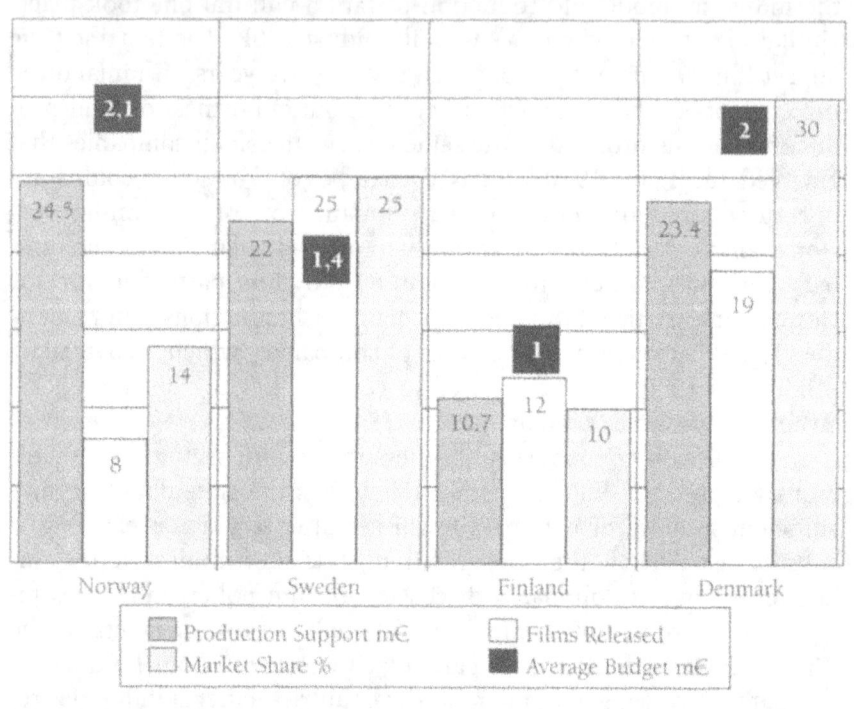

Source: Erkki Astala, Finnish Film Foundation.

zine *SESinfo* such as "We Are Witnessing a Turn of Events" and "Stronger Self-Esteem" reflect a conscious lifting of spirits in the film sector and also indicate that a difficult crisis of legitimacy had been overcome. The positive mood at the foundation was further strengthened by the fact that the state budget of 1997 included an added EUR 1.2 million of support for cinema. What's more, audience figures for national films at the end of the 1990s had increased markedly, leading to great public excitement about a "Finnish film boom." The national television reported on most national premieres, and audience figures for individual films were discussed in the daily newspapers in a way that further fed the boom: "*Gold Fever in Lapland* (Åke Lindman, *Lapin kullan kimallus*) Reaches 100,000 Viewers" (*Helsingin Sanomat* 1999) or "*Restless* (Aku Louhimies, *Levottomat*) Earns 1.5 Million Euros on Its Premiere Weekend" (*Helsingin Sanomat* 2000).

The Finnish film boom is a more complex phenomenon than simply an increase in audience figures for national films, however. The boom also marks the emergence of a positive attitude toward national cinema, which the national cinema—and above all cinema policy—had for a long time lacked. During the 1980s, "foundation film"—meaning films supported by the film foundation—became a byword for slow, difficult, and affectedly artistic film. Throughout the 1990s, public conversation concerning national cinema was dominated by the notion that the national cinema was in crisis. Much was written about the crisis in the newspapers, which tended to focus on decisions made by the Finnish Film Foundation and "scandals" related to films it had supported. If not about these issues, press coverage was about vanishing audiences. What is more, cinema received more attention than any other art form. The boom ended this period of criticism; for the first time since the 1960s, the Finnish Film Foundation and the national cinema received mainly positive publicity. The *Objectives for the National Cinema* program stated the following: "While the reputation and public image of Finnish cinema at home was at an all-time low point only a few years ago, it has now secured a steady curve upward, and almost every new film released has positive expectation attached to it. Internationally, the Finnish cinema, feature films, short films, and documentaries are widely appreciated, although sale figures have so far been modest" (*Suomalaisen elokuvan tavoiteohjelma* 1999).

The European cinema tradition has to a great extent coalesced around masterpieces and has overwhelmingly been an auteur tradition. European film has been very dependent on state support; its distribution network has been built on the existence of film festivals and prizes, and its exhibition sector has been constituted largely by art house theaters (Mattelart 1998). Whether the goals of economic growth and a breakthrough into the international market are realistic or not, the notion that a transformation of the existing tradition needs to occur has figured prominently in recent film policy debate. In Finland, those who advocated internationalization received significant institutional support at the end of the 1980s, when the Committee on Culture and Communication released a report stressing the economic importance of audiovisual culture, underscoring the significance of maintaining national identity and preventing "culturally distant" forms from gaining too much influence (*Viestintäkulttuuritoimikunnan* 1989, 15).

In *Nordic National Cinemas,* Tytti Soila, Astrid Söderbergh Widding and Gunnar Iversen approach Nordic cinema's national element from the vantage point of its circumscribed circulation: "As opposed to several other countries' film cultures, Nordic cinema has been national in the specific sense that it has not, or only to a limited extent, been exportable to other countries" (1998, 2). This gloomy situation seems to be on the verge of changing—at least in some Nordic countries. Lukas Moodysson has given Sweden its biggest success at the international level in many years with his first feature-length film, *Show Me Love* (1999, *Fucking Åmål*), which portrays contemporary teenage life in a small-town setting. The renewed international visibility of Danish cinema is mainly due to the prize-winning Dogma movement of the late 1990s and associated figures such as Lars von Trier, Thomas Vinterberg, and Søren Kragh-Jacobsen. On the other hand, the international recognition of Danish cinema has significantly intensified with commercially successful coproductions shot in English, such as *Breaking the Waves* (1996), *Dancer in the Dark* (2000), *It's All about Love* (2003), and *Skagerrak* (2003).

Finnish movie production, by contrast, has had to survive, up until this point, on the mercies of the domestic market, and there are no guarantees that the new millennium will change the existing export situation. The most successful film of the 1980s, *The Winter War* (Pekka Parikka, 1989, *Talvisota*), was exported with great advance planning and effort; despite the work, the chief result of this expensive process was the bankruptcy of the production company National-Film. In the 1990s it is undoubtedly Aki Kaurismäki, the maker of pure auteur-films, who has been the most visible Finnish cultural export. However, Kaurismäki's audiences are small, his appeal narrow. Only his latest feature film, *Man without a Past* (2002, *Mies vailla menneisyyttä*), Grand Prix winner in Cannes and the first Finnish film ever to be nominated for an Oscar (Best Foreign Language Film), has enjoyed commercial success, reaching some 2 million viewers around the world. The Finnish Film Foundation therefore maintains that "Aki Kaurismäki-type art-house films" and films meant for a narrow audience segment, such as the children's movie *Tommy and the Wildcat,* have a reasonable chance of being internationally successful (Hellman 2000). Films like *Ambush* (Olli Saarela, 1999, *Rukajärven tie*) and *The Wild Ones* (Aleksi

Art or Industry?

Mäkelä, 1999, *Häjyt*), which describe Finnish historical events or ideas closely related to national image and identity, are not viewed as likely export successes, despite their domestic popularity. They nevertheless carry a great significance, "for they are important as emblems of national values" (Hellman 2000).

"LESS ARTISTIC SKILL, MORE COMMERCIALISM": THE NEW DIRECTION OF FINNISH FILM POLICY

The Finnish Film Foundation's head of distribution, Harri Ahokas, describes the new era of the national cinema business in remarks published in the finance pages of *Helsingin Sanomat* on August 6, 2000. Ahokas underscores the significance of new types of marketing: "Actually, it's only with *Restless* and *Badding* (Markku Pölönen, 2000) that cinematic marketing strategies have been successful, as they should be. In other words, films need to be made with the market situation as their point of departure: a film is a product that must be made for an audience." According to Ahokas, the new era began when "attitudes dating back to the 1970s, which saw noncommercial films as being somehow better and more valuable than commercial ones, disappeared." Ahokas's view intersects with discussions in the 1980s concerning the gap between filmmakers' aims and audience tastes, in which the implication was that filmmakers need to make films "for the people" instead of producing them solely to please film critics and funding administrators among the intelligentsia.

In 1980, the first managing director of the Finnish Film Foundation, Veikko Korkala, presented the first clear program for promoting production. In his model, the only criterion for subsidy was quality: "The commercial cinema has its place and its mission, but the purpose of the foundation is primarily to support national, culturally significant film. If the line between these two categories becomes too blurred, it needs to be deliberately clarified" (Ylänen 1980). Korkala's remark completely rules out the possibility of a national cinema that is also commercially successful—that is, one appealing to big audiences while maintaining its roots in domestic cultural traditions yet simultaneously generative of new cultural dynamics. Korkala defined "quality" in the way the 1960s art film tradition saw it: according to the views of the director. A quality film is hence "a film that is created and originated from a genuine need; the director has real views and a developing relationship with his work." Korkala defined national film by looking at the taste of its makers, dismissing the possible preferences of the finished product's receivers: "If the film only reflects already existing views and taste, then it will stop evolving" (Eteläpää 1981). Entertainment industry filmmakers criticized the Finnish Film Foundation for this policy. The debate surrounding the art/entertainment question was at times very heated. For example, in April 1981 the filmmaker Spede Pasanen publicly chopped up the negatives of his first three films with an ax, because his latest popular comedy—part of the *Uuno Turhapuro* series of farces—was deemed to be of insufficient quality to receive financial support.

Before resigning from the foundation, Korkala also spoke of the importance of diversity in production in the national cinema. These later comments stood in contrast with the opinions he expressed in the early 1980s. The profile of Finnish cinema should be changed in order to eliminate a tendency toward artistic similarity, he suggested. It seems that Korkala's vision (*Uusi suomi* 1981) of a national production profile has become current practice. The *Objectives for the National Cinema* program reprises and elaborates these views:

> Diversity of film production as a method of survival also means that films should be offered to various different audiences and groups, both smaller and larger. Changes in assumptions about the national, unified culture suggest that there is no single "right" audience. Rather, it has been pluralized. ... The requirement for continuous development and reforms ensuring the creative potential of films means that we must also have the ability to produce artistically ambitious, individual films that will touch smaller audiences. However, national cinema cannot remain viable unless there are films that reach the big audiences. (*Suomalaisen elokuvan tavoiteohjelma* 1999)

Toward the end of the 1980s the cinema policy discussion began to include other ingredients. In addition to supporting film production, issues related to marketing and distribution received increased or new attention. These new areas of attention can be seen as indicating a shift away from filmmakers' influence and toward greater concern with viewers and consumers. In short, the receivers of film products received more attention. Korkala's successor, Jukka Vilhunen, took the problems of production companies increasingly into consideration.

Art or Industry?

Dedicating attention to audiences' preferences was undoubtedly one way of responding to the financial difficulties companies were increasingly facing.

The turn of the decade also witnessed an intellectual trend that put relations between high and popular cultures under revisionist scrutiny. The boundaries between art and entertainment were tested and breached deliberately and self-consciously by the film foundation. Vilhunen's policy agenda clearly indicated that he thought entertainment films should receive financial support. A key for enacting this "less artistic vision, more commercialism" program was the creation of a type of product aimed at attracting younger audiences (Sinisalo 1989). This new program was never unanimously accepted in the film sector, however. In 1994, for example, foundation subsidies granted to popular comedies met with widespread public disapproval. What upset people most was that the film sector's search for lost audiences and the identity of national cinema seemed to have embraced the cheapest possible strategy: adoption of cinema's commercial tradition, and in particular films that resembled popular sitcoms.

Clearly, the "less artistic vision, more commercialism" debate showed that something essential was changing in Finnish cinema policy. When Marianne Möller became managing director of the Finnish Film Foundation in 1992, she addressed as her first task the supposed division between art and industry. Möller's wish that film could simultaneously be understood as art and industry was at that time still highly provocative, though it has now become a basic tenet of cinema policy liturgy.

TO EUROPE, EUROPE!

The 1990s cinema policy debate turned not only on the art/entertainment question but also on the line between international (European) and national elements of cinema. Finland joined the Media program of the European Union in 1993. The program aims to create a stronger basis for the European film and television industry, strengthening its competitiveness against the American film industry. Despite all the efforts to create a competitive industrial sector, the European Union's audiovisual policy continues to have two sides, combining *free market ideology* and *regulation;* E.U. policy stresses the cultural agenda because the open market can be seen as a distinct threat to the audiovisual production of the European Union (Soramäki and Okkonen 1996, 11).

A significant proposal made in 1991 for the revision of Finnish cinema funding favors a move toward Europeanization. Jukka Vilhunen proposed that subsidizing film production should be an automatic process instead of one based on funding applications and discretion. This "European" reform proposal was a clear step away from filmmaker- and content-centered cinema policy. Vilhunen suggested that production support for any project that had already acquired a sufficient level of financing should be guaranteed. As Vilhunen described it, "As soon as we move away from Finland and the safety of the Nordic welfare state, we find this type of thinking. The cultural nation-states of Europe are not interested in observing the content of film productions. They are in a transition toward clearer models of finance" (Ylänen 1991). The grand idea was that the foundation would no longer be the sole judge of "quality" and hence of films worthy of support. The subsidy reform was carried out in 1992; it maintained support based on consideration and grants while adding new automatic production support. In practice, the model did not work, because the funds available for distribution were insufficient. However, even though the automatic support system failed, its presence in the proposal was evidence of a new cinema policy. It also provided clear evidence that the concept of cinema as industry had won out over that of cinema as art. The foundation's decision was characterized in public as "a tough European model, which would cut short the film sector's breast-feeding and incest" (Ylänen 1991).

How did this talk about the tough European model originate? As a term, the *European model* referred in particular to the discussion of, and changes in, subsidy policy among the big European film countries (France, Germany, and Great Britain); the main aim of these discussions and changes was the reformation of European cinema into a more commercial form. Supporters of the new European industrial agenda unanimously agreed on the cause of the long-term illness of the Continent's film industry. They maintained that European cinema policy had for decades solely concentrated on using public support to maintain the production sector in order to safeguard national art cultures, to deleterious effect. In his work *Europe, Europe: Developing the European Film Industry,* Martin Dale describes a straightforward way of curing the chronic illness of the European film industry: Europeans should make films that follow the simple principles of American films.

Art or Industry?

In the Europe of the 1990s, conversation about a European film *industry* employing Hollywood's tactics of competition returned to the spotlight—especially in the big film production states. The discussion underlined the problems that had emerged from reliance on public support aimed at safeguarding national cultures to the neglect of economic views. The obsessive concern with protecting European cinema has, according to many—for example, Angus Finney—prevented Europeans from seeing the great benefits an economic point of departure could provide European cinema (1996, 68). David Puttnam agrees, claiming that the ubiquity of state-support policy has led Europeans to concentrate on supply instead of demand, on financing filmmakers' needs instead of the changing wishes of consumers (1997, 344–45).

In Finland the main issue has been how to export cinema. National identity and its ties with Finnish cinema remain extremely strong. For Finland, joining the European Union's Media program was an important stimulus for conversation about economic growth and expansion beyond domestic markets. The Finnish cinema and audiovisual sector are dependent on developments in the subsidy systems of Nordic and European countries, because Finnish cinema cannot develop if it relies solely on the domestic market. Naturally, the domestic audience and domestic distribution channels are important for us, but they alone are insufficient to create growth in the sector (Möller 1995, 1).

During the 1990s there was a lot of talk about the need for production companies capable of turning out film on a consistent basis. A key element for these companies is their ability to dislodge themselves from the 1960s ideology of funding each project individually. The proposed ideal for production companies is long-term commitment to production that recognizes the significance of preproduction and marketing. Before she was laid off in 1995 as managing director of the film foundation, Marianne Möller argued that one of the problems Finnish production companies were experiencing arose from the fact that producers and filmmakers had to work intensively for short periods, concentrating on one project at a time. She suggested that changes in subsidy policy, which led to a more even distribution of labor over different phases of the production process from planning to scriptwriting and marketing, would offer a solution to these problems (1995, 1). The issue of production concentration noted by Möller also intersects with questions about the role of directors and producers. There was a tendency in the 1990s toward a transformation in the role of the director, which pulled him from the pedestal to which he was elevated during the 1960s. In this connection, Angus Finney has argued that the "crisis of the European cinema" is partly caused by the "auteur-problem," that is, an overemphasis on the role of the director at the expense of scriptwriters and producers (1996, 5; see also Dale 1992, 85). Möller, who steered Finnish cinema on a course toward Europe, has expressed a similar criticism of the director's role: "Finland is now part of the European Union. The old mechanisms and systems for controlling interest have to be replaced by new ones. We see the audiovisual sector as being too influenced by directors" (Husa 1995). It seems we have come full circle, and cinema in Finland has once again been defined as an *industry,* even though opposition to the cinema-as-industry ideology was the main reason for legitimizing public financial support for cinema during the early 1960s.

"FINNISH PEOPLE NEED FINNISH CINEMA"

> State efforts to financially support, above all, the largest part of audiovisual production expenses are justified both from a cultural-political and an industrial point of view. High-quality, ambitious drama and documentary films are an integral part of the national culture. At the same time, funding is a part of productions that have export potential. By purposefully concentrating on this part of the production, we are strengthening the structure of the entire industry and its capacity to offer domestic products in response to increasing demand in the market. . . . The audience has pluralized, because of changes in the unified, national culture. Still, the quality of an experience and the justification for the existence of an artwork can never be simply tied to the number of people enjoying the experience or work. (*Suomalaisen elokuvan tavoiteohjelma* 1999)

Even today, demands for additional funding have not been made solely on industrial and economic grounds. What, then, are the cultural-political reasons that make it beneficial for the state to invest in national cinema now? The answer can be found in the *Objectives for the National Cinema* program, quoted above. An important point in the program is made as follows: "Finnish people need Finnish cinema" and "a strong cinema is a national resource." It is reasonable to observe, then, that the cultural grounds for financial support of the cinema have remained the same for the last eighty years, despite many other changes in the industry.

When discussing national cinema and its financial support, one argument always seems to be the strongest: national cinema is valuable to the cultural life of the nation. This argument, however, has not been entirely free of conflict. In the 1950s "film-culture activists" questioned the cultural values of the national cinema, as they maintained that the film sector's approach to production sought to produce entertainment with a "captive nation as the audience." Later, the 1960s New Wave's affirmation of artistic views and projects met with difficulties in the mid-1970s. Depending on the point of view, this was due either to a lack of audience or a lack of state support. Many argued that the New Wave of cinema had, through its cultural preferences, managed to scare away the audience.

In the case of the Finnish cinema, different films—in different eras—have been accepted as being representative of national cinema. In the first era, all domestic films qualified. There was no direct support from the state, and as a result domestic cinema could itself determine how national cinema would be defined; national cinema could be "entertainment unifying the nation," a viable industry offering jobs, or art that belonged side by side with older, more distinguished art forms (Laine 1993, 11–12). Problems began to occur in the 1950s when experts outside the film industry, such as critics committed to modernism, put themselves forward as representatives of a true understanding of the essence and function of film. Cinema concepts elaborated during the 1950s such as "art" and "industry" were no longer innocent labels that could be attached as they had been previously but ideologically complex notions, which could have negative or positive meanings, albeit hardly ever both at the same time. In the second era, when the art concept increasingly acquired supporters, national cinema, underwritten by the state, was synonymous with the noncommercial art film. In the 1970s, further requirements, such as "radical" and "socially critical," were added.

In the third era, following the Finnish Film Foundation's purposeful and determined adherence to the art film during the 1980s, the concept "national cinema" once again came to include all domestic films. For example, the Finnish film boom can be explained in part by the fact that the debate on it lumped all domestic films together under the rubric of "national film," from popular comedies to Aki Kaurismäki's cinema. This use of the category closely resembles the connotations that national film carried during the studio era. Today, even the Finnish film magazine *Filmihullu*—which during the 1970s was one of the chief proponents of noncommercial and socially critical art film—has dedicated a theme issue (2000) to the Finnish boom's popular new films such as *Gold Fever in Lapland* and *A Charming Mass Suicide* (Ere Kokkonen, 2000, *Hurmaava joukkoitsemurha*). The issue speaks of these films as building blocks for a new Finnish cinema. Evidence like this suggests real change is occurring. At least for the moment, normative claims concerning the content of national cinema seem to have diminished.

All this is also connected with an attitude change among filmmakers. It has been proposed that one of the reasons for the Finnish film boom is the fact that new actors in the cinema field no longer see a conflict between artistic motivations and the need to look for audiences. The new policy line at the Finnish Film Foundation has also been praised as one of the biggest factors behind the success of national cinema. Managing director Jouni Mykkänen describes the professionalism of the foundation: "Previously, funds were divided more amateurishly and a lot of compromises were made. Now this has become a very businesslike organization" (Arolainen 1999).

From an economic and industrial viewpoint, since the late 1950s the Finnish film industry has been an unbalanced, fragmented industry stretched around an aggregate of small businesses. The Finnish film industry—more accurately Finnish film production—is also the product of the government's subsidy policy. It mainly operates at a loss, and not even the successes, neither the "grand national films" nor even the "film boom" films, have been able to change that. The three pillars of national cinema are still feature films aimed at large audiences and based on national topics or history, such as Saarela's *Ambush* or Pölönen's *A Summer by the River* (1998, *Kuningasjätkä*), brand comedies, and art films—the latter two usually being nonexport material. Hence the map of national cinema still mainly includes only the domestic market. Elsewhere in Europe, the project of industrialization has been taken further. The search for strong producers can be seen as a clear indication that the concept of the "director's film" has become outdated. On the other hand, it is typical of Finnish film culture to find "heroic directors" who, it is assumed, can solve any current crisis in national cinema and draw audiences back into the cinemas. At the moment the search for a director who could win international acknowledgement for Finnish film continues.

The most significant change in question here, for both cinema and art in general, is a transformation in the relationship between perceptions of art and markets. Previously seen as opposites, it is now perfectly acceptable to talk about industry and trade when discussing cinema; in making and supporting film, economic aspects are considered more carefully than ever before. While it is increasingly acceptable to speak about money in relation to cinema and art, it continues to occur covertly and in disguise, concealed by rhetoric of national cultural preservation. Appealing to national values and culture has always been a sort of superjustification, which has been immune to historical contingency and changes in cinema policy discourse. By contrast, decision makers at the Film Foundation have all repeated the same message in the past: the success of Finnish cinema ultimately depends on money, which means additional support from the state. In the words of Erkki Astala: "Money attracts money. The more society is willing to invest in production, the more money will pour in from elsewhere. That dynamic creates a real industry" (Kauppinen 2000).

WORKS CITED

Arolainen, Teuvo. 1999. "Elokuville haetaan nyt yleisön suosiota." *Helsingin Sanomat*, April 24.
Astala, Erkki. 2003. "Suomalaisen elokuvan tulevaisuus." *SESinfo* (January).
Dale, Martin. 1992. *Europe, Europe: Developing the European Film Industry*. London: Academie Carat and Media Business School.
Eriksson, Bengt. 1994. *Selvitys audiovisuaalisen liiketoiminnan kehittämisestä*. Helsinki: KPMG Management Consulting.
Eteläpää, Heikki. 1981. "Veikko Korkala elokuvatukikahakoista: Laadun vaatimus ainoa tuotantotuen jakoperuste." *Uusi Suomi*, June 1.
Finney, Angus. 1996. *The State of European Cinema: A New Dose of Reality*. London: Cassell.
Hellman, Heikki. 2000. "Elokuvan tukeen halutaan 30 mmk:n tasokorotus." *Helsingin Sanomat*, January 15.
Helsingin Sanomat. 1999. "Lapin kullan kimalluksella jo satatuhatta katsojaa." October 9.
———. 2000. "Levottomat keräsi ensi-iltaviikonloppunaan 1,5 miljoonan lipputulot." February 1.
Husa, Mikko. 1995. "Puhu hiljaa teollisuudesta." *Aamulehti*, May 19.
Kauppinen, Eeva. 2000. "Saisiko olla 32 lisämiljoonaa elokuvalle." *Kaleva*, January 15.
Kupoli: Kulttuuripolitiikan linjat. 1992. Committee report 36. Helsinki: Opetusministeriö.

Laine, Kimmo. 1993. "Kotimainen työ, Lapatossu ja Helsingin olympialaiset 1940." *Lähikuva* 3, no. 4: 5–16.

Mattelart, Armand. 1998. "European Film Policy and the Response to Hollywood." In *Oxford Guide to Film Studies*, ed. John Hill, 478–85. Oxford: Oxford University Press.

McGuigan, Jim. 1996. *Culture and the Public Sphere*. London: Routledge.

Möller, Marianne. 1995. "Muuttuvat ympäristöt." *SESinfo* (February).

Moran, Albert. 1996. *Film Policy: International, National, and Regional Perspectives*. London: Routledge.

Pantti, Mervi. 2000. *"Kansallinen elokuva pelastettava": Elokuvapoliittinen keskustelu kotimaisesta elokuvasta itsenäisyyden ajalla*. Helsinki: Suomalaisen Kirjallisuuden-Seura.

Puttnam, David. 1997. *The Undeclared War: The Struggle for Control of the World's Film Industry*. London: HarperCollins.

Sinisalo, Kati. 1989. "Vihoviimeisen säätiöelokuvan uudistaja." *Uusi Suomi*, October 28.

Soila, Tytti, Astrid Söderbergh Widding, and Gunnar Iversen. 1998. *Nordic National Cinemas*. London: Routledge.

Soramäki, Martti, and Kirsi-Marja Okkonen. 1996. *Taloudellinen integraatio ja EU:n audiovisuaalinen politiikka*. Helsinki: Yleisradio.

Suomalaisen elokuvan tavoiteohjelma. 1999. Suomen elokuvasäätiö, December 9, http://www.ses.fi

Suomen kinolehti. 1938. "Mitä hyvältä elokuvalta vaaditaan." June–July.

Uusi suomi. 1981. June 1.

Valtioneuvoston päätös valtion elokuvapalkintojen jakamisesta. 1962. Suomen asetuskokoelma, 212.

Viestintäkulttuuritoimikunnan I mietintö: Kansallisen elokuva-, televisio- ja videotuotannon ja –jakelun edistäminen. 1989. Committee report 15. Helsinki: Opetusministeriö.

Ylänen, Helena. 1980. "Elokuvasäätiön uusi tuotantopäällikkö: Laatu ratkaiskoon mitä elokuvaa tuetaan." *Helsingin sanomat*, January 26.

———. 1991. "Vastuu taiteesta palautetaan elokuvantekijöille." *Helsingin Sanomat*, August 22.

CHAPTER 7

From Epiphanic Culture to Circulation: The Dynamics of Globalization in Nordic Cinema

Mette Hjort

The concept of national cinema has no doubt always been something of a regulative idea, a vision in tension to a certain extent with the transnational realities of cinematic production that have characterized filmmaking for many decades. At a time when globalization and its implications for the nation-state are drawing attention to cultural hybridity and various transnational connections, it is easy to forget that any coincidence of the national with the cinematic is to be found, not in some anterior and clearly separate historical moment, but in various normative conceptions that may have been more or less successful in guiding earlier cinematic practices. In a context of overblown claims about transnationalism and its novelty, careful historical accounts (such as that by Tim Bergfelder [2000] of European coproduction agreements in the 1950s and 1960s) serve an important corrective function, for they make a persuasive case for seeing cinematic transnationalism—as informal practice as well as formally institutionalized arrangement—as a phenomenon with a rather long history. Equally suggestive is Philip Schlesinger's (2002) contention that an excessive reliance in film studies on assumptions derived from sociological theorizations of a national communicative space has made it difficult properly to register the transnational and syncretic nature of much of what counts as national cinema. Yet, Schlesinger's call for new theoretical approaches *is* motivated by a sense that the old models, while never *fully* appropriate, are *particularly* flawed at this point. The view, clearly, is that the theories and assumptions need to change because transnationalism, much more so than in earlier periods, is now the order of the day.

While transnationalism in the cinema has a long history, it currently has a ubiquity that is without precedent. What is more, cinematic transnationalism is now linked in various ways to certain types of globalization, a claim that cannot plausibly be made in connection with earlier instances of transnational collaboration. While generalizations about the dynamics of globalization are helpful up to a certain point, there seems to be little hope of grasping the specificity of various *kinds* of globalization without the revealing details that case studies can provide. This commitment to theorizing in and through concrete cases provides the rationale for focusing the present discussion of transnationalism and globalization on key developments in the Nordic countries over the past fourteen years or so.

In 1993 Jøergen Ljungdalh (at that time a consultant for the Danish Film Institute) made the following insightful—indeed, prescient—remark: "In fifty years' time people watching the Danish films being produced today will no doubt be struck by just how tight the family ties between the Nordic countries became in the course of the 1990s" (cited in Andersen 1997, 351). What Ljungdalh had in mind here was, of course, the prevalence of Nordic coproductions since the late 1980s. To grasp the specificity of globalizing tendencies in the North is, I contend, to understand the motivations for and impact of especially institutionally codified forms of cinematic collaboration across national borders of the kind that provide the basis for Ljungdalh's remark. The central goal, then, is to chart the implications of the tightening bonds evoked above for the Danish case, to pinpoint the nature and dynamics of the process of *denationalization* that has been one of the results of transnationalism, understood both as a response to and as a means of globalization.

In many ways the Nordic Film and TV Fund provides the institutional bases for the crucial transformations that need to be identified. Indeed, the distance separating the original vision for the fund from its current modus operandi provides pointers for understanding the changing face of Nordic globalization. Denationalization, as we shall see, involves more than a simple de-emphasizing of national in favor of transnational elements, for in the present context the relevant process includes a denationalization of the transnational itself. Whereas in the early 1990s cinematic transnationalism in the North favored the kinds of concepts of deep as well as epiphanic culture that are consistent with and indeed support many a national conception of communicative space, the mid- to late 1990s saw a preference quite simply for cooperation and circulation. The performative effect of the shift from an epiphanic culture (that discloses or reveals the favored or sedimented narratives of certain nations) to a "mere" circulation of audiovisual works, people, and monies is becoming evident at the start of the new millennium. What we are witnessing, more specifically, is the emergence of a genuinely transnational communicative space with a newfound tolerance for cultural hybridity. While it may indeed be the case, as the authors of *Global Hollywood* insightfully point out, that "co-production treaties are . . . clear legacies of nation-state formations under modernity," our Nordic example thus clearly contradicts the related contention that "such treaties institutionalise normative and static conceptions of national culture in the very process of international collaboration" (Miller et al., 2001, 89). Cinematic globalization in the North is a complicated phenomenon stretching over more than a decade and involving changing views on the desirability of various forms of transnational collaboration, only some of which are reducible to the pursuit of national culture by other means.

The suggestion that *transnationalism* might be synonymous in certain instances with *globalization* is by no means self-evident and thus calls for some definitions in relation to salient features of the empirical case under discussion. The attempt in the early 1990s on the part of Danish filmmakers, producers, and filmmaking institutions not only to appeal to audiences beyond national borders but also to involve other nations in the very production of Danish films on a regular basis was prompted by the growing costs of cinematic production, a problem to which a pooling of economic resources in the form of coproduction arrangements seemed a plausible solution. Soaring costs are linked in this case to the perceived necessity of certain production values, which makes Hollywood's strategy of globalization, understood in essence as the pursuit of global markets by means of the "ultra-high-budget film" (Balio 1998, 59), a key element in the story. Indeed, the decision, for example, on the part of the Danish Film Institute increasingly to operate within a Nordic rather than a purely national context was in many ways a response to globalization, Hollywood-style. Yet, it is important to note that the response in question is also an instance of globalization, for as Mark Juergensmeyer insightfully suggests, "regional alliances" (2002, 6) are one of the many forms that globalization can take. In this sense the creation of the Nordic Film and TV Fund (NFTF) in 1990 in order to stimulate coproductions among the five Nordic nations clearly links transnational filmmaking in the North to a set of globalizing strategies.

As an initiative of the Nordic Council, the NFTF represents a kind of top-down attempt to change some of the institutional parameters of filmmaking in the North. What we have here is an example of what might be called *reactive* globalization, for the aim was to ensure that Nordic culture would continue to find cinematic expression in a global media culture dominated by Hollywood, that budgets for Nordic film projects would be such that the production values of Nordic films would meet audience expectations shaped largely by Hollywood products, both in the North and globally. The council's provisions were not, however, necessarily taken up in the way that policy makers intended. Indeed, in 1994 a report published by the council called attention to the phenomenon of "sleeping partners," the tendency on the part of producers to short-circuit a vision focused on regional integration, but also on the ideal of a more global Nordic presence that a prioritization of transnational culture and cooperation was to make real (1994, 29). The evidence points to what is essentially a resistance to globalization, the maxim governing this kind of stance being that of the quid pro quo: "If you contribute a million to my film, I'll contribute a million to yours, and then we can both apply to the NFTF for support" (Andersen 1997, 345). In short, the globalizing impulse from above was reframed so as to allow national filmmaking to continue largely unchanged, albeit with the enhanced budgets that a simulated and purely economic transnationalism released. At this point, the tone is set by neither reactive globalization nor the resistance to globalization. The NFTF, for example, is less defensive about Nordic culture, while directors, producers, and decision makers at the various Nordic Film Institutes automatically situate their activities in relation to a Nordic context. The current situation, as Pil Gundelach Brandstrup and Eva Novrup Redvall (2003) have pointed out and elaborate in the present volume, is one in which filmmaking as a genuinely transnational practice is very much a reality, rather than a vision to be implemented or strategically circumvented. The Danish facts speak for themselves: half of the feature-length films produced between 1990 and 1999 (with a Danish company as the major producer) were coproductions, an increase of about 600 percent compared to the 1980s. At this point, coproductions are no longer reducible to national cinema by other means.

From Epiphanic Culture to Circulation

While all Nordic coproductions are potentially relevant to the study of cinematic globalization in the North, some are clearly more interesting than others—more likely, that is, to shed light on distinctive transnationalizing and denationalizing processes. The subset that I have in mind here is that of all Nordic coproductions that can be described as somehow "culturally marked." "Unmarked" coproductions develop story-worlds that, while culturally inflected in the sense that they are necessarily situated in a given cultural context, are not intended or likely to appeal to a given group's sense of *cultural ownership*. Films, on the other hand, that qualify as "culturally marked" typically foreground language and heritage as elements requiring special attention on the part of a given group that can reasonably be assumed to have something at stake in the cultural elements in question. In some cases coproductions could be said to emerge as "culturally marked" not as a result of specific authorial intentions, but because they involve a particular mix of cultural elements that audiences, for whatever reason, find distracting or "noisy." I would like, however, to reserve the term "marked" for those coproductions that are intentionally designed to mobilize a sense of cultural ownership and to a certain extent realize the intention in question. Now why, one might ask, give pride of place to the culturally marked coproductions? The quick answer, which I hope to spell out below, is that the culturally marked coproductions help to identify the particular conception of the transnational that was operative during the earliest phase of Nordic globalization as well as the effect of a revised approach to transnational filmmaking in the North from the mid-1990s onward. Of particular interest are the culturally marked coproductions that are best characterized as self-defeating, for in their particular failings we discern the kinds of commitments on the part of audiences that are very much a feature of a nationally defined communicative space—commitments, as we shall see, that will gradually dissolve as a transnational communicative space based on circulation begins to instill a deep tolerance for cultural hybridity or for a significantly denationalized national culture.

The story I want to tell here about globalization in the Nordic countries begins with a number of films made just before the creation of the NFTF and during the early years of its existence: *Wolf at the Door* (Henning Carlsen, 1986, *Oviri*), *Hip, Hip, Hurra!* (Kjell Grede, 1987), *Pelle the Conqueror* (Bille August, 1987, *Pelle Erobreren*), *The Prince of Jutland* (Gabriel Axel, 1994), and *Two Green Feathers* (Henning Carlsen,

1995, *Pan*). August's Oscar-winning film is particularly important inasmuch as it initially helped to frame arguments in favor of the creation of a Nordic Film and TV Fund in 1990 and subsequently served as a concrete example of what the institution aimed to achieve. My story ends with Ole Bornedal's English-language adaptation of the celebrated Norwegian writer Herbjørg Wassmo's canonized novel, *Dina's Book*. Bornedal's film, it is worth noting in passing, is one of a spate of English-language Danish films released at the start of the new millennium: Lars von Trier's *Dogville* (2003), Thomas Vinterberg's *It's All about Love* (2003), Nicolas Winding Refn's *Fear X* (2003), Lone Scherfig's *Wilbur Wants to Kill Himself* (2002), and Søren Kragh-Jacobsen's *Skagerrak* (2003).

THE EARLY MODEL: EPIPHANIC CULTURE AND THE IMMANENCE OF NATIONALLY INFLECTED PERSPECTIVES

When the Nordic Film and TV Fund was first created, the assumption was that its role would be to stimulate transnational cooperation in the form of "natural coproductions." This model was conceived not in the realm of abstract speculation but in the wake of the galvanizing impact of August's *Pelle,* a film that seemed to policy makers, administrators, and producers alike to incarnate an ideal mode of Nordic cooperation. The term *natural coproduction* was coined in connection with *Pelle* on account of the way in which the film's story-world called for cultural participation on the part of two nations (Denmark and Sweden), the cultural involvement in question constituting a kind of "natural" invitation to economic collaboration. That is, in this heavily canonized story about peasant migration from Småland in Sweden to the Danish island of Bornholm, the nationality of the central characters clearly identified certain nations as the "natural" investors. Reflected in August's film, as well as in the canonized literary work by Martin Andersen Nexø that it adapts, is the interconnected history of the Danish and Swedish peoples in the form of patterns of migration and virtually coinciding languages. What we have here is a kind of palimpsest of shared culture, for the literary text from which the film derives a kind of ready-made appeal is not simply about a particular period in the history of interaction between Swedes and Danes but is itself a Nordic rather than a merely Danish literary classic. The concept of natural investment that underwrites the relevant coproduction model relies on two senses of the term *investment*. For the point is to mobilize economic capital through what we may loosely call a "libidinal economy," a mix of psychological factors in this case that makes transnational collaboration desirable at some deep level. One way of getting at the psychic dimension would be to say that the natural coproduction model favored by the NFTF during its early years presupposed the existence of overlapping epiphanic cultures, the overlapping being a matter not of trivial traits or experiences but of the kinds of significant texts or events that figure centrally in various heritage discourses because they are understood somehow to reveal or make manifest an enduring national identity.

When the Nordic Film and TV Fund first announced its guidelines in the late 1980s, eligibility for funding required the participation of at least two Nordic countries in the production process as well as a certain Nordic content (Andersen 1997, 342). The Nordic Council report published in 1994 ("Undersøgelse af film og TV distribution i Norden") was one of a series of documents that prepared the way for the revised conception of funding eligibility that is operative today. As of 1995 the emphasis was placed on distribution rather than production requirements, provisions for distribution in at least two Nordic countries being a sine qua non for funding.[1] The 1994 report explored a concept of broad appeal that is interesting both in light of the early history of the NFTF and in relation to recent developments. For a proposed film to be viewed as likely to appeal widely throughout the Nordic countries, the report argued, at least three of the following factors would have to be generally known to the relevant audiences: the film's basic idea, its theme, its story, its scriptwriter (or, in the case of adaptations, the original literary work on which the cinematic work was based), the actors, the filmmaker, or the producer (19).

Inscribed within the very concept of a natural coproduction, the favored model for Nordic collaboration during the initial phase of globalization, was a preference for what we might call a "content-driven" rather than a "person-driven" approach to transnational appeal. When I use the term *content*, here the intention is to refer to what audiences take a given film to be about in a very broad sense. "Aboutness" may, then, encompass not only the story-world of a film but also various well-established conceptions of why the story-world and its original creator (a canonized author, for example) matter to a given community. A film's "aboutness" does not, however, typically include thoughts about those who somehow facilitate the film as the specific means of its production: the actors, producers, or director. A person-driven approach to appeal foregrounds the facilitators, as we shall see, in a way that a content-driven emphasis on epiphanic culture does not.

The vision that excited policy makers in the late 1980s and early 1990s was that of cinematic works that would be able to move Nordic audiences by making salient forms of deep cultural content that are "multiply claimed" inasmuch as they sustain national imaginings in more than one Nordic nation. In the NFTF's ideal scheme of things, natural coproductions would be structured in such a way as to make culturally authentic modes of engaging with various types of heritage content or culture available to at least two national audiences while drawing attention to cultural differentiation along national lines. While the envisaged model presupposes some form of shared culture, it is clear that attitudes toward the cultural texts or narratives in question may diverge to various degrees. The concept of a natural coproduction hinges, in short, on the existence of multiple perspectives (arising from various national identities) on key cultural events or achievements that animate the nations in question.

At this point, the NFTF explicitly states that funding does not hinge on "pan-Nordic thematic requirements, national quotas, or requirements in regards [sic] to the artistic or technical staff" (http://www.nftf.net/AboutNFTF.html). Yet, it is not a matter of abandoning the above-mentioned concept of broad appeal but of devising new ways of ensuring that the desired appeal exists. The points identified in the formula for ascertaining broad appeal are as relevant now as they were in the early 1990s, but it is the ability to broker distribution agreements, rather than the NFTF's analysis of a proposed project in terms of some quasi-mathematical calculation, that provides evidence of likely appeal. Yet, the shift from production to distribution considerations does coincide with the increasing importance of what sociologists would call "action roles," and of the persons who assume these roles, as compared with sedimented and enduring cultural formations. That is, cinematic transnationalism in the North no longer rests on the existence of a perspectivally inflected epiphanic culture that can be cinematically explored, for viewers' knowledge of and interest in specific professionals whose sphere of operation is Nordic, rather than national, are now key. In short, the NFTF's decision to shy away from Nordic content in order to emphasize Nordic cooperation as such, as well as the visibility of the resulting projects in the North, has had the in many ways predictable effect of making people qua actors, directors, and producers the motor-force of Nordic transnationalism. From the mid-1990s onward, distribution potential has been increasingly connected to the intensified circulation of people who are willing and able to respond to opportunities for continued professional involvement throughout the North. And it is to this ongoing and growing circulation of people that we must look if we are to understand how communicative space in the Nordic countries has been genuinely transnationalized and, by the same token, denationalized.

SELF-DEFEATING COPRODUCTIONS

The argument I am developing hinges on a contrast between successful natural coproductions and what I want to call self-defeating coproductions. What is striking, in my view, is the radical shift that has occurred in the way in which audiences respond to elements of cultural hybridity in Nordic coproductions. In the response to Bornedal's Nordic blockbuster, *Dina*, we find a means of measuring the relevant changes, for here is a film that in all likelihood would have qualified as a self-defeating coproduction had it been made in the late 1980s or early 1990s. I shall turn to *Dina* and what it tells us about Nordic communicative space toward the end of my discussion. At this stage what is needed is a few clear examples of self-defeating coproductions.

A self-defeating coproduction is essentially a form of cinematic cooperation in which paradoxical use is made of the basic principles of cultural ownership and authenticity that are embedded in the concept of a natural coproduction in the account offered above. A paradigmatic instance of a self-defeating coproduction is Kjell Grede's *Hip, Hip Hurra!* which focuses on the so-called Skagen artists, a colony of Danish, Swedish, and Norwegian artists who were drawn, at the turn of the last century, to the northernmost tip of Jutland in Denmark, where the painters in question found a natural luminosity in line with their artistic vision and practice. The community included the Swedish painter and composer Hugo Alfvén, the Danish painters Anna Ancher and Michael Ancher, the Swedish painter Oscar Björck, the Danish painter and author Holger Drachmann, the Danish painter Viggo Johansen, the Norwegian painter Christian Krogh, the Swedish painter Johan Krouthen, the Norwegian-born Danish painter Peder Severin Krøyer, the Danish painter Marie Triepcke (who would become Krøyer's wife), the Danish painter and art historian Karl Madsen, and the Norwegian painter Eilif Peterssen. The focus in *Hip, Hip, Hurra!* is squarely on Krøyer, who, along with Anna and Michael Ancher, is typically understood to have been a particularly central and animating presence. Krøyer, who was born in a madhouse in Stavanger in Norway and later adopted by the established Danish zoologist Henrik Krøyer, was educated at the Royal Academy of Art in Copenhagen, where he worked with Fredrik Vermehren and Wilhelm Marstrand. That the film is a biopic is clearly signaled by the choice of title: *Hip, Hip, Hurra!* is the title of Krøyer's first masterpiece from his Skagen period. Painted in 1883, the impressionist *Hip, Hip, Hurra!* depicts the Skagen artists gathered for a summer luncheon in an idyllic garden setting.[2] The film explores the ways in which a rare and positively childlike ability to experience joy combines in Krøyer with a madness that in all likelihood was a symptom of syphilis and that would result in his being committed to an asylum in Zealand later in life. The drama of the film stems in large measure from the depiction of the painter's tempestuous relation to his wife, Marie Triepcke, a person with depressive tendencies who would ultimately leave him for Alfvén. Joie de vivre, artistic genius, madness, and passion—both reciprocated and unrequited—are the key ingredients in the Swedish director's historical narrative.[3] The aim, Grede claims, was somehow to capture and explain the almost mythical quality that surrounds the term *Skagen* in Nordic culture and not, as he underscores, to provide a kind of cinematic reconstruction of the genesis of "the paintings that the artists painted and that people have so loved" (1986). Grede was at pains throughout, he insists, to avoid the temptations of kitsch—temptations, we are to assume, that arise easily in a context involving natural beauty, sensibilities that respond at a deep level to that beauty, and artworks of an impressionist nature. The decision to ask Sten Holmberg to assume the responsibilities of cinematographer was in large measure prompted by the belief that he would be able, as he indeed was, to capture the beauty by which the artists were moved, as well as the defining features of their art, without embracing an aesthetics of kitsch.

It is important to note that the mythical quality that Grede associates with Skagen and that he identifies as a motivating artistic factor is linked to a strong, preexisting pan-Nordic "love" for the paintings and artists who lend symbolic meaning to the geographical term in question. At a press conference held in Copenhagen on May 30, 1986, Grede remarks on the extent to which the Skagen painters constitute a heritage culture that is still very much alive throughout the northern countries: "The idea of making a film about the Skagen painters is in no way unique and has been around a long time. But why is the interest in this period so intense among ordinary citizens, why does the National Museum attract six thousand visitors per day during the winter months when they have a special exhibit?" If the Skagen artists are a matter of heritage constructions, they are so on a national as well as a Nordic scale, and it is in this complexity of scale that we find the rationale for a natural coproduction.

Hip, Hip, Hurra! as Jesper Andersen points out, was originally conceived but not ultimately realized as a natural coproduction:

> Part of the strength of this joint Nordic project involved having a Swedish actor play the Swedish composer Hugo Alfvén, a Norwegian actor the Norwegian painter Christian Krogh, and so on. Yet, in choosing the lead, this principle was abandoned inasmuch as P. S. Krøyer is played by the Swedish Stellan Skarsgård. This no doubt helps to explain why the film failed to draw viewers in Denmark. *Hip, Hip, Hurra!* foreshadowed a problem of linguistic authenticity that would also hit later Nordic coproductions. (1997, 343)

Andersen's point is this: the film focuses on Søren Krøyer, a figure who has been canonized as a Danish painter, yet in the fictionalized biopic Krøyer is Swedish, not Danish. While the thwarting of common knowledge about the nationality of the central persona may not exhaust the reasons for the film's poor performance at the Danish box office, there can be no doubt that it played an important role. That Grede's Danish-Swedish-Norwegian coproduction should have sold a mere 49,948 tickets in Denmark, a context where a film that is successful in box office terms sells about 250,000 tickets, is indeed striking, a prima facie anomaly requiring explanation along precisely the lines suggested by Andersen.

The self-defeating nature of Grede's cinematic project, I wish to contend, has to do with the contradictory injunctions or invitations that it issues to the envisaged national audiences. These audiences are expected to be interested in—indeed, they are implicitly *instructed* to be interested in—the film's fictionalized account of the lives of historical figures who are part of an institutionally constructed and officially sustained heritage culture. Although the artists' lives and contributions are institutionalized as heritage culture on both a Nordic and a national scale, national audiences are assumed to be most invested in, and most familiar with, the achievements of their respective compatriots. The point, precisely, is to use the concept of a significant historical compatriot to leverage interest in the biopic.

The rationale for natural coproductions, which at one level is that of Grede's film, brings to mind aspects of set theory. The situation is precisely one of overlapping sets, with each set encompassing a national culture, a national audience, and at least one canonized national figure. The area of overlap, which arises in this instance as a result of interaction among the various national figures, has the effect of framing these individuals as vehicles for a Nordic identity and thus as having an inherent pan-Nordic appeal. But the point is that the Nordic appeal in question is predicated not on a syncretism of cultures that effaces the national dimension but rather on a convergence of national interests. In a manner that is wholly characteristic of the natural coproduction, *Hip, Hip, Hurra!* invites careful attention to issues of national culture and the role played by remarkable individuals in its creation. Having prompted the form of "caring" or involvement in question, the film then goes on to violate the very principle of appeal on which it relies. The message, in short, is very much a contradictory one, for it is both a matter of investing in national culture and of overlooking the ways in which the film's story-world disregards the phenomenon of citizenship or nationality that is a central element in the standard historical accounts with which viewers are expected to be familiar. It is not, of course, a matter of claiming that self-contradictory injunctions constitute the *sole* reasons for the film's failure at the box office. Other factors that would have to be considered in any exhaustive account of the work's reception history would be its broadly modernist style and generally depressing themes.

Minor cinemas, it can be argued, abound with self-defeating coproductions for reasons that are linked to the ever-present desire and need somehow to access audiences that transcend the level of the purely national.[4] In some instances the self-defeating dimension may be imposed, against the will of the director, by the accidents or formal provisions of a given coproduction arrangement. In other cases the element of contradiction may arise as the unintended effect of a strategy of multiple address involving, for example, an attempt to engage global audiences as well as national audiences. In the context of minor cinema, there is a recurrent temptation, it would appear, to leverage national interest through deep epiphanic culture and to stimulate global interest by sacrificing the authenticity of the cultural configuration in question. Before attempting a succinct and more analytic recapitulation of the self-defeating coproduction's defining features, let me quickly point to two other examples, both of which take us outside the framework of Nordic collaboration and into a European context, where, of course, the concept of a natural coproduction, and hence the possibility of its contradictory instantiation, also arises.

Wolf at the Door (*Oviri*, 1986) is a Danish-French coproduction directed by Henning Carlsen, a venerable Danish filmmaker who achieved international acclaim many decades ago with his adaptation of the Norwegian writer Knut Hamsun's *Sult* (*Hunger,* 1966). Like *Hip, Hip, Hurra! Wolf at the Door* is a biopic, the focus in this instance being on the French painter Paul Gauguin and his relation to his Danish wife, Mette Gad. Carlsen's account of his reasons for making the film are moving and personal:

> *Wolf at the Door* finds its starting point in 1980 when I was hospitalised in Svendborg for a few weeks and actually hovered between life and death for a while. One night, around half past three or four o'clock in the morning, I woke up, and it was exactly as though there was a projector behind me, and this projector was projecting a scene with a charabanc driving through a forest onto the wall. As the charabanc reaches the curve in the road it comes to a standstill and out gets Paul Gauguin, who raises his hat and takes his leave. He's speaking Danish, and then he simply walks away in the direction of the hospital windows while the charabanc drives in the direction of the hospital door. What I saw there on the wall was the clearest of visions. I knew immediately that it was Gauguin. At that point I'd never seen a picture of Gauguin and I knew almost nothing about him. (Hjort and Bondebjerg 2001, 51)

Carlsen's research, much of it conducted at the Bibliothèque nationale in Paris, led him to question the official and largely critical account of Paul Gauguin's life, the result being a biopic that amounts to a defense of the painter's decisions and actions. Gauguin's neglect and abandonment of his Danish wife and children, for example, are interpreted not as symptoms of personal vice but rather as the product of a cultural divide that makes certain quintessentially Danish national traits appear in a deeply off-putting light.

A real history of communication between cultures, however problematic, is thus the starting point for the film, which involves precisely the combination of Danish and French monies that one might expect. A key casting decision intervenes, however, to disturb what might otherwise have been a "natural" relation between economic and cultural investments:

> Originally the idea was that the film would be a 50/50 co-production involving my own company and Gaumont in France. Gaumont was very pleased with the script we handed in, but the discussions about who should play the various roles were endless. When Jean-Claude Carrière and I wrote the script in French, we modelled Gauguin on Donald Sutherland without for a second imagining that he would ever play the role. But I finally proposed Sutherland after all and he was very accommodating. In fact, I'd called him in England and he read the script that very same night. The next day he said that he thought it was a good script, but that he'd like to make a quick trip to Paris, where his family was. He said he'd be leaving that weekend, and then we could talk once he got back. I thought Donald Sutherland spoke French, and I hadn't for one second thought about the language issue, which was, of course, rather naive on my part. . . . But after having visited his family he called me in order to decline the role because he'd tried out some of the scenes in French with his wife as a spectator and she'd laughed her head off. I then suggested that we could resort to dubbing, but he didn't want any part of that. When I subsequently called Gaumont, they suggested that we make the film in English. (Hjort and Bondebjerg 2001, 52)

An oversight in the form of an automatic yet ultimately unwarranted attribution of competence in French results in the adoption of English as the language of the film's story-world. Alongside Sutherland, viewers find established Danish actors, such as Ghita Nørby, who plays the mother of one of Gauguin's French models. The fourteen-year-old girl in question, Judith Mollard, is herself played by Sofie Gråbøl, who has since gone on to become one of the stars of the new Danish cinema. For Danish viewers the challenge is to make believe that the heavily accented English spoken by Nørby (a significant and very Danish presence in Danish national cinema) in a supposedly French setting in fact is French, just as French audiences face the task of convincing themselves that the English-speaking Sutherland is a French-speaking Gauguin. The language-based obstacles to make-believe are further compounded by visual properties derived from the film's production design. That Henning Carlsen should choose to characterize the situation as "paradoxical" is, as we shall see, very suggestive indeed: "It was of course a little paradoxical to be making the film in English, when all the shooting was to take place in Copenhagen, and 95 percent of the action, which concerns a French artist, was supposed to occur in Paris. Everything was done in Denmark. There's nothing, not a single shot, from France; the entire Parisian milieu was constructed in a studio in Valby" (Hjort and Bondebjerg 2001, 53) . . . and it shows! The film thwarts the memories and conventions associated with a Parisian look from the earliest moments of the film, which draw attention to cobblestones unlike any to be found in Paris or its well-known representations. *Wolf at the Door,* not surprisingly, did very poorly in the countries that were to have provided it with "natural" audiences—France and Denmark (in Denmark, for example, the film sold only 34,259 tickets). That Carlsen's biopic fared well in the United States is interesting and a clear indication that an appropriation or reframing of the life as international rather than national heritage has the effect of neutralizing and effacing authenticity concerns that are directly linked to nationally inflected expectations and memories.

Another striking example of a self-defeating work is Gabriel Axel's *The Prince of Jutland,* a film that is typically listed as a Danish/British coproduction, although some of the funding was derived from Dutch, French, and German sources as well as from the supranational Eurimages program. The film is a reworking of the Hamlet story, drawing on Saxo Grammaticus's medieval account of prince Amled, which also inspired Shakespeare. Inasmuch as the Danish Amled spends a significant amount of time in England, the tale of this prince and his deeply effective strategy of revenge against his uncle Fenge (Gabriel Byrne)—for the murder of his father and seduction of his mother (Helen Mirren)—provides a perfectly "natural" basis for a coproduction involving Danish and British monies.

Various interviews with Gabriel Axel, including one with the present author in the summer of 1994, clearly suggest thinking in line with what I elsewhere, following Charles Taylor, have called "a politics of recognition" (Hjort 1996). The idea, in brief, was to reclaim a narrative originally told by a Dane from the effective history that institutionalizes it as a canonized English classic: to make salient, and invite recognition for, aspects of Danish heritage culture as part of an international dialogue of cultures. Axel traces his interest in the Amled story to its roots in what he construes as an enduring *ethnie,* to his perception of Saxo and the tale this monk recounts as quintessentially Danish. The project of retrieval in which Axel saw himself as engaged involved a thoroughgoing reconceptualization of the Hamlet figure, Amled having been depicted by Saxo as a decisive figure capable of engaging in effective means-end deliberations. The aim, that is, was to provoke interest in the original, and in its national origins, through a contrast between the paralysis commonly associated with Shakespeare's Hamlet and Amled's qualities as a kind of action hero *avant la lettre.*

It took Axel literally decades to secure funding for his Amled project, and for many, many years the plan was to use Danish as the language of the film's Danish story-world. The shift from Danish to English, and to a cast featuring prominent English-speaking actors, was a direct result of the financing package that was finally pieced together. Axel himself admits that "he misses the Danish language in the film. It is part of the tone that he has established." But he goes on to justify the use of English nonetheless: "But that's the way it is. And as a matter of fact the choice of English probably isn't such a bad one, because at that time the Danish language was probably closer to English than what we today understand as Danish" (Moe 1994). The film was a colossal failure, both at the box office and with critics, who pointed to wooden acting, laughable dialogue, and a generalized sense of amateurism. *The Prince of Jutland* sold a pathetic 7,914 tickets in Denmark, prompting the following explanation from Jesper Andersen: "Gabriel Axel's *The Prince of Jutland* . . . would no doubt also have appealed more to a Danish audience if it had been filmed in Danish. The only identifiable Danish actor is Jess Ingerslev, who only survives for four minutes and only manages to utter two sentences before exiting the film with a knife in his back" (Andersen 1997, 354).

Together, *Hip, Hip, Hurrah! Wolf at the Door,* and *The Prince of Jutland* provide the basis for a more analytic discussion of the defining features of self-defeating coproductions. We are essentially dealing here with a mode of actual or perceived address that is more or less related to phenomena such as mixed messages, contradictory injunctions, or double binds, the latter being strictly speaking paradoxical in much the same way that the "performative antinomies" discussed by George Lakoff (1972) are. Carlsen's use of the term *paradoxical* in the passage cited above is suggestive because it points to contradiction as a distinguishing feature of self-defeating coproductions. Yet, it is important to note that contradictions are not necessarily paradoxes, although there is a tendency in ordinary parlance to assume an unproblematic conflation or equivalence of these terms.

The point that self-defeating coproductions involve contradiction, not paradox, is best made by way of contrast with the properly paradoxical double binds analyzed by Paul Watzlawick and his colleagues (1967). In their classic study, *Pragmatics of Human Communication*, a double bind is said to arise when the following three conditions obtain:

1. Two or more persons are involved in an intense relationship that has a high degree of physical and/or psychological survival value for one of them. . . .

2. A message is given which is so structured that (a) it asserts something, (b) it asserts something about its own assertion and (c) these two assertions are mutually exclusive. . . . The meaning of the message is, therefore, undecidable. . . .

3. The recipient of the message is prevented from stepping outside the frame set by this message, either by metacommunicating (commenting) about it or by withdrawing (212).

It is worth noting that film spectatorship in no wise meets the first condition, which presupposes a kind of captive audience unknown to the cinema. Nor is the second condition met by self-defeating coproductions, for the intended or inferred messages cannot be said to be undecidable in the way, for example, that the self-referential "Don't obey this order" is, where obedience automatically and instantly generates disobedience, which in turn automatically and instantly generates obedience, and so on ad infinitum. Unlike the victims of the pernicious double bind, film audiences can opt out of the communicative situation with which self-defeating coproductions present them. They are also at liberty to metacommunicate about the film's mixed and other messages through reviews or the kind of informal discussion that can seal a film's fate at the level of "word of mouth."

The problem with self-defeating works is that they are perceived as involving an intolerably contradictory mode of appeal, which perception prompts bad press and serious indifference. The contradictory injunctions that undermine a given work's appeal are, of course, only implicit and never fully anticipated by the makers. A work is self-defeating, then, as a result of viewers' tendency to construe its appeal as contradictory, the assumption on the part of the makers having on the contrary been that the film would appeal in ways that would not in fact give rise to an unsettling or simply tedious tension between mutually exclusive psychological states. As far as the makers of the works are concerned, the national audiences being targeted are invited to adopt what might be called the stance of the *rootless nationalist*. This is a stance that rests on injunctions of the following kind: (1) Engage with your national heritage; (2) Ignore any denationalizing, fictionalizing, or deauthenticating moments that might be necessary for aesthetic reasons or for reasons having to do with the practical constraints of filmmaking. At the level of reception, however, the injunctions are reframed as mutually exclusive, as contradictory and irksome: (1) Care about your national heritage; (2) Ignore travesties of your national heritage.

The divide separating the understandings of those engaged in the craft of filmmaking from those of viewers highlights the extent to which self-defeating coproductions represent a particular kind of communicative breakdown. The idea that self-defeating coproductions are characterized by a particularly nefarious relation between intent and uptake is likely to be uncontroversial. What is more difficult to determine is why the divide in question arises in some cases but not others. General explanations are unlikely to be of much help here, for there is a host of factors that might explain why the stance of the flexible nationalist is deemed enticing or, on the contrary, deeply off-putting. In some cases, for example, the breakdown arises as a result of an entrenched nationalism and generalized intolerance toward cultural difference, particularly if it begins to impinge on areas that are commonly understood in terms of cultural purity. Formal cinematic properties, such as sound, editing, or framing, may also play a decisive role. If, for example, these basic cinematic elements have been mobilized in a particularly skillful or seductive manner, then even audiences committed to various forms of cultural authenticity might be willing momentarily to suspend their commitments in favor of a more flexible stance.

The largely positive reception of Bornedal's *Dina* is striking precisely because this film instantiates many of the same elements of cultural "impurity" that caused films like *Hip, Hip, Hurra!* or *Wolf at the Door* to fail. The striking difference in response points, in my view, to an emerging tolerance for cultural hybridity and a growing tendency among Scandinavian audiences to invest in transnational Nordic identities. What is also evident here is the willingness increasingly to settle for (and perhaps even prefer) a "more or less" account of national culture as compared to the "all or nothing" model favored by the more national audiences of the 1980s and early 1990s. If *Hip, Hip, Hurra! Wolf at the Door,* and *The Prince of Jutland* are any indication, the choice some twenty years ago was between exploring heritage in what would pass for an authentic mode or not exploring it at all. In the contrast between Grede's self-defeating *Hip, Hip, Hurrah!* and Bornedal's popular *Dina* we find clear signs of a transnational communicative space in the North—the key question, then, being how essentially national audiences operating within a series of nationally defined communicative spaces (marked significantly by only one "Other," namely Hollywood) came to understand themselves in transnational terms. The answer, I believe, is to be sought, among other things, in the performative effects of the circulation-based model of Nordic cooperation that replaced conceptions centered on epiphanic culture.

THE SUCCESSOR MODEL: HOMOPHILY AS THE BASIS FOR CIRCULATION

There is a good deal of evidence to suggest that the problems encountered with the "epiphanic" model gradually resulted in a quite different approach to cinematic globalization in the North. Comments by various directors are revealing in this respect. Henning Carlsen, for example, is delighted to note that the coproductions that once drove cinematic transnationalism in the North have given way at this point to films that are merely cofinanced. The contrast, in his mind, hinges on the way in which coproductions are expected somehow to make the fact of significant cultural collaboration manifest in the actual film, whereas cofinanced films are freed from any such epiphanic requirements (Hjort and Bondebjerg 2001, 54). Susanne Bier, director of the award-winning Dogma film *Open Hearts*, is similarly attuned to the more recent emphasis on collaboration without cultural strings attached: "When we made *Family Matters*, co-productions were very much in their infancy and I have the feeling that a different co-production model has emerged in the meantime. . . . I don't believe in writing stories aimed at co-productions, but I do believe, on the other hand, that there's a much greater degree of exchange now than there used to be and that many more things get off the ground than just ten years ago" (Hjort and Bondebjerg 2001, 243). What Bier draws attention to is the emergence of strong networks for the circulation of ideas, people, money, and films. Jesper Andersen makes a similar point from the perspective of someone who, as an employee of the Danish Film Institute, is attuned to ongoing dialogues among Nordic producers and consultants: "Whereas previously it was mostly individuals—directors, actors, or technicians—who crossed borders, the possibilities for international financing have created a valuable network among Danish and foreign producers and film consultants, not least in the North" (Andersen 1997, 346).

From the mid-1990s onward the cinematic articulation of discrete instances of partially overlapping and preferably significant national culture gave way to a culturally much more flexible model of collaboration extending well into the area of reception in the form of an intensified circulation of cinematic works within the North. Underwriting the idea of a Nordic space in which people, monies, and films circulate easily is the principle of homophily, which quite simply presupposes the existence of affinities at some deep and in many ways banal level. Commonality is now the taken-for-granted basis for collaboration rather than some regulative ideal that is to be made compelling and real through an epiphanic cinematic culture. In his influential study titled *Dynamics of Intercultural Communication*, Carley H. Dodd defines homophily as "the tendency to communicate with those similar to us" (1998, 178), the idea being that intercultural relationships depend on concepts of similarity and difference, communication across national borders being viewed as agreeable, for example, to the extent that some form of similarity is salient. Dodd distinguishes usefully between four kinds of homophily: similarities having to do with the way people look, with their backgrounds, their attitudes, and, finally, their values. The assumption, expressed by filmmakers, producers, and policy makers from the mid-1990s onward, is that cooperation across national borders is far easier in the Nordic context than it is in other cases on account of these different kinds of homophily. As Søren Kragh-Jacobsen, the director of the Dogma film *Mifune*, remarks: "After all, we speak the same language. We like each other. We know one another.... We have the same mentality" (interview with Hjort, Summer 1998). The existence of various forms of taken-for-granted homophily is here identified as the basis for regular and relatively unproblematic cinematic cooperation in the North. Statistics provide further evidence of the phenomenon in question: at the outset of the new millennium 80 percent of coproductions with a Danish major involved collaboration with Sweden, followed by Norway in a clear second place (Brandstrup and Redvall 2003). Whereas an insistence on making shared Nordic cultures and identities visible turns out to be a self-defeating gesture, the more self-confident assumption of a banal commonality stimulates circulation in a way that has precisely the kind of denationalizing effect that makes a genuinely transnational culture possible.

That circulation, rather than epiphanic culture, is the key to understanding Nordic globalization today is clearly suggested by the NFTF's decision to make distribution in two Nordic countries (rather than the "manifest" and preferably culturally motivated participation by two Nordic countries in the production process) the sine qua non of funding eligibility. The creation of new collaborative networks in the area of distribution does not, of course, leave the sphere of production or creation untouched, for the roles of producer and distributor may well coincide (as they increasingly do in the case of Nordic TV stations). Indeed, circulation pertains to all aspects of cinematic culture. The transnational flow of money has generated networks of producers with shared understandings and experiences, which in turn facilitates and intensifies cooperation in other areas, as agents positioned within multiple networks begin to share their contacts. At the same time, the growing tendency for directors and actors to circulate among the Nordic countries literally transforms the communicative space in which they operate from a series of interconnected national spaces to an increasingly integrated transnational arena. Bille August, a Dane schooled in Sweden and with a long history of making films in both Denmark and Sweden, was once an exceptional case, but this is no longer true. The much younger Swedish filmmaker Åke Sandgren, was, for example, trained at the Danish Film School and is now a fully participating and nationally recognized member of the Danish film community (largely as a result of his Danish Dogma film, *Truly Human* [2001, *Et rigtigt menneske*]). Susanne Bier is another case in point, for not only is she equally at home in Swedish and Danish contexts of filmmaking, she has a clear sense of how a given project might be best served by one of the relevant frameworks (Hjort and Bondebjerg 2001, 243). Dagur Kári, the Icelandic director of the much-praised Icelandic-Danish coproduction *Noi, the Albino* (2002), graduated from the Danish Film School in 1999. And the list goes on. The point is that as circulation of all kinds becomes the norm, national audiences cease to approach the results of various collaborative efforts with the kinds of expectations that are prompted by and indeed constitutive of national cinemas.

The increasingly transnationalized attitudes of Nordic audiences are a key factor in the emergence of an integrated Nordic communicative space, a point that is tellingly reflected in the Nordic Council's fiftieth anniversary celebrations in 2002. A Nordic Film Award, which went to Aki Kaurismäki for *The Man without a Past* (2002, *Mies vailla menneisyyttä*), was created to mark the anniversary, and there is talk of turning the award into a permanent institution. Film Festival initiatives, such as the "Nordisk Tävling" competition at the Göteborg Film Festival, serve a similar agenda.[5] Multiple identifications, crisscrossing the Nordic arena and loosening the hold of national conceptions of belonging, are, in short, the performative effect of a model emphasizing circulation on a transnational scale. Stars—be they directors, actors, or even producers—are the key vehicles of the ongoing tendency toward denationalization and transnationalization. As such they provide support for Richard Dyer's insightful contention that "Stars are . . . embodiments of the social categories in which people are placed and through which they have to make sense of their lives" (2000, 604). To the categories identified by Dyer—class, gender, ethnicity, religion, and sexual orientation—we can thus add that of citizenship, not in a strictly legal sense but in the informal sense explored by Yasemin Soysal (2002) and Riva Kastoryano (2002) in their influential work on changing conceptions of citizenship in an increasingly transnational world.

The shift from epiphanic culture to circulation helps to explain how a film that once would have registered as a self-defeating coproduction can emerge in this day and age as something of a Nordic success story. Let me conclude, then, with a few words about Bornedal's *Dina*, a story about a young girl who accidentally causes the gruesome

From Epiphanic Culture to Circulation

Dina (Marie Bonnevie) and Jacob's (Gérard Depardieu) wedding among the Norwegian fjords in Ole Bornedal's *I Am Dina* (2002)

death of her mother and finds herself emotionally rejected by her father, who simply cannot forgive the child. The Danish director's adaptation of the Norwegian Wassmo's canonized novel is the result of collaboration between "two of Scandinavia's most experienced film producers. . . . Danish producer Per Holst of Nordisk Film, and Norwegian producer Axel Helgeland of Northern Lights" (http://www.iamdina.com/-eng/production/production.html). The cast is an international one, with a heavy emphasis on actors from both Denmark and Norway. The grown Dina is played by Marie Bonnevie, the daughter of the Norwegian actress Jannik Bonnevie and the Swedish actor Per Waldvik. Bonnevie's training includes a particularly formative year at the Folk High School on the Danish island of Aerø as well as several years at the prestigious Dramaten in Stockholm. Her international breakthrough came as Gertrud in one of the Dane Bille August's successful Nordic productions, *Jerusalem*. In addition to Bonnevie, Bornedal's cast includes a number of other Nordic stars: Bodil Udsen (a prominent Danish actress), Jørgen Langhelle and Bjørn Floberg (two well-known Norwegian actors), and Pernilla August (one of the most established of Swedish actresses). When Gérard Depardieu, Hans Matheson, and Kate Hardie are thrown into this mix, along with the decision to make an eclectic mix of accented Englishes the language of the film, there can be little doubt that we have all the ingredients here for a bona fide Europudding standing in clear tension with heritage constructions on a national scale and the expectations they generate.

The lines of ethnic and cultural affiliation that Nordic audiences once took for granted in the form, for example, of preferences for a *correspondence* between actors' and filmmakers' nationalities and the national identity of the relevant heritage elements are clearly—yet, it turns out, unproblematically—disrupted in the case of *Dina*. The figures on cinema admissions in Scandinavia were as follows as per December 31, 2002:

Norway: 310,905
Denmark: 264,141
Sweden: 32,524
Finland: 19,558

The Danish ticket sales placed *Dina* on the list of top twenty films in Denmark (http://www.nftf.net/Newsletter/NL-030311.html). A press release described *Dina* as "by far the most popular film in Norwegian cinemas in the Spring of 2002" and went on to note that the film won five Danish Robert prizes (awarded by the Danish Film Academy) and an Amanda for Best Actress (the equivalent of a Norwegian Oscar) (Helgeland 2002). The press was for the most part very favorable in both Denmark and Norway, unlike in Sweden, where hostile reviews were dominant. *Dina* may not be a pan-Nordic blockbuster, but it is a film that manages, in spite of its hybridized cultural dimensions, to perform unusually well in at least two Nordic countries.

Predictably enough, interviewers repeatedly asked Bornedal to justify his decision to make use of what Wlad Godzich, in an interesting article on the nature and dynamics of Global English, calls a "disglossic" strategy (1999, 44), a strategy that here registers as an almost cheeky insistence on a cacophony of accented Englishes. The justification, unsurprisingly, has to do with "reach," with the ambition of global appeal. As Bornedal puts it: "To people who ask why we didn't shoot in Norwegian, I say, why didn't they shoot *Doctor Zhivago* in Russian? If they had perhaps 200,000 people would have seen the movie" (http://www.iamdina.com/eng/director/bornedal.html). Yet the interviewers' questions were not necessarily framed as objections to the use of Global English, and any possible objections along these lines certainly left audiences in Denmark and Norway largely indifferent.[6] Bornedal's dramatic departure from the genre conventions of costume dramas and heritage film appear to be important elements in *Dina's* appeal. The fact that the flamboyant refusal to establish a pattern of clear national links between relevant heritage constructions and the various purveyors of the film's story-world proved acceptable to audiences no doubt also points to the pervasiveness of Global English as a contemporary cultural force, as compared with the period during which *Wolf at the Door* or *Hip, Hip, Hurra!* were released. The ongoing denationalization of Nordic media spaces, there is reason to believe, may well be the combined effect of Global English and one of the responses (Nordic globalization through and as circulation) originally generated by Hollywood's globalization.

It is important to note that the questions of cultural ownership that once framed certain coproductions as natural persist in *Dina's* diverse contexts of reception, but in a significantly *transmuted* form. Norwegian audiences emphasized the film's relation to a Norwegian classic. Danish audiences focused on Bornedal's role as an ambitious and flamboyant Danish director, while Swedish audiences paid special attention to the actress Bonnevie. Yet Norwegian audiences were also attuned to Bonnevie's qualities as a Norwegian and Swedish star, just as Swedish and Danish audiences acknowledged Wassmo's role as a Nordic writer. More important, the investments completely bypass the idea of cultural correspondence that informs the "all or nothing" conception of the epiphanic model. Instead we find a highly eclectic mix of engagements and a striking tolerance for cultural hybridity. Norwegians, for example, appear more than happy to enjoy Wassmo's classic tale in a form that is "more or less" recognizable when it comes to national characteristics. Compare this situation to the one experienced in the mid-1990s by Henning Carlsen in connection with his Hamsun adaptation, *Two Green Feathers*:

> I've had exactly the same problem with *Two Green Feathers* which was mostly a Norwegian production, although some Danish money was involved too; I'd also invested some of my own money in it. So the Institutes simply decided to classify *Two Green Feathers* as a Norwegian film with a Danish director. But the Norwegian Film Institute has never promoted it internationally, because when it's time to send out a film that represents Nor-

way, they always opt for a film with a Norwegian, rather than a Danish, director. There's a way in which films simply die as a result of being co-productions. (Hjort and Bondebjerg 2001, 54)

The emergent and performative effect, it would appear, of abandoning earlier commitments to overlapping epiphanic cultures in order to foster circulation of various kinds is precisely the sense of Nordic belonging that Carlsen found lacking in 1995. In the reception of Bornedal's *Dina* some seven years later we discern the contours of a new and genuinely transnational communicative space in the North.

NOTES

1. It is interesting to note that the recent Nordic tendency to focus on distribution and circulation rather than production mirrors developments on a European level. In their account of Media, Media II, and Media Plus, Toby Miller and George Yúdice clearly suggest that "the tactic was a concentration on film distribution rather than production" (2002, 182).
2. The sketch for the painting is part of the Skagen Museum's holdings, while the final work is housed in the Göteborg Art Museum.
3. See Löthwall 1987 for background information on the film.
4. On the concept of a minor cinema, see Hjort 1996.
5. The identified strategies find clear parallels on a European level, the European Film Academy having introduced the "People's Choice Awards" in 1997 in an attempt to create a transnational cinematic imaginary (http://www.europeanfilmacademy.org/htm/3peopl.htm). The shooting star nominations submitted by national film bodies in connection with the Berlin Film Festival are also noteworthy in this connection.
6. Ebbe Iversen's position on the language issue is interesting, for it draws attention to the film's status as a "pudding" while suggesting that irritations typically associated with the category in question are neutralized by pleasures having to do with visual style, generic innovation, and powerful acting: "Unfortunately people talk in the film, and let us quickly deal with the most important criticism of Ole Bornedal's ambitious film. It takes place in Norway in the 1800s, but because it is a European coproduction—a so-called europudding—it is filmed in English with an international cast that speaks with varying degrees of accent, from French to Danish. And this is hardly conducive to realism, believability or the audience's ability to identify with the film. . . . The film's visual dimension is so impressive, however, that one almost forgets the awkward accents along the way" (2002).

WORKS CITED

Andersen, Jesper. 1997. "I lommerne på Europa: Internationaliseringen af dansk filmproduktion." In *Dansk film, 1972–97*, ed. I. Bondebjerg, J. Andersen, and P. Sche-

pelern. Copenhagen: Munksgaard/Rosinante.
Balio, Tino. 1998. "'A Major Presence in All of the World's Important Markets': The Globalization of Hollywood in the 1990s." In *Contemporary Hollywood Cinema*, ed. S. Neale and M. Smith. London: Routledge.
Bergfelder, Tim. 2000. "The Nation Vanishes: European Co-Productions and Popular Genre Formulae in the 1950s and 1960s." In *Cinema and Nation*, ed. M. Hjort and S. MacKenzie. London: Routledge.
Brandstrup, Pil Gundelach, and Eva Novrup Redvall. 2003. "Fra *Babettes gæstebud* til *Unit One*: Internationaliseringen af nyere dansk film." In *Nationale spejlinger: Tendenser i ny dansk film*, ed. A. Toftgaard and I. Hawkesworth. Copenhagen: Museum Tusculanums Forlag.
Dodd, Carley H. 1998. *Dynamics of Intercultural Communication*. Boston: McGraw-Hill.
Dyer, Richard. 2000. "Heavenly Bodies: Film Stars and Society." In *Film and Theory: An Anthology*. Oxford: Blackwell.
European Film Academy. http://www.europeanfilmacademy.org/htm/3peopl.htm.
Godzich, Wlad. 1999. "L'anglais mondial et les stratégies de la disglossie." *boundary 2* 26, no. 2: 31–44.
Grede, Kjell. 1986. "Presskonferens i Köpenhamn." May 30.
Helgeland, Axel. 2002. Press release. "*Jeg er Dina* med storslagen premiere i Frankrike." E-mail: axel.helgeland@nordiskfilm.com.
Hjort, Mette. 1996. "Danish Cinema and the Politics of Recognition." In *Post-Theory: Reconstructing Film Studies*, ed. D. Bordwell and N. Carroll. Madison: University of Wisconsin Press.
Hjort, Mette, and I. Bondebjerg. 2001. *The Danish Directors: Dialogues on a Contemporary National Cinema*. Bristol: Intellect.
I Am Dina (A Film by Ole Bournedal). http://www.iamdina.com/eng/director-/bornedal.html; http://www.iamdina.com/eng/production/production.html.
Iversen, Ebbe. 2002. "æstetisk udsøgt og rasende kulørt." http://www.berlingske.-dk/popup:print=167564
Juergensmeyer, Mark. 2002. "The Paradox of Nationalism in a Global World." In *The Postnational Self: Belonging and Identity*, ed. U. Hedetoft and M. Hjort. Minneapolis: University of Minnesota Press.
Kastoryano, Riva. 2002. "Citizenship and Belonging: Beyond Blood and Soil." In *The Postnational Self: Belonging and Identity*, ed. U. Hedetoft and M. Hjort. Minneapolis: University of Minnesota Press.
Lakoff, George. 1972. "Performative Antinomies." *Foundations of Language* 8: 569–72.
Löthwal, Lars-Olof. 1987. "Informationsmaterial Kring *Hip, Hip, Hurra!*" Swedish Film Institute, April 4.
Miller, Toby, et al. 2001. *Global Hollywood*. London: British Film Institute.
Miller, Toby, and George Yúdice. 2002. *Cultural Policy*. London: Sage.
Moe, Helene. 1994. "En livsdrøm på plakaten." *Kristeligt dagblad*, August 19.
Nordic Council. 1994. "Undersøgelse af film og TV distribution i Norden." *TemaNord*.
Nordic Film and TV Fund. http://www.nftf.net/AboutNFTF.html; http://www.nftf.net/-Newsletter/NL-030311.html.
Schlesinger, Philip. 2002. "Media and Belonging: The Changing Shape of Political Communication in the European Union." In *The Postnational Self: Belonging and*

Identity, ed. U. Hedetoft and M. Hjort. Minneapolis: University of Minnesota Press.
Soysal, Yasemin. 2002. "Citizenship and Identity: Living in Diasporas in Postwar Europe?" In *The Postnational Self: Belonging and Identity,* ed. U. Hedetoft and M. Hjort. Minneapolis: University of Minnesota Press.
Watzlawick, Paul, et al. 1967. *Pragmatics of Human Communication: A Study of Interactional Patterns, Pathologies, and Paradoxes.* New York: Norton.

PART III
Auteurism and Genre in Transnational Context

CHAPTER 8

Globalization and the Auteur: Ingmar Bergman Projected Internationally

Linda Haverty Rugg

The study of cinematic auteurism is also necessarily the study of globalization, for the auteur has been by definition a filmmaker of international stature who is understood paradoxically as representative of a national culture while at the same time transcending national boundaries. The very use of the term *auteur* in English, when one could just as well say *author,* points toward a history, spearheaded in France, of international production, distribution, and reception related to the role of the art cinema director.[1] But, to paraphrase a question by Foucault, what is an auteur, precisely? One might begin by saying that an auteur is an individual, usually acting both as director and screenwriter, whose artistic vision is projected through his or her films. But the reception of an auteur's work seems to operate on a plane that exceeds an individual artist's vision. For instance, in "The Transpositions of a Filmmaker," an essay on Bergman reception in Sweden and abroad, Birgitta Steene describes what she calls the "assimilation stage" of reception, "when a foreign mind absorbs a cultural product so totally that its foreignness disappears. In such a moment," she adds, "Ingmar Bergman's creative persona, embedded in the work itself, communicates directly with another human being" (1998, 127).

Steene's article is an excellent study of Bergman reception in five countries—Sweden, the United States, France, Brazil, and India. But what I would like to do here is leave behind a strict account of diverse national patterns of viewership and cultural reception to follow up instead on Steene's idea of a "creative persona" that somehow "communicates directly with another human being" to the point that the "foreignness" of a foreign film "disappears." What is it in the reception of auteurist films and in the very fabric of such films that creates the illusion of a dissolution of boundaries, both national and personal? In order to answer this question I will first turn to Bergman's role in the birth of auteurist cinema, with close attention paid to the original definitions of the cinematic auteur. This will involve reading Bergman through Jean-Luc Godard and François Truffaut. Then I will move on to a reading of Bergman's pathbreaking film *Persona* of 1966 as an experiment in the dissolution of boundaries. In order to imagine how the auteur's creative persona enters into the consciousness of the viewer, it is useful to consider evidence of the transfiguration of Bergman's persona in the works of other auteurs from outside Sweden; this provides artistic expression of what Steene calls the disappearance of foreignness. And so I will discuss Bergman's presence in the films of François Truffaut in the first section and in the work of Woody Allen in the third.

BERGMAN À LA MODE

When François Truffaut, writing as a twenty-two-year-old for the French weekly *Arts*, proclaimed his subscription to a *politique des auteurs*, he was actually inventing the term. His credo constituted the foundation of this peculiar realm of "politics," and it seems important here to recuperate that part of his invention that was not precisely lost but dropped in translation. While Truffaut and his colleagues at the *Cahiers du cinéma* pursued an active program of defining and expanding the notion of the *politique des auteurs*, Andrew Sarris, who was the first major proponent of auteurism in the United States, proposed dropping the "politique" for his American readership. To his mind, the "auteur theory" promoted film as a high aesthetic medium (the "art film"), and an overt reference to politics would only muddy the waters. Sarris imagines politics and aesthetics as two separate realms, a typical position in American cultural criticism of that time. Besides, it seemed that if Truffaut had any political aim in the creation of the "politique," it was to overthrow the dominant norms and reigning figures of the French cinematic world, not the government.

Truffaut biographer Serge Toubiana, in prefacing a collection of the *Cahiers* essays that introduced, expanded, and critiqued the notion of the cinematic auteur, is suspicious of the term *politique des auteurs*. He writes: "One could interpret the word 'politics' in this sense, as a profound irony, as an indication of the *disengagement* demanded by this critical practice (at a moment when the mainstream intellectuals had nothing but the word 'engagement' on their lips). The only politics of the *Cahiers* consisted in talking about cinema, auteurs, and the mise-en-scène" (de Baecque and Toubiana 1999, 7). To the exclusion, that is, of explicitly "political" discussion. But nevertheless a political implication remains embedded in the studiously apolitical aesthetics of auteurism: the idea of an international cinema. François Truffaut, Jean-Luc Godard, and Eric Rohmer, for instance, paved the way for their own careers as internationally recognized auteurs by lionizing in the pages of *Cahiers* such foreign directors as Roberto Rossellini, Fritz Lang, Alfred Hitchcock, John Ford, and Howard Hawks. Truffaut especially wanted to refute mainstream criticism by insisting that the work of Lang, Hitchcock, Renoir, and Buñuel did not suffer during their respective emigrations but retained the ineffable quality of each man's cinematic genius. That the economic structure, culture, geography, and language that produced a film should be immaterial to this genius is in itself a political claim. And in fact, the critical reception that grew out of the *politique des auteurs* nurtured the international art cinema movement to the degree that art films were most successfully marketed and always reviewed as the products of an auteur: a Truffaut film, a Hitchcock film, a Bergman film.

Ingmar Bergman was a key figure for the group of young French New Wave filmmakers who launched the auteur theory. As a director from a marginal European nation, working in a language and culture none of them knew, he represents the aspect of the *politique des auteurs* that posits film as a "universal language." In writing of Bergman's early films in an adulatory essay, "Bergmanorama," Jean-Luc Godard seems, even as he writes, to abandon language as a rational medium: In the history of film there are five or six films of which the critic can say nothing more than "This is the most beautiful of films! . . . To say that [it is] the most beautiful of films is to say everything. Why? Because it is so. And cinema alone can quite openly make use of this infantile reasoning. Why? Because it is the cinema. And the cinema is sufficient unto itself" (2001, 85; author's translation). What does it mean to say that cinema is sufficient unto itself? And how does Bergman's work provide the vehicle for such a statement?

Three things become clear when one looks back at the formulation of the *politique des auteurs* as it took shape in the *Cahiers*. First, the photographic image is meant to speak for itself. There is a devotion to photography as iconography among the French New Wave filmmakers that seeks to blast cinema out of the confines of text, of literature, of cultural inheritance. To do this Godard, for instance, implicitly refers to the indexical nature of photography. A photograph does not explain or narrate but simply shows, as Roland Barthes would have it, what *has been there* (1981, 76). A beautiful film is simply a beautiful film. There is no language to explain this; only the experience of looking at the film itself will bring the point home. Godard's insistence on the nonlinguistic way in which we view cinema points toward an understanding of the image as independent of words. He pursues this point further by emphasizing Bergman's cinematic construction of time.

Bergman, argues Godard, is the "filmmaker of the instant." His films, like the literary work of a Proust or a Joyce, take as their point of departure the snapshot, the moment captured at the click of a photographic shutter. The trick is to enlarge upon and extend this moment without losing the sense of the instant. "A film by Ingmar Bergman is, one might say, a twenty-fourth of a second that undergoes a metamorphosis and stretches into an hour-and-a-half. It is a world between two blinks of an eyelid, sadness between two beats of a heart, the joy of living between two claps of the hands" (2001, 88). Godard means that the "real" presence of the world, captured in each photograph, infuses the film; the images become, in aggregate, a reality. This is in the spirit of Godard's maxim that "cinema is truth twenty-four frames per second"—the "truth" here resides in part in a naïve belief in photographic truth. But Godard is also interested in the cinematic machine, the projector. The metaphors Godard employs—the blink of an eye, the beat of a heart, and so on—place the viewer's body in alignment with the cinematic apparatus. It is not by chance that he writes of a Bergman film mystically occurring within a twenty-fourth of a second; film passes through the projector at the rate of twenty-four frames per second, so that a single image would be projected for that brief moment in time. Bergman himself seems to echo Godard when he writes of his own fascination with the illusory nature of film: "No other art bypasses our conscious minds as film does, going straight to our feelings, deep into the twilight chambers of our souls. A tiny glitch in our optic nerve, a shock effect: twenty-four illuminated squares a second, with darkness between, but the optic nerve does not register the darkness" (1987, 89). It is the photographic capture of time and the cinematic extension of photography into movement that forms the foundation, as Godard sees it, of Bergman's art. This leads to a visceral connection between the viewer and the film, according to both Godard and Bergman; the Swedish director speaks of a direct line into the viewer's soul, while the French director eroticizes the cinematic act and writes of love. He ends his essay with an amorous declaration: "I love *Summer Interlude*." This brings us to the second characteristic of auteurism, which depends upon the first: the creation, projection, and consumption of film should form a direct link between the auteur and the viewer.

Further, it follows from Godard's remarks that the auteurist vision exists apart from the context of space (cultural geography) and time (social history). As Truffaut's argument about the works of auteurs in exile attests, the auteur's films represent an intensely *personal* vision, identified with artistic genius, which is always already separate from such concerns as national literary traditions, studio requirements, economic limitations, and so on. In one of his early manifestos on the subject of cinematic auteurism, Truffaut writes:

> The film of tomorrow appears to me as even more personal than an individual and autobiographical novel, like a confession, or a diary. The filmmakers will express themselves in the first person and will relate what has happened to them. . . . The film of tomorrow will not be directed by civil servants of the camera, but by artists for whom shooting a film constitutes a wonderful and thrilling adventure. The film of tomorrow will resemble the person who made it and the number of spectators will be proportional to the number of friends the director has. The film of tomorrow will be an act of love. (1957; quoted in de Baecque and Toubiana 1999, 110)

Once again, we should note that we see here the direct, visceral connection between the viewer and the film embodied in the cinematic "act of love." In this romantic description of the film utopia of "tomorrow," Truffaut seems to describe a kind of cinema verité, perhaps made with a handheld camera for a group of select friends. But in fact he remains deeply attached to narrative film created for the broadest possible audience—the world audience. The film of tomorrow, as Truffaut subsequently imagines it in the creation of his breakthrough film *The 400 Blows* (1959, *Les quatre cents coups*), is both intimate (autobiographical, personal) and fully public, an exposure of the auteur's hidden past and innermost fears and desires to an international audience.

Truffaut's mother and stepfather, deeply aggrieved at what they considered distorted and negative portraits of themselves and their son's childhood in *The 400 Blows*, demanded that Truffaut publicly refute remarks he had made in prerelease interviews indicating that the film accurately depicted his childhood. Truffaut honored their wishes by publishing an article in *Arts* on the day of the film's release, denying the film's autobiographical nature. Yet it was clear to viewers and critics alike that Truffaut's earlier characterization of the film as an account of his childhood was the more honest position. How does a viewer know this?

The notion of autobiographical narrative film, which Truffaut raises with romantic fervor in his description of the "film of tomorrow," is rather more complicated than a director's simple "relation of what has happened to him." While the neighborhood, events, and characterizations of *The 400 Blows* were close enough to the reality of Truffaut's childhood to offend his parents, it is obvious that the child actor of the film is not Truffaut, and that the scenes of Paris of the 1950s, devoid of any signs of Nazi occupation, are not precisely the streets of Truffaut's youth. An autobiographical theory purist like Philippe Lejeune (1987) would object that *The 400 Blows* lacks the foundation for autobiography: an absolute identification between the person narrating the life and the person within the narration.[2] And for Lejeune there is also the problem that the film unfolds in a photographed present that is always necessarily a mere reconstruction of the past. But perhaps the disruption of the usual relationship between persons and between past and present is precisely the point. If we follow Godard's (irrational) logic to say that cinema occurs in an expanded moment of time, we have to understand films as something quite different from textual narrative, which takes shape in a duration, a chronology. Film should be understood primarily as a spatial expression of time, "sculpting in time," as Russian director Andrei Tarkovsky would have it. Not only is the cinematic moment or instant, the photographic snapshot, in the foreground—history is understood cinematically as a function of both the present and the past.[3] How does this work?

In *The 400 Blows*, Truffaut consistently alludes to cinema directly and to the cinematic apparatus more subtly. His young "self," Antoine Doinel, loses himself in moviegoing (which was, as Truffaut's biographer tells us, Truffaut's lifelong obsession as well). We see the boy watching films we cannot see; Truffaut places the cinematic screen in the viewer's position, which gives us the opportunity to both position ourselves behind the screen and "see ourselves" in the viewing audience. At one point, as the truant Antoine and his friend René leave the theater, Antoine quickly snatches a promotion photograph from an outdoor display. The camera does not dwell on the image he steals, but it is recognizable as a still from Bergman's *Summer with Monika* (1953, *Sommaren med Monika*)—the famous photograph in which Harriet Andersson, sheathed in a tight sweater with a plunging neckline, sits sunning herself on a rock. *Summer with Monika* was released when Truffaut was twenty-one. In other words, this event in the film both reflects an action from his childhood, when he skipped school to go to the movies, and a symbolic act from his adulthood, when he "steals" an image from Bergman.

The "theft" from Bergman's *Monika* finds cinematic expression in the final moments of *The 400 Blows*. At the end of the film, the juvenile delinquent ("bad boy") Antoine Doinel escapes from a detention center and runs desperately for freedom. His flight takes place in part along a country road lined with trees placed artistically, in the European fashion, at regular intervals. The camera observes his run from behind the screen of this row of trees, creating the cinematic visual effect mentioned above of a periodic flashing of black between "frames" of action. Finally the boy comes to the sea, both a goal (he has never seen the ocean before) and the ultimate barrier. (The sea also happens to be the means of Monika's escape from the strictures of Stockholm to the archipelago.) He stops and turns, apparently confronting the camera, engaging the gaze of the viewer in a final freeze-frame. This use of the direct gaze is a quotation from the conclusion of Bergman's *Monika*, when Monika, the "bad girl" of the film who has run away from her husband and child, looks directly into the viewer's eyes. Truffaut's film, then, is not just about a (fictionalized) episode from his childhood but also an account of his own persona as filmmaker in relation to a "father" filmmaker: Père Bergman. The self portrayed in the film is both the child who skipped school to go to the movies and the young man who proposed a new kind of cinema that would draw on the work of such models as Bergman. Godard's comment about the expansion of time in film narrative could have an application here; Truffaut's narrative of childhood is situated *both* during his own childhood (the events at school during and at home occur as he remembered them, in the neighborhoods of his youth) and during his infancy as a filmmaker (during the 1950s, when he receives/steals his inspiration from artists like Bergman). The time frame of a single instant (the theft of the movie still, for instance) expands to encompass the approximately ten years between such actual, juvenile thefts and the adult "theft" of the Monika image for use in Truffaut's own filmmaking.

Beyond the temporal claims of cinema proposed by Godard, *The 400 Blows* also offers evidence of the personalized, even erotic nature of cinema as described/prescribed by Bergman, Godard, and Truffaut. Through the writings of all three critic-filmmakers drifts the notion of cinema's direct line of contact between image and viewer, with the implication of a point of origin in the auteur. Both Bergman and Truffaut draw on the idea of connection by apparently breaking through the illusionistic fourth wall of naturalist performance tradition to have their characters "look back" at the audience. The gaze exchanged between a defiant Monika and the entranced moviegoer François channels into Antoine Doinel's gaze into the eyes of Truffaut's audience. Of his own obsessive moviegoing, Truffaut writes, "I felt a tremendous need to enter *into* the films. I sat closer and closer to the screen so I could shut out the theater" (de Baecque and Toubiana 1999, 33). Much later in Truffaut's career, he made a film in which he plays a director making a film: *Day for Night* (1973, *La nuit américaine*). At one point, the director receives an eagerly anticipated packet of books, and when he opens them and takes them out, we see that they are books by and about famous auteurs: among others, Rossellini, Fellini, Hitchcock, and Ingmar Bergman. Truffaut's citations, both implicit (in *The 400 Blows*) and explicit (in *Day for Night*), point to a relationship with Bergman formed entirely through viewing and making films. In this relationship Truffaut both retains his claims to selfhood—projecting his own childhood and even appearing as an actor playing a director—and dismisses the idea of a distinct, fully integrated artistic vision that emerges from a single consciousness. Despite the apparent claims of auteurism, that auteurist films are the clear product of a particular "genius," a countervailing power circulates here between Bergman and Truffaut, implying that this "genius" cannot be identified absolutely with a single individual but is shared among filmmakers and between filmmakers, actors, the audience, and the mechanism of film technology. Essentially, it seems that auteurist filmmaking can challenge not only given notions of nation and culture but selfhood as well. This is perhaps the only way to understand how the idea of an auteur, so imbued with romantic notions of artistic genius, can apply to cinema. The model of selfhood engaged in the eighteenth and nineteenth centuries—the individual subject—becomes the twentieth-century post-Nietzsche, post-Freud model: a subject divided within itself and fully dependent on intersubjective, collaborative construction. I will explore this further in the following section.

BERGMAN'S *PERSONA*

In 1966 Bergman had the idea to make a film about two women sitting on the beach, wearing hats and comparing hands. That he thought of his new film in such schematic terms may have had something to do with the fact that he had just undergone a spell of aphasia—after an intense bout of illness, Bergman lost the power of speech and found himself grappling with wordless images (Bergman 1987, 238–39). In *Persona* (1966), the film that emerged from this episode of muteness, one of the two protagonists is a woman who either cannot or will not speak, embodying Bergman's autobiographical experience: "One day I discovered that one of the women [in my vision] was mute, like myself" (239). And recalling Godard's remark about Bergman as the "filmmaker of the instant," we see that Bergman claims to craft his film from a single, wordless image. Not only was no language necessary in envisioning this film—no language was possible. Then, as he struggled to realize his hand-comparison project, Bergman was presented with a photograph of two women, one an actress with whom he had worked and who had been his lover (Bibi Andersson) and one an actress from Norway whom he had never met (Liv Ullmann). What struck him about the image was "how devilishly alike" the two women were. For this reason, he felt he needed to make the film centered on them. Thus from this single moment—two women at the beach who resemble one another, wearing hats and comparing hands—Bergman's most experimental film evolved.

In Bergman's imagination the relationship between the two women of *Persona* arises from their physical resemblance to one another, which makes a confusion of selfhood visually possible. While in terms of their roles the two female protagonists are quite different (the silent, manipulative actress Elisabet Vogler played by Ullmann and the talkative, pragmatic nurse Alma played by Andersson), their physical resemblance allows their faces to be forged together into a single, uncanny image at the point in the film's narrative when it seems that the boundaries between their psychic selves have been dissolved. This story of the merged subjectivities of two women makes up the "story" of the film. But *Persona* also represents the ways in which different "realities" merge in film—not only does the boundary between two individuals blur in a frighteningly disorienting fashion but the boundary between the "real" world and the projected film world is also breached by the film. To underscore the film's concern with identity and guises, one need look no further than the title, *Persona*, which refers to both mask and character. But the working title of the film was *Kineotography*, which suggests that *Persona* is in fact also about film. From the opening frame sequence showing the interior of a movie projector to the "subliminal" messages flashed during the credits to the "breaking" of the film midnarrative to the sudden insertion of a shot of a director and cameraman toward the film's end, this is a film that relentlessly calls attention to itself as a cinematic work of art. The question is: How does the story surrounding the two women (the *Persona* story) collude with the story surrounding the film and its projector (the *Kineotography* story)? Scholars and critics have provided numerous answers to this question.[4] For my purposes here I will focus on why the idea of film's ability to visually produce a merged subjectivity seems so vital to an auteurist filmmaker like Bergman.

Filmmaking, despite the idea of the auteur as lone genius, is an intensely collaborative act. If it is true, as Truffaut proposes, that the auteur makes films in the first person, we have to imagine that first person as an aggregate. Bergman had, for instance, an extraordinarily strong partnership in many of his films (including *Persona*) with cinematographer Sven Nykvist, who could almost be imagined as Bergman's eyes, a vehicle through which Bergman creates his vision. Further, a dependable group of actors followed Bergman from film to stage to film and back, offering their faces, bodies, and gestures to the creation of Bergman's universe. That both of the women playing the central roles in *Persona* were at one time (either before or during the filming) Bergman's lovers underscores the erotic nature of the film's story (the interaction between Alma and Elisabet is highly sexualized) and the nature of filmmaking; as Bergman writes in his autobiography: "Film work is an intensely erotic business" (1987, 199).

One of the protagonists of *Persona*, Liv Ullmann, explains filmmaking's eroticism in terms of the cinematic close-up:

> The closer a camera comes, the more eager I am to show a completely naked face, show what is behind the skin, the eyes; inside the head.... When the camera is as close as Ingmar's sometimes gets, it doesn't only show a face, but also what kind of life this face has seen. Thoughts behind the forehead, something the face didn't know about itself, but which the public will see and recognize. Privately we long for exactly this kind of recognition: that others should perceive what we really are, deep inside. To make a film with Ingmar is, for me, to have this experience. (1977, 224)

While what we actually see in the frame is a flat image, we somehow "recognize" what is "behind." We penetrate the persona on-screen, using the eye of the camera.

The frame of *Persona*'s narrative, in which, among other things, a young man caresses a large screen upon which shifting images of the two female protagonists are projected, points directly toward the desire to penetrate film's enigmatic surface. And yet another "frame" is implied; not only is there the world of the boy outside the film's narrative, but the "real world" of filmmaking is brought in through the image of the projector, the "jammed" filmstrip, and a fleeting glimpse of a cameraman and director "making" the film. Of course, none of the frames can really access the "real world." The film cannot film itself being made or broken. Nor can the film "see" the spectators, as is implied in the sequence in which Elisabet points her camera "at the audience." But Bergman wants to play at transgressing the boundaries between filmmaker and film, film and spectator. When the cameraman and director suddenly appear toward the end of the film, the audience has only enough time to register the fact that there is *a* cameraman and *a* director in the frame. We assume on some level that these men are *the* director and *the* cameraman, that is to say, of *Persona*. But when one looks closely at the image (after repeated viewings or using the "pause" button), the identities of the men remain unclear. First, in order to identify the two men as director and cameraman, the viewer must recognize these two "real people" from sources outside the film. And even supposing one possesses that knowledge, the face of the man behind the camera is obscured by the camera. He is, in effect, masked—possibly Bergman, possibly someone else entirely, but not Nykvist, as the man operating the camera is not blond. The man to his right on the crane (his right-hand man) is not Bergman; he is a very blond man, possibly Nykvist. This little moment, when God seems to descend from the machine (in fact, another camera rises to meet the figures on the crane and film them) does not reveal the face of God. Nor do we know the identity of the "voice of God" (that is, an authoritative cinematic narrator's voice) that speaks in a voice-over earlier in *Persona*. It is only through outside reading (in Kawin 1978, 122) that we learn that the voice is actually Bergman's.

Thus Bergman plays an elaborate game of hide-and-go-seek in *Persona* using possible traces of his own body (his image? his voice?) to complicate further the relationship between the viewer's space (the real world in which Ingmar Bergman lives) and the narrative space of the film. There are several points to be made here in relation to the significance of the cinematic auteur and his connection to the audience. *Persona* breaks boundaries between persons and between "worlds" or "realities"—but it can do so only as part of the machinery of illusion: the trick photograph that "merges" the faces of the two actresses, the apparent breaking and burning of the film. These things do not actually happen but only seem to happen, and upon reflection the viewer realizes that they cannot have happened. It may be, as the film suggests, that there are no fixed subjectivities, no "you" or "I" that exist in independent isolation. The very pronouns "you" and "I" only serve to mark position points, not individuals. And it may be that confusion can occur between projected realities, as there may be no fixed "original" reality—everything may in fact be a projection, as the film's use of iconic symbolism hints. But in order to understand this web of illusion the filmmaker must resort to illusion, the optical trick that Bergman cites as film's direct pathway into the soul of the viewer. In unmasking the illusory nature of film in *Persona*, Bergman points toward the illusory nature of personhood and reality. This applies perhaps especially to the notion that we can somehow access the auteur through his films. *Persona* implicitly challenges the idea of a single genius behind the making of auteurist films (which are collaborative, which are illusions) by challenging our understanding both of individual identity (what is an auteur?) and cinematic "reality." Rather than waiting for film theorists to deconstruct the idea of the cinematic auteur, in *Persona* Bergman deconstructs himself.

BERGMAN ON WRY

At the climax of Woody Allen's late noir comedy, *Shadows and Fog* (1992), the protagonist, Max Kleinman (played by Allen), escapes from a serial killer by running into a circus tent. Inside the tent is a magician, and Kleinman, it turns out, is a great admirer of magicians, having hoped to become one as a child. When Kleinman urgently explains that the killer is on his way and they have not a second to lose, the magician invites Kleinman to escape with him into his "mirror of illusion." The magician drags him up to a tall narrow mirror and, entering the reflection himself, he urges Kleinman to join him. "Yump, young man!" he shouts (for he is a magician with an unaccountably Scandinavian accent), "Yust yump!" The two of them confront the killer from "inside" the mirror; the murderer can see them making faces at him and see a dim reflection of his own face, but he can't touch them. Thus in his own way, Allen stages the problem presented more seriously in *Persona* of the boundary between the world on-screen and the "real" world, paying particular attention to the desire (in this case, the killer's) to penetrate an illusion. That Allen himself was an amateur magician as a boy, that Ingmar Bergman has been one of Allen's cinematic idols throughout his career, that Bergman has equated filmmaking to a circus and to a magic show in several films, that in the end of one of them (*The Magician*, 1958, *Ansiktet*) there is a "mirror of illusion," and that the strange magician who knows how to work the "mirror of illusion" has a Scandinavian accent seem to point toward a subtle connection between Bergman and Allen. In other Allen films, the connection is less subtle.

How did a relationship spring up between "a young boy with red hair and black-rimmed glasses" from a middle-class, Jewish family in Brooklyn and the son of a Lutheran pastor who served the Swedish royal court? In his *New York Times* review of Bergman's autobiography *Magic Lantern*, Woody Allen recalls that he had heard there was nudity in Bergman's film *Monika: The Story of a Bad Girl*, as *Sommaren med Monika* was called in the United States. Allen's impetus for seeing a Bergman film for the first time was the motivation for most filmgoers at the time; as the doctored English title suggests, *Monika* was marketed as soft porn, a film that had slipped into the heavily censored U.S. market through a foreign loophole. English titles for subsequent

Bergman films (*The Naked Night* for *Gycklarnas afton/Night of the Clowns* [1953] or *Illicit Interlude* for *Sommarlek/Summer Game*) indicate how distributors continued to try to attract viewers with Allen's inclinations to films that in fact were more artistic than salacious. The problem with titles and their translation indicates one of the roadblocks that language stubbornly places in the way of auteurist film, which is supposed to transcend language through image.

When Allen was a bit older and apparently more mature (or at least more aesthetic) in his moviegoing, he went to another Bergman film with, as he puts it "the unpromising title *Wild Strawberries*" (1957) (1991, 27). The original Swedish title of the film, *Smultronstället* ("the wild strawberry patch") does not speak to someone from Brooklyn; for a Swede it means both literally a place where one can find the elusive wild strawberry and a secret place where one tastes pleasure. Because wild strawberries (like wild mushrooms) are difficult to find, one shares the secret of the strawberry patch location only with one's most intimate circle, and because of the erotic value of sensual strawberries and their location in the hidden spots of the summer forest, the title carries a hint of romantic tryst and escape from the mundane into the blissful. Further, the place is a location stored in memory to be called up for future reference, a place to which one hopes to return to remembered happiness. And all of these associations are linked to the story of the film, in which the elderly professor Isak Borg returns to the strawberry patch of his youth, where he is able to conjure forth magically the people and places of his past. The title of the film, meaningless to Allen, provides a neat summary of the work for Swedes, which indicates the way in which language and cultural difference can block reception of some levels of auteurist film.

Yet Allen does understand *Wild Strawberries* through the film's images: "Only [when I saw *Wild Strawberries*] did I lock into what was to become a lifelong addiction to the films of Ingmar Bergman. I still recall my mouth dry and my heart pounding away from the first uncanny dream sequence to the last serene close-up. Who can forget such images?" (1991, 27). It is important to note here the visceral, physical response the future filmmaker experiences when confronted with Bergman's films; Allen's heart pounds as Isak Borg's seems to do on the soundtrack of the dream sequence. While watching *The Seventh Seal* ("always my favorite film") "with a small audience at the old New Yorker Theater," Allen sits "riveted like a child at a harrowing fairy tale" (27). The movie house, the others in the audience, the seat against his back, all are part of Allen's reception of Bergman's films, which seem to stream into his consciousness in just the way Bergman imagines they would, straight into the soul.

Allen's first reference to Bergman is a parody of an image from his "favorite film," *The Seventh Seal*. This particular image, the figure of Death and his chess game with the Knight, has been one of the most popular targets of parody in film history. Americans seem particularly incapable of resisting the urge to create scenes in which Death challenges a film's protagonist to badminton (*De Düva*, George Cove, 1968), Battleship or Twister (*Bill and Ted's Bogus Journey*, Peter Hewitt, 1991), or simply a contest of wits (Allen's *Love and Death*, 1975). In these parodies Death appears suddenly and frighteningly, always in flowing robes, like the Death figure of *The Seventh Seal*. But he also always speaks in a sonorous, portentous voice, while Bengt Ekerot, the actor who portrays Bergman's Death, has a light, gentle, and rather high-pitched voice that seems out of character with his black robes and grim mask. This lack of congruity between the parodies and Bergman's original points toward what seems like a misinterpretation of Bergman by his parodists. Bergman's Death is already something of a parody. Bergman's Knight recognizes Death because he has seen paintings of the figure in churches. The original inspiration for *The Seventh Seal* was just such a painting, which depicted the Dance of Death leading a line of plague victims into the netherworld. Bergman quotes this painting in the final scene of his film, "one of the most memorable shots in all movies," according to Allen (1991, 27). When one returns to *The Seventh Seal*, one sees that the images of Death are often lightly satiric; Death has a sense of humor and also a secret store of vanity, which the Knight is able to manipulate to his own ends. It is in part Bengt Ekerot's intonation in his line "Ja, jag är faktiskt en ganska skicklig schackspelare" (Yes, I am actually a rather skillful chess player) that leads to the viewer's understanding that Death in this context is both comedic and vulnerable at some level. Taken from the world of pure and ghastly image on a church wall and moved into the realm of language and narrative in film, the medieval Death figure acquires a modern, sardonic tone. American filmmakers who have parodied Bergman's Death perhaps missed the language and tone of the original, which was not an original in the first place.

Allen's later treatments of Bergman motifs grow more serious, to the dismay of his fans, who were drawn to the comedy of Allen's early films. One of the things Allen admired about Bergman was his ability to be both a "showman" (Allen 1995, 28) and a serious artist. Bergman, Allen writes, "evolved a style to deal with the human interior, and he alone has explored the soul's battlefield to the fullest" (28). In *Interiors,* Allen's first fully dramatic film, he attempts to follow his Swedish mentor into the depths of the human psyche, using the paradoxically flat and impenetrable cinematic surface as his vehicle. Allen's film, like many of Bergman's, makes use of the geographical and architectural setting of a claustrophobic house situated on a barren shore, and his cinematographer, Gordon Willis, creates a cold, clean look through the use of light, reminiscent of Sven Nykvist's work in *Persona.* The criticism surrounding *Interiors,* in fact, was that it was too close to Bergman (even in the plot design of three sisters and their relationship to an absent mother, as in Bergman's *Cries and Whispers*) and not close enough to Allen. In other words, Allen sacrificed his own showmanship (which derives from his background as stand-up comic) to a Bergmanesque rendering of serious art. Thus one auteur disappears behind another; in Allen's case, a quite literal disappearance, since he is physically absent from *Interiors.*

A more successful and subtle foray into Bergman's world occurs later in Allen's career with *Crimes and Misdemeanors* (1989). The theme Allen treats in the film—getting away with murder—addresses the problem of guilt and the question of God's existence, which permeate much of Bergman's work. But a more specific parallel can be drawn between a particular scene in Allen's film that recalls a scene from Bergman's *Wild Strawberries,* the film that had led to Allen's "addiction" to Bergman thirty years before. In *Wild Strawberries,* the old man Isak Borg, on his way to receive an honorary doctorate at Lund, stops off at the house where his family spent their summers during his childhood. When he finds the old strawberry patch of those long-ago summers, he is drawn into the past: "I don't know how it happened, but the reality of the clear day dissolved into the even more clear reality of memories that rose before my eyes like a true occurrence." In the film, Isak is able to watch the people from his past as if they were on film; they are unable to see or hear him. These are not precisely memories, however, because he witnesses events from the past that he would not have been able to see at that time (his beloved Sara flirting with his brother, a birthday party that took place while he was out fishing with his father). When the family is summoned to the house for Uncle Aron's birthday breakfast, the elderly Isak rises from the strawberry patch and goes into

Globalization and the Auteur

Isak Borg (Victor Sjöström), as though gazing at the illuminated spectacle from the theater in Ingmar Bergman's *Wild Strawberries* (1957)

Rosenthal (Martin Landau), transfixed by a childhood Passover Seder in Woody Allen's *Crimes and Misdemeanors* (1989)

the house, standing in the dark of the hall at a doorway that opens into the almost impossible brightness of a large dining room filled with white furniture, blond people, and summer light. There is a curtain beside the door that assists him in hiding but also emphasizes what is already clear—that Isak's position as voyeur hidden in the dark mirrors the film viewer's position, gazing at the illuminated spectacle from the theater. He watches the comedic scene played by his family, and when Sara runs out of the room crying, he tries to comfort her, but she cannot see or hear him. He remains a spectator, though a deeply implicated one.

In Allen's *Crimes and Misdemeanors,* his protagonist Judah, guilty of having asked his brother to hire a contract killer in order to murder his mistress, finds himself driving in the neighborhood where he and his brother grew up. He stands gazing at their childhood home until the present occupant invites him in. She accommodates his need for solitude ("Mind if I just take a minute?" he asks. "Everything seems to be flooding through me") and leaves him standing just outside the dining room. Suddenly he hears the murmur of Hebrew prayers, and he walks into the doorway of the dining room to listen. To his surprise, a Passover Seder from his childhood is taking place, with his father at the head of the table and his young self seated next to his young brother. While the Swedish breakfast scene included an imperious matriarch, the Jewish Passover scene features the dominating voice of Judah's aunt, a Marxist atheist who finds the religious aspect of the meal repellent. She enters into an argument with Judah's father, who protests that there is a God who punishes the wicked. Her answer, that Hitler murdered 6 million Jews and got away with it, prompts Judah to ask from his position on the threshold, "And if a man commits a crime? If he kills?"

This is of course a significant departure from Bergman's model, since one of the points seems to be that Isak cannot enter into dialogue with the "film" or "play" of his past. Everyone at the Seder table looks up at Judah, and his father responds, "Then one way or another he will be punished. Murder will out." In Allen's film, the spectator enters easily into the spectacle. Judah's father even recognizes the man standing in the doorway as his son; when Judah's aunt claims that a murderer who remains undiscovered can have a clear conscience, he says, "Your aunt has a brilliant mind, but she's had a very unhappy life, Judah." In the meantime, we have a reaction shot from the young Judah sitting at the table that indicates his interest in the aunt's position, the position the older Judah will embrace in order to live out his life.

One way to account for the difference in the two treatments of this essentially similar event is a difference in religious and cultural practice. In Lutheran rituals, as in Catholicism and mainstream Protestantism, laypeople usually occupy a spectator position. Aside from scripted responses and hymns, in which the voice of any one member of the congregation is obscured among the voices of the group, there is no audience participation and certainly no questioning. Jewish tradition, on the other hand, highlights the importance of asking questions. Individuals are asked to reflect on and ask about the meaning of a given ritual practice or passage of scripture. This is particularly true of the Passover Seder, in which the youngest child of the household is called upon to ask ritual questions: "Why is this night different from all other nights?" and so on. The Haggadah, a script for the Passover ritual, underscores in many ways the practice of questioning; one of the four sons described in the ritual is "the son who does not yet know how to ask questions." Therefore Judah, as one of the sons of the family, does not precisely interrupt what is going on. He phrases his question as a Talmudic hypothetical: "And if a man kills?" That his father seems unruffled both at the adult Judah's presence and the nature of his question speaks to the "natural" way that boundaries between actors and spectators (rabbi and congregation) are supposed to be breached in Jewish tradition when important questions must be asked of scripture.

Another interpretation of Judah's entrance into the scene returns to the idea I have explored extensively in this essay: the current that flows between filmmaker and viewer through the medium of film. Woody Allen, watching *Wild Strawberries* in the late 1950s in New York, absorbs the film's images and reframes them in his own cultural setting thirty years later. Judah's ability to breach the boundary between spectator and spectacle parallels the way in which Bergman's film penetrates Allen's consciousness and then is reprojected for Allen's viewers. A similar action takes place in Antoine Doinel's theft of the image of Monika in *The 400 Blows*. Truffaut, immersed in Bergman's images, doing his best to sit close to the screen and "enter" the film, takes away impressions that he will reproject in his first important narrative film, a film that others take for a projection of his life. Truffaut, like Allen, also enters a number of his films as an actor. The circulation of motifs, images, lines, even actors and technicians (Allen has employed Bergman's frequent collaborators Sven Nykvist and Max von Sydow in his films, for instance) point toward a construction of auteurism that imagines the filmmaker as part of an aggregate force. This is true in terms of intertextuality, in terms of the use of the same actors and technicians, but also in terms of shifted paradigms for art (collaborative) and selfhood (intersubjective). Yet paradoxically, the distribution and reception of art films depend on the idea of the auteur as an individual stable entity with a singular artistic vision.

The directors I have discussed in this brief study of auteurism pull their viewers' attention toward the contested origin of the auteurist vision—the auteur's body—but in doing so, they paradoxically undo the body's coherence with its work. Of the three, Bergman offers the most attenuated version of self-exhibition—we catch only a brief glimpse of a director (is it *the* director?) and hear a snatch of a voice (the author's voice) in *Persona*. Woody Allen and François Truffaut, on the other hand, appear frequently in their own films. When the director appears as actor, there is an immediate confusion of the "real" and its projection. The audience can identify the figure on-screen with both the origin of the cinematic vision and its product. The identification with Woody Allen (the "real" person) and his persona on film is so complete that there may be no possible recuperation of a "real" Woody Allen; a documentary film by Barbara Kopple (1997) on Allen and his "other life" as a Dixieland jazzman reveals him to be, in his "real" life, essentially the Woody Allen of *Stardust Memories,* with a train of aggressive fans, Fellini grotesques. Both Truffaut and Allen make films about directing films in which they themselves play the director (*La nuit américaine* and *Hollywood Ending,* respectively). And as they play the director within their films, these directors transform themselves once again into viewers—the first viewers of the film they are in the process of making.

When Birgitta Steene discusses the "assimilation stage" of reception, the point at which "a foreign mind absorbs a cultural product so totally that its foreignness disappears," she refers to the experience of a viewer watching a film by an auteur such as Bergman. After considering the strategies of merging, reflection, projection, and appropriation in the work of these three auteurs, we might say that assimilation is an integral part of viewing and producing film. The desire to enter into the frame and, in turn, bring the projected world back into the real one finds repeated expression in auteurist cinema, a form that proclaims the primacy of the image as a conduit to the heart and soul of the viewer, regardless of national identity. The recurrence of misreadings of cultural details and garbled or purposefully misleading titles or subtitles indicates that the circuit between film and viewer cannot be as direct as Godard or Bergman would have it. But the failings of language only echo the essential problem of a globalized auteurist vision: The auteur is, despite dogged self-projection, always absent, may not even exist, and is certainly not accessible as a human being. Any message to the contrary belongs to the realm of shadows and fog, the mirror of illusion. What we can say about the auteur's globalizing power is that it represents a desire, the desire that pulls the scattered and diverse cohort of filmmakers and viewers into a network of mutual assimilation.

NOTES

1. German in fact translates *cinéma des auteurs* as *Autorenkino*.
2. This argument is also central to Elizabeth Bruss's seminal article of 1980.
3. This idea of history echoes Walter Benjamin's notion of history as a photographic flash, a moment in which the present and the past illuminate one another.
4. See, for example, Sontag 1968; Kawin 1978; and Blackwell 1986.

WORKS CITED

Allen, Woody. 1995. "Through a Life Darkly." In *Ingmar Bergman: An Artist's Journey on Stage, on Screen, in Print*, ed. Roger W. Oliver, 25–30. New York: Arcade.
Barthes, Roland. 1981. *Camera Lucida: Reflections on Photography*. Trans. Richard Howard. New York: Farrar, Strauss and Giroux.
Bergman, Ingmar. 1987. *Laterna Magic*. Stockholm: Norstedts.
Blackwell, Marilyn Johns. 1986. *Persona: The Transcendent Image*. Urbana: University of Illinois Press.
Bruss, Elizabeth W. 1980. "An Eye for I: Making and Unmaking Autobiography in Film." In *Autobiography: Essays Theoretical and Critical*, ed. James Olney. Princeton, N.J.: Princeton University Press. 296–320.
de Baecque, Antoine, and Toubiana, Serge. 1999. *Truffaut: A Biography*. Translated by Catherine Temerson.Berkeley: University of California Press.
Godard, Jean-Luc. 2001. "Bergmanorama." In *La politque des auteurs: Les textes*, ed. Antoine de Baecque and Gabrielle Lucantonio, 85–93. Paris: Cahiers du cinema.
Kawin, Bruce. 1978. *Mindscreen: Bergman, Godard, and First-Person Film*. Princeton, N.J.: Princeton University Press.
Kopple, Barbara. 1997. *Wild Man Blues*. Jean Doumanian Productions, Cabin Creek Films, Sweetland Films.
Lejeune, Philippe. 1987. "Cinéma et autobiographie: Problèmes de vocabulaire." *Revue belgedu cinéma* 19 (Spring): 7–14.
Sontag, Susan. 1968. "Bergman's Persona." In *Styles of Radical Will*, 62–85. New York: Farrar, Strauss and Giroux.
Steene, Birgitta. 1998. "The Transpositions of a Filmmaker: Ingmar Bergman at Home and Abroad." *TijdSchrift voor Skandinavistiek* 19, no. 1: 103–28.
Truffaut, François. 1957. "Vous êtes tous témoins dans ce procès: Le cinéma francais crève sous de fausses légendes." *Arts*, May 15.
Ullmann, Liv. 1977. *Changing.*. Trans. Liv Ullmann, Gerry Bothmer, and Erik Friis. New York: Knopf.

CHAPTER 9

"I'm a Lumberjack and I'm Okay": Popular Film as Collective Therapy in Markku Pölönen's *A Summer by the River*

Thomas A. DuBois

Expectations were running high among Finnish filmgoers at the beginning of 1998, as the premiere of Markku Pölönen's latest film approached. Pölönen, who divides his time between making feature films and television commercials, became a household name in Finland through the success of his 1993 film *Land of Happiness* (*Onnen maa*), a nostalgic look at Finnish tango culture, steeped in rural imagery and romance. Although not a box office success, *Land of Happiness* struck a chord with the Finnish public once it was aired on television. In 1995, Pölönen's adaptation of Heikki Turunen's novel *The Last Wedding* (*Kivenpyörittäjän kylä*) drew record numbers to the theaters and established Pölönen as a voice interested not only in celebrating Finnish rural life but also in examining its conflicts and processes of change. Now *A Summer by the River* (*Kuningasjätkä*), billed as an examination of rural log floaters' lives during the 1950s, promised the same powerful mix of nostalgia and realism, a recipe for success in a country where the forest and the logger hold long-standing economic and symbolic significance.[1] In the months that followed its premiere, *A Summer by the River* met and surpassed viewers' expectations, garnering record viewership and attracting nominations for numerous Finnish as well as international film awards. It gave its Finnish audience, I argue in this chapter, a means of collectively reenvisioning certain seemingly threatened pillars of Finnish national identity: the forest, the logger, and (at the deepest and most resonant level) masculinity itself. *A Summer by the River* revises the lumberjack of earlier Finnish literature and film to adhere to the emerging ideals of masculinity in 1990s popular culture and psychology. By doing so, Pölönen is able to reassure his audience that the "soft," intimate man of the 1990s—provided he has learned to also be "fierce"—is not a *perversion* but a *continuation* of the Finnish man of the past. Pölönen's film becomes a tool for collective therapy, a soothing response to the pervasive notion of a crisis of masculinity in late-twentieth-century popular culture. As such, it gives us a fascinating glimpse into the collective functions that popular film can play in a small society.

THE FOREST AND THE LOGGER: HISTORICAL REALITIES

First, in examining the symbolic uses of the lumberjack in any piece of Finnish literature, art, or film, it is important to recognize the clear economic centrality of forestry within Finnish society for most of the last two centuries. As Reunala (1989) points out, the forest has always figured as a source of livelihood and sustenance for Finns. Already in the sixteenth century Finns had begun to export timber to Sweden—both as firewood and as lumber—an industry that grew in the course of the next two centuries with the development of water-powered sawmills and improved saw blades. The introduction of steam-powered mills in the mid-nineteenth century created a boom in the timber industry, which expanded to include pulp mills and paper factories as well. Both landowning farmers and landless itinerant workers rushed to fill the voracious maws of the new mills, felling trees at an unprecedented rate, marking them with identifiable company symbols and then floating them downstream to be redeemed for cash. By its peak in the 1940s, the timber industry accounted for 90 percent of Finnish exports. In the immediate postwar era, this important industrial engine served as the principal means of generating income to rebuild the country and pay off its war debts. It remains an important industry today, despite the country's diversification of industry and livelihood during the second half of the twentieth century and the massive urbanization of its populace. Wise planning by late-nineteenth-century legislators ensured that the forest has been treated as a renewable resource rather than as a good to be extracted and abandoned, a further point of pride for Finns.

Snellman (1996) traces the history of logging in the northern Finnish Kemijoki area's watershed from the 1890s to the mid-1960s, examining the development of unique varieties of social life that unfolded in and around the lumber camp, much as in the case of Scottish bothy culture or the culture of American cowboys. In contrast to these foreign examples, however, the Finnish logger's world—with its skills, stories, songs, and forms of competition and celebration—could truly be described as a *common* experience among rural Finns, who still made up the majority of the nation's population. In the 1950 census, fully 70 percent of rural men reported having worked within the industry for some period (Virtanen and DuBois 2000, 99). And it is arguable that the timber industry might not have become such a prominent part of Finnish cultural identity if it had not been for the vast number of people it actually employed. Firsthand knowledge lent it the kind of resonance within Finnish culture that wartime experiences came to hold in American popular culture and film during the early postwar era. Those who had not worked in the industry themselves or been involved in supplying food or other services directly to loggers at least knew people who had, and nearly everyone had heard stories of the adventures of friends and relatives in the industry for much of their lives.

As widespread mechanization reduced the need for timber workers, however, familiarity with the logging livelihood waned. The obsolescence of older skills like log rolling and ax wielding further drove a wedge between what older Finns regarded as the "real" logging and the "debased" machine tending of the progressively more mechanized modern industry. Pölönen, who had done fieldwork in preparation for a documentary on the timber industry during the 1970s (Ahonen 1998), chose to locate his film's action in the 1950s, the period that could be seen as the beginning of the end of logger culture per se and the heyday of its romanticization in popular film.

Both Snellman (1996, 1998) and Pöysä (1997) explore the economics of the logger's life and the tensions it created in Finnish rural society. Owning land and remaining a fixture within a locale had long been an ideal of Finnish peasant life, supported by turn-of-the-century land reforms that sought to extend that possibility to an ever greater proportion of the rural populace (Reunala 1989, 48). Strangers and itinerants were viewed with distrust, and a landless man was particularly distrusted if he showed interest in courting a local farmer's daughter. Courtship, in fact, was regarded as a sober affair; as marriages were the means by which farms were passed from one generation to the next, they had to be decided with prudence and foresight. The timber industry, however, created a reason for mobility within the countryside and introduced wage earning as an alternative means of livelihood that could compete with the income generated by farming. Even though, in practice, most timber workers spent most of their year doing farm work themselves, the image of economic freedom that the logging industry afforded made a strong impression on the popular imagination. The notion of men who could now be footloose and still earn a living seemed to threaten the very ideals of farm society, particularly if they showed themselves possessed of a roving eye and a keen wit. With a likelihood of having traveled widely—including working sojourns in Sweden, Canada, or the United States—the logger represented a new breed in the Finnish imaginary. A potentially dangerous free radical, whose impermanence, love life, and attitude toward industry were to be questioned, the logger was more a source of anxiety than entertainment for the first half of the twentieth century. As such, he was precisely the kind of figure that attracts literary and filmic attention.

THE LUMBERJACK IN FINNISH LITERATURE AND FILM

Complex issues of livelihood and identity clustered around the logger in Finland, as they did around his counterparts in northern Sweden (Johansson 1994) and North America. Already in the 1870s, depictions of lumberjack life were beginning to appear in Finnish literature (Pöysä 1997, 95), and by the turn of the century, these had crystallized in several particularly influential works. In keeping with Spicer's (2001) exploration of male types in British cinema, we can view these early representations as establishing a series of overlapping—sometimes conflicting—images of the lumberjack, ones that later literature, popular music, and film would expand, modify, parody, and transform. The most paradigmatic texts of this initial period were Teuvo Pakkala's *Tukkijoella* (On the Logging River, 1899) and Johannes Linnankoski's *Laulu tulipunaisesta kukasta* (*The Song of the Blood-Red Flower*, 1905). Pakkala's text, a play in four acts, is studded with popular songs that aggrandize the lumberjack, his bravery, and his love life. Typical of these is a stanza sung spontaneously by a chorus of cheerful lumberjacks:

> Oh the lumberjack he knows no sorrow
>   He shoots the rapids and sings.
> He goes where he will and walks where he would
>   And with the girls has flings. (Pakkala 1952, 87; author's translation)

In the love story at the core of the play, the heroic lumberjack, Turkka, wins the heart of a landed farmer's daughter, Katri, eventually revealing at the play's surprise ending that he, too, is a landowner. The play was made into a film in 1928 and remains one of the most popular works in Finnish theater history, enjoying regular revival in summer repertoires as well as amateur theater. Its songs, set to music by the Finnish composer Oskar Merikanto, remain some of the best-known pieces in Finnish popular music.

Linnankoski's novel, on the other hand, takes the lumberjack figure one step farther, depicting its hero, Olavi, as a lady's man, charming even the haughtiest of local maidens and finding a new conquest in every village. Similarly filled with popular songs and daring feats, it portrays the lumberjack as carefree but crafty, a man to protect one's daughter from, a man to dream of late at night. While Olavi reforms by the novel's end, it is his escapades before that which gave the work its popular appeal. The novel enjoyed widespread popularity, going through some twenty-seven editions before being incorporated into the author's collected works in 1952 and undergoing translation into nearly two dozen other languages. It also attracted the disapproval of conservative and moral elements in Finnish society, however, and its importance as a work of Finnish literature is often discredited (for example, Ahokas 1973, 170; Laitinen 1981, 332). This conflict between popular embrace and highbrow disdain becomes a persistent fixture of lumberjack images in Finnish literature and affects to a certain extent the choice of images and audience in *A Summer by the River* as well.

A mark of the appeal of Linnankoski's novel is the fact that it was made into a film not once but five times, three times in Sweden and twice in Finland (1919, 1934, 1938, 1956, and 1971). As Soila (1994) has shown, these filmatizations map interesting shifts in the notion of film romances and the treatment of lumberjack themes. Scenic landscapes and stereotyped romance decline in importance over the various film versions, as filmmakers seek to unearth a believable romantic relationship in what had become by the 1950s a highly contrived plot.

In fact, by the decade of the 1950s, a new, more parodic image of the lumberjack was taking hold in Finnish popular cinema, one that played off earlier representations but made light of the morals, drinking habits, and sexual escapades of its woodsman heroes. Known collectively as the "Rillumarei" films, these included works by singer/screenplay writer Reino Helismaa, including his *Rovaniemen markkinoilla* (At the Rovaniemi Market, 1951) and *Lentävä kalakukko* (The Flying Casserole, 1953) (Peltonen 1996). Key to the success of these unabashedly lowbrow popular films was their incorporation of popular music. Justeeri's (Kauko Käyhkö) single "Rovaniemen markkinoilla" was the number one–selling record in Finland for 1951. Its nonsensical refrain *ruma-relluma-rilluma-rei* came to stand for the entire genre of films and entertainment. Tellingly, however, the song was banned from airplay on the Finnish National Broadcasting system (Yleisradio) for most of the 1950s, due to its "errors" in Finnish grammar and presentation (Peltonen 1996, 17). Also typical of this parodic vein were popular songs like the Finnish American Hiski Salomaa's Finnglish hybrid "Lännen lokari" (The Logger of the West, 1930). The song's main character takes the Olavi figure to a comic extreme, depicting his exploits across the entirety of North America:

> Here's a logger come from the woods of the West
> I've traveled almost everywhere.
> I've been to Butte and St. Cloud,
> Red Lodge and Miami.
> I've traveled seas and continents
> And even Alaskan tundra
> And everywhere I've gone the hot girls all know
> The logger of the West. (Westerholm 1983, 70; author's translation)

Salomaa's record made its way back across the Atlantic to become one of the most popular songs of its era, a signature piece on the new Metsänradio (Forest Radio) broadcasts that ran in North Karelia and northern Finland from the mid-1940s (Pöysä 1997, 102). Esa Pakarinen played off the song in another of Helismaa's films, *The Brother of the Logger of the West* (1952, *Lännen lokarin veli*), which follows the adventures of the savvy Esa Coolman, newly returned from his time in America (339). Slapstick, irreverent, and extremely popular, the Rillumarei films established a new lowbrow idiom in Finnish popular cinema, one that would irritate Finnish critics but find ample replication in the works of later Finnish film comedians, for example, Uuno Turhapuro (Peltonen 1996).

While the lumberjack thus became a favorite figure of comic popular culture in the 1950s, the logging livelihood itself began its decline. Sensing its passing, folklorists began to collect logger lore at the close of the 1950s, organizing collection competitions and festivals of logger culture, initiating the nostalgia that would soon overtake popular conceptions of the logger's life (Pöysä 1997). By the 1970s, the logger could become the focus of serious realist films such as Mikko Niskanen's *Eight Fatal Shots* (1972, *Kahdeksan surmanluotia*) and adaptations of the writings of the Finnish memoirist Kalle Päätalo. Now depicted as a disempowered wage slave, the 1970s filmic lumberjack can be seen as strongly colored by a nostalgia for the seemingly empowered carefree life of early lumberjack depictions. And as the viewing public grew continually more urbanized and distanced from the wilds of the Finnish woods, the forest could at last become the conceptual space for imagining a therapeutic, exotic, and spiritual experience of the "wilderness" (Saarimaa 1994; Virtanen 1994; Sepänmaa 1993).

A SUMMER BY THE RIVER IN CONTEXT

Given the importance of the lumberjack image in Finnish literature and film, then, Pölönen has little trouble invoking it in his own work. Most often, however, he does so through self-conscious parodies that shed ironic light on both the romantic and the comedic treatment of the livelihood in earlier films. The protagonist, Tenho Ovaska, and his coworkers become a gallery of lumberjack stereotypes that Pölönen sets out to deflate, one by one.

Pölönen mentions in interviews his readiness to accept some of the basic assumptions of the lumberjack image. In comparing loggers to American cowboys, for instance, he remarks: "Cowboys herded cattle and lumberjacks herded trees, but they have the same occupational identity and they regard the same things as valuable in their work. Both value freedom. Life and work are hard, demanding, and cold, but freedom is what's most important" (Ahonen 1998; author's translation). Their struggle with the environment and work make them tough and determined, Pölönen states: "No limp-muscled guy could make it out there. Put him to work for a couple of days doing logging: then you'll see who is really Finland's strongest man!

Popular assumptions such as these, however, are only the starting point in Pölönen's exploration. At the outset of the narrative, for instance, after the death of Tenho's wife and the loss of his job and apartment (apparently due to drinking), Tenho (Pertti Koivula) and his young son Topi (Simo Kontio) set out for North Karelia, intending to earn cash that will buy Tenho a car and Topi a bicycle upon their return to Helsinki. We are presented, then, with the image of log floating as a source of ready income, a job that will float a man until he can find a better situation. Early on in the film, however, we are shown the hard labor involved, and the elder Hannes (Esko Nikkari) reminisces with Tenho about the harsh conditions and near starvation of timber workers in the past, a stark contrast to the film's present (the 1950s) but also a deflation of the audience view of logging as easy earnings. Tenho's desperate clutching of his earnings and hand-to-mouth existence in the camp depart markedly from the idealized images of earlier works.

The image of lumberjacks as musical performers is deftly dismantled as well. At the moment of their first appearance in the film, the logging crew does produce a token amount of music: one of the crew members tunelessly sings a couplet from a logging song. This performance is immediately eclipsed, however, by the arrival of the ukelele-playing Kottarainen (Peter Frantzén), who strums his small instrument pathetically and then makes further sounds with his zipper. Throughout the film, Kottarainen is shown singing not Finnish lumberjack songs but Hawaiian luau music, which combines somewhat incongruously with his black beatnik clothing and verbal dexterity. The crew's leader, Tohkanen (Heikki Kujanpää), later admits his own secret desire to be a professional singer, but in the outdoor dance near the climax of the film, we see that Tohkanen's idol is not Reino Helismaa or Hiski Salomaa but the tango crooner Olavi Virta. Virta's own performance is interrupted by the obligatory brawl scene, in which Kottarainen storms the stage and at last sings a jaunty Rillumarei number about wasting one's pay on a Saturday night. The eventual arrival of the popular song is thus strongly ironized: it becomes part of the *image* of the lumberjack within the surrounding farm community rather than a product of the distinct logger culture that the audience has witnessed for the bulk of the film. As an angry woman swats Kottarainen with her purse, he shows evident enjoyment in the creation of a persona that is as patently fictitious as any of the other personas he takes on in the film, including a temperance preacher and tribal healer.

The notion of the lumberjack as footloose and carefree is called into question through the character of Hilteeni (Vesa Mäkelä). Where Esa Pakarinen played the stereotyped Coolman newly returned from the States, Hilteeni represents an embittered and frustrated returning migrant whose only acquisitions from his time in America are a pair of broken sunglasses, a tendency to punctuate his speech with the English *you know,* and a familiarity with American comedy routines like those of Charles Chaplin and Buster Keaton. His dream of becoming a wealthy farmer in America has been shattered, and he has returned to the world of log floating filled with a resentment that he aims at Tenho. Far from representing the lumberjack as one who has chosen a life of mobility and adventure, Pölönen depicts Hilteeni sniveling in envy as he watches the local farmers tending their land. The image of the wage slave of 1970s portrayals is evident in Hilteeni, yet his comic sniffling and disagreeable personality parody this sense of filmic seriousness as well.

Finally, Pölönen's portrayal of the logging crew's love life is a pointed deflation of the stereotype lumberjack lover of earlier eras. Pölönen evokes images of the erotic lumberjack in the scenes leading up to the local dance. The loggers, with Kottarainen as their spokesman, address two rather plain farm girls who are doing their wash by the riverside. Kottarainen's broad sexual innuendos cause the girls to giggle, enraging local farmers who are watching. In a highly parodic sequence, the logging crew marches resolutely toward the open-air dance stage, the crewman Puukko (Sulevi Peltola) reciting a lumberjack poem while a panicking farmer shuts his beguiled daughter up in a barn, causing her to spill her basket of fruit. The local store owner forbids his daughter Hilkka (Anu Palevaara) to attend the dance because of the loggers, trying to compel her to pay attention to the local farmer Lavikainen instead, who would represent a more suitable match. Yet in the scenes that surround this moment, it is clear that Tenho alone of all the loggers manages to meet or even dance with a woman. And further, it is Hilkka, encouraged perhaps by Topi, who takes the leading role in the romance, kissing a shy and uneasy Tenho and ensuring that, by the end of the film, they will have established a serious relationship. The film lacks entirely the easy romance or conquests that typify literary and filmic representations of the lumberjack, even while it invokes and plays off these in its own depiction of the film's single romance. Given that Tenho hardly qualifies as a "real" logger, Pölönen's film suggests a far less idealized image of the erotic adventures of the randy lumberjack.

MATKA MIEHUUTEEN: THE JOURNEY TO MANHOOD

In a certain sense, then, Pölönen's film seeks to distance itself from earlier images of the Finnish lumberjack, even while it relies upon these for much of its immediate comprehensibility and appeal to a Finnish audience. Its self-conscious treatment of representation and narrative construction can be seen as a mark of postmodern aesthetics, yet it also clears the stage for an alternative construction. In the conceptual space cleared of earlier stereotypes, Pölönen attempts to create a new image of the lumberjack, one in keeping with 1990s ideas regarding masculinity and its development.

Pölönen's *A Summer by the River* makes ready use of the ideas of the then-topical men's studies movement in Finland, particularly as derived from Robert Bly's immensely popular exploration of masculinity, *Iron John: A Book about Men* (1990). Translated by Leena Nivala in 1993 as *Rautahannu: Matka miehuuteen,* the book's subtitle ("A Journey toward Manhood") could well serve as the title for Pölönen's film.

Bly's work proceeds from the assertion that the "1990s man" is psychologically defective in certain ways due to a disvaluing of male role models in his development and a compensatory (but destructive) increase in the importance of female role models instead. According to Bly, men and women will not know happiness in the 1990s until men recover rites of initiation in which men lead other men toward an embrace of the "wild," "hairy," "warrior" masculinity that their mothers have tried to keep them from. These rites, Bly maintains, are common in traditional societies and reflected widely in ancient myths and tales such as the Grimm's version of *Iron John*. Exploring this particular tale from a Freudian and Jungian perspective, Bly finds in it a map for male initiation and growth and the basis for the recovery of new rites of passage for the modern man. He took his message on the road throughout the United States, running men's weekend seminars that were already finding replication in Finland by 1993 (Kauranen 1993). As I will argue below, Pölönen's *A Summer by the River* makes careful use of the narrative progression set forth in Bly's book and offers his Finnish audience a Finnish version of the Iron John tale, carefully crafted to reinforce popular understandings of Finnish manhood, landscape, and history.

Pölönen's film follows Bly's narrative framework faithfully. Where Bly alternates between discussion of masculine development in boys versus young adult men, Pölönen gives his audience one of each, allowing it to witness the parallel maturation of both father and son. The Tenho-Topi pair at the narrative's outset is grieving and incomplete, a situation caused ostensibly by the death of the wife/mother, but in fact revealing Tenho's deeper defects as a man. As he slips into paralytic depression, losing his home and job, Tenho exemplifies what Bly labels "the soft man" (1990, 4). As Bly puts it: "He was nurturing, but something else was required—for his relationship something *fierce* is needed once in a while" (4). Bly's aspersions on the nurturing attitudes of the 1990s man are abundantly illustrated by Tenho: he is shown reading his son a bedtime story, talking softly and reassuringly to him, and spending his free time in private conversation with him. Although he warns his son that crying is of no use in *miehen maailma* (a man's world), he is shown repeatedly crying in the film himself, both out of pain and in relief. Clearly, within the narrative's framework, both Tenho and Topi are in need of some "fierceness" that would allow them to weather the storms of life. This masculine quality, nationalized in the film's ethos as *sisu* (Miettinen 1999)—the storied Finnish quality of tenaciousness, resourcefulness, and guts—is the energy that Topi will try to evoke from his father in dealing with the bullies in the logging crew. When an angry Topi demands to know why Tenho takes so much abuse from Hilteeni, Tenho speaks in nurturing, "soft" tones, saying that as a younger man he will strike only if Hilteeni hits him first. And when Topi pulls a knife to try to defend his father, the latter responds by severely scolding (but not hitting) his son. The "flawed" Tenho is portrayed as a specimen of the kind of man whom Bly finds painfully incomplete: "A grown man six feet tall will allow another person to cross his boundaries, enter his psychic house, verbally abuse him, carry away his treasures, and slam the door behind; the invaded man will stand there with an ingratiating, confused smile on his face" (146). To remedy Tenho's lacks, an initiation ritual must occur.

For Bly, male initiation begins through "absentation" from the ordinary world (filled with feminine influences) and contact with the "Wild Man," a composite archetype of assertive masculinity ("hairyness") that the "young man" can discover through being led to it by older men. The powerful control of the maternal, operative in the civilized world, must be escaped so that a specifically masculine training in the wilderness can commence. In Pölönen's film, Tenho has sensed his need and seeks his Wild Man experience through returning to the trade and know-how of his woodsman grandfather. Tenho and Topi journey into the wilds of North Karelia, leaving their urban and urbane past behind them, as they share seats with a Wheels-on-the-Bus menagerie of colorful and uncouth rural figures: men with baskets of eggs, fat ladies who barf and burp, driver's assistants who deliver newspapers without a moment's decrease in speed, passengers who get out and push the bus up hills. Festive accordion music over the radio recalls Metsänradio broadcasts. And final arrival at their destination necessitates hitchhiking, a situation that puts them in contact for the first time with the assertive and self-confident truck-driving, pack-hauling Hilkka. Hardly an epitome of 1950s femininity, Hilkka nonetheless appeals to both Tenho and Topi, 1990s men reinserted in a 1950s world.

According to Bly, male initiation must next involve an act of scarring: the conferral of some physically noticeable but emotionally pivotal wound, which, Bly posits, allows the young man to access again all the other wounds of his prior life (1990, 15). In Pölönen's film, this wounding occurs in the process of hazing, in which the greenhorn Tenho is subjected to ever more brutal treatment, ridicule, and ostracism as he tries to learn the ropes of log floating. At a highly charged moment in the film, Hilteeni leads the crew to capture Tenho and repeatedly bash his rump on the ground, causing him intense pain that leads him to walk with a limp and a cane for the next several scenes. The wounding scene is not only visually prominent in the film, it is also portrayed as part of Finnish tradition, a time-honored means of humiliating a man on the outs. Withdrawing from Topi, Tenho enters a state of self-searching, which, Hannes informs the worried Topi, is part of what he has to do as a man, a view which could as easily have been delivered by Bly himself. The Finnish logging crew seems fully equipped with an array of initiatory rituals, which, Bly states, characterize a society with a healthy notion of masculinity.

At a turning point in the film, Hannes seems to pronounce the hazing period over, beckoning Hilteeni to him for a whispered conference. Immediately thereafter, the entire crew noisily and cheerfully piles out to help Tenho with his work—freeing a massive logjam that has stopped the crew's progress for some time. With great bustling and camaraderie, the jam is soon freed, and the men shout in triumph: a rather heavy-handed symbol of the conclusion of Tenho's period of testing and new acceptance within the community of men. Pölönen later undermines the seriousness of this image by having Hannes admit that he deceived Hilteeni into believing Tenho was an inspector from the lumber company. His initiation has thus come not out of the men's desire to incorporate him but from their fear of reprisals from the company's upper management. Nevertheless, Pölönen depicts the psychological work as having occurred according to Bly's model: Topi now reports that his father is serene again, like someone "of whom you could ask questions when you don't know how things work." The wound has been received and accepted, its implications worked through, so that Tenho in turn can serve as a proper mentor to his son.

Once this "welcoming" has occurred, Bly states that men involved in initiation must share their stories, pooling the wisdom contained in experiences and tales. Writes Bly: "The older men teach him the myths, stories, and songs that embody distinctively male values: I mean not competitive values only, but spiritual values" (1990, 15). Pölönen's characters do just that, sharing with the camera a range of narratives that delineate and define the male experience. Tohkanen tells of his spiritual experience of female beauty, destroyed by his ideal's untimely fart. Hannes recounts his courting of a proud farmer's daughter, whose rejection of him he sets out to avenge with a cruel but ribald prank. Kottarainen tells of his having been attacked by a bear, a harrowing experience that has left a physical scar on his head and presumably accounts for his psychological peculiarity. Tenho and Topi are distinct in the company in that they, as the newly initiated, are virtually the only men who do not tell personal stories. Pölönen makes these male narratives overt in his film, paring away the pretense of interpersonal discussion or context so that the characters often speak nearly directly to the camera. At least some Finnish reviewers found these scenes irksome disjointed monologues (for example, Review of *A Summer by the River*, 1998), yet their function within the film's portrayal of men's initiation is essential: the kinds of self-sharing advocated in 1990s men's seminars has its counterpart in the campfire talks of the past, even if the narrators couch their stories in cynical or self-parodic guises.

Also crucial in this reinscription of the Finnish man of the past is the assertion of his inherent sensitivity, a characteristic that Pölönen's film appears intent on revealing. Where Bly views the "1950s male" as also defective (describing Reagan as "a sort of mummified version of this dogged type" [1990, 1]), Pölönen seeks to rewrite the lumberjack so that he shows all the positive qualities of the 1990s man as well. He appreciates not only women's bodies but also women's souls (1), and he is man enough to be in touch with his own "feminine side." Tenho manages to get hired on the crew not because of his skills but because of Tohkanen's soft spot toward Topi. Hannes's eyes go teary when he recalls his drowned son Jussi. A patient and tender Hilteeni tells Topi a far-fetched bedtime story while the rest of the crew goes to the dance. Both Topi and Tenho eventually become incorporated into a warm and loving group of men who watch out for their needs and are keen to nurture and love the growing boy. This element, again, is a 1990s insertion into the lumberjack of the past. Its purpose is to reassure the Finnish audience that the patriarchy of old was in fact quite kind: a pervasive, uptight, rural institution but one barely masking a soft, domestic core.

The man's process of self-realization, however, cannot end in Bly's terms with the man's acceptance into the company of men. Still to come must be the "Meeting with the God-Woman in the Garden," the woman who will benefit from the man's newfound masculine prowess. As Bly describes the experience: "He is about to meet the feminine in nonmaternal form, in its powerful, blossoming, savvy, wild, instigating, erotic, playful form. She is the savvy woman on the earth plane" (1990, 123). In Pölönen's film, this narrative turn can only involve Hilkka, the only female character in the entire film with a speaking part. We have met her earlier in the film as the rather butch, crate-slinging truck driver who gives them a lift. Now, however, she reappears as the progressively more feminine daughter of the local shopkeeper. When Topi is bullied at her father's store (the victim of antilogger prejudices), Hilkka comes to his aid. She also inspects the bump on Tenho's head after the local farmers have tried to sabotage the crew's log cache. Topi and Hilkka frolic in a meadow together, but it is clear that he regards her as potential surrogate mother material, given that her voice sounds like that of his own deceased mother. Topi prods his father into going to the dance, where he is able to charm Hilkka with his competent dancing, stealing her away from her dislikable farmer suitor. Later he appears as a nocturnal visitor below her window, until he is chased away by Hilkka's irate father. The couple's romance is filled with stereotyped filmic images—embracing in meadows, kissing while skinny-dipping, necking on top of Hilkka's truck. And by the end of the film, they have formed a new nuclear family, as man, woman, and son wave in grateful satisfaction at the departure of the crew of men, silhouetted against the calm waters of the flowing river.

This tale of male maturation would not be complete, however, without Tenho's recovery of his "inner warriors" (Bly 1990, 146–79). According to Bly, the man must learn the valor of doing battle for things that matter: "sovereignty" as a man, commitment to ideals, and defense of one's own. In Pölönen's film, Tenho recovers his warriors at the rapids. No longer a greenhorn at the periphery, he leads the crew as a squadron of brave boatmen, rowing to save a stranded Topi from the rage of the river. To the accompaniment of male open-throat singing, Tenho and his crewmates rescue the threatened boy, whom they pronounce "Kuningasjätkä" (The King of the Lumberjacks). Tenho has brought his warrior self to life again in the act, but now he must gain the confidence of acting singly as well as in a group. So he challenges Tohkanen to an audacious wager, shooting the rapids alone on the back of a single log. He too thus earns the title "Kuningasjätkä," as the amazed and excited men hurl him into the air in triumph, a visual reversal of the earlier humiliation he had suffered at their hands. Tenho is now complete: rid of his inner wounds, initiated, in touch with his hairy and warrior self, coupled with a God-Woman, and fully able to defend his cherished loved ones. Now, at last, he and his family can live happily ever after.

Appealing to a popular audience entails first getting people onto the same page with regard to characters, conflicts, and likely narrative turns—or, to put it in a filmic metaphor, helping an audience "get the picture." From this point of view, both established images (types or stereotypes) and current trends represent useful building blocks. Past images allow a filmmaker to evoke an audience understanding with a minimum of detail. Current ideas under discussion in the mass media offer the filmmaker the opportunity of appealing to the audience's latest interests and curiosity. Where a filmmaker with art film aspirations may eschew established images, current sound bites, or popular psychology, the filmmaker who hopes to reach a wide audience is foolish to discard such resonant and ready-to-use materials. In this sense, the popular film is always more "of the moment" than its more aloof and encrypted counterpart.

In the case of *A Summer by the River*, Pölönen seeks to offer therapy to his audience, redefining the lumberjack of the past so that he can remain an ideal for Finnish men of the present. In so doing, he engages in the kind of paradigm-setting that Spicer describes in popular British cinema: Tenho and his crewmen represent the same kind of reinscription of the working Everyman that Gaz and his unemployed steelworker mates represent in Beaufoy's *The Full Monty* (Peter Cattaneo, 1997) (Spicer 2001, 190). Despite his film's occasional parody of lumberjack images, however, Pölönen does not seek to "subvert masculinity" in the way that some of the films discussed by critics in the volume edited by West and Lay (2000) do. Rather, his is a presentation of the intersection of hegemonic national identity and masculinity, akin to that of the Australian *Crocodile Dundee* films (Peter Faiman, 1986, 1988, 2001) (West 2000). While "softening" the Finnish lumberjack of the 1950s, Pölönen reassures his audience that assertive women and "real" men can indeed coexist, and that no "crisis of masculinity" in fact is occurring so long as we "remember" the 1950s man in an altered fashion. Male initiation is essential for psychic growth, but Finns—Pölönen seems to argue—have always had it. The lumberjack of the past was not a defective male jerk, because he possessed hidden 1990s sensitivity. The man of the 1990s is not defective either, since he represents a continuity with the secure 1950s man. And male reliance on occupational identity, although seemingly problematized in an era of long-term high unemployment, works after all: we can all be lumberjacks at heart.

NOTES

1. Throughout this essay, I use the term *logger* for actual timber workers and *lumberjack* for literary or filmic representations. As Pöysä (1997) shows, however, the Finnish term *jätkä* covers an extremely broad range of meanings in contemporary Finnish, encompassing the concepts "logger," "guy," "good sport," "worker," "Joe," and so on. As we shall see, this semantic latitude is important for the uses that Pölönen makes of the characters in his film.

WORKS CITED

Ahokas, Jaakko. 1973. *A History of Finnish Literature*. Bloomington: Indiana University Press.

Ahonen, Kimmo. 1998. "Markku Pölönen—Supisuomalainen tarinankertoja" Interview. http://www.film-o-holic.com/haastattelut/polonen_kuningasjatka.htm

Bly, Robert. 1990 *Iron John: A Book about Men*. Reading, Mass.: Addison-Wesley.

Johansson, Ella. 1994. *Skogarnas fria söner: Maskulinitet och modernitet ii norrländskt skogsarbete*. Stockholm: Nordiska Museet.

Kauranen, Anja. 1993. "Jätkät—Uhanalainen laji" *Helsingin Sanomat* 11, no. 2.

Kirby, David. 1989. "The Labour Movement." In *Finland: People, Nation, State*, ed. Max Engman and David Kirby, 193–211. London: Hurst.

Laitinen, Kai. 1981. *Suomen kirjallisuuden historia*. Helsinki: Otava.

Linnankoski, Johannes. 1905. *Laulu tulipunaisesta kukasta*. Reprint, Porvoo: WSOY, 1952.

———. 1921. *The Song of the Blood-Red Flower*. Trans. W. Worster. New York: Moffat, Yard.

Miettinen, Raimo. 1999. Review of *Kuningasjätkä*. *Film Goer*, http://www.leffa-

"I'm a Lumberjack and I'm Okay"

arviot.com/arvostelut/k/kuningasjatka/
Pakkala, Teuvo. 1899. *Tukkijoella: Nelinäytöksinen laulunsekainen huvinäytelmä.* Reprint, Helsinki: Otava. 1952.
Peltonen, Matti, ed. 1996. *Rillumarei ja valistus: Kulttuurikahakoita 1950-luvun Suomessa.* Helsinki: Suomen Historiallinen Seura.
Pöysä, Jyrki. 1997. *Jätkän synty: Tutkimus sosiaalisen kategorian muotoutumisesta suomalaisessa kulttuurissa ja itäsuomalaisessa metsätyöperinteessä.* Helsinki: SKS.
Reunala, Aarne. 1989. "The Forest and the Finns." In *Finland: People, Nation, State,* ed. Max Engman and David Kirby, 38–56. London: Hurst.
Review of *A Summer by the River.* 1998. http://www.uta.fi/~csmaso/elokuvat/Kuningasjatka.htm
Saarimaa, Riika. 1994. "Metsänhoitajan metsä—Puuta ja jotain muuta. In *Metsä ja metsänviljaa.* ed. Pekka Laaksonen and Sirkka-Liisa Mettomäki, 141–50. Kalevalaseuran vuosikirja 73. Helsinki: SKS.
Sepänmaa, Yrjö. 1993. *The Beauty of Environment: A General Model for Environmental Aesthetics.* Denton: Environmental.
Snellman, Hanna. 1996. *Tukkilaisen tulo ja lähtö: Kansatieteellinen tutkimus Kemijoen metsä- ja uittotyöstä.* Oulu: Pohjoinen.
———. 1998. "Miksi Kuningasjätkä?" http://www.tsl.fi/~perinne/tyovaentutkimus/1998/snellman.html
Soila, Tytti. 1994. "Five Songs for the Scarlet Flower." *Screen* 35, no. 3 (Autumn): 265–74.
Spicer, Andrew. 2001. *Typical Men: The Representations of Masculinity in Popular British Cinema.* London: I. B. Tauris.
Virtanen, Leea. 1994. "'Suomen kansa on aina vihannut metsiään.'" In *Metsä ja metsänviljaa,* ed. Pekka Laaksonen and Sirkka-Liisa Mettomäki, 134–40. Kalevalaseuran vuosikirja 73. Helsinki: SKS.
Virtanen, Leea, and Thomas A. DuBois. 2000. *Finnish Folklore.* Helsinki: Finnish Literature Society.
West, Russell. 2000. "'This Is a Man's Country': Masculinity and Australian National Identity in *Crocodile Dundee.* In *Subverting Masculinity: Hegemonic and Alternative Versions of Masculinity in Contemporary Culture,* ed. Russell West and Frank Lay, 44–66. Amsterdam: Editions Rodopi B. V.
West, Russell, and Frank Lay, eds. 2000. *Subverting Masculinity: Hegemonic and Alternative Versions of Masculinity in Contemporary Culture.* Amsterdam: Editions Rodopi B. V.
Westerholm, Simo, ed. 1983. *Reisaavaisen laulu Ameriikkaan: Siirtolaislauluja.* Kansanmusiikki-Instituutin Julkaisuja 11. Kaustinen: Kansanmusiikki-Instituutti.

CHAPTER 10

Learning from Genre: Genre Cycles in Modern Norwegian Cinema

Gunnar Iversen

On February 21, 2003, the Norwegian low-budget horror movie *Wilderness* (Pål Øie, *Villmark*) debuted in Norwegian theaters. Critics applauded the film, and a largely youthful audience loved the story about how four young people, two women and two men, are terrorized in the dark Norwegian woods. The four young people are supposed to work together on a reality TV series, and their producer, an older man, takes them to an isolated cabin in the woods. He wants to test the youngsters to see if they fit the job. However, a mentally disturbed killer is also loose in the area, testing the survival skills of the youngsters more effectively than the old TV producer.

The story of *Wilderness* is well known, sounding like numerous other genre movies; more than anything, it is a Norwegian version of a movie like *The Blair Witch Project*. When the Norwegian film critics praised the film, and the audience loved it, it was not because the film was special or original—on the contrary, it was because it was one of the few examples of an effective and competent genre movie produced in Norway. For example, the critic for the daily newspaper *Dagbladet* ended his review with a note of surprise: "Anyway, the film is an achievement: It is possible to make a good low-budget horror film in Norway" (Wiese 2003).

To critics and audiences alike, it has been something of a surprise each time a successful genre movie has been made in Norway. Since the mid-1980s we have seen several production cycles of genre movies in Norway, producing movies that use successful genre formulas and formats from the American film industry and try to exploit these genre formulas in a Norwegian context. Most of these films have failed at the box office, unable to compete with American imports, and failed as films, unable to use genre formats to tell a good story that not only entertains but also tells us something about Norwegian society in a local or global context.

In this chapter I will discuss a specific production trend in Norwegian cinema since the mid-1980s, the indigenous genre film: films that imitate well-known Hollywood genres such as thrillers, westerns, and horror movies. There have been at least two production cycles of such genre movies, in the mid-1980s and the late 1990s, and a new cycle may well have started with the success of *Wilderness*. After an initial discussion of the film production situation in modern Norwegian cinema, with a consideration of the international trend in Norwegian cinema since the mid-1980s and the two genre cycles in the 1980s and 1990s, I will focus especially on the director Nils Gaup. His films, and especially the big-budget production *Pathfinder* (*Veiviseren* in Norwegian, *Ofelas* in Sami), illustrate the paradoxes of the genre film in a local production context, a context where state subsidies are supposed to bring both economic and cultural benefits, and most of all where state subsidies are supposed to strengthen a film production rooted in a national cultural identity.

FILM PRODUCTION IN NORWAY

The film production sector has always been extremely fragmented and insecure in Norway, a cottage industry living from hand to mouth. Producers have struggled from one production to the next, unable to plan for a slate of films to play off against each other, each film having to stand on its own terms. Such instability has dogged Norwegian film production since its start in the early 1910s. The impoverishment of the Norwegian production sector can be explained on the basis of five elements: (1) the small size of the Norwegian domestic market, which makes it difficult to recoup costs locally; (2) the aversion of the Norwegian financial sector toward high-risk investment, leading to a subsequent lack of corporate or equity financing; (3) the dominance of Hollywood movies in the Norwegian market; (4) the unintegrated structure of production, distribution, and exhibition sectors in Norway; and (5) the municipal cinema system, which entails that most cinemas are municipally owned, hence directing their profits to county budgets. This system makes it difficult to fold distribution revenue back into production.[1]

Until 1950, the Norwegian state had little interest in establishing a viable production infrastructure, and film production was dominated by a project-by-project, cottage industry approach, with small production companies being forced to start from scratch with each project. State subsidies for Norwegian film started in 1950, and today all films produced in Norway benefit from some form of state subsidy. The state production system of 1950 made film production a national project and guaranteed continual domestic film production. Although this system has gone through several changes and refinements, subsidies and other supports have been important since 1950.[2] Still, very few movies produced in Norway make a profit.

Today, two basic types of public support for the production of Norwegian films are in operation: *production support* and *box office bonus*. Production support is awarded selectively by the newly established Norwegian Film Fund, an organization created in 2001 as a part of the New Norwegian Film Policy intended by the Norwegian Ministry for Cultural Affairs to renew and modernize the film sector, combining the three national institutions—the Norwegian Film Institute Production Support, the Audiovisual Production Fund, and Norwegian Film, Ltd.—that had previously distributed production support to Norwegian film producers. Production support was principally intended to provide a source of funding for films with artistic aspirations, although funding was not limited to art cinema productions exclusively. The latter aim can be seen in the New Norwegian Film Policy, which added a "50/50 scheme" modeled on the Danish system.[3] This funding structure provided automatic advance support to feature films for which producers have managed to raise a minimum of 50 percent of the capital to cover the budget.

The explicit aim of the new policy was to provide the national film production sector with more freedom and with increased accountability for policy implementation. The policy resulted in an immediate boost of output, with nearly twenty feature films premiering in theaters in the year 2003. At the same time, the government wanted more films for its money and thus no longer emphasized the aspects of artistic aspiration or national cultural identity as clearly as before.

The other state support for Norwegian films is a box office bonus, which is based on the ability of the individual film to attract an audience, awarded as a general measure. Thus all Norwegian feature films premiered in Norwegian cinemas are entitled to a ticket subsidy of 55 percent of the box office gross. Films for children are entitled to 100 percent. Box office bonus has an upper limit, calculated for each individual film, and is based on the amount of financial risk taken by the producer's financial share in the production.

These two types of public support, plus various funds for project development for feature films, guarantee a continual film production in Norway. In general, very few Norwegian films cover their production costs or make substantial profits at the box office. The recent successes of the feature film *Elling* (Petter Næss, 2001) and the feature-length documentary *Cool and Crazy* (Knut Erik Jensen, 2001, *Heftig og begeistret*) have shown that indigenous films can successfully compete on the national or regional level with Hollywood cinema and make large profits at the box office, but such successes are exceptions to the rule. It is impossible for Norwegian producers to survive on a commercial footing, and government support and subsidies are absolutely necessary.

During the 1980s an average of nine feature films were produced in Norway annually; by the 1990s this had risen to ten films annually, but production trends remained generally the same: literary adaptations, coming-of-age films, comedies, art cinema productions, and crime films or thrillers. The only significant new production trend of the 1990s was that feature-length documentaries once again became a vital part of production and distribution, and after 1995 several feature-length documentaries made an artistic and economic impact in Norway.

In both decades Norwegian audiences enjoyed short, but much hyped and discussed, production cycles of indigenous genre films: examples of market-driven film production, trends based not on cultural or artistic aspirations but on an understanding of the sorts of films that the most frequent cinemagoers desire and that therefore will generate the most profit. One of the reasons why these particular production trends emerged was the wish among filmmakers to capture a larger audience—first and foremost a national audience but also, if possible, an international audience. This desire to "go international" grew out of the 1980s and triggered the first cycle of genre movies in Norway.[4]

NORWAY GOES INTERNATIONAL!

The year 1980 was a particularly low point in Norwegian film production. Although ten films premiered that year, none found a substantial audience, and discussions soared high in the newspapers and on television about the incompetence of Norwegian film and film directors. Reviewer after reviewer wrote about the provincialism and dilettantism in Norwegian film production, questioning the policy of state subsidy. One reviewer even dared to ask whether it was worth the effort and the money to make films in Norway at all (Skagen 1980, 4–7).

In the same year, director Oddvar Bull Tuhus, who had started as a filmmaker specializing in political social realist films in the early 1970s, made the nostalgic feature *1958*. This Norwegian pastiche of *American Graffiti* (George Lucas, 1973) signaled a new trend in Norwegian film. After a decade of political or artistic "idea films," where ideas were more important than plots, Norwegian film slowly started to learn to tell a good story again. During the 1980s, idea films were replaced by "story films": films that set a good story as first priority, with ideas about society in second place. A trilogy of films by Oddvar Bull Tuhus—*1958* (1980), *Fifty-Fifty* (1982), and *Hockeyfeber* (1983, Hockey Fever)—paved the way for more genre-oriented films and the first cycle of indigenous genre films with an international orientation.[5]

During the late 1980s, a new economic situation emerged regarding "tax-shelter production" in Norway, allowing finance houses to write off film production costs and providing a new source of stimulus for Norwegian film producers and directors. Money was suddenly available from wealthy investors, provided the films performed at the box office. Investors could now obtain considerable tax advantages together with the prospect of a possible profit if the film earned more than its production cost. For a short period Norwegian cinema changed from being a cultural zone without an audience and subsidized by the government to a sector for hot investments by banks or investment companies. The year 1985 proved to be one of the most interesting and significant years for Norwegian film production. Several high-quality productions in different genres created international interest, attitudes among producers and directors seemed to change drastically, and Norwegian films once again were huge successes at the box office in Norway. There was a new slogan in the Norwegian film business: Norway goes international!

An important landmark in the early 1980s was the film *Orion's Belt* (Ola Solum, 1985, *Orions belte*), which signaled a new international orientation in Norwegian cinema. The production of *Orion's Belt* required more capital than the State Production Committee, which awarded production support in the 1980s, was willing to give, so the producer invited a financial company to draw upon other sources. The success of *Orion's Belt* resulted in a short gold rush situation. Foreign companies like Goldcrest and Buena Vista as well as Norwegian production interests used the limited partnership and tax-shelter benefits to finance film projects.

This led to a new situation. On the one hand, Norwegian capital was used to partly finance American movies like *Revolution 1776* (Hugh Hudson, 1986) and *Flight of the Navigator* (Randal Kleiser, 1986).[6] On the other, Norwegian films were more internationally oriented, striking examples being the film noir pastiche *Blackout* (Erik Gustavson, 1986), set in a studio world complete with its own Chinatown, far from Norwegian society and culture, and *Turnaround* (Ola Solum, 1987), which did not even use the Norwegian language and was thus finally denied state support. The social realism of the 1970s had been replaced by a cycle of action-oriented genre movies, often intended for an international audience. Norwegian film culture, which five years earlier had seemed doomed, now vibrated with excitement.

Orion's Belt was the first, and one of the most successful both economically and artistically, of these new action dramas. This political thriller tells the story of three Norwegians on board a freighter who make their living from dubious assignments on the coast of Spitsbergen. By coincidence, they discover a Soviet listening post for submarine detection in a cave. Caught red-handed by a Soviet helicopter, two of the Norwegians are killed in a battle in which the helicopter is shot down. The lone survivor reaches Spitsbergen, and the listening post proves extremely interesting for the Norwegian Secret Service. In the end the discovery has to remain top secret for diplomatic reasons, and the lone survivor is pursued through the streets of Oslo—no doubt by agents of the Norwegian government who want to obliterate all traces of the unfortunate boat crew.

Orion's Belt was Norway's most expensive production to date, and the commercial success and international acclaim of the film immediately led to similar projects, which won support from eager investors now willing to invest money in a film culture "going international." This period in modern Norwegian film history is often referred to as "the Helicopter Period," and a cycle of crime- or paranoia-thrillers followed. Action films like *Etter Rubicon* (Leidulv Risan, 1987, Rubicon), *Blücher* (Oddvar Bull Tuhus, 1988), and *The Dive* (Tristan de vere Cole,

1989, *Dykket*) were classic race-against-time thrillers, dealing with a NATO neutron bomb explosion in the north of Norway, the hunt for secret papers on a sunken German warship, and a diving accident on an oil rig in the North Sea, respectively. Many of these thrillers were well produced but could easily have been made in almost any Western country. This new orientation toward extreme action and international tone, an imitation of classical Hollywood cinema, was also evident in films like *Blackout, Turnaround,* or *Karachi* (Oddvar Einarson, 1990); the titles themselves reveal something about their international orientation.

The most successful of these action thrillers of the late 1980s were *Orion's Belt* and *Pathfinder.* Nils Gaup's film from 1987 was the first feature film ever to be shot in the Sami language and had to be subtitled in Norway, but the film owes much of its international fame to its close resemblance to the western genre and is often referred to in Norway as a "cod western."

The excitement in Norwegian film production seemed to wear off after a few years. The government changed tax laws, no longer enabling finance houses to write off film production costs, and the Klondike feeling disappeared. Even though thrillers and genre films became a stable part of film production in Norway, directors and producers as well as the audience were no longer as interested in this kind of film.

Thus, a first cycle of indigenous internationally oriented genre films ended in the late 1980s, but at the same time, Norwegian film production was revitalized. Other film types were made, mostly for the national audience. Ten years after *Orion's Belt,* Norwegian cinema again met with international interest and acclaim. The art cinema productions *Eggs* (Bent Hamer, 1995) and *Junk Mail* (Pål Sletaune, 1996, *Budbringeren*) were selected for the Critics' Week at the Cannes Festival, and *Junk Mail* won the top prize in its category. These films found a ready public at home and abroad and were followed by more action-oriented crime films like *Insomnia* (Erik Skjoldbjærg, 1997), remade in Hollywood by Christopher Nolan in 2001, or *Blessed Are Those Who Thirst* (Carl Jørgen Kiønig, 1997, *Salige er de som tørster*). *Insomnia* and the street thriller *Schpaa* (Erik Poppe, 1998) were the most successful, artistically as well as economically, of a new cycle of internationally oriented genre films in the years 1997 and 1998. Suddenly, once again, many Norwegian filmmakers wanted to reach the global as well as the local market, with the production of films carefully designed for an international market.

The film *Scared to Death* (Are Kalmar, 1997, *Livredd*), a street thriller about drugs and murder, does not leave the big city, but the other movies in this cycle used Hollywood myths and elements from American horror and crime films to create a contrast between the cool big-city life and the isolated and backward countryside. In films like *Isle of Darkness* (Trygve Allister Diesen, 1997, *Mørkets øy*), *1732 Bloody Angels* (Karin Julsrud, 1998, *Høtten*), *Cellophane* (Eva Isaksen, 1998, *Cellofan*), and *Weekend* (Erik Gustavson, 1998), the Norwegian countryside is transformed into a Texaslike landscape of horror and crime, inspired by films like *Easy Rider* (Dennis Hopper, 1969) and *Deliverance* (John Boorman, 1972). None of these films found a large audience, and they were not shown outside of Norway. Many critics reacted to this stereotyped and genre-oriented way of depicting communities outside of the capital, Oslo, questioning whether the genre conventions that were intended to make it easier to reach a youthful audience instead made communication and identification impossible (see Tennø 2002). The kinds of arguments used in the heated debates of 1998 were largely the same that had been voiced when Nils Gaup's *Pathfinder* premiered in 1987.

THE DIRECTOR NILS GAUP

Nils Gaup was born in 1956 and grew up in a small Sami community of only three thousand inhabitants, Kautokeino, in the north of Norway. There were no cars or television at the time, and Gaup is fond of portraying Kautokeino as a border town in a western movie: "There were storytellers, though, and plenty of drinking and fights. People would wear knives in their belts just as cowboys wore guns" (Cowie 1999, 40). Gaup resolved to become an actor, and at the age of nineteen he enrolled in the Norwegian Theater Academy. After graduation he worked as an actor in the theater.

Nils Gaup was dissatisfied with the Norwegian films of the 1970s, which he found too political and boring. He wanted to tell good stories, like the storytellers of his childhood, so he turned to his Sami heritage for his debut *Pathfinder* in 1987. He had no previous experience with filmmaking other than as an actor in the social realist film *The Second Shift* (Lasse Glomm, *Det andre skiftet*) in 1978. Gaup storyboarded each scene and each angle of his film, convincing the producer John M. Jacobsen to raise the money. Though *Pathfinder* had the most expensive budget accorded a Norwegian film up to that time and was definitely a big-budget film in the Norwegian production context, in the international context, the film was closer to a low-budget film. *Pathfinder* was a huge success in Norway, and the film achieved distribution in numerous countries. *Pathfinder* was the first Norwegian film to achieve distribution in the United States and England, hitherto regarded as impossible to breach. The film was also nominated for an Oscar the year that *Babette's Feast* won the Academy Award as Best Foreign-Language Film, an event that changed Gaup's life completely. In an interview he mentions that "I received about one action script a month, including both *RoboCop II* and *Waterworld*" (Cowie 1999, 41).

Nils Gaup next accepted an assignment from Disney to make *Shipwrecked* (1990, *Håkon Håkonsen*), an adventure movie for children. In his following film, Gaup returned to Norway and also to a smaller budget. *Head above Water* (*Hodet over vannet*), from 1993, is a suspense thriller with lots of black humor. A couple, Einar and Lene, enjoys a dream vacation on an island off the southern coast of Norway. They are alone on the beautiful summer island, save for Bjørn, Lene's childhood friend who occupies the only other summerhouse on the island. Einar and Bjørn leave on a fishing expedition. Lene enjoys the solitude until Gaute, her former psychiatrist and lover, arrives. He dies suddenly, apparently in his sleep, and Lene hides his corpse in the potato cellar, thus starting a macabre comedy with many surprising plot twists, ending with violence and murder.

Head above Water was a success, and not only at the box office in Norway; the film impressed Kevin Costner enough for him to purchase remake rights under his Tig Films banner in Hollywood. The remake, starring Harvey Keitel and Cameron Diaz and directed by Jim Wilson in 1996, had all the plot twists but none of the charm of the Norwegian movie and was not very successful in the United States or elsewhere. In 1996, Gaup himself directed the French-American coproduction *Tashunga*, or *North Star*, a western set in 1899 during the American gold rush period. In this internationally financed production, sometimes labeled a "revisionist thriller," James Caan plays a corrupt miner pitted against a half-Indian trapper played by Christopher Lambert. Weak script and casting resulted in a film that did not find commercial success.

Nils Gaup's most recent film is *Misery Harbour* (1999). This ambitious film, more of an art cinema production than a genre picture, is the story of young Espen Arnakke. Stifled by the little town of Jante, he flees to sea, looking for adventure and freedom. Life on the boat is even worse than in his hometown, so he jumps ship in Newfoundland, where he finds love and friendship. But love turns to jealousy and friendship to hate, and he kills a man. Based on the life and work of the Danish-Norwegian author Aksel Sandemose, one of the most controversial Scandinavian writers in the pre- and postwar years, the film discusses Sandemose's well-known "Jante Law," a depiction of the ten commandments of small-town, small-minded oppression and conformity. Since *Misery Harbour*, Nils Gaup has directed *Nini*, a TV series for the public broadcaster NRK and has been trying to finance a big-budget historical epic about a Sami insurrection in the 1850s. Gaup is perhaps the most successful Norwegian film director of the 1980s and 1990s. Most of his films have become both critical and box office hits, but he has been criticized for his use of genre formats; after his debut with *Pathfinder*, several critics warned about a "genrification" of Norwegian cinema.

PATHFINDER

Pathfinder is based on a Sami story about a young boy, Aigin, who sees his parents and little sister slaughtered by a raiding party of evil Tchudes, a fictional people that evoke aspects of early Viking-age Nordic cultures. He is wounded by an arrow but escapes the Tchudes and skis to a Sami camp. At the camp, Aigin realizes that he inadvertently may have shown the Tchudes the way to these other families. When the families flee to the coastal area, Aigin and other young men stay behind to fight the ferocious Tchudes. In the fight, the other Sami youngsters are killed. Aigin is taken prisoner and forced to act as a pathfinder for the evil raiders. The boy manages to trick his captors and lead them over a cliff to a violent death. The Sami families have lost their shaman pathfinder, Raste, in the battle against the Tchudes, and in the end Aigin takes his place, becoming the new pathfinder. *Pathfinder* is a simple but economic and effective story. It is good box office material, and it has all the ingredients of good narrative: chases and fights, violence and deceit, magic and natural scenery, but also depictions of how the Sami people stick together and men sacrifice them-

Pathfinder (1987) (courtesy of Norwegian Film Institute)

selves for the good of the community. It even has the contours of a love story between Aigin and the young woman Savve, the only tribe member who always believes in Aigin. Around these story elements, almost universal in their simplicity, is the fierce natural beauty of northern Norway and the "exotic" authenticity of the Sami people, their magic, customs, and way of life.

Nils Gaup skillfully structures his story in parallel actions to enhance identification and the feeling of vulnerability that characterizes the good Sami people in their fight against the evil Tchudes. The relationship between the two groups is depicted in black-and-white contrast. The black-clad Tchudes, all older men with weather-bitten, ugly faces, seem to lack any feeling of community. They are like a pack of wolves, a comparison the Sami people make several times. In contrast, the Sami people care for each other, are clad in white or light-brown fur clothes, and their children and women play major roles. An important scene occurs one-third of the way into the film, when the shaman Raste lectures Aigin about the invisible ties that bind the Sami people together; this scene not only works as a way of differentiating between the two people, expressing important ideas about human relationships, but also points to the coming-of-age theme underlying the film.

Peter Cowie has stated that "growing up lies at the heart of modern Norwegian cinema" (1999, 18). This is an important observation; since the 1970s not only Norwegian cinema but all Nordic cinemas have depicted every phase of childhood and adolescence in numerous films about the pains of growing up. This central theme in modern Norwegian cinema, young persons coming to terms with the challenge of adulthood, is most dramatically depicted in *Pathfinder*. Aigin becomes a man and takes the most important position in the community when he tricks the Tchudes to their death in the fierce mountains above the Sami camp. This points to another central, and universal, theme in the film. The Sami people are not only a people with decent human feelings and relationships, they are also more closely connected to nature than the Tchudes. These close connections are depicted from the start of the film. A short prologue, or flash-forward, shows the shaman Raste telling Aigin, and the audience, that he has seen the bull reindeer for the third time. This is a fateful premonition for Raste, but it also reveals how Raste can read the signs of nature. Raste's magical power is naturally transferred to Aigin at the very end of the film, when he too sees the magic bull reindeer against the blazing northern light after the Tchudes have been defeated. Another important aspect of the film, crucial in understanding Gaup's way of handling the fine line between universality and cultural specificity, is its style. Gaup uses close-ups or medium shots with surprisingly few long shots. This not only gives the story an enhanced intensity, it also contributes to the universality of the story. Gaup has carefully avoided a feeling of "tourist information." He selects very few long shots of the beautiful Norwegian nature and landscape and does not "anchor" the story in a specific cultural and natural landscape. The story could be set in nearly any place in the northern part of the world, and even the snow and ice can be read allegorically as the fierce surroundings and milieu that the Sami people must face to survive. In this way *Pathfinder* is both a moral fable, lecturing us about human relationships and the importance of a relationship with nature, and an exciting action-oriented story about violence and deceit, magic and love, and the victory of good over evil. The film skillfully combines the "exotic" authenticity of the Sami people and the landscape and natural setting with a simple story universal in its appeal.

THE RECEPTION OF *PATHFINDER*

Pathfinder was a huge success in Norway, and most Norwegian critics applauded the film. In the newspaper *Morgenbladet* the reviewer stated: "Yesterday Nils Gaup's *Pathfinder* premiered. This date should be remembered as a new *day one* of Norwegian film" (Dahl 1987; term in italics emphasized and in English in the original). Most other critics described the film as an event, something they never had seen the likes of, at least not in Norwegian cinema. Gaup was compared to the biggest directors in film history: Kurosawa, Leone, Ford. *Pathfinder* was used by the Norwegian critics to state that it was possible, even in a little country like Norway, to make professional, world-class movies.

Though *Pathfinder* met with great success in Norway, some critics pointed out a paradox inherent in the film. A return to colorful indigenous sources after a decade of social realist idea films, *Pathfinder* incorporated unique material from Sami tradition while at the same time using genre formulas well known from American cinema, borrowing especially from the western. Gaup's film is a spectacular historical epic, with dramatic imagery and sound effects, but apart from the exotic "surface" or scenery of the story, it could have been made or set anywhere in the Western world. One reviewer pointed to the fact that the film is "a sort of Indian-western in Nordic surroundings, a *northern*" (Dahl 1987). A point of discussion after the premiere was the perceived loss of collective identity when traditional material is used without examining the conventions according to which the past is represented or rethinking the ambiguities of the genre. Most paradoxical about the film is the fact that even in Norway it had to be subtitled because its sparse dialogue was in the Sami language, while the story itself was immediately comprehensible even without words because it was so familiar from American movies. This tale from around the previous millennium, based on an ancient legend, seemed to lack historicity almost entirely (Alm and Svendsen 1987).

In several debates in the late 1980s, *Pathfinder* was used to discuss the problematic paradox of "genrification" of the Norwegian cinema. New internationally oriented genre film production in Norway turned to genre elements and formulaic stories because the Norwegian cinema seemed to have lost necessary narrative competence after years of making idea films, not story films. Filmmakers wanted to communicate to a larger audience, national and international, and genre elements helped secure narration, communication, and market access. In this process originality and cultural specificity came second. The major problem, however, was that Norwegian cinema had little to offer a national or an international market except its *difference* from European or American genre films. It could not compete in terms of budget or competence, so most genre films ended up being box office failures. The strategy of "instant" communication turned out to block communication as well as originality and authenticity. It had nothing, at least nothing new, to tell its audience. And nothing that American films couldn't do better. Few films managed to breathe life into the formulaic stories—*Orion's Belt* and *Pathfinder* being the major exceptions. Few films dared to recontextualize familiar genre elements and clichés.

The question many asked was whether there was anything genuinely Norwegian in these films apart from the occasional beautiful shots of natural scenery. *Pathfinder* posed the question of national identity in a more paradoxical way: a film that was genuinely Norwegian, in terms of having sprung from a Sami legend almost one thousand years old, but at the same time nearly identical to any American western film. Critics pointed to the fact that if you exchanged the Tchudes for Indians and the Sami for settlers, you would have a traditional western. But what sort of a western is *Pathfinder*?

PATHFINDER AS WESTERN

Pathfinder was the first Norwegian film to achieve distribution in the United States, where it was a moderate success. There are numerous reasons why Gaup's film achieved distribution and financial success, including, for example, its Academy Award nomination, but *Pathfinder* was obviously more than just a good picture. It was also the right film at the right time.

One of the contextual factors that helps account for the success of *Pathfinder* in the United States was the revival of the western genre in the 1980s. Very few westerns were released in the early 1980s, and in 1984 westerns were recorded as having a market share of 0 percent in the cinema in the United States (Neale 2002). During the next year, however, things started to change, as films like *Pale Rider* (Clint Eastwood, 1985) and *Silverado* (Lawrence Kasdan, 1985) attempted to revive the western genre. From 1986 on several successful miniseries and telefilms, among them the adaptation of *Lonesome Dove* (Simon Wincer, 1989), appeared on television, and a new and varied cycle of westerns was produced (Neale 2002; Prince 2000).

In his essay "Westerns and Gangster Films since the 1970s," Steve Neale (2002) distinguishes between two trends in the western cycle of the 1980s: the neotraditional and the new revisionist western. The neotraditional western tries to revive the genre, blending traditional elements with minor up-to-date attitudes, while the new revisionist western recontextualizes familiar western genre elements and clichés, especially by telling the stories from the point of view of Native Americans. Despite not using the usual iconographic elements that traditionally have defined the western, like six-shooters and cowboys, *Pathfinder* has many of the themes of the genre: the male hero as defender of community and family, mobilization of a frontier mythology, an expansive sense of space. Gaup's film has revisionist ambitions in his telling of a Sami legend from a Sami point of view, but most of all it is a neotraditional western. In mixing these two trends in the same film, it effectively incorporates both trends that characterize the American western in the 1980s, and this is perhaps one reason why the film was so successful.

This might even explain some of its popularity in Norway. One of the greatest commercial successes of a Norwegian cultural product since Ibsen was a series of eighty-three western novels about the lonesome ranger Morgan Kane. The series was extremely popular in Europe: "By May 1987 the series had sold an estimated 14,013,000 books all in all, including 6,967,000 outside Norway. The series, or separate titles, have appeared in Denmark, Sweden, Finland, Iceland, England, France, Germany, the Netherlands and Spain" (Gripsrud 1989, 135). The Morgan Kane series, published since 1965, also blends a neotraditional and a new revisionist approach to the hero and the genre, thus appealing to different reader groups and providing a core audience for a film like *Pathfinder*. Indeed, a film based on the Morgan Kane series was scheduled for production in Norway in 1987, but the production company, Scandinavian Motion Picture Syndicate, did not manage to raise the necessary capital for the big-budget western to be shot in Mexico, so the film was never made.

The western cycle in Hollywood in the mid-1980s and the significant success of the Morgan Kane series in Europe provide an important contextual background for the reception and success of *Pathfinder*. Gaup tells a good story that blends different reworkings of a paradigmatic Hollywood genre. He breathes life into formula and balances the thin line of commercial globalism and cultural specificity, creating a western that is also a *northern*.

LEARNING FROM GENRE

Under the New Norwegian Film Policy, Norwegian films today benefit from two basic types of state subsidy. This policy was implemented to protect and promote national culture in a climate increasingly geared to what is perceived as an undifferentiated commercial global culture. Local production brings both economic and cultural benefits. At the same time, public funds are not so clearly limited to filmmakers pursuing artistic and cultural agendas as earlier, and the new Norwegian Film Fund wants more films for its state support. Since the first genre cycle in the mid-1980s, a paradox has characterized parts of the Norwegian film production and its relationship to the state support system and the film policy of the Norwegian government: many of the films produced do not strengthen or disseminate local culture at all but instead look like just another Hollywood movie except for the language used by the actors. The directors do not rework genre clichés in a local context, extend them as source material, or invest them with greater resonance, except in the rare instance of a film like *Pathfinder*. Since the 1980s Norwegian film directors have wanted to "go international," using genre conventions and formulas to produce several cycles of indigenous genre films. One reason for this was a genuine insecurity among Norwegian film directors about how to tell a good story on film after a long period of political and social realist idea films and in a production climate without a viable production infrastructure dominated by a project-by-project situation. Many directors turned to genre to recapture a lost audience, but the results were not always popular films that could find that audience. Many reviewers and critics have questioned these films and questioned whether government support should be awarded to such productions.

The recent "50/50" funding policy strengthens the commercial production sector in Norway and will surely result in more indigenous genre films in the years to come, films that try to be both local and global at the same time. Films like *Pathfinder*, or the recent horror film *Wilderness*, show that this balancing act is possible, but the big question remains. Will this result in the further erosion of a national culture already dominated by American cultural products, or will it paradoxically strengthen Norwegian culture?

NOTES

1. For more information about the municipal cinema system in Norway, see Iversen 1998.
2. For more information about state support and the production systems of 1950, 1955, and 1964 in Norway, see Iversen 1998.
3. For further information on Danish film funding policies, see Ib Bondebjerg's chapter 4 in this volume.
4. An exception to this discussion is the comedy, as one can easily define several cycles of comedies, but these films are more national and local in subject matter than the internationally oriented genre cycles I want to discuss here. For a discussion of the most important comedy cycle in Norwegian film production through the 1950s and 1960s, see Larsen 1998.
5. For an analysis of Oddvar Bull Tuhus's films in the early 1980s, see Iversen 1993.
6. For a humorous description of this gold rush situation from an English point of view, see Eberts and Ilott 1990, 586–88.

WORKS CITED

Alm, Richard, and Trond Olav Svendsen. 1987. "Tsjudene vender tilbake!—Notater om 'Veiviseren.'" Z 4: 4–5.
Cowie, Peter. 1999. *Straight from the Heart: Modern Norwegian Cinema, 1971–1999*. Kristianslund/Oslo: Kom Forlag/Norwegian Film Institute.
Dahl, Henning Kramer. 1987. "En film som viser vei." *Morgenbladet*, October 2.
Eberts, Jake, and Terry Ilott. 1990. *My Indecision Is Final: The Rise and Fall of Goldcrest Films*. London: Faber and Faber.
Gripsrud, Jostein. 1989. "Masterson's Male Masterpiece: The Penetrating Story of a Norwegian Western (or Two)." In *Media Fictions*, ed. Michael Skovmand, 135–48. Aarhus: Aarhus University Press.
Iversen, Gunnar. 1993. "Det Amerikanske Idealet." Z 2: 12–17.
———. 1998. "Norway." In *Nordic National Cinemas*, ed. Tytti Soila, Astrid Söderbergh Widding, and Gunnar Iversen, 102–41. London: Routledge.
Larsen, Leif Ove. 1998. *Moderniseringsmoro—Romantiske komedier i norsk film, 1950–1965*. Bergen: Universitetet i Bergen.
Neale, Steve. 2002. "Westerns and Gangster Films since the 1970s." In *Genre and Contemporary Hollywood*, ed. Steve Neale, 27–48. London: British Film Institute.
Prince, Stephen. 2000. *A New Pot of Gold: Hollywood under the Electronic Rainbow, 1980–1989*. Berkeley: University of California Press.
Skagen, Sølve. 1980. "Septembermordet." *Filmavisa* 3, no. 4: 3–7.
Tennø, Marit Aakre. 2002. "1732 Bygda—Marerittet har eit postnummer." *Syn og segn* 4: 49–55.
Wiese, Andreas. 2003. "Villmark." *Dagbladet*, February 21.

Aki Kaurismäki's Crossroads: National Cinema and the Road Movie

Andrew Nestingen

Road movies figured prominently in Nordic cinemas, both auteurist and popular, at the millennium. Mika and Aki Kaurismäki are perhaps the most noteworthy auteurs associated with the genre. Their road movies include *The Clan* (1984, *Klaani—tarina sammakoiden suvusta*), which Aki wrote and his brother Mika directed, Mika Kaurismäki's film *Rosso* (1985), in which an Italian hit man is caught in a seemingly endless and finally fatal traversal of the Finnish countryside, and Aki Kaurismäki's *Ariel* (1988), *Leningrad Cowboys Go America* (1990), *Leningrad Cowboys Meet Moses* (1993), and *Take Care of Your Scarf, Tatiana* (1994, *Pidä huivista kiinni, Tatjana*). "Aki Kaurismäki," observes Jonathan Romney, "has taken the road movie genre more to heart than any European director save Wenders" (2003, 43). Other Scandinavian auteurs have also embraced the genre. As Birgir Thor Møller argues in his discussion of Fridrik Thór Fridriksson in chapter 12 of the present volume, Fridriksson uses the road movie to explore the balance between cultural geographies of rural and urban, tradition and postmodernity, national and transnational in *White Whales* (1987, *Skytturnar*), *Children of Nature* (1991, *Börn náttúrunnar*), *Cold Fever* (1994), and *Falcons* (2002). A younger generation of personal filmmakers has employed the genre as well, as Katrin Ottarsdóttir does in *Bye Bye Bluebird* (1999), a road film set in the Faroese Islands. These auteur films exploit the road movie's fixation on mobility and encounters with the unfamiliar to grapple with cultural identities, borders, and liminal spaces between identities in the present-day Nordic region.

The road movie has furnished popular Nordic cinema a critical edge as well, where it has provided a frame for consideration of the ongoing reconstitution of these nation-states through the transnational circulation of images, capital, and people. *The New Country* (Geir Hansteen Jorgensen, 2000, *Det nya landet*), which first appeared on Swedish television as a four-part miniseries and was later released as a feature, is the most well-known example of popular uses of the road movie. The film takes up a tangle of tensions, struggles, and questions linked to migration, relating the odyssey of Massoud and Ali (forty-something Iranian and teenage Somali asylum seekers) as they scour Sweden for the money, connections, and documents to aid them in escaping to Canada, where they believe they'll find a more accepting, less racist society. Lukas Moodysson, who directed *Show Me Love* (1998, *Fucking Åmal*) and *Together* (2000, *Tillsammans*), was a coproducer and screenwriter of the project. He has described the film as an effort to foreground issues of political justice, immigration, and diaspora in Sweden (Björkman, Lindblad, and Sahlin 2002). Another film that typifies the prominence of the road movie is Thomas Vinterberg's reflection on criminality and family in the road movie *The Greatest Heroes* (1996, *De største helte*). The Norwegian Harald Østgård-Lund's *Halfway to Haugesund* (1997, *Halveis till Haugesund*), in which a punk rocker travels from Oslo to the Telemark region of Norway to play a gig, meeting a Norwegian of Pakistani background who runs a business doing genealogical research in the area for Americans in search of long-lost roots, combines the road movie with a dose of comedic self-reflection.

When Scandinavia's auteur and popular cinema embrace the road movie, it seems pertinent to ask what the significance of the genre might be in millennial Nordic national cinemas. The trend is particularly intriguing in relation to the semantics of the road movie. Road films from *Easy Rider* (Dennis Hopper, 1969) to *Thelma and Louise* (Ridley Scott, 1992), from *Mad Max* (George Miller, 1979) to *Central Station* (Walter Salles, 1998, *Central do Brasil*), have drawn on panoramas of open frontiers and images of spatial enormity (Laderman 2002). In contrast, Nordic road movies appear claustrophobic, for even though the Nordic countries as measured by area are among the largest in Europe, their landscapes are diminutive in comparison to the frontiers of the United States, Australia, or Brazil. The images of the road movie and Nordic national landscapes fit together in an intriguing and thought-provoking connection.[1] Their disjunction is cause to consider more carefully how genre and national cinema fit together.

In raising such questions there's good reason to examine Aki Kaurismäki's *Leningrad Cowboys Go America* and *Take Care of Your Scarf, Tatiana*. As Kaurismäki is the most famous and celebrated of Finnish filmmakers, the "nationality" of his cinematic images has been much discussed. As Kimmo Ahonen et al. point out in a volume on contemporary Finnish cinema, Aki Kaurismäki has become something of an ambassador, his films a symbol of success, an engine for the development of Finnish cinema (2003, 7).[2] Paradoxically, they observe, his entire career has resisted, undermined, and critiqued such a reception. In a global media environment in which commodified images attract enormous attention, create powerful leverage, and earn billions of dollars, Kaurismäki's cinema carries great importance for Finland. But when we examine his road films, it becomes evident that their relation to national cinema is far more complex than has been understood. Kaurismäki's cinema has been categorized as national, because scholars have argued it's about familiar characters, attitudes, conflicts, and places, which express postwar Finnish cultural consciousness. Even *Leningrad Cowboys Go America,* for some critics, is not so much an image of the American South as an expression of Finnishness (Toiviainen 2002; von Bagh 1997). While there are admittedly good reasons to interpret Kaurismäki's films in this way, Kaurismäki's use of road movie semantics and syntax situate these films in a postmodern welter of images, which, it is generally argued, cannot be characterized on the basis of the image's expression of its ostensible referent but rather must be considered on the basis of the image's embeddedness in a web of other images (Jameson 1991). That is to say, situating Kaurismäki's films in terms of national expression, or, by contrast, in relation to other images, draws on divergent understandings of the image's status. These understandings lead to distinct assessments of the significance of these films in relation to the cinema and cultural history of a Nordic region in transition. The categorization of Kaurismäki's cinema in national terms should be reconsidered, because his multilayered films, especially in their intersection with genre, include images that need to be situated within a web of other images, even if their referents remain relevant.

NATIONAL CINEMA

In contrast to my argument, critics and scholars largely agree that Aki Kaurismäki's films are best understood as cinematic expressions of Finnish culture. What do they mean? After all, national cinema can connote a range of notions. In the first place, in speaking of Finnish cinema, it is prudent to keep in mind the argument that discourses of national cinema have continually transformed during the history of the medium (Laine 1999; Pantti 2000, chapter 6 in this volume). National cinema as an institution is more complex than the on-screen representation of language, attitudes, beliefs, and practices typically associated with a nation-state (Crofts 1998; Chow 1998; Miller et al. 2001). Andrew Higson has written an influential analysis of the plurality of national cinema (mentioned in the introduction to the present volume) in *Waving the Flag*, where he attributes a fourfold meaning to national cinema: it can be defined economically, in terms of audience taste, by way of production and marketing strategies, or in terms of a canon as defined by a national intelligentsia (1995, 4–9). Higson omits a fifth element, what Mette Hjort has called "banal nationalism," meaning that texts of the national cinema intersect with what citizens of a nation-state would generally agree were features of the national culture—language, regional differences, institutions, and the like (Hjort 2000; Billig 1995). Higson underemphasizes banal nationalism in part, perhaps, because his concern with differentiating U.K. from U.S. cinema marginalizes the significance of language in defining national cinema. Since critics and scholars have argued so consistently for a categorization of Kaurismäki in national terms, it's useful to refer to Higson to raise several points that contest their categorization.

A brief examination of financing, relative dislike of Kaurismäki's films in Finland, and his films' production and marketing strategies complicate the films' national categorization. First, while Kaurismäki's films have received extensive funding through the Finnish Film Foundation, they tend to be cofinanced in cooperation with French, German, Danish, Swedish, and European Union underwriters. Kaurismäki's films rely on the most diverse financing schemes in Finnish cinema and compare to von Trier's well-known transnational financing schemes (Brandstrup and Redvall 2003, 109). By contrast, recent popular Finnish cinema—for example, the films that figured in the Finnish film boom of 1999–2001—have been funded entirely with Finnish money (Nestingen 2003; Pantti, chapter 6 in this volume).

Second, Kaurismäki's films have not been popular among Finnish theatergoers. Rather, they are often seen by Finnish audiences as examples of inscrutable, unappealing art cinema, "foundation films," to recall Pantti's remarks. Indeed, the films have proven markedly less popular in domestic distribution than they have in European distribution. While Kaurismäki's 1996 *Drifting Clouds* (*Kauas pilvet karkaavat*) attracted 49,700 theatergoers domestically, for instance, it reached 453,700 in European distribution; while it was an also-ran for domestic audiences, it belonged to the top ten most popular European films of the year (*Suomalaisen elokuvan markkinat* 1999, 83). The silent film *Juha* (1999) (the filmatization of a canonical Finnish novel) received a similar reception, seen by some ten thousand viewers in Finland but reaching hundreds of thousands in Europe, including a several-month theater run in Paris (83). *Tatiana* and the *Leningrad Cowboys* films exhibit a similar pattern: significantly more popular abroad than at home. To be sure, domestic audiences know Kaurismäki's films will be screened on Finnish national television, and it is often suggested that this fact discourages potential viewers from attending his films in theaters, while maintaining a large domestic audience. In sum, however, his films are not popular with Finnish theater audiences.

Third, the marketing of the films has not sought to package them as Finnish, either for domestic or international audiences, even if a Finnish setting sometimes features in their commercial packaging or is related to their narrative content, as in the case of *Juha*. Comparatively, national origin figures much less prominently in the marketing of Kaurismäki's films than of many other recent Finnish films, for example, *Ambush* (Olli Saarela, 1999, *Rukajärven tie*), *Badding* (Markku Pölönen, 2000), and *Rose of a Rascal* (Timo Koivusalo, 2001, *Rentun ruusu*). Most often Kaurismäki's films are associated with his image as an idiosyncratic auteur, a notion echoed in his self-deprecating interviews. The films are produced and marketed for art house distribution, with their primary audience outside Finland. To be sure, in interviews Kaurismäki often speaks of national aspects of the films and presents himself as the world's most melancholic Finn (Romney 1997, 2003; Kaurismäki, 1991). Yet financing, audience reception, and marketing of Kaurismäki's films do not indicate that they ought to be categorized solely as national films.[3]

It seems reasonable to suggest, then, that one reason Kaurismäki has been received primarily as a national filmmaker is that scholars and critics have stressed the significance of this category in their interpretations of his films. It is necessary to recognize the influence of a national intelligentsia whose cinema discourse both describes and produces the category of national cinema in relation to Kaurismäki. Pantti remarks in chapter 6 in this volume and in her "*Kansallinen elokuva pelastettava*" (2002) on the importance that Finnish cinema discourse has attached to the emergence of a messianic national auteur. For many commentators, Kaurismäki is Finnish cinema's "outstanding hope," as a wave of Finnish press coverage following his *Grand Prix* at Cannes 2002 suggests (Ahonen et al. 2003, 7). What kinds of arguments do these commentators make in categorizing the films as national? Most often, they have argued that the films' narrative themes, dialogue, and characterization capture an ineffable and unique national identity. The films' sparse dialogue and dark humor, for instance, are held to reflect on and simultaneously affirm Finns' famous silence.[4] The art critic Mika Hannula relates an anecdote about a talk given by prominent Finnish film scholar and critic Peter von Bagh about Kaurismäki in Berlin, which neatly crystallizes many critics' assessments. Von Bagh gestured passionately to the audience, writes Hannula, "to underline his feelings, emphasizing the stark realism of [Kaurismäki's] films, their accurate image of Finnish reality"; von Bagh went on to suggest that "to an outsider these films can never totally open up. Their world, larger than life, and their universe epitomize such genuine, raw Finland and Finnishness" (1998, 106–7). Von Bagh contends that even Kaurismäki's films set outside Finland—the *Leningrad Cowboys* films, *I Hired a Contract Killer,* and *La vie de Bohème*—are "genuinely Finnish" (1997, 6). Tommi Aitio speaks of *Tatiana* as distilling an expression of postwar Finnish culture (1994, 26). The literary scholar Pirjo Lyytikäinen interestingly suggests the films might well be placed within the venerable Finnish literary tradition of realist and neorealist national self-portraiture (1999, 164).

Scholars working outside Finland have also supported the national expressionist reading. René Prédal, for example, agrees that "in a certain way, each film by Aki Kaurismäki constitutes a sort of documentary of the development of Finnish mentalities" (1999, 39).[5] In what will likely stand as the canonical assessment of Kaurismäki's work between 1980 and 2002, Sakari Toiviainen's history of contemporary Finnish cinema, *Levottomat sukupolvet,* the author maintains that Kaurismäki's melancholic vision is only fully understood as a uniquely national expression (2002, 96–97).[6] These arguments hold that Kaurismäki's settings, humor, nostalgic tone, and laconic characters express a collectively shared attitude, consciousness, and outlook, and spring from a Finnish *Weltanschauung*. At least they indicate a consensus among commentators on Kaurismäki.

My point is not that these readings don't offer a plausible and in many ways insightful account of Kaurismäki's films. Clearly, national elements turn up in the films under consideration in this essay, too. *Leningrad Cowboys Go America* opens with panoramas of familiar national landscapes from Finland's Ostrobothnian region (see Toiviainen 2001; von Bagh 1997). The characters' nostalgia for home, their endless toleration of mild tyranny, their music, their drinking, and, not least, the exchange that opens the film—between a music promoter (a cameo by Peter von Bagh) and the cowboys' manager, Vladimir (Matti Pellonpää)—evoke conventions of self-deprecation among Finns about their "peculiar" national culture ("no commercial potential"). *Tatiana* plays the same chords, using coffee and liquor, masculine diffidence and barn dances, with an array of 1960s material culture as props, to render a national imaginary on-screen. Banal nationalism—settings at the harbor, the bank, the unemployment office, the bar, and the roadside café (and of course language)—also figures prominently. And Kaurismäki often amplifies banal nationalism with quirky characters who embody national clichés. However, to omit consideration of the films' many layers to underscore national expression fails to recognize the complexity of the films and the complexity of national cinema discourse. As the philosopher Sara Heinämaa remarks in a discussion of the films: "I find it absurd to interpret the Kaurismäki brothers' films as depictions of Finnish identity; because I simply fail to see what is distinctly Finnish in the world they depict. Okay there are certain national elements there . . . but [they] are the least interesting level to their films" (quoted in Ehrnrooth et al. 1998, 70). Or, as Jonathan Romney remarks about *Tatiana,* in a less polemic tenor: "Despite taking place in a fantasy pasta dream of Kerouac gone Nordic—*Tatiana* is revealing about Finnish culture, about the thirst for Americana on the one hand and the fascination with the neighboring former USSR on the other" (2003, 45).

When we complicate the categories by which national cinema is conceptualized and take into consideration comments like Heinämaa and Romney's about the on-screen images in Kaurismäki's films, it becomes clear that a critique of the categorization of Kaurismäki's films would surely provide a fuller understanding of how they might be more richly situated in relation to their historical moment. At the same time, films consist of multiple elements, and viewers may ascribe different significance to the various levels. Turning to the syntax and semantics of genre provides a handle that might help us unpack these multivalent films. Given the prominence of interpretations of Kaurismäki in terms of national expression, it's useful to read Kaurismäki's on-screen images in relation to genre, to make evident their multivalence.

GENRE

It might seem that genre would be a peculiar way to approach Kaurismäki's cinema. He makes self-conscious art films, is known for his unique vision and humor, and stresses in interviews his interest in auteurs such as Charles Chaplin, Robert Bresson, Luis Buñuel, Carl Th. Dreyer, Rainer Werner Fassbinder, Jacques Tati, Teuvo Tulio, and Wim Wenders, among others. What's more, he's also well known for his summary dismissals of the "high concept" (Wyatt 1994) genre cinema of the New Hollywood. Yet on the other hand, Kaurismäki invites the viewer to place his national themes and images in relation to intertextual connections with genre implications. About writing *Drifting Clouds,* Kaurismäki comments: "When I began to write the film, I put Frank Capra's sentimental redemption story *It's a Wonderful Life* (1946) as the limit on one end, and De Sica's *Bicycle Thieves* (1948) on the other, and Finnish reality in the middle. It was necessary to find optimism without losing touch with reality, to make contemporary neorealism in color" (quoted in Bacon 2003, 89). *Drifting Clouds* can well be seen as a mishmash of the syntax around which Capra's film is organized, the individual's recuperation of meaning, and the semantics of De Sica's unemployed Milan, which together articulate Finnish reality. When we turn to Kaurismäki's road movie, whose syntax and semantics are more clearly linked to a corpus of genre films, questions about categorization become especially relevant and intriguing.

In film studies, genre has tended to be defined by identifying a corpus of films that share semantic or syntactic features, which lend themselves to taxonomic classification.[7] So, the road movie might be identified by its semantics: images of the car, shots of dialogue in the car's interior, contrasts between rural and urban spaces, sweeping panoramas with fast panning shots, location shooting. Syntactically, the genre might also be defined as a series of conflicts between fixity and mobility, belonging and marginality, attachment and emancipation (see Laderman 2002). The genre works by deploying semantic and syntactic elements in recognizable patterns. That these patterns can not only be recognized but are a source of pleasure for audiences is taken to indicate that film industries produce films by genre blueprint, and that their production correlates with categories of reception (labels) that can aid and guide an audience in identifying and consuming films. This notion of genre implies that genres are obvious and have unchanging definitions. Obviously, it also requires some further elaboration in relation to Kaurismäki, who on this definition wouldn't seem like a genre filmmaker. It's necessary to examine a few assumptions to differentiate conventional notions of genre from the revisionist account of genre I'll use to discuss Kaurismäki.

Does genre mean the same thing to people over time and in different cultural contexts? How might we make sense of how genre works in a variety of circumstances? Some scholars have suggested that concern with textual form and typology has tended to obviate genre's penchant to mean different things to different viewers. The most suggestive argument of this sort appears in Rick Altman's 1999 study *Film/Genre*. Altman argues that genre is not determined only by producers, but is also constituted by viewers' negotiation of semantic and syntactic elements of genre. What's relevant here is that Altman tries to explain how genres are not immutable structures intrinsic to the text but are discursive networks, always being revised and revamped by different groups making and receiving cinema (98–99).

The linchpin of Altman's argument is his notion of the generic crossroad, which provides a term for defining the dynamics by which semantics and syntax are balanced in the production and reception of genre. A generic crossroads occurs in a text when different narrative pleasures are set in opposition, to which viewers may respond in creative, divergent ways. "Each one of these moments depends on a crucial opposition between two paths open to a spectator. Strategically simplifying, we may say that one fork offers a culturally sanctioned activity or value, while the other path diverges from cultural norms in favor of generical pleasure" (1999, 145). Crossroads can invoke semantics and syntax of genre to create different routes to viewing pleasure. Semantics and syntax often keep cultural norms in play while opening the way to escape from them through juxtaposed genre-coded semantics and syntax. Tension incrementally accrues over the course of a film, as the outcomes of each crossroad are registered with viewers. An example might help here. In Kaurismäki's *Ariel*, the film's opening offers a crossroad in which semantics and syntax generate a tension between culturally sanctioned behavior and genre glee. The film opens with the destruction of the mine in which Taisto (Turo Pajala) and his father work, which is followed by the abrupt suicide of Taisto's father. Before shooting himself, the father gives his son the keys to his inheritance, which proves to be a whale of a white Cadillac. The closed mine, snowy landscape, deserted barroom, and laconic characters can well be seen as culturally familiar national images, semantically. But, we learn, the keys give access to the semantics of the road movie, made evident by the images of the long, white Cadillac standing in the garage. At the crossroads, the tension mounts as the audience wonders: Which semantic markers will appear, and what syntax do they necessitate? Will Taisto accept the inheritance as a symbol of his father's hope for him and responsibly take up his father's legacy in the culturally sanctioned outcome? Or will he affirm the beautiful image, the road, a new style that rejects his past? The lines of narrative development are held in tension (which tends to be indicated by the mixture of bewildered silence and loud guffaws in audiences at screenings), prompting the viewer to consider various possibilities.

Yet, typically, the opening sequence of *Ariel* affirms genre: Taisto pulls the rumbling Caddy out of the garage, which immediately collapses, and, after a moment of pause that allows the audience to focus on the Cadillac, Taisto guns the engine, spins the tires, and heads onto the road. The semantics and syntax of the road movie are evident from the outset: the Caddy and the conflict between fixity and mobility. Generic pleasure quickly builds as the open convertible cruises the deserted, winter highway, with 1970s Finnish rock by a Kaurismäki favorite, Rauli Badding Sommerjoki, playing nondiagetically. Audience members are offered images of the road movie, which appear as surprising and out of place in this wintry mining country as the scarf-shrouded Taisto might appear to another driver. In the crossroads, writes Altman, "one side continues to judge as culture has taught us to judge, while the other bases its judgments on generic criteria, often diametrically opposed to cultural norms" (1999, 147). In *Ariel*, familiarity with the road movie allows the viewer to overlook the injustice of the economic changes that force Taisto to leave home and to ignore his callous attitude toward his father's death (he doesn't bother to hang around for the funeral) and his indifference to the rural mining-village community. The viewer can chuckle at the opening of this bizarre road movie and anticipate more to come. There are also salient cultural political implications here, to which I'll return later.

It's not the film but the interaction of viewers and film that is key to the crossroad dynamics. This implies that variant emphases on the semantics and syntax of a film lead to different ways of making sense of it.

> Genres don't provide the energy necessary to generic experiences; that must instead come from viewers, who, being different, can be expected to invest their energy in extremely diverse modes. What genres are adept at, however, is funneling toward a homogeneous experience those viewers who invest in a similar type of generic pleasure. . . . The ability to choose one's genre pleasure lies at the very heart of generic operations. (Altman 1999, 151)

The economy of genre as "choose your own adventure" lies in the way the crossroads fuel an escalation of tension between the choices available, sanctioned by cultural norms or generic ones. Altman's concept of genre is helpful in relation to Kaurismäki because it helps us recognize the way different sorts of pleasure are offered through the tensions that feed the films' narrative development. There are genre semantics and syntax as well as national semantics.

One of the problems with this line of argument is that it would seem to make genre so situational and contingent that it would obliterate the generic object itself. How can we know a road movie, for example, if genre is not a stable object of analysis, and "we do better . . . to treat genre as a complex situation, a concatenated series of events regularly repeated according to a recognizable pattern" (84)? Why, then, should genre be an object of study?

Altman's argument does not eliminate the notion that genre has a connection to constituent elements but prompts us to consider the way we organize the significance of those elements in arguing about genre's social significance. Altman resolves this issue pragmatically, arguing that when we attribute significance to ultimately contingent semantic and syntactic elements, we make sense of them pragmatically by nesting them in other discourses: for example, genre, an auteur's style, or national cinema. For just as one might argue about the beginning of *Ariel* that its semantics invoke the road movie, so too a critic might work up a chain of connections to connect the static camera in the sequence to Kaurismäki's style, his body of work, and his auteur style. Altman uses the sentence as a metaphor to clarify this pragmatic explanation of genre (1999, 210). As a sentence consists of certain semantic elements joined together according to certain syntactic rules, which can be used in a variety of ways (for example, phatically, performatively, ironically), the meaning-making function of this grammar is relevant insofar as users contingently connect parts and wholes in meaningful ways.

While I'm stressing the significance of genre, the larger point I wish to make here, like Heinämaa and Romney, is that the many levels of Kaurismäki's cinema are not served well by situating them in relation to singular categories like nation—a master-narrative if ever there was one. Rather, by attending to the interlarded levels in the film, we begin to see the many paradoxes that arguably are most significant to Kaurismäki's cinema. In considering these composites, it's instructive that the Finnish film scholar Henry Bacon notes the same quality, arguing that disjunction is a key to understanding the cultural politics of Kaurismäki's films. He points out, for example, that the films' representation of Helsinki, of time, and of character are paradoxical, presenting the viewer with contradictory images. Helsinki is stripped of its symbolic features, while the style and shape of its buildings and streets indicate that it is Helsinki (2003, 92–93). The historical moment in which the films are set is also disjointed, because references to current events and headlines are common, but they are juxtaposed with anachronistic styles, institutions, and attitudes—such as the many musicians who haven't heard of rock 'n' roll or the inclusion of tram models no longer in use. The characters, too, points out Bacon, are out of place, insofar as they are unemployed, anachronistic, rejected, forgotten (93). Through these disjointed images, argues Bacon, the films foreground a humanist solidarity, which is not visible in the fashionable images of the day, but which becomes visible through Kaurismäki's aesthetic. Another way of putting this is to say that Kaurismäki uses the image ironically, always saying something slightly different than he means. My point is not entirely different than Bacon's; it is only that I have sought to use genre crossroads as a way of situating the images of these road movies in order to make sense of the paradoxes he identifies. Yet, I would also argue, an account of the status of the image must be a part of any attempt to historicize Kaurismäki's cinema and its cultural politics. Let's take up these issues in more detail by looking at Kaurismäki's road movies.

ROAD MOVIES

The syntax of the road movie intersects with that of earlier quest narratives, from Homer's *Odyssey* to the pilgrimages in saints' lives, from the Icelandic sagas' narratives of travel as a catalyst for maturation to the picaresque novel's episodic accounts of travel, and on to the Bildungsroman and its many later revisions, such as Kerouac's *On the Road* (Laderman 2002). The conflicts arising from travel and mobility in quest narratives are related to the crossroads that figure prominently in the road movie. Yet, the road movie also marks a break from these literary narratives. Scholarship on the road movie generally links its emergence to the rise of the New Hollywood during the late 1960s and early 1970s, situating the road movie in relation to 1960s counterculture, the Brat Pack's embrace of European auteur cinema, and Hollywood's economic struggles and efforts to refashion itself for the newly emergent baby boomer audience (Cohan and Hark 1997; Laderman 2000, 2002). To map out the crossroads in Kaurismäki's road movies, then, it is necessary to identify and examine them and their conflicts with some historical specificity. Situating Kaurismäki in that way indicates that his films feature crossroads that offer the semantics of the generic image but also gesture to an authenticity discussed by Bacon.

In his study of the road movie in *A Cinema without Walls,* Timothy Corrigan (1991) distinguishes between the quest narrative and the road movie by differentiating between forms of representation. He sees them as sharing syntactic similarity yet differing in semantic significance because of the way the image represents the protagonist. The journey offers insight by separating the protagonist from the familiar, suggests Corrigan; it relocates the protagonist by projecting him onto a course of movement that allows him to see the social terrain from an alternative perspective. "The familiar is left behind or transformed through the protagonist's movement through space and time, and the confrontations and obstacles that he encounters generally lead . . . to a wiser individual and often a more stable spiritual or social state" (144). Crucially, for Corrigan, in the quest narrative *the psychic and bodily experience* of the journey is the *site* of relocation, as attainment of a new perspective for the subject is associated with departure and arrival of the body. Similarly, in the major book-length study of the road movie genre, David Laderman's *Driving Visions* (2002), the author argues that through the dynamic mentioned by Corrigan, the journey narrative often articulates a critical commentary on its historical moment. Laderman observes that by separating protagonists from a "stable social context . . . they become more able to critically observe social mores" (7). He supports this argument by citing Cervantes's *Don Quixote* (1615), Voltaire's *Candide* (1759), Defoe's *Moll Flanders* (1722), and Fielding's *Tom Jones* (1749). It might be mentioned that the spatial dislocation on which the journey narrative is built figures in the originary moments of Finnish literature. The first novel in Finnish, Aleksis Kivi's *Seven Brothers* (1870, *Seitsemän veljestä*), for example, uses flight from society to critique contemporary structures of authority (the state church in particular), identifying sources of national self-consciousness outside then dominant institutions. Corrigan and Laderman argue that by dislodging the subject from an immanent social context, journey narratives imply that a transcendental distance (cultural, economic, political, religious) can be attained, which leads to deeper understanding and perspective. While this notion does not fit with postmodernist and poststructuralist criticisms of transcendence, it nevertheless remains an important historical impulse in the modern West.

An echo of these arguments is evident in some of the readings of Kaurismäki's road films. Peter von Bagh's comments (1997) that even the films set outside Finland, such as the *Leningrad Cowboys* films, express a profound national consciousness suggest that separation, articulation, and identification lead to a rediscovery of a national perspective. While von Bagh is speaking of how a critic reads the films, it is reasonable to see his argument as also implying that these road movies' narratives use the journey outside the national space to reflect on the nation itself, creating a distanced position from which the viewer comes to value his or her national culture through the films. Separation causes longing, which brings into focus the object of one's longing, and one's identity with it, suggests von Bagh.[8]

Yet, can the journey narrative be seen as continuous with the journey in the road movie? Might theorizing and historicizing the film genre help us better understand the crossroads that figure in Kaurismäki's road movies? In Corrigan's poststructuralist and psychoanalytic account, a distinction between the journey narrative and the postwar road movie is salient because in the latter, the humanist subject is no longer the key site of relocation and differentiation of perspective. In the road movie, argues Corrigan, the automobile becomes the semantic icon of knowledge, experience, and consciousness—the image of subjectivity, in short. If Sal Paradise and Dean Moriarty are physically on the road becoming subjects through their journeys (albeit with cars like Dean's Hudson figuring as important allegorical symbols), then in the road movie, according to Corrigan, it's the vehicle itself that becomes the subjective image of travel that marks the journey; the *image of the car* is a posthuman *site* for the fashioning of identity (see also Laderman 2002, 9–11).[9] This point leads Corrigan to argue that the road movie can no longer be seen as simply the narrative representation of a subjective experience of the historical moment (as in the quest narrative): "The commodification of the image as vehicle underlines, in brief, the central crisis that is developing: it increasingly marks the separation of human perspective and the genre from any sort of logical or natural relation with the history of culture, forcing each to take as its subject only its own symptoms, the material excess of a culture's failure to naturalize its rituals" (148). In other words, when modern forms of subjectivity and travel become embedded in a flow of images of velocity, travel, and being, the distinction between subject and image becomes indistinct. In this case, we're talking not about a subject's expression through images but of the manipulation of the image as the locus of identity. It is helpful to situate Kaurismäki's crossroads in relation to Corrigan's argument because of Kaurismäki's road films' fixation on the image.

Corrigan's argument compels us to ask, then, How do Kaurismäki's road films engage "the history of culture," the "commodification of the image as vehicle," and the continuum between them? The tension between these poles (not unlike the tension between De Sica and Capra) pervades the road films. On the one hand, the focus on down-and-out characters from a recognizable national past articulate a desire to opt out of the culture of the image and the transnational capitalist system that generates it. On the other, the films are replete with stylized images of the past, careful selections of popular culture, semantic and syntactic genre references, inside jokes that self-reflexively indicate a savvy appreciation for global popular culture in the postwar period. The publicity material for *Ariel* calls all this neatly to mind: "[*Ariel* is] a film that begins as an unemployment story, turns into a hanging-out movie, has a touch of a love story about ordinary people, becomes a crime and prison film before ending up as over-romantic melodrama. Contains the truth about life in a typical Western 'everything-for-sale' society. Some drama included" (quoted in Connah 1991, 479). The film can be seen as a serious critical examination of the structural transformation of the Finnish economy during times of globalization, yet it can also be seen as delightful commentary on B-movie uses of the image of the car as a site of subjective transformation, on the aesthetics of the criminal image, and on cinematic narratives of romantic love and the family (Toivianen 1994, 2002; Nestingen 2002). By looking at *Leningrad Cowboys* and *Tatiana*, we can spell out in more detail the significance of this tension for the categorization and historicized understanding of Kaurismäki.

LENINGRAD COWBOYS GO AMERICA

The Leningrad Cowboys themselves are a composite of semantic excess not irrelevant to the road movie. By excess here, I'm speaking of the term not in its psychoanalytic usage, but of the way Kristin Thompson uses it, roughly, to denominate unmotivated exceptions to the stylistic patterns that comprise a film (1999). Taking the concept of excess "up another level" in relation to genre will also prove helpful in Kaurismäki's case, allowing the semantics in his films to be pragmatically situated in relation to patterns of the genre's semantics. This move aids in understanding the cultural politics in question. The Cowboys' rock 'n' roll style plainly enough has its roots in films like *Easy Rider*, but whereas films like *Natural Born Killers* (Oliver Stone, 1991) attack the commodification of this rock 'n' roll style to sell crime spectacle, *Leningrad Cowboys* embraces a self-reflexively cracker-barrel version of it. Casting, costume, and props are characterized largely by semantic excess in terms of the style of the genre: the draconian manager Vladimir (Matti Pellonpää), the backward players (they arrive in New York to tour the United States playing "Siberian" dance tunes, unaware of rock 'n' roll), the band's odd musical makeup, from their torpedo bouffants to their balalaika player to their preferred mode of transport, enormous Cadillacs. The characters who cross their path are also uniformly caricatures, whether the arrogant rock promoter (Richard Boes), the motor-head used car dealer (a cameo by Jim Jarmusch),[10] or the enthusiastic lost cousin (Nicky Tesco). The trip that provides the movie's premise, from New York to Mexico, also offers genre excess, comically glossing the last journey to Mexico of Jack Kerouac's *On the Road*. The southern setting, and the characters the cowboys run across, also allude to the denizens of the rural South in *Easy Rider* and *Bonnie and Clyde*, among others. The film's characters, journey, and setting consist of a thick fabric of genre connections.

The film's excess is obvious, but its significance is ambiguous. Consequently, many viewers respond indifferently, for it is difficult to determine whether one should take the excess seriously or treat it as a joke. There is little tension in the crossroads, because they are submerged in the constant superfluity of genre pleasure. Still, the film's playful exaggeration of road movie clichés—such as the used car dealer, rock 'n' roll attitude on the road, the exploitative nightclub owner, stylish cars, and the journey to freedom as a critique of the status quo left behind—offer pleasure to any viewer familiar with the icons of postwar popular culture, many of which figure in the conventional road film (Laderman 2002). In this sense pleasure springs from the opportunity the film offers for reflection on popular culture and the road film genre itself. One might think of this as a goofy sort of metacinema, oddly reminiscent of the metacinematic motif that figures in Wim Wenders's *Kings of the Road* (1976, *Im Lauf der Zeit*). That film famously opens with Bruno Winter (Rüdiger Vogler) repairing a movie projector, chatting with the theater owner, a former Nazi. The opening sequence comments on the repair of cinema as an institution, part of Wenders's and the New German cinema's project, which is figured in the film through Bruno's repair of cinemas (Laderman 2002, 264). If Wenders's film seriously aims to come to terms with the past and present of German national cinema, speaking to a national guilt and desire for reconstruction (as the German title's emphasis on temporality suggests), Kaurismäki's commentary does not carry the same fixation on the national past and reconstruction. *Leningrad Cowboys* is a metacinema that affirms the image as the site of a humorous yet self-conscious detour between present and past. To press the point further, whereas Corrigan (1991) sees a crisis issuing from the displacement of the subject by the image (which, for example, Wenders might also be seen as trying to repair), Kaurismäki's road images display little anxiety. Yet, here we might recall Bacon's (2003) remarks about irony: the excessiveness of the generic images set in juxtaposition with the films' search for authenticity indeed creates an ironic gap.

In an intriguing contrast to the excessiveness of genre semantics, the film's settings are strikingly mundane, left-behind places; absent from the film are any sites of power-saturated, glamorous images. By contrast, the prominence of commodified images in a road film of about the same era, Wenders's *Paris, Texas* (1984) stands out: the latter film's fascination with the commodification of the image and identity is evident in the billboards that figure centrally in the film as well as in Jane's (Natasha Kinski) employment as an erotic dancer. *Leningrad Cowboys* uses setting to turn away from the commodified image, structuring the Cowboys' journey from New York to Mexico as a panorama of rural poverty and down-and-outers in the southern United States. The Cowboys' journey meanders around the South in what seems like an effort to include as many forgotten rural landscapes and townscapes as can be packed into its seventy-eight minutes.[11] These panoramas belong to the road movie but are shorn of their usual romanticization: boarded-up shops, biker bars, city skylines, out-of-season beaches, junkyards, corner bars, pulp mills, oil refineries, and honky-tonks. The playful performance of a New Orleans jazz funeral, for example, lacks all the commonplace images of celebration and sorrow associated with it and ends in the arrest of the Cowboys.

The film's picture of the United States includes pictures of the least well-to-do, many of whom were nonprofessional actors cast on site. Whether the diffident barber the Cowboys meet, the threatening motorcyclists who take them in, or their final arrival at the festive Mexican wedding, these moments in the film express a sense of gravity absent from the tongue-in-cheek playfulness with genre that pervades most of the film. These moments express a wish for subjective authenticity. By the term, I mean to refer to Charles Taylor's use of it in his *Sources of the Self* (1989) and *Ethics of Authenticity* (1991). Taylor traces his use of authenticity to Rousseau's and Herder's preromantic arguments about authenticity as self-expression that adequately articulates one's own sense of identity, which is the basis for being recognized by others in ways that are true to oneself and one's circumstances. By authenticity, then, I mean satisfying self-definition and recognition in dialogue with others (Taylor 1991, 36–37). Dialogue must not be forgotten, because it entails that self-definition occurs continually in relation to other forms of meaningful self-definition. Without going into further detail about Taylor's rich argument, we simply need to note that the juxtaposition of excessive images and down-and-outers is a dialogue that is at once humorous and serious. The articulation of authenticity in *Lenin-*

grad *Cowboys* comes through in the latter, and I think it's fair to say it invokes a deep concern with ethical responsibility to others—a theme that becomes more pronounced in later films such as *Drifting Clouds* and *The Man Without a Past*.

Dialogue comprising authenticity, it must be pointed out, is highly relevant to the cultural politics in these films about lovable Finnish losers. These losers are not prolix. Interestingly enough, silence, while often mentioned in connection with Finnish national identity in a humorous way, has been a point of historical stigma. Historian Matti Peltonen (1998) has demonstrated how Finnish nineteenth-century elites constructed silence as a lack—associating it with deficient education, heavy drinking, and rural backwardness. The folklorist Satu Apo speaks of this cultural politics as part of a "stigmatization tradition" (1998). By characterizing silence as a lack, elites justified their programs of amelioration, transformation, and nationalization of the people. Peltonen argues that while this dynamic subsided in the welfare state period, it has recently reemerged as Finland has sought to retool itself as a globalized economic zone. So, for example, Finnish businesspeople take courses in wine, fashion, and small talk. The Cowboys offer an alternative model. If, as Taylor suggests, authenticity has to do with self-expression, then Kaurismäki's films are wary of the obstacles to "self-expression" in a culture of the image, like that of the small-talk course. How can images of national expression and authenticity be made for the screen, when these same images are the most precious commodity of postmodernity, for sale themselves? As his playful gloss of the stigmatization tradition suggests, inversion of received images creates multiple possibilities for response and use of the films.

TAKE CARE OF YOUR SCARF, TATIANA

If cultural hybridity underpins *Leningrad Cowboys*, can the same be said about *Take Care of Your Scarf, Tatiana*? Of all Kaurismäki's films, *Tatiana* might be seen as the most fully developed version of the national auteur's picture of the national past. The film is packed with national elements. Its country-bumpkin protagonists' journey through the Finnish summer; the film's rural settings replete with old-fashioned bars and hotels; its televised performances by the smash-hit band of the moment, the Renegades; its material culture, from Husqvarna motorcy-

Images of speed in the opening credits of Aki Kaurismäki's *Take Care of your Scarf, Tatiana* (1991)

On the road in style: Tatiana (Kati Outinen), Reino (Matti Pellonpää), Klavdia (Kirsi Tykkyläinen), and Valto (Mato Valtonen) in *Take Care of your Scarf, Tatiana*

cles to Volga automobiles to Iittala beer mugs; and the characters' tendency to fill their mouths with coffee and spirits instead of words. All this playfully draws a caricature of Apo's stigmatization tradition. The non-Finns in the film note this. Russian hitchhiker Klavdia (Kirsi Tykkyläinen) and Estonian Tatiana (Kati Outinen) speak about Valto (Mato Valtonen) and Reino (Matti Pellonpää) as "dumb Finns," berating their diffidence, lack of manners, and silence. Nevertheless, as in *Leningrad Cowboys*, the national is one layer in a composite that situates the film in a broad field of cultural meaning making.

A key juxtaposition is established in the opening sequence. The credits are preceded by images of men riding motorcycles in protective attire, women riding on the back of their motorcycles—calling to mind such "speed films" as Carl Dreyer's *They Reached the Ferry* (1948, *De nåede færgen*) and the motorcyclists of *Easy Rider*, metonymically signaling the road movie through a privileged speed image. The frenetic opening images contrast starkly with the introduction of Valto, staunch and middle-aged, anchored at a sewing machine. The action begins when he locks away his mother for refusing his request for more coffee. Valto heads off for supplies, stopping to pick up his repaired Volga station wagon from a mechanic friend, leading to a several-day test drive, fueled by coffee and liquor. But if the road film often cultivates social criticism, for Valto and Reino, the road does not offer freedom but rather the space to act young and carefree. Their beleaguered efforts are warmly comical, not sharply social critical. In contrast to the stylish opening images, their tired-out adolescent fantasies seem quaint.

Valto and Reino are often presented in a way that underscores the semantics of the road movie, which becomes the focus of the film. It's helpful to locate the characters' embrace of the *roku* (rocker) look of the early 1960s, since this is the source of their image. The significance of their style is indicated by the film's soundtrack, which is comprised of numerous rockabilly hits performed by the Renegades, a Liverpool band who enjoyed Beatlemania-like popularity in Finland in the early and mid-1960s—and which are included on the soundtrack of a number of Kaurismäki films. Most of Reino's energy goes toward performing the authenticity of his rocker credentials: Brylcremed hair, leather jacket, hard drinking, ready to fight. Valto is a phlegmatic homebody by comparison, gamely playing along. The film comically and self-consciously derives humor from the generic nature of the then emergent rocker style. Rock 'n' roll challenged the predominance of the dominant *iskelmä* music (*Schlager*) by offering a subculture of rebellious difference, with a fashion and attitude repertoire, with which its participants could affiliate themselves through taste and choice. Connecting oneself with the music, like that of the Renegades, situated one in a space of a self-defined youth culture (Bruun et al. 1998). By contrast, Valto and Reino are older than the image that Reino would like to conjure about themselves. Hence his fondness for rocker slang—for example, his drunken monologue at the beginning of their journey—grates against his decaying, forty-year-old body.[12] The prominence of slang in the film carries particular importance because of its rarity in Kaurismäki's work, marking the style of the characters in this film. The element is finally highlighted by Valto's terse and slangy dismissal of a waiter's insult at the conclusion of the film. By contrast, Kaurismäki's characters often speak a schoolbook Finnish, a rarity something akin to the stilted English spoken by Margaret (Margi Clarke) in *I Hired a Contract Killer* (1990). *Tatiana*, then, creates a good deal of its humor, and pleasure, through its framing of style and speech. One might even argue that Valto is a foil for making Reino's excess more obvious. To return to the image that opens the film, then, its excess opens a gap between image and authenticity that the characters strut around in over the course of the film. Given the prominence of rock 'n' roll road movie semantics in *Tatiana*, it might seem appropriate to connect the film to Corrigan's argument, seeing it as a humorous consideration of less glamorous performance of genre images like "on the road" and "rocker." To connect the point to the larger theme in the essay: What is the relation between image, authenticity, and nation in *Tatiana*? The question brings back into focus a cultural politics of authenticity.

To answer the question it's helpful to compare *Tatiana* with some recent films that treat rock 'n' roll of the same period in a much different tone and with different aims. These films are not paradoxical, in the way Kaurismäki's are, but use the image to paper over their relation to genre, authenticity, and nation. Early Finnish popular music has featured centrally in biopics like *Rose of a Rascal* (Timo Koivusalo, 2001, *Rentun ruusu*), *Badding* (Markku Pölönen, 2000), and *The Swan and the Wanderer* (Timo Koivusalo, 1999, *Kulkuri ja joutsen*). These hagiographic treatments revivify and recuperate popular figures from the time during which *Tatiana* is set, making them larger than life on screen, their image the performance of a national mythos, packaged conveniently for the theater. As DuBois argues in chapter 9 in this volume, these projects are sometimes gendered, employing sentimentality to recover ostensibly lost, or crisis-ridden, masculinities. By contrast, Kaurismäki revels in disjunction (of the sort evident in Reino's character), not in the seamless presentation of the prehistory of contemporary Finnish popular culture, as though the image were identical with the erstwhile reality. By juxtaposing excessive images with vulnerable efforts at self-definition, he forestalls the sentimentality of the biopics. He offers not National Identity but disjunction. By underlining the disjunction, *Tatiana* pushes to the foreground the component parts of early rock 'n' roll youth culture. This approach links the film to the music and its social significance, as opposed to telling its story as part of a national narrative of development. It leaves the crossroads open.

This argument might seem counterintuitive in relation to a film whose panorama shots and characters locate the film squarely within a national rubric. The panoramas of country roads and their surrounding fields that figure in the film bring to mind both the social significance of the countryside in postwar Finland and its cinematic significance. Sakari Toiviainen (2001) has pointed out the significance of uses of national landscapes in efforts to elevate national cinema as a valid form of the national cultural expression in the 1930s. The lumberjack became a generic figure connected with these notions, as DuBois argues in his contribution to this volume (chapter 9). During the cold war, rural life was lionized, as maintaining a productive national agriculture and forest industry became matters of national security (Eskelinen 2003, 7). Settings in the film call all this to mind, and it is surely right to see this as a "national" road movie on account of its iconography. One could go on to list other cherished national symbols prominent in the film.

One way of making sense of these paradoxes is by recalling Bacon's irony. Yet, it's become evident that the irony in *Leningrad Cowboys* and *Tatiana* is also Socratic, or postmodern, rather than simply a trope that can be neatly decoded in clear national terms, as Bacon implies. Perhaps recalling the reemergence of the stigmatization tradition noted by Peltonen, the irony of Kaurismäki's films can be seen to seek to open a space for many voices in discussions of authenticity, rather than trying to favor a singular one. This argument suggests, then, that Kaurismäki's cinema is most richly situated in a plural, transnational cultural terrain, whereon pragmatic meaning making depends on intersections with many discourses.

CONCLUSION

Aki Kaurismäki is coowner of two bars in Helsinki, Corona and MOCKBA. The latter has turned up in several of his films, including *The Man without a Past*. In the film M goes to MOCKBA for a drink after his release from police incarceration. In reality, MOCKBA is built around design and material culture that make it a delightful Soviet pastiche. The bar brings the ambivalent relation of image and authenticity that has figured in this essay into focus. The tiny bar is filled with 1970s Soviet touches, from the absent sign for the bar (MOCKBA is printed on a paper hung next to the door) to the lush lace curtains that hang in the windows to the samovar behind the stainless steel bar and the rye and salami sandwiches preserved on a covered plate, unrefrigerated. Vladimir Vysotsky and Georg Otts are in regular circulation on an ancient jukebox. One would not err in noting semantic excess.

The bar, like the films discussed in the essay, combine image and authenticity in a fusion that is full of pleasure, yet simultaneously dialectically seeks to articulate authentic self-definition. This can only occur, in times of globalization, within a culture of the commodified image. The films squeeze enormous pleasure from teasing and ironizing such commodified images. They smartly employ genre in a way that invites multiple pragmatic uses. Yet their humor leavens the films' quest for authenticity. The tension between pleasure in the image and search for authenticity makes the theme of self-definition more complex—and also more effective in speaking about economic, political, and cultural entanglements of the present day in a global media culture. In looking at Kaurismäki's road movies and noting the contrasts and paradoxes they use to generate crossroads moments, it becomes richer to see Aki Kaurismäki in the context of Finnish cultural history and cinema but also as part of a Nordic cinema in transition between the national and transnational.

NOTES

1. I use "national landscape" here in a critical way, recognizing the way it is itself a "medium" constructed historically. For discussion of this issue, see Mitchell 2002.
2. Thanks to Pietari Kääpä and Mervi Pantti for calling this volume to my attention.
3. Similarities between Kaurismäki and Lars von Trier are evident in their shared auteur references across lines of national cinema, multinational funding schemes, relative unpopularity at home and success abroad, and distinct auteur stamp. In contrast, Von Trier's international successes, including awards at Cannes for *The Element of Crime* (1984, *Forbrydelsens element*), *Europa* (1991, *Zentropa*), *Breaking the Waves* (1996), and *Dancer in the Dark* (2000) and the number of English-language films in his oeuvre perhaps make him a less "national" director than Kaurismäki.
4. The argument that silence is a form of Finnish expression has been made in other contexts, for example, by Peter von Bagh in his article "Silents for a Silent People," where he maintains that while the silent cinema in Finland was not a period of prolific production, silence on-screen might be seen as a form of national expression, as with Kaurismäki's *Juha* (1999).
5. "D'une certaine manière, tout film d'Aki Kaurismäki constitue une sorte de documentaire sur l'évolution des mentalités finlandaises."
6. Toiviainen sums up other scholarly arguments concerning the Finnishness of Kau-

rismäki's films (Aitio 1999, 29; Serceau 2000, 59; von Bagh 1991). One of the most sophisticated of these studies is Satu Kyösola's dissertation study (2001) of Kaurismäki's films as a dynamic of melancholic repetition, appearance, and disappearance. The films attempt to revivify endlessly a lost past, expressing a melancholic fixation on the image of a missing object of that past.
7. See Altman's survey of this tendency in *Film/Genre* (1999, 15–16. "Whether the topic is the musical (Feuer [1982]), the Western (Cawelti [1975]), the biopic (Custen [1992]), the historical adventure film (Taves [1993]), the war film (Basinger [1986]), or even British genre films (Landy [1991]), the generic corpus is assumed to be a given, preconstituted by industrial fiat" (16).
8. This is the basic dynamic behind Kyösola's study (2001) of melancholy in Kaurismäki.
9. David Cronenberg's 1996 film *Crash* might be seen as an explicit meditation on this theme.
10. With this cameo, Kaurismäki invokes Jarmusch's *Mystery Train* from the same year as well as Jarmusch's cast of retro characters first appearing in *Stranger than Paradise*. In some ways, the Cowboys are kindred spirits to the Japanese rock 'n' rollers who appear in *Mystery Train*. There is a nexus of influences between Kaurismäki, Jarmusch, Wenders (*Paris, Texas*), Fridriksson (*Cold Fever*), and Hal Hartley (*No Such Thing*), discussed by Birgir Møller in his chapter 12, "In and Out of Reykjavik," in this volume.
11. The Cowboys arrive in Memphis from New York, from where they drive south to New Orleans before heading back north to Natchez, Mississippi, only to turn southwest to Galveston, Texas, from where they head south again to Mexico by detouring north through Houston.
12. Matti Pellonpää was forty-three years old during the shooting of the film.

WORKS CITED

Ahonen, Kimmo, Janne Rosenqvist, Juha Rosenqvist, and Päivi Valotie, eds. 2003. "Saateeksi." In *Taju kankaalle: Uutta suomalaista elokuvaa paikantamassa*, 5–7. Turku: Kirja-Aurora.
Aitio, Tommi. 1994. "Tatjana ja Anita: Suomi silloin ja nyt." *Filmihullu* 2: 26–27.
———. 1999. "Vieras mies tulee taloon." *Filmihullu* 1: 28–30.
Altman, Rick. 1999. *Film/Genre*. London: British Film Institute.
Apo, Satu. 1998. "Suomalaisuuden stigmatisoinnin traditio." In *Elävänä Euroopassa: Muuttuva suomalainen identiteetti*, ed. Pertti Alasuutari and Petri Ruuska, 83–128. Tampere: Vastapaino.
Bacon, Henry. 2003. "Aki Kaurismäen sijoiltaan olon poetiikka." In *Taju kankaalle: Uutta suomalaista elokuvaa paikantamassa*, 89–97. Turku: Kirja-Aurora.
Basinger, Jeannine. 1986. *The World War II Combat Film: Anatomy of a Genre*. New York: Columbia University Press.
Billig, Michael. 1995. *Banal Nationalism*. London: Sage.
Björkman, Stig, Helena Linblad, and Fredrik Sahlin. 2002. *Fucking film: Den nya svenska filmen*. Stockholm: Alfabeta Bokförlag.

Brandstrup, Pil Gundelach, and Eva Novrup Redvall. 2003. "Fra *Babettes Gæstebud* til *Blinkende lygter:* Internationalisering af dansk film." In *Nationale spejlinger: Tendenser i ny dansk film,* ed. Anders Toftgaard and Ian Hawkesworth, 109–38. Copenhagen: Museum Tusculanums Forlag.

Bruun, Seppo, Jukka Lindfors, Santtu Luoto, and Markku Salo. 1998. *Jee jee jee: suomalaisen rockin historia.* Helsinki: WSOY.

Cawelti, John G. 1975. *The Six-Gun Mystique.* Bowling Green: Bowling Green University Press.

Chow, Rey. 1998. "Film and Cultural Identity." In *Oxford Guide to Film Studies,* ed. Jonathan Hill and Pamela Church Gibson, 169–75. Oxford: Oxford University Press.

Cohan, Steven, and Ina Rae Hark, eds. 1997. *The Road Movie Book.* London: Routledge.

Connah, Roger. 1991. *K/K, a Couple of Finns, and Some Donald Ducks: Cinema in Society.* Helsinki: VAPK.

Corrigan, Timothy. 1991. *A Cinema without Walls: Movies and Culture after Vietnam.* New Brunswick, N.J.: Rutgers University Press.

Crofts, Stephen. 1998. "Concepts of National Cinema." In *Oxford Guide to Film Studies,* ed. Jonathan Hill and Pamela Church Gibson, 385–94. Oxford: Oxford University Press.

Custen, George F. 1992. *Bio/Pics: How Hollywood Constructed Public History.* New Brunswick, N.J.: Rutgers University Press.

Ehrnrooth, Jari, Mika Hannula, Sara Heinämaa, and Jyrki Siukonen. 1998. "Discussion." In *Aavan meren tällä puolen/ Härom de stora haven/ This Side of the Ocean,* ed. Maaretta Jaukkuri and Tuija Kuutti, 37–92. Helsinki: Museum of Contemporary Arts.

Eskelinen, Heikki. 2003. "Maaseutu—Rasite vai resurssi?" *Hiidenkivi* 2: 6–9.

Feuer, Jane. 1982. *The Hollywood Musical.* Bloomington: Indiana University Press.

Hannula, Mika. 1998. "Kulman kautta—Puheesta tekstiin/ Om hörnet—Från det talade ordet till det skrivna/ Through an Angle—From Talk into Text." In *Aavan meren tällä puolen/ Härom de stora haven/ This Side of the Ocean,* ed. Maaretta Jaukkuri and Tuija Kuutti, 105–14. Helsinki: Museum of Contemporary Arts.

Higson, Andrew. 1995. *Waving the Flag: Constructing a National Cinema in Britain.* Oxford: Clarendon Press.

Hjort, Mette. 2000. "Themes of Nation." In *Cinema and Nation,* ed. Mette Hjort and Scott MacKenzie, 103–18. New York: Routledge.

Jameson, Fredric. 1991. *Postmodernism, or, The Cultural Logic of late Capitalism.* Durham: Duke University Press.

Kaurismäki, Aki. 1991. "Työmiehen muotokuva." Interview by Peter von Bagh. *Filmihullu* 5: 4–11.

Kyösola, Satu. 2001. "Des ombres et des nuages: Dynamiques mélancoliques dans l'oeuvre d'Aki Kaurismäki." Diss., Université Paris III–Sorbonne Nouvelle.

Laderman, David. 2000. "The Road Movie Rediscovers Mexico: Alex Cox's *Highway Patrolman.*" *Cinema Journal* 39, no. 2: 74–99.

———. 2002. *Driving Visions: Exploring the Road Movie.* Austin: University of Texas Press.

Laine, Kimmo. 1999. *Pääosassa Suomen kansa: Suomi-Filmi ja Suomen Filmiteollisuus*

kansallisen elokuvan rakentajina, 1933–1939. Helsinki: Finnish Literature Society.
Landy, Marcia. 1991. *British Genres: Cinema and Society, 1930–1960*. Princeton, N.J.: Princeton University Press.
Lyytikäinen, Pirjo. 1999. "Birth of a Nation: The Literary Inscription of Finnishness." In *Europe's Northern Frontier: Perspectives on Finland's Western Identity*, ed. Tuomas M. S. Lehtonen, trans. Philip Landon, 138–65. Sitra 230. Helsinki: PK Kustannus.
Miller, Toby, et al. 2001. *Global Hollywood*. London: British Film Institute.
Mitchell, W. J. T., ed. *Landscape and Power*. 2nd ed. Chicago: University of Chicago Press, 2002.
Nestingen, Andrew. 2002. "Leaving Home: Kaurismäki's *Ariel* and Global Circulation." *Journal of Finnish Studies* 6, nos. 1–2: 5–26.
———. 2003. "Nostalgias and Their Publics: The Finnish Film Boom, 1999–2001." *Scandinavian Studies* 75, no. 4: 539–66.
Pantti, Mervi. 2000. *"Kansallinen elokuva pelastettava": Elokuvapoliittinen keskustelu kotimaisen elokuvan tukemisesta itsenäisyyden ajalla*. Helsinki: Suomalaisen Kirjallisuuden Seura.
Peltonen, Matti. 1998. "Omakuvamme murroskohdat: Maisema ja kieli suomalaisuuskäsitysten perusaineksina." In *Elävänä Euroopassa: Muuttuva suomalainen identiteetti*, ed. Pertti Alasuutari and Petri Ruuska, 19–40. Tampere: Vastapaino.
Prédal, René. 1999. "Réalisme intérieur à la finlandaise: Un comique vide, froid, raide, et lent." *Contre bande* 5: 39–48.
Romney, Jonathan. 1997. "The Kaurismaki Effect." *Sight and Sound* (June): 10–14.
———. 2003. "Last Exit to Helsinki." *Film Comment* 39, no. 2: 43–45, 47.
Serceau, Daniel. 2000. "Une esthétique du raccourci et de la segmentation." *Contre bande* 5: 99–108.
Suomalaisen elokuvan markkinat ja kilpailukyky. 1999. Helsinki: F & L Research. http://www.flms.com/elokuva.pdf
Taves, Brian. 1993. *The Romance of Adventure: The Genre of Historical Adventure Movies*. Jackson: University of Mississippi Press.
Taylor, Charles. 1989. *Sources of the Self: The Making of the Modern Identity*. Cambridge: Harvard University Press.
———. 1991. *Ethics of Authenticity*. Cambridge: Harvard University Press.
Thompson, Kristin. 1999. "The Concept of Cinematic Excess." In *Film Theory and Criticism: Introductory Readings*, 5th ed., ed. Leo Braudy and Marshall Cohen, 487–98. New York: Oxford University Press.
Toiviainen, Sakari. 2001. "Paradises Lost." *Books from Finland* 35, no. 1: 33–37.
———. 2002. *Levottomat sukupolvet: Uusin suomalainen elokuva*. Helsinki: Suomalaisen Kirjallisuuden Seura.
von Bagh, Peter. 1991. "Oloissamme kumma heppu." *Filmihullu* 5: 3.
———. 1997. "Introduction: The Comedy of Losers." In *Shadows in Paradise: Photographs from the Films by Aki Kaurismäki*, by Marja-Leena Hakkanen, 5–21. Helsinki: Otava.
———. 1999. "Silents for a Silent People." In *Nordic Explorations: Film before 1930*, ed. John Fullerton and Jan Olsson, 86–90. London: John Libbey.
Wyatt, Justin. 1994. *High Concept: Movies and Marketing in Hollywood*. Austin: University of Texas Press.

In and Out of Reykjavik: Framing Iceland in the Global Daze

Birgir Thor Møller
Translated by Rune Christensen and Trevor G. Elkington

It seems difficult, if not impossible, for the international press to frame and describe Icelandic art, music, or film—no matter what period it belongs to—without referring to the country's larger-than-life landscape, history, or folklore, even if for understandable reasons. Today, this contextualizing strategy may be an attempt to provide an anchor point in times of globalization and postmodern circulation, cross-pollination, borrowing, and hybrids. In these flows, all that is peculiar and from Iceland becomes an instance of "odd Iceland." Examples are many, but pop icon Björk is surely the most well known. Because Björk's voice is as singular as her self-fashioning, and she must be defined or at least placed—and parallels seem absent—she easily becomes the untamed natural phenomenon, the Icelandic troll. This contextualizing strategy is typical in relation to Icelandic film, too, and is evident in relation to the first and foremost figure in Icelandic film, Fridrik Thór Fridriksson,[1] the Oscar-nominated child of nature and celluloid, who'll be the focus of this essay. Unfortunately, the dearth of scholarly discussion available on Icelandic cinema and the influence of romanticized framings of its popular culture in cultural journalism have obscured the history of Icelandic cinema. This essay seeks to illuminate that history, scraping away the romanticization.

In light of this project, a more provocative, though no less accurate, title might have been, *"Children of Nature* or *101 Reykjavik?"* It would undoubtedly stress the nexus between nature and city—thereby providing a more nuanced frame for Icelandic film than the romanticized one. And, notably, it would outline the tension, more specifically, between the nation's native soil, which among other things is the foundation for Fridriksson's *Children of Nature* (1991, *Börn náttúrunnar*), and the capital's downtown, which is represented in Baltasar Kormákur's *101 Reykjavik* (2000). A contrast between country and city, differentiating the traditional (and often romanticized) Iceland from the modern Iceland, is evident not just in these films and their titles, but in the majority of the seventy-four feature films that have appeared since Ágúst Gudmundsson's *Land and Sons* (1980, *Land og synir*) had its premiere on January 25, 1980—Iceland's first film after the creation of the Icelandic Film Fund (IFF) in 1979, when domestic film production can be said to have begun in earnest.

The average of three feature films produced a year since the establishment of the IFF may not sound like much. It's salutary to remember, however, that for a population of 280,000 Icelanders, the number is in fact high. Icelandic cinema's symbolic significance has become especially important. The Icelandic film milieu received a new and more widespread attention throughout the 1990s, as more films were released on a clearly more heterogeneous scene. One had barely written "2000," which saw the premiere of six Icelandic films, before a third generation of filmmakers appeared with new ideas about how to capture the nation's portrait on the silver screen. And not just for the local scene: the 1990s also witnessed the internationalization of Icelandic film, not least Fridrik Thór Fridriksson's breakthrough with the Oscar-nominated *Children of Nature*.

It is too early to judge this new generation of filmmakers, although some of them have already received international accolades and recognition—in particular Baltasar Kormákur for his *101 Reykjavik,* which was followed quickly by a second feature, *The Sea* (2002, *Hafid*). But there are tendencies and directions in these films that call to mind the country-city nexus.

This essay does not aim to disregard the Viking films (or other period dramas), nor to ignore their importance in Icelandic cinema, but keeping in mind the country-city division, this essay will emphasize films that have tried to capture modern Iceland, the impact of modernization, and now globalization on Iceland and Icelandic cinema. The focus is justified in part by Iceland's hasty modernization—and especially urbanization—during the twentieth century, which is a pronounced theme in Iceland's contemporary literature and film. Most salient, however, is that this conflict is the decisive axis of Iceland's short film history, as evident in the films of Fridrik Thór Fridriksson.

He stamped the 1990s as his era, becoming the nation's most internationally respected and active director and producer. Fridriksson's films are the central point of the essay after a short overview of Iceland's somewhat odd path to and from the international screen.

THE FRAME: FROM THE SCANDINAVIAN TO THE NATIONAL

A prominent figure of the now classic period of Scandinavian silent film arguably inaugurated Icelandic cinema, Sweden's Victor Sjöström. Sjöström's *The Outlaw and His Wife* (1918, *Bjerg-Ejvind och hans hustru*) is based on the Icelander Jóhann Sigurdsson's play. The film set the Icelandic feature film's historical cycle in motion. Iceland began, then, as a supplier of stories and landscapes for Scandinavian (co)productions, not becoming a regular film-producing nation until 1980.[2] The following decade was dominated by the national film, both economically and thematically speaking. During the 1990s, however, Icelandic film production became a part of the international scene, dominated by cofinanced or coproduced films. In that sense the Icelandic film industry has resembled the development of the other Scandinavian cinemas—although only after the 1980s.

No regular Icelandic feature film production occurred before the founding of the IFF in 1979. But Icelanders were not unfamiliar with being portrayed on screen. Sporadic reportage and scenic films can be found from the first half of the twentieth century. These are effectively attractions, however. They presented to Icelanders familiar scenes in well-visited theaters, providing popular amusement to an entertainment-poor and otherwise young Reykjavik, also furnishing a window on the wide and in every respect distant world. Likewise, the 1950s offered amateurish but popular films (farces, family films, dramas, and documentaries) by Loftur Gudmundsson, Óskar Gíslason, and Ásgeir Long. Loftur Gudmundsson's melodrama *Between Mountain and Shore* (1949, *Milli fjalls og fjöru*) is the first entirely Icelandic feature film as well as the nation's first color talkie.

However, Óskar Gíslason's farce *The Bakka Brothers in Reykjavik* (1951, *Reykjavíkurævintýri Bakkabrædra*) serves as a better example in this context, bringing the rural and simpleminded Bakka brothers to modern Reykjavik. In various brief episodes, they meet the new world, the attractions and apparatuses of which they entirely fail to grasp. Their encounters with everything from one-way traffic to an elevator, a refrigerator, a boutique window full of lingerie, and the fictive world of the theater become a humorous collection of sketches. At the same time, the film is a sightseeing tour of postwar Reykjavik. Shot entirely on 16 mm black-and-white film, primarily in long takes, without editing within the episodes and very minimal, scratchy sound quality, the film remains amusing in its naïve way. It also provides a good film-historical picture of the period. Yet its main attraction to audiences of the time was the fact that it was Icelandic. Otherwise, it was through coproductions that Icelanders sought more or less recognizable reflections of land and country.

A typical example of such coproduction is Arne Mattsson's Swedish film adaptation of Nobel Prize winner Halldór Laxness's novel *Salka Valka* (1954), for which cinematographer Sven Nykvist shot exteriors in Iceland. The novel is a contemporary, critical, social-realist tale describing the life and events of a small fishing community. It was coproduced by the Icelandic company Edda-film. During the postwar years the company was headed by the National Theater's director, Gudlaugur Rósinkranz, who undertook three productions that can be seen as indicative of tendencies in Icelandic film over the rest of the century. In the 1960s, Rósinkranz's gift for persuasion convinced Erik Balling at Nordisk Film to assemble his team of technicians around an adaptation of Indridi G. Thorsteinsson's *The Girl Gogo* (1962, *79 af stödinni*), which, unlike Balling's popular Danish films, was a fatalistic and dark social-realist account of a farmer's son's attempt to establish himself, economically and romantically, in a depraved Reykjavik. *The Girl Gogo* was made in Iceland, with Icelandic actors, and—not least—shot in the Icelandic language.

Edda's last project was the pretentious, expensive, and unsuccessful "Nordic pudding" *The Red Mantle* (1967, *Den røde kappe*), directed by Gabriel Axel. Axel directed the Russian actor Oleg Vidov, as well as Swedish, Danish, and Icelandic actors each speaking their own language. In postproduction the film was synchronized entirely in the respective languages and released as *Den røde kappe* (Denmark), *Den röda kappan* (Sweden) and *Rauda skikkjan* (Iceland). *The Red Mantle* wasn't as much a Viking film as a romantic love story from the eleventh century with (inadvertently comic) blood and gore. Hollywood's Vikings, such as Kirk Douglas in Richard Fleischer's *The Vikings* (1958), had seemed hilariously foreign to Icelandic eyes. But it was the *The Red Mantle*'s Vikings, who in their romantic and boyish—to some eyes, even androgynous—manners sparked the dream of authentic Viking films: that is to say, raw and unromanticized Viking films as told by the saga island's own. In fact, the making of *The Red Mantle,* in addition to providing an eighteen-year-old Hrafn Gunnlaugsson with a summer job on the set and in the effects department, inspired and provoked him. Eighteen years later Hrafn Gunnlaugsson enjoyed his international breakthrough with the Viking film *When the Raven Flies* (1984, *Hrafninn flýgur*).

LAND AND SONS

Icelandic national cinema, and more specifically the IFF, can well be seen as a consequence of the century's patriotic spirit. It can be traced to the national awareness and pride generated by Iceland's declaration of independence on June 17, 1944, when Iceland became a republic independent of Denmark. More directly, however, the fund was the result of work by a group of ambitious young filmmakers who returned home during the 1970s after study in Sweden and England, primarily. The short films and the TV production put into motion by the Icelandic state's television channel RUV in 1966 did not satisfy them. They wanted to make feature films for domestic exhibition, which has traditionally been dominated by Hollywood. Passion and commitment were clearly the motivational forces. But legitimacy was based upon the idea (not unpredictably) that Iceland lacked a truly national response to popular American film and in general lacked a national mirror to reflect the country's traditional and newly emergent hybrid cultural forms.

In 1978, Reykjavik's first film festival was held, initiated and organized by, among others, two figures who would later become notable. One was the twenty-four-year old Fridrik Thór Fridriksson, who at the time led the nation's only existing film club, where he promoted art films and classics of film history; this experience comprised the entirety of his education as a filmmaker and cineaste. The other was the thirty-year old Hrafn Gunnlaugsson, who had been educated at Dramatiska Institutet, the national school of drama in Stockholm. He had distinguished himself at the nascent Icelandic national TV station. He also directed the first Icelandic adaptation of Halldór Laxness with his short film *Lilja,* which had its theatrical premiere at the festival, where Icelandic short films were presented along with film art from abroad. The prominence attained by the local, if numerically few, participants in the festival received a stamp of legitimacy from Wim Wenders in remarks he made during the concluding address of the festival. Wenders's encouragement earned him the moniker "Godfather of Icelandic Film," for his comments provided some of the impetus for the establishment of Kvikmyndasjódur Íslands—or the IFF. It was founded the following year, with funding provided by parliamentary finance laws. The fund received what was calculated to be the cost of one film, the sum of which was to be divided into three projects. The paltry $50,000 (at the 2000 exchange rate) provided a long-awaited boost for zealous filmmakers, even if its impact was more on morale than on actual film finance.

A relevant consequence of the lack of financing for Icelandic feature film was high theater ticket prices, although these did not seem to discourage attendance. Initially, the public paid twice the price for a ticket to an Icelandic film than for a foreign one; at the time of writing, a price difference of around 30 to 40 percent is still the rule. Nevertheless, both Ágúst Gudmundsson's *Land and Sons* and Hrafn Gunnlaugsson's *Father's Estate* (1980, *Ódal fedranna*) were sensational audience magnets. Gudmundsson's adaptation of Indridi G. Thorsteinsson's social-realist portrait of the generation gap and dissolution in 1930s-era agrarian Iceland drew some 110,000 viewers.[3] Hrafn Gunnlaugsson's *Father's Estate* addressed the same topic in a more political and controversial fashion. His film was a critical, contemporary account of a farmer bound by the cooperative movement he started. Together with the likewise popular but very amateurish family film, *The Fishing Trip* (Andrés Indridason, 1980, *Veidiferdin*), these films generated great optimism about domestic cinema—which has sometimes reached fever pitch. In the course of the 1980s, twenty-seven films were produced, the vast majority of which saw a box office deficit, some of which bankrupted their production companies. Of the twenty-seven, three were Viking films, two were thrillers, one a children's film, and ten were comedies, while the rest were dispersed between existential, political, or everyday life dramas, often inspired by the European art film and (particularly Scandinavian) social realism. The contrast between country and city in these films is striking. In contrast to *Land and Sons*, where Reykjavik is the dream and goal of the young characters, although it is never shown, in the majority of these films the city is presented as a stronghold of pervasive economic and political corruption that undermines hardworking people, their land, independence, and future. Examples of these include *Father's Estate* and the more left-oriented films such as Thorsteinn Jónsson's adaptation of Laxness's polemic problem novel from 1948, *Atomic Station* (1984, *Atómstödin*) and Thráinn Bertelsson's *Deep Winter* (1985, *Skammdegi*).

Roughly, then, the birth of domestic cinema in Iceland occurred through the work of a handful of directors who were born during or just after the war and educated outside Iceland during the 1970s in the context of the (often anti-American) aftershocks of 1968.[4]

FROM THE UNDERGROUND AND EXPERIMENTATION

Fridrik Thór Fridriksson (b. 1954), a somewhat younger, autodidactic, and experimental filmmaker, stood at the margin of the founding group of Icelandic filmmakers. Yet he belonged to the local avant garde, or more precisely the Fluxus movement, which had found its way to Iceland. In diminutive Reykjavik, this small movement was able to attract attention via happenings and similar arrangements in the capital city, blending diverse talents and many media. Fridriksson announced himself with a literal adaptation *The Saga of Burnt Njal* (1980, *Brennu Njáls saga*), in which the audience, uncertain of what awaited them in the country's largest theater (Háskólabíó, with 976 seats), witnessed a hand leafing through the pages of this national treasure, which, in keeping with the work's climax, went up in flames! A cultural shock therapy in twenty minutes, the film is an affront for which some have yet to forgive Fridriksson. He followed up with, among other things, the controversial documentary film *Rock in Reykjavik* (1982, *Rokk í Reykjavík*), in which a sixteen-year-old Björk (Gudmundsdóttir) appears among punk rock and New Wave bands that perform and circulate in the city's secluded underworld, speaking openly about taboo subjects such as drugs. The film was the first to depict the youth of Reykjavik and was seen by 20,000 primarily young viewers.

Fridriksson has continued to have close connections to the underground and rock scene, music that he has always blended with the soundtracks of his feature films (diegetically and nondiegetically). Fridriksson was one of the early advocates of the Icelandic quartet Sigur Rós, whose melodies have been characterized as ambi-sound pictures—or even as sound landscapes, to remind us of the above mentioned nexus. They sing their peculiar, falsetto vocals in a homegrown language that lacks true lyrics but may sound to foreign ears like Icelandic. Sigur Rós's music figures prominently in Fridriksson's *Angels of the Universe* (2000, *Englar alheimsins*), where they collaborate with his usual composer, Hilmar Örn Hilmarsson. After Hilmarsson received the European music award, the Felix, for the music in *Children of Nature*, which blends Icelandic church and folk traditions with the late romantic (which is the cornerstone of Hilmarsson's music as well as that of more traditional classic film music), he worked far and wide, but chiefly in Scandinavia and always with Iceland as his base. Fridriksson portrayed popular music's diffuse Iceland even further with *Icelandic Cowboys* (1984, *Kúrekar Nordurins*), showing events during the nation's country festival at a country hotel in the remote Skagaströnd, whose singing cowboys also participated in *Cold Fever* (1995, *Á köldum klaka*) eleven years later.

By the mid-1980s, nobody in their wildest dreams could imagine that the "dirty hippie," as Fridrik Thór Fridriksson was once called, would be described just ten years later by the international press as the personification of the Icelandic film industry, but he was not alone in his experimentation with the otherwise expensive and therefore often formidable screen. Hrafn Gunnlaugsson's controversial *Inter Nos* (1982, *Okkar á Milli—Í hita og thunga dagsins*) provoked a straitlaced Iceland that was not accustomed to jazzed-up or punked-out versions of the national anthem, children's songs, or, even worse, Icelandic nudity! In explicit, recurring, and insistent shots from the main character's point of view, the characters' sexual impulses and fantasies also become the spectators'. Gunnlaugsson ignited discussion, and not for the last time.

Kristín Jóhannesdóttir (b. 1948) set high ambitions for herself, with a less provocative but even more experimental feature film debut.[5] *Rainbow's End* (1983, *Á hjara veraldar*) amounts to the nation's most experimental and formalistic endeavor, both on the whole and specifically in relation to the country and city theme. The film stylizes and fragments the country-city division through a series of sequences, which, as self-standing but not always entirely successful tableaus, draw sharp contrasts in the film's dreamlike and cautionary vision.

INTERNATIONALIZATION

During the mid-1980s, Icelanders stopped streaming into the theaters every time an Icelandic film debuted. The novelty had dissipated. Being a filmmaker became all the more difficult, insofar as financing for the lion's share of projects increasingly depended on private financing, sometimes on mortgaging an apartment. Even though the establishment of the commercial subscription TV station Stöd 2 in 1986 provided the hard-pressed industry a new source of contracts and a few more *krónurs* were added to the film fund, only nine of the aforementioned twenty-seven films were produced in the last half of the decade. The optimism of the early 1980s was suddenly replaced by a prevalent pessimism, which pretty much marked the years until the early 1990s, when international funds, notably Eurimage (1989) and the Nordic Film and Television Fund (1990), made their entrance with a perceptible impact on the film milieu and not least on the films—both in terms of quantity and quality. The only genre that proved successful throughout the 1980s was the folk comedy. Although these films contained some satire, their stereotypes were too local to attract international attention. Thráinn Bertelsson, who had had great success with *New Life* (1983, *Nýtt líf*) and its two sequels *Pastoral Life* (1984, *Dalalíf*) and *A Policeman's Life* (1985, *Löggulíf*), first received international attention and a certain amount of acknowledgment with his sixth film, *Magnús* (1989), a touching and warm comedy with an eye for the absurd elements of everyday life and life itself.

In contrast to the films of the 1980s and some of the early 1990s, most films of the 1990s are marked by the work of experienced craftspeople and actors, which is evident in the films' comparative technical superiority and confident, deliberate sense of craft and art. Their quality makes the weaker films from the early 1990s look even worse. So even though, for example, *Men's Choir* (1992, *Karlakórinn hekla*) and *Behind Schedule* (1993, *Stuttur frakki*) were dependable popular successes in Iceland, they do not in any way reflect the professional craftsmanship evident in Gudný Halldorsdóttir's Scandinavian costume drama *Honour of the House* (1999, *Ungfrúin góda og húsid*) or Gísli Snær Erlingsson's internationally recognized children's films *Benjamin Dove* (1995, *Benjamín dúfa*) and *Ikingut* (2000). The "baddies" of early 1990s suffer in comparison also because they lack the naïve, and often charming, enthusiasm of earlier "baddies." In the case of the latter, uneven sequences (and entire films) can be offset or balanced by the intimacy created or captured by the era's deprived and minimal, but nevertheless charming, style. In the best examples, it results in a careful, fundamentally beautiful poetic realism, as in *Land and Sons*.

Conversely, in the 1980s, it became evident that a lack of money and experience would prevent production of films reminiscent of large international productions, as both Egill Edvardsson's thriller *The House* (1983, *Húsið*) and Thorsteinn Jónsson's *Atomic Station* expensively illustrated. Edvardsson realized his dream of an international quality film with the grandly constructed coproduction *Agnes* (1995), which was about the last woman to be executed in Iceland, in 1830. On a slightly less ambitious scale, Jónsson captured the chaos of family life in the successful children's film *The Sky Palace* (*Skýjahöllin*) in 1994, which was commercially distributed in Europe and made an Icelandic contribution to the tradition of Nordic children's film.

Among the directors who emerged in the 1980s, only Hrafn Gunnlaugsson successfully broke out of the confines of realism. His *When the Raven Flies* is raw and expressive in comparison with *The Red Mantle*'s carefully coifed blonde youth, and also in comparison with Ágúst Gudmundsson's *Outlaw, the Saga of Gísli* (1981, *Útlaginn*), an unremarkable word-for-word adaptation of the saga. Despite capital from Hrafn Gunnlaugsson's devoted Swedish partner, the producer Bo Jonsson and his company, Viking Film Ab, and the Swedish Film Institute, which smoothed the way for Gunnlaugsson to win the Swedish Guldbagge film prize, the film was a low-budget production. But the limits of a low budget suit the raw style of Gunnlaugsson, and his style seems like an appropriate aesthetic for the harsh life of the Viking era. The style is unpolished and expressive, which meshes with the dirty characters, their harsh experiences, and filthy living conditions. It can well be seen as the "unromanticized" or "authentic" cinematic representation of the Viking era that Gunnlaugsson and other Icelanders advocated at the time. Since the Guldbagge award for *When the Raven Flies*—discussed in this collection in chapter 13 by Bjørn Sørenssen, "Hrafn Gunnlaugsson: The Viking Who Came in from the Cold?"—his productions have received both greater funding and wider distribution. In his larger-scale productions, however, the simplicity so effective in *When the Raven Flies* is less evident.

In the same way, neither can Ari Kristinsson's gentle cinematography and Renaissance-inspired use of filters disguise the fact that nothing remains unsaid or hidden between the lines in his medieval drama, *Flames of Paradise* (1999, *Myrkrahöfdinginn*). Paradoxically, this film was produced by his previous film rival, Fridrik Thór Fridriksson, and his Icelandic Film Corporation (IFC). This coproduction also relied on Bo Jonsson's Viking Film, together with the IFC's network of coproducers, which includes Peter Rommel Productions in Germany and Filmhuset in Norway, and has otherwise been tightly connected to Lars von Trier's and (particularly important in the Icelandic context) Peter Aalbæk Jensen's Danish company Zentropa Entertainments. These coproductions create networks of cooperation that strongly influence Iceland's place in international cinema. After a suggestion from Fridriksson at Cannes in 1998, Hal Hartley shot parts of *No Such Thing* (2001, aka *Monsters*) in Iceland, where his Possible Films entered into close cooperation with the IFC under the American Zoetrope, with Francis Ford Coppola as executive producer.

The current state of Iceland's film culture has also attracted official Iceland into active participation in the international film scene, not just the IFF. Since 2001 the Ministry of Industry has subsidized foreign filmmaking in Iceland (with a 12 percent reimbursement policy), as it did for Hal Hartley's *No Such Thing*. By comparison, then, in 1996 Fridrik Thór Fridriksson's IFC participated in Lars von Trier's *Breaking the Waves* as the only Icelandic financier, whereas in 2000 both Fridriksson's IFC and the IFF participated in financing *Dancer in the Dark*. Although Fridrik Thór Fridriksson became the biggest Icelandic producer in the 1990s—indeed, the very personification of the Icelandic film industry—it is his reputation as a director that earned him this position.

ANGELS OF THE UNIVERSE

Fridrik Thór Fridriksson's adaptation of his childhood friend Einar Már Gudmundsson's internationally acclaimed novel, *Angels of the Universe*, premiered on January 1, 2000. Expectations were high, for the novel had won the Nordic Council's Literature Prize in 1995. The novel tells the unique and idiosyncratic story of Páll, who lives only for art, music, and poetry but suffers from worsening schizophrenia. (Einar Már Gudmundsson's older brother Pálmi Örn was schizophrenic.) The bleak story is nevertheless warm, free of pedantry or moralizing. It is narrated in the first person by Páll, primarily through voice-over. The technique stands in contrast to Fridriksson's prolific documentary production, in which he had eschewed voice-over. Furthermore, Fridriks-

Fridriksson's *Angel of the Universe* (2000)

son's magical mise-en-scène illustrates the hallucinatory world—or universe—of the narrator (without point of view shooting). Momentarily he invites the spectator to experience it.

In Iceland, despite the serious and challenging topic, the film sold some 90,000 tickets. It also performed well internationally, both at festivals and in art house distribution, where Fridriksson's films have found their international audience. Although the film touched many, some foreign critics found it difficult to categorize. Páll's peculiar life and journey into the infinite caused comparisons with the classic *One Flew over the Cuckoo's Nest* (Milos Forman, 1975), an unfortunate though understandable comparison.

The film also stands as an anomaly in Fridriksson's work up to that point. Thus it could easily be seen as the beginning of a new chapter in his life and career, which up until *Angels of the Universe* had focused thematically on contrasts in modern Iceland, which swings between modern and traditional, the American and the Icelandic, film and the folk tale, city and country. These contrasts comprise Fridrik Thór Fridriksson's point of departure; as the child of the city, cinema, and nature, he creates a mosaic in his cinema, which will now be the focus.

In and Out of Reykjavik

ON THE ROAD

Fridriksson's first feature film, *White Whales* (1987, *Skytturnar*), is a "reverse" road movie, inasmuch as it narrates the journey of rural characters into the city, in contrast to the usual trajectory of the road movie, which sees urban characters venture into the countryside. The film sends two whale hunters on a fatalistic journey to Reykjavik, where they never find peace. Through these two "white whales," who conflict with the other species, Fridriksson vaulted beyond his reputation as a documentarist. Although the film was not a domestic success, it received international attention at festivals, where many perceived Fridriksson as an iconoclast, reminiscent of Jim Jarmusch, Wim Wenders, or Aki Kaurismäki. Through their outsiders and other such loner types, these directors display the alienation of modernity in an unfamiliar New York, Berlin, or Helsinki, where Aki Kaurismäki—inspired by *White Whales*—made *Ariel* in 1988. They also picture the rapid changes of the postwar period, focusing in particular on outsiders and the alienated. In Fridriksson's case, this has much to do with his biography.

Fridriksson was born in Reykjavik in 1954, only ten years after Iceland achieved its independence. He grew up in one of the capital's many new neighborhoods, where rapid developments washed over the tiny community, bringing radical change. Urbanization created wide and deep effects, and the American military at Keflavik introduced and prompted interest in popular culture. The base had its own radio and television station, which broadcast to the capital eleven years before the creation of the Icelandic RUV in 1966. The American presence divided the nation in two. Some enjoyed American popular culture and the wealth that the base created. Others saw the base and its influence as a threat to the country's recently gained independence and sovereignty.

Fridriksson was a product of this turbulent time, and it was this period he chose to illuminate on the screen in the 1990s. *Movie Days* (1994, *Bíódagar*) and *Devil's Island* (1996, *Djöflaeyjan*) describe the changes and contrasts between the old and the new, the familiar and the foreign in postwar Iceland. In *Movie Days,* we experience the events through the eyes of a child and in *Devil's Island* through the saga of a poor family from Reykjavik's borderland, which can well be seen as a borderland of modernity. In the two road movies *Children of Nature*

(1991) and *Cold Fever* (1995), Fridriksson tears us from modern, rational life as it appears in Reykjavik and Tokyo, projecting it against the traditions of the past and the (super)natural life of the country. He shows us the landscape's open and seemingly untainted beauty as well as its recalcitrant mysticism.

His mythology is somewhat similar to the American western and Dennis Hopper's pioneering road movie, *Easy Rider* (1969). Freedom for the individual can be found in neither the civilized nor corrupted (but just natural) landscape—which in Iceland, according to folk belief, is haunted by spirits and other more or less friendly life-forms. And Fridriksson, much like the authors Gudmundsson and Einar Kárason, his childhood friends and coscriptwriters, does not doubt his characters' stories and anecdotes. His cinema might be called a sort of magical realism that springs from everyday antiheroes' experiences. It never takes place in imaginary spaces, as in South American magical realism, but occurs through the poetic or lyrical meeting between the magical and the ordinary. This intersection produces "incredible" folktales for the contemporary moment.

CHILDREN OF NATURE

In *Children of Nature* we encounter a lonely old peasant, Thórgeir, who shuts the farm down after the year's harvest to go to Reykjavik, where his daughter and her family live in one of the city's numerous apartment complexes. But there is absolutely no room for the old man and his way of life in the modern family's hectic routine. He ends up in a nursing home—set aside, parked, out of the way. In the nursing home, he meets an old lover who wants to revisit the place where they grew up one last time. One spring night they abscond. In a stolen jeep, pursued by the police, they search for freedom and their roots. Assisted by nature and its magic—such as when the jeep disappears, or rather dissolves into nature, only a few hundred meters from the puzzled policemen—they once again become children of nature. Finally, they find peace at their childhood home and leave our world. After burying his beloved, Thórgeir enters the final stage, assisted by Bruno Ganz, reprising his role as angel in Wim Wenders's *Wings of Desire* (1987, *Der Himmel Über Berlin*).

Children of Nature is a short and warm film of only eighty minutes, with sparse dialogue and only about three hundred camera posi-

The old farmer Thórgeir returning to his point of origin in Fridrik Thór Fridriksson's Oscar-nominated road movie *Children of Nature* (1991)

tions (as opposed to the nine hundred of *Devil's Island*, which seems to be its antithesis). It can be viewed as a road movie starring old rebels, a love story, or as a quiet and poetic reminder of the fact that some people's goals and values do not always fit into the hectic pace of modern-day society. The story is also about love and old age as well as the importance of our roots. As in Bergman's *Wild Strawberries* (1957, *Smultronstället*), its message is universal and common, which probably appealed to the international audience.

The first fifteen minutes of the movie lack any dialogue whatsoever. In extended and well-composed images, we follow old Thórgeir and monitor how the slow and steady rhythm of his daily life is incorporated into the film. The film stands in stark contrast to the noisy life that the audience members leave behind when they enter the movie theater. It lyrically transports the audience away form the city noise, be it that of Reykjavik or Los Angeles. The film's shooting location played a key role in this connection. It was set in the Icelandic countryside, serving as something of a tourist brochure abroad—and at home. Suddenly, nature was everywhere.

It appears somewhat strange that *Children of Nature,* along with *Movie Days,* was dragged into a colorful Icelandic debate in the 1990s about the movie industry's aesthetic and thematic use of nature. A number of people argued that the nation's film industry focused too much on nature, presenting an overly romanticized picture of the old and poor peasant community.[6] Most significantly, the debate provided a forum for arguing that in Iceland, too, modernity was a reality, and that one should not always complain about it as a cultural threat but affirm it. The discussion also created and intensified awareness about cinema's capacity to shape the image of Iceland—at home and abroad. To be sure, international attention generated a certain degree of satisfaction—and no one was, or is, ashamed of the traditional representation. On the contrary, Icelanders tend to be extremely proud of the nation's cultural heritage. On the other hand, many wished to bring the image of the country up to the present, showing modern Iceland and its urban life on its own terms and as a full-grown member of the modern world.

The debate also reflects thematic changes of the period in Icelandic cinema. The country and city divide has become less of an opposition in films of the 1990s and later. In the films of a group of "young and wild" directors,[7] such as in Júlíus Kemp's *Wallpaper* (1992, *Veggfódur*) and Óskar Jónasson's *Remote Control* (1992, *Sódóma Reykjavík*), Reykjavik appears more corrupt and criminal than ever before. Yet it appears so through images of the city alone, not set in contrast to the rural countryside, traditionally romanticized as the honorable, untouched, and authentic Iceland. The movies of the 1990s do not portray the country and city dichotomy as a choice between two cultures, two lives. Instead, the contrast is referred to as present and past, and the Icelandic highway, which connects rural with urban life and figures prominently in the majority of Icelandic films, becomes an escape or search route, as in the road movie. *Children of Nature,* for example, does not portray Reykjavik as either decadent or Americanized. In the film modernity functions more as a fragmented and systematic alienation of the individual, which is symbolized through architecture—for instance, in the city's blocks and streets—or institutionally, through the nursing home and the police. By contrast, in the films of the early 1980s such as *Land and Sons, Father's Estate,* and *Atomic Station,* or even Balling's

The Girl Gogo from 1962, the contrast is an irreversible crossroad, part of a national debate about turning points, common to an earlier social realism. These newer films deal with change, giving perspective to the duality that makes up modern Iceland.

Movie Days, on the other hand, showcases these new developments and the brave new world of American popular culture in particular—for example, in the city's theaters, on TV and radio—and compares these references with their counterparts in Icelandic traditions. Naturally, the two sides compete, but everything is experienced through the eyes of a naïve and easily fascinated eight-year-old, for whom traditions and new impressions of the city are equally alien. The adults' reactions to the rapid changes entertain us as much as they puzzle the child. His open, but also somewhat suspicious, eyes are also the global spectator's (including the youngest Icelanders'), inasmuch as they view the traditional way of life in the country. That said, one should not forget that *Movie Days* is first and foremost Fridriksson and his generation's look back at the island of their childhood, and in that sense, it is also a somewhat nostalgic reminiscence about roots, made up of both city and nature, of the modern and the traditional. And *Movie Days* has parallels in Icelandic film, for example, with Thorsteinn Jónsson's *Dot, Dot, Comma, Dash* (1981, *Punktur punktur komma strik*) or with Hrafn Gunnlaugsson's *The Sacred Mound* (1993, *Hin helgu Vé*). As is typical of Gunnlaugsson, however, his memories primarily deal with his and everybody else's deep roots in the rural, untamed life. Yet *Movie Days*'s warm and ironic humor also links it to films like Woody Allen's *Radio Days* (1987) and Giuseppe Tornatore's *Cinema Paradiso* (1989, *Nuovo cinema paradiso*). These seem more appropriate for a comparison than the similar Scandinavian semiautobiographical stories about "that summer when life changed"—among which one might mention the Norwegian *Cross My Heart and Hope to Die* by Marus Holst (1994, *Ti kniver i hjertet*), *My Life as a Dog* (1987, *Mitt liv som hund*) by Lasse Hallström, or the Dane Nils Malmros's portrayal of growing up in Århus, *The Tree of Knowledge* (1981, *Kundskabens træ*).

COLD FEVER

In 1989 Fridriksson brought Jim Jarmusch's *Mystery Train* to Reykjavik's Film Festival, of which Fridriksson served as director in the 1990s. The producer Jim Stark and the actor Masatoshi Nagase came along as the film's representatives. Both of them became infatuated with the country, its sights and curiosities. Stark immediately came up with an idea for a film. Nagase should go on another mysterious journey, this time through Iceland. Fridriksson, who in his youth had worked for a headstone carver and as a cemetery assistant and whose films always feature a funeral, came up with the idea for *Cold Fever*. The story was inspired by an article about a group of Japanese geologists who drowned in a remote Icelandic river. Their family members had consequently traveled all the way to Iceland to perform a Buddhist burial ritual.

Cold Fever is a comedy and a road movie with mythological overtones. Yet it was the representation of national character that caught the attention of the Icelandic public and vaulted the film into an important position in the country's film history. A heated debate ensued over what kind of Iceland and Icelanders were represented in *Cold Fever*'s coproduction. The film was discussed in this way not so much because it is internationally cofinanced (it was made independently of the IFF), but because the film can be seen as the view of an outsider like Jim Stark, a catalogue of Icelandic curiosities and clichés that stress the oddity of the Icelandic. There is a lot of Iceland, and especially odd Iceland, in *Cold Fever*. As the film progresses, the protagonist, Hirata, finds it more and more difficult to answer the question, "How do you like Iceland?"

Maybe *Cold Fever* stood out as too Icelandic, too odd or even weird, or too much Fridriksson's picture of Iceland. Was the film, its production and portrayal of Iceland, just pure speculation about the Icelandic character? Was it an auteur film or just a sales gimmick, "the best Icelandic/Japanese road movie you'll see all year," as the poster read? These questions were not raised in connection with other, more classical coproductions, like Hilmar Oddsson's visually loaded portrayal of the composer Jón Leifs (1899–1968) in *Tears of Stone* (1995, *Tár úr steini*) or Edvardsson's *Agnes*. The emotional debate seemed to originate from Icelanders' perception that Fridriksson was not only using them as a sales gimmick but also making fun of them. Fridriksson himself remarked, "[Icelandic] national feeling [is] subdued by an inferiority complex due to the size of the rest of the world. On the other hand, we also suffer from megalomania. So the nation is somewhat schizophrenic, and that is what I play around with. Or, I enjoy finding it in myself. So, on the screen it probably looks like I am making fun of people. But in all honesty, I am mostly making fun of myself" (Møller 1997).

Fridriksson's *Cold Fever* hit a sore spot with Icelanders, even though it is arguably a typical example of then current cinematic postmodernism in the United States and Europe. Everything from black humor to introverted irony marked cinematic themes during the 1980s and 1990s. Postmodernism found its way into films made by realists and serious formalists, featuring in the work of directors who expose the absurd in surroundings that had previously been portrayed as dull and gray. On that point, directors like Mike Leigh in England, Pedro Almodóvar in Spain, Jarmusch and David Lynch in the United States, or Aki Kaurismäki in the other corner of sensible and somewhat gloomy Scandinavia resemble Fridriksson a great deal.

Masatoshi Nagase Hirata's role in *Cold Fever* as involuntary tourist in Iceland, which Gísli Snær Erlingsson had tried a few years before in *Behind Schedule*, became more common and accepted in times of globalization. In one sense, foreigners have become spectators of the domestic audience, and on the other hand, they are the international audience's proxy to Icelandic magic and lunacy. This is a trend that turns up, for example, in Baltasar Kormákur's *101 Reykjavik* and *The Sea*. The foreigners' presence, along with their questions and objections, delineates difference, in contrast to which the "uniquely" Icelandic personality comes into focus.

DEVIL'S ISLAND

The alienating effects of modernity can be seen as a common thread running throughout Fridriksson's road movies. Alienation is combined with rootlessness, which is also found among younger Icelandic filmmakers (Kemp and Jónasson). Fridriksson's *Devil's Island*, and later Kormákur's *The Sea*, present a young, alienated, and rootless generation as a part of a larger whole but always from the perspective of people living in the peripheral spaces of modernity—that is, the postwar barracks and the increasing number of abandoned, or almost abandoned, fishing villages.

French sociologist Pierre Sorlin has analyzed how the Italian neorealists used shantytowns in their films about social problems in postwar Rome. Sorlin explains:

> The filmic version of the poorest neighborhoods which developed mostly in the 1960s and 1970s was ambiguous. It tended to give a realistic, critical version of the derelict areas excluded from the benefits of contemporary

welfare in countries where prosperity was increasing. At the same time, shantytowns were presented as fairly different, as another world. . . . The cinema disclosed something that most viewers had good reason to be unfamiliar with because neither politicians nor the media wanted to unveil it. (1994, 129)[8]

In these neighborhoods, different generations' respective dreams of better living conditions and a constant, consequence-free escapism through popular culture are imagined, realized, and shattered. In these places, the community either proves it can continue to exist or disintegrates. Keeping this in mind, maybe it was not just an off-the-cuff remark when Fridriksson presented *Devil's Island* to the international press and the audience at Berlin's International Film Festival in 1997 with the film-historical reference, "This is my birth of a nation!"

Even though Sorlin's analysis concerns contemporary portrayals, it captures *Devil's Island*'s scenario and its function quite precisely. To begin with, the point is that the war—cynical as it sounds—was great business for Iceland. Part of the occupying force stayed on after the war as a part of NATO. The new Keflavik Airbase (some forty kilometers from Reykjavik) patronized local businesses, especially the construction industry. Furthermore, the postwar period was one of growth for Iceland because of fish prices on the international market. Throughout this time the barracks, which had housed thousands of soldiers during the war, remained. Abandoned by the army, they provided a solution to the immediate housing problem that heavy urbanization—part of the period's rapid modernization—had caused in young and still growing Reykjavik. The barracks and camps, however, also framed and reflected—as did the Italian shantytowns—the social problems that arrived with the new world—or the adverse effects of the new world. (It would be hard to claim that the barracks represented postwar economic growth, except by being demolished.) Furthermore, in a similar way to the point Sorlin makes about marginal neighborhoods, the barracks were situated on the margin of the new development, "as another world." Yet, they also figure the country as a whole, which the title of the film so gently suggests.

What *Devil's Island*'s Icelandic audience might have recalled—or heard—about Camp Thule and life in the barracks probably did not correspond with the image that the film portrayed. The film was anything but glamorous in its portrayal of the neighborhood, where the young, ruthless, and restless generation of wild ones never seemed to miss an occasion to booze heavily—often with broken bones and furniture as the result. On the other hand, *Devil's Island* also emphasized the everyday struggle as it evoked empathy when recalling yesterday's hard times. In Reykjavik today, however, one cannot find so much as a trace of the barracks, even though they are an important part of Iceland's modern history. And Camp Thule certainly was not the only one. In reality, as Fridriksson has explained, "there were thousands who lived in the barracks that the Americans left behind, which the authorities are so ashamed of that they do not even show it at the Reykjavík Museum" (Møller 1997). Life in marginal spaces like the barracks, or "shantytowns," is forged around collective belonging, whether this comes from positive community building or shared deprivation. Sorlin remarks that films that use these places do so to provide a background for "an intensive collective life. In fact, these films re-enact some stereotypes of the 'popular' neighborhoods previously developed in the nineteenth century's popular novels with open-air dances, feasts, games of chance, and violence. Life is supposed to be hard but free in these faraway districts" (1994, 127).

Even though *Devil's Island*'s portrayal of the community, which has clear parallels to Italy's Ettore Scola's *Ugly, Dirty, and Mean* (1977, *Brutti, sporchi e cattivi*) and especially Visconti's *Rocco and His Brothers* (1960, *Rocco e i suoi fratelli*), is of a life both violent and unfortunate, it is still marked by Fridriksson's bittersweet humor. His humor originates in his humanism and his persistent sympathy for main characters, who—like the outsiders they are—struggle for a place in a newly rich society. In *Devil's Island*, the sense of community remains, though it is badly shaken, when the barracks are torn down and the family moves to the building of the future—the apartment complex that has been visible behind the barracks throughout the film, symbolizing the changing times. Despite its harsh portrait of Iceland, a sensational 86,000 Icelanders bought tickets for the film in 1996, beating out *Independence Day* (Roland Emmerich, 1996) as the year's top blockbuster.[9]

Baltasar Kormákur's contemporary Icelandic group portrait, *The Sea*, reprises many of the themes and conflicts from Fridriksson's earlier film. In a small town, a patriarch and owner of the town's fishing industry calls his children home to settle family matters and discuss the future. Though it has a different starting point, one is reminded of Thomas Vinterberg's *The Celebration* (1998, *Festen*) and Per Fly's *The*

Heritage (2003, *Arven*), when the family's firstborn—and the film's central character—returns from Paris, where he is more occupied with music than his business studies. Over the course of a weekend in *The Sea*, the family's hidden skeletons are pulled from the closet, overturning the family itself and the entire society.

In its portrayal of tumultuous insanity and destruction of a community at the periphery of Iceland and modernity, *The Sea* echoes *Devil's Island*. The old antennas have been exchanged for satellite dishes, and the family lives in a modern and lonely villa on the side of the mountain. Their home sits above a town of scattered buildings, which house industry as well as immigrant workers. There is a gas station, a dive bar, a women's lingerie store, and a pizza delivery. Furthermore—and on top of the film's recurring "How do you like Iceland?" theme and its concern with local politics—*The Sea*, again like *Devil's Island*, furnishes an active commentator: the chain-smoking, foul-mouthed grandmother remarks on everything and everybody. Elevated above life's banal reality, she has survived everything—and everybody—and constitutes a witness to the dramatic developments within the family and the nation over the course of the century. She arguably replaces the iconographic figure of Iceland's unsullied purity, the innocent blonde, a good, naïve farmer's daughter. In contrast to Sweden, which entered the American consciousness as a nation of sexual liberation through images of Hariett Andersen on the run, the Icelandic blonde stayed at home, for example in *Land and Sons*. Or she was defiled and impregnated by men of power, as in *Atomic Station* or as in *Wallpaper's* play with the cliché in 1992.

The Sea testifies to the fact that industrialization belonged to the fishing industry in Iceland. This theme resonates with *Salka Valka* and especially Ásdís Thorodssen's *Ingaló* (1992). But even if it was out on the sea that the Icelanders forged their connection to the modern world, it was in the city where they gathered and experienced it. Therefore, it is not so strange that Reykjavik has always represented the new—both in literature and film. In contrast, fishing towns stand out as cold ports, temporary camps, or merely stations. Like the aforementioned barracks, they are situated in the borderland between past and present, the known and unknown, always on the brink of dissolution, season after season. Ultimately, as on the ships themselves, which Fridriksson also addressed in his debut *White Whales* (1987), they are sites of instrumental economic activity. The people occupying these

In and Out of Reykjavik

Hlynur Björn, down and out, in Baltasar Kormákur's portrait of Generation X in *101 Reykjavík* (2000)

towns' dull spaces of labor and leisure must transport their dreams elsewhere to realize them.

101 REYKJAVIK

Gunnar Sommerfeldt's Danish cinematic adaptation of Gunnar Gunnarsson's *The Story of the Borg Family* (1920, *Borgslægtens historie*) premiered January 22, 1921 in Reykjavik's Gamla Bíó, which today houses the national opera. Back then, approximately 20,000 out of 95,000 Icelanders lived in the capital. Today, approximately 180,000 of some 280,000 Icelanders live in Reykjavik and surrounding areas. Among the cafés, the nightclubs, cinemas, and theaters, one can still find houses that remind you that today's downtown Reykjavik, with the zip code 101, used to comprise the entire city.

The significance and fascinating aspects of this quick and late urbanization do not seem to impress or concern the young characters of Iceland's millennial cinema, yet like the older generation of *Children of Nature*, they are deeply affected by these changes. The young generation—like rootless teenagers, small-time criminals, or unemployed daydreamers, whose greatest taste is for nightlife and quick, indifferent intoxication and pleasure—detest bourgeois values, steadiness, and the struggles and routines of everyday life. Hlynur Björn is one of them in Baltasar Kormákur's film adaptation of Hallgrímur Helgason's Generation X novel from 1996, *101 Reykjavik*. It was a film with international appeal, and indeed success. Part of its success can be attributed to the role of Pedro Almodóvar's favorite actress, Victoria Abril. The film was also helped by music written by the former Sugarcube, Einar Örn Benediktsson, and by Blur's lead singer, Damon Albarn. Albarn's participation marks a partnership of another sort. He is coowner of a trendy Reykjavik café with the actor, theater entrepreneur, and director of *101 Reykjavik*, Baltasar Kormákur (b. 1966).

Hlynur Björn is thirty-four years old. He is unemployed and spends his afternoons surfing the Internet or cable TV channels. He spends his evenings and nights in Reykjavik's lively nightlife, sleeping his mornings away before more surfing. He lives with his mother and evidently plans no major changes. Suddenly, his life takes an unexpected turn. His mother reveals that she is a lesbian and has begun a relationship with Lola (Abril). Lola turns out to be pregnant, as is Hlynur's would-be girlfriend Hofi. And Hlynur has slept with both of them. On the face of it, Hlynur Björn and old Thórgeir in *Children of Nature* appear worlds apart. But when it comes down to it, they are both lost in Reykjavik's chaos, without any foothold, aims, or means. Essentially, Hlynur Björn is just as alienated and out of sync with the modern city's everyday life as the old farmer is. Apparently, it does not help to be online with the rest of the world, at least as that world appears through the prism of the Internet or cable television. Hlynur's snappy remarks, sarcasm, and irony shatter like a porous facade when reality gets too close and demands attention and engagement.

Just as in Fridriksson's portrayal of a generation and a subculture in *Rock in Reykjavik* in 1982, the youngest generation of Icelandic directors frame their Iceland through the modern city of Reykjavik. Their counterculture has been formed in opposition to historical Iceland and is affiliated with scattered cities and youth cultures around the globe. This raises a classic question. What is the future of their past? While this is a counterfactual question, many cultural texts will emerge from the conflicts generated by a generation that has begun with a more open, but also more fragmented, frame of reference than any previous generations. *The Sea* points to some of the issues that will be relevant. Will a demand for national nostalgia arise? Or will this generation make a home in the global daze? And what about Iceland, the roots, the odd Iceland? During the postwar period, pressures associated with modernization and Americanization compelled Icelanders to investigate Iceland afresh. Today, Reykjavik has been accepted on its own terms, as just as authentic as the rural Icelandic landscape and mise-en-scène, whereas before, the city was considered only a temporary resting place for modernity. The films discussed reflect Reykjavik's acceptance and its effect on Icelandic self-understanding. At any rate, and although the rural and original Iceland has lost neither its authenticity nor its force of attraction, the changing understanding of Reykjavik has breathed new life into Icelandic cultural production, which has produced more complex images that dismantle the polarized and stereotypical representations of country and city. On that note, the new films do not merely echo transnational and international movements. Yet, banal though it may be, the films of Gunnlaugsson, Fridriksson, and Kormákur are as dialogical as any statement: they are just as much a product of the time and place they reflect as of the eyes that look at them, be they in Reykjavik, Berlin, or L.A.

FALCONS

Fridrik Thór Fridriksson's 2002 road movie *Falcons* requires consideration in closing, for it marks a transformation in the concerns of *Children of Nature*, echoed in Kormákur's *101 Reykjavik*. *Falcons* is a lyrical fable with a simple plot. In that sense it resembles *Children of Nature* more than any other of Fridriksson's works. In the film, a depressed jailbird, Simon, played by Keith Carradine, returns to a remote Icelandic village, where he once worked, to commit suicide. Upon reaching the village, he meets the young artist Dúa (dove), who has found a subject in the local birds. Her exhibits consist in part of recordings of their songs, which, when presented at the local community center, generate disbelief on the part of the locals. Through Dúa, the worn-out jailbird slowly rediscovers his desire for life. She also turns out to be his daughter. But inevitably, her outsider status causes trouble, and Dúa eventually ends up butting heads with the local sheriff. Father and daughter must flee together. The two outsiders gradually become attached to one another as they travel across the roads of Iceland and

Europe. They also carry Iceland's most sacred—and legally protected—bird, the falcon. Dúa has cared for the bird since finding it lying wounded. The American Simon plans to sell the bird to the highest bidder to achieve financial security. Instead, Dúa releases the bird in Germany's multicultural Hamburg.

It is easy to think of the film as an allegory of Fridriksson's own experiences with *Cold Fever.* Upon its release, Icelandic critics accused him (and his American cowriter and producer) of selling the nation's soul to foreign investors who were only interested in commodifying the rare and unique, the exotic and awkward. But *Falcons* is a universal fable about finding, accepting, and affirming one's place in life's cycles. Traveling through the countryside of Iceland and Europe, the film suggests that Fridriksson is through, for now at least, with the idea of the Icelandic mentality as a thematically significant synthesis of the modern and the traditional. It is as if the artist, who up through the 1990s portrayed his roots, has gotten to know himself and his position well enough to work as the autonomous character he always has been: as the young and provocative outsider working on the sidelines of the domestic cinema throughout the 1980s, as Iceland's internationally acclaimed director of the 1990s. Presently, his frame of reference places him both vertically in his own country's history and horizontally in international film history. But even though he is an artist in a global world, he still has a corner to which he can retreat: an anchor point, which is his point of origin and departure. Ultimately, we can conclude that Björk is not the only odd *and* Icelandic wave breaking in the darkness of the global theater.

We've seen fit to include a filmography and a selected bibliography on Iceland itself as well as on Icelandic cinema and directors with this essay because Iceland's is the least known of the Nordic cinemas. Moreover, because no satisfactory treatment of Icelandic cinema has been available in English until the present time, despite the international prominence of popular culture with Icelandic connections, we hope this filmography and bibliography might provide a point of departure for further inquiry.

Table 12.1
Icelandic feature releases from January 1, 1980, to January 25, 2003

Date	Original title (Icelandic spelling)	English title	Director (Icelandic spelling)
January 25, 1980	Land og synir	Land and Sons	Ágúst Gudmundsson (Guðmundsson)
March 8, 1980	Veiðiferðin (Veioiferethin)	The Fishing Trip	Andrés Indridason (Indriðason)
June 21, 1980	Óðal feðranna (Óðal feoðranna)	Father's Estate"	Hrafn Gunnlaugsson
March 13, 1981	Punktur punktur komma strik	Dot, Dot, Comma, Dash	Thorsteinn (Þorsteinn) Jónsson
October 31, 1981	Útlaginn	Outlaw: The Saga of Gísli	Ágúst Gudmundsson (Guðmundsson)
December 26, 1981	Jón Oddur og Jón Bjarni	The Twins	Thráinn (Þráinn) Bertelsson
April 11, 1982	Sóley	Sóley	Róska & Manrico Pavelettoni
August 14, 1982	Okkar á milli—í hita og þunga dagsins (Oðkar á milli—í hita og þunga dagsins)	Inter Nos"	Hrafn Gunnlaugsson
December 18, 1982	Með allt á hreinu (Með allt á hreinu)	On Top	Ágúst Gudmundsson (Guðmundsson)
March 12, 1983	Húsið (Húsið)	The House	Egill Edvardsson (Eðvarðsson)
April 2, 1983	Á hjara veraldar	Rainbow's End	Kristín Jóhannesdóttir
September 29, 1983	Nýtt líf	New Life	Þráinn (Þráinn) Bertelsson
December 17, 1983	Skilaboð til Söndru (Skilaboð til Söndru)	Message to Sandra	Kristín Palsdóttir
February 4, 1984	Hrafninn flýgur	When the Raven Flies"	Hrafn Gunnlaugsson
March 3, 1984	Atómstöðin (Atómstöðin)	Atomic Station	Thorsteinn (Þorsteinn) Jónsson
September 30, 1984	Dalalíf	Pastoral Life	Þráinn (Þráinn) Bertelsson
December 26, 1984	Gullsandur	Golden Sands	Ágúst Gudmundsson (Guðmundsson)
March 16, 1985	Hvítir Mávar	Cool Jazz and Coconuts	Jakob Magnússon
April 6, 1985	Skammdegi	Deep Winter	Þráinn (Þráinn) Bertelsson
December 19, 1985	Löggulíf	A Policeman's Life	Þráinn (Þráinn) Bertelsson
March 22, 1986	Eins og skepnan deyr	The Beast	Hilmar Oddsson
October 18, 1986	Stella í orlofi	The Icelandic Shock Station	Þórhildur Þórleifsdóttir (Þórhildur Þórleifsdóttir)
February 14, 1987	Skytturnar	White Whales"	Fridrik Thór Fridriksson (Friðrik Þór Friðriksson)
August 25, 1988	Foxtrot	Foxtrot	Jón Tryggvason

Table 12.1 (continued)

Date	Original title (Icelandic spelling)	English title	Director (Icelandic spelling)
October 23, 1988	Í skugga hrafnsins	In the Shadow of the Raven[a]	Hrafn Gunnlaugsson
February 25, 1989	Kristnihald undir jökli	Under the Glacier[a]	Guðný (Guðný) Halldórsdóttir
August 11, 1989	Magnús	Magnus	Þráinn (Þráinn) Bertelsson
September 1, 1990	Ævintýri Pappírs Pésa	The Adventures of Paper Peter[a]	Ari Kristinsson
December 27, 1990	Ryð (Ryð)	Rust[a]	Lárus Ýmir Óskarsson
July 31, 1991	Börn náttúrunnar	Children of Nature[a]	Friðrik Þór Friðriksson (Friðrik Þór Friðriksson)
November 1, 1991	Hvíti Víkingurinn	The White Viking[a]	Hrafn Gunnlaugsson
February 8, 1992	Ingaló	Ingaló[a]	Ásdís Þóroddsen
April 4, 1992	Ævintýri frá Norðurslóðum (Ævintýri frá Norðurslóðum)	Northern Tales[a,b]	Maariu Olsen, Katrín Óttarsdóttir, Kristín Pálsdóttir
May 11, 1992	Svo á jörðu sem á himni (Svo á jörðu sem á himni)	As in Heaven[a]	Kristín Jóhannesdóttir
August 6, 1992	Veggfóður (Veggfóður)	Wallpaper	Júlíus Kemp
October 8, 1992	Sódóma Reykjavík	Remote Control	Óskar Jónasson
December 19, 1992	Karlakórinn Hekla	Men's Choir	Guðný (Guðný) Halldórsdóttir
April 6, 1993	Stuttur Frakki	Behind Schedule[a]	Gísli Snær Erlingsson
October 29, 1993	Hin helgu vé	The Sacred Mound[a]	Hrafn Gunnlaugsson
June 30, 1994	Bíódagar	Movie Days[a]	Friðrik Þór Friðriksson (Friðrik Þór Friðriksson)
September 29, 1994	Skýjahöllin	The Sky Palace[a]	Þorstein (Þorsteinn) Jónsson
February 10, 1995	Á köldum klaka	Cold Fever[a]	Friðrik Þór Friðriksson (Friðrik Þór Friðriksson)
March 31, 1995	Ein stór fjölskylda	One Family	Jóhann Sigmarsson
August 9, 1995	Einkalíf	Private Life	Þráinn (Þráinn) Bertelsson
September 15, 1995	Tár úr steini	Tears of Stone[a]	Hilmar Oddsson
October 5, 1995	Nei, er ekkert svar	No Is No Answer[a]	Jón Tryggvason
November 9, 1995	Benjamín dúfa	Benjamin Dove[a]	Gísli Snær Erlingsson
December 22, 1995	Agnes	Agnes[a]	Egill Eðvarðsson (Eðvarðsson)

Table 12.1 (*continued*)

Date	Original title (Icelandic spelling)	English title	Director (Icelandic spelling)
March 21, 1996	*Draumadísir*	Dreamhunters[a]	Ásdís Thoroddsen
October 3, 1996	*Djöflaeyjan*	Devil's Island[a]	Fridrik Thór Fridriksson (Friðrik Þór Friðriksson)
August 14, 1997	*Blossi 810551*	Blossi 810551[a]	Júlíus Kemp
September 26, 1997	*María*	Maria[a]	Einar Heimisson
October 11, 1997	*Perlur og svín*	Pearls and Swine[a]	Óskar Jónasson
December 26, 1997	*Stikkfrí*	Count Me Out[a]	Ari Kristinsson
August 27, 1998	*Sporlaust*	No Trace[a]	Hilmar Oddsson
September 23, 1998	*Dansinn*	The Dance[a]	Ágúst Gudmundsson (Guðmundsson)
September 24, 1999	*Ungfrúin góða og húsið (Ungfrúin góða og húsið)*	Honour of the House[a]	Gudný (Guðný) Halldórsdóttir
November 26, 1999	*Myrkrahöfðinginn (Myrkrahöfðinginn)*	Flames of Paradise[a] (aka Witchcraft)	Hrafn Gunnlaugsson
January 1, 2000	*Englar alheimsins*	Angels of the Universe[a]	Fridrik Thór Fridriksson (Friðrik Þór Friðriksson)
March 10, 2000	*Fíaskó*	Fiasco[a]	Ragnar Bragason
May 31, 2000	*101 Reykjavík*	101 Reykjavík[a]	Baltasar Kormákur
September 27, 2000	*Íslenski draumurinn*	The Icelandic Dream	Róbert I. Douglas
November 24, 2000	*Óskabörn Þjóðarinnar (Óskabörn þjóðarinnar)*	Plan B—Report	Jóhann Sigmarsson
December 26, 2000	*Ikingut*	Ikingut[a]	Gísli Snær Erlingsson
January 19, 2001	*Villiljós*	Dramarama	Inga Lísa Middleton, Dagur Kári, Ragnar Bragason, Ásgrímur Sverrisson, Einar Thór (Þór) Gunnlaugsson
October 20, 2001	*Mávahlátur*	The Seagull's Laughter[a]	Ágúst Gudmundsson (Guðmundsson)
January 4, 2002	*Regína*	Regina[a]	María Sigurdardóttir (Sigurðardóttir)
February 1, 2002	*Gemsar*	Made in Iceland (aka Cell)	Mikael Torfason
March 28, 2002	*Reykjavík Guesthouse—Rent a Bike*	Reykjavík Guesthouse—Rent a Bike	Björn Thors & Unnur Ösp Stefánsdóttir
August 16, 2002	*Maður eins og ég (Maður eins og ég)*	A Man Like Me	Róbert I. Douglas

Table 12.1 (continued)

Date	Original title (Icelandic spelling)	English title	Director (Icelandic spelling)
September 13, 2002	Hafið (Hafið)	The Sea[a]	Baltasar Kormákur
September 27, 2002	Fálkar	Falcons[a]	Fridrik Thór Fridriksson (Friðrik Þór Friðriksson)
December 21, 2002	Stella í framboði (Stella í framboði)	Stella Runs for Office	Gudný (Guðný) Halldórsdóttir
January 25, 2003	Nói Albínói	Nói the Albino[a]	Dagur Kári

Sources: Titles as recorded in films, IFF newsletters, and festival publications, 1992–2002 (including www.iff.is/www.icelandicfilmcentre.is); dates of premier as reported in Icelandic newspapers, primarily *Morgunbladid*, 1980–2003 (www.mbl.is).

[a] Denotes a film internationally coproduced or cofinanced to any degree.

[b] *Northern Tales* is not precisely an Icelandic film so much as a "northern anthology"; it consists of three short films by female directors from, respectively, Greenland (Maariu Olsen), the Faeroe Islands (Katrín Óttarsdóttir), and Iceland (Kristín Pálsdóttir).

In and Out of Reykjavik

NOTES

1. For sake of reference and clarity, all Icelandic names and titles are provided in their international form; please refer to table 12.1 for the original spellings with Icelandic characters.
2. Besides *The Outlaw and His Wife*, the most frequently discussed films from the silent era are Gunnar Sommerfeldt's Danish adaptation of Gunnar Gunnarsson's novel *Borgslægtens Historie* (1920, The Story of the Borg Family); Gudmundur Kamban and Gunnar Robert Hansen's codirected adaptation of Kamban's tragedy *Hadda Padda* (1924), of which the exteriors were shot in Iceland with Clara Pontoppidan in the lead role; and Kamban's *Det sovende hus* (1926, The Sleeping House), a drawing-room play that takes place entirely indoors and in Denmark. *Det sovende hus*, like the other two films, was produced by Nordisk Filmkompagni but is notable as the first feature film based on an original manuscript written by an Icelander.
3. No official estimations exist for audience numbers before 1995, but producers and theaters have provided such numbers to, among others, Cowie 2000. See http://www.producers.is for further information.
4. These directors include first and foremost Ágúst Gudmundsson (b. 1947), who made four films between 1980 and 1984, only to pop up on the silver screen much later with the coproduced period film *The Dance* (1998, *Dansinn*), a film adaptation of the Faeroese author William Heinesen's novel, and *The Seagull's Laughter* (2001, *Mávahlátur*), a universal story about women's struggles before feminism, based on Kristín Marja Baldursdóttir's novel; and Hrafn Gunnlaugsson (b. 1948), who after *Father's Estate* depicted an existential crisis (most likely his own) in *Inter Nos* (1982, *Okkar á milli—Í hita og thunga dagsins*), before devoting himself to his Viking films, a passion held since childhood, as his *The Sacred Mound* (1993, *Hin helgu vé*) shows, the year before Fridrik Thór Fridriksson captured his inspirations and roots as a storyteller in the childhood film *Movie Days*. Additionally, Thorsteinn Jónsson (b. 1946), previously known as a documentarist, impacted the milieu with a coming-of-age film from the postwar years, wherein both young people and the young nation face difficult choices, all while freedom and independence billow in the breeze, in the ascetic adaptation of Pétur Gunnarsson's *Punktur punktur komma strik* (1981, Dot, Dot, Comma, Dash), which lies in an entirely different ballpark than his second film, the much more ambitious *Atomic Station*. Otherwise, the early 1980s are distinguished by less active, and therefore less distinctly profiled, directors like Kristín B. Pálsdóttir (b. 1948) or Thórhildur Thórleifsdóttir (b. 1945), who directed a social satire by the later very active director, producer, and scriptwriter Gudný Halldórsdóttir, *Stella í Orlofi* (1986, The Icelandic Shock Station). And then there was the hyperactive and humorously humanist Thráinn Bertelsson (b. 1944), locally just as popular, who made six films between the years 1981 and 1989.
5. Kristín Jóhannesdóttir's follow-up film, *As in Heaven* (1992, *Svo á jördu sem á himni*), is a masterpiece, a play between epochs held together by a girl who in the 1930s experiences a tragedy from the fourteenth century.
6. The debate I refer to took place mainly in public newspapers. In a country of this

size, many people express their opinion about all sorts of topics in letters to the editor or other newspaper sections—with contributions of varying quality. The internal debate within the film industry is also expressed in the bimonthly film publication *Land og synir.* The discussion eventually faded out, but it still existed during my stay in 1997, when the head of the National Film Archive of Iceland, Bödvar Bjarki Pétursson, drew my attention to it. Pétursson participated in the debate himself (especially in connection with the international advertising agencies' use of Iceland as a setting); see Pétursson 1996.
7. Besides Kemp (b. 1967) and Jónasson (b. 1963), who—as the first in a group of young, wild filmmakers—paved the way, Jóhann Sigmarsson (b. 1969) directed *One Family* (1995, *Ein stór fjölskylda*) and *Plan B* (2000, *Óskabörn thjódarinnar*), Ragnar Bragason (b. 1971) directed *Fiasco* (2000, *Fíaskó*), and the somewhat older Hilmar Oddsson (b. 1957) contributed *No Trace* (1998, *Sporlaust*). All the films deal with modern urban life in Reykjavik but always through its underworlds, centered around fast nightlife and the various subcultures.
8. Sorlin provides a comparative sociohistorical investigation of European film in which he raises a number of questions about the images that (modern) European film uses to portray its contemporary time. Sorlin's work outlines the foundation for my parameters, and it is supplemented satisfactorily by Orr 1993.
9. That 86,000 (out of 268,000 in 1996) saw *Devil's Island* was a sensation. Not since *Land and Sons* and the first year of the industry, when 30 to 40 percent of the population saw a film just because it was Icelandic, had an Icelandic film attracted so many people to the theater—that is, if we disregard the popular comedies like Bertelsson's *New Life* trilogy, 1983–85 or Halldórsdóttir's *Men's Choir,* which seemed to go against the development and as late as 1992 attracted an audience of almost 100,000.

WORKS CITED

Cowie, Peter. 2000. *Icelandic Films, 1980–2000.* Reykjavik: Icelandic Film Fund.
Land og synir. 1996. 6 (November–December).
Møller, Birgir Thor. 1997. "Skál: An Interview with Fridrik Thór Fridriksson." *Scope,* May 9, http://www.Scope.dk
Orr, John. 1993. *Cinema and Modernity,* Cambridge: Polity Press.
Sorlin, Pierre. 1994. *European Cinemas, European Societies, 1939–1990.* London: Routledge.

SELECTED BIBLIOGRAPHY

On Iceland

Gíslason; Gylfi Th. 1994. *Ad vera Islendingur—Vegsemd thess og vandi.* Reykjavik: Setberg.
Hjálmarsson, Jón R. 1999. *Islands Historie—Fra bosættelsen til vore dage.* Reykjavik: Iceland Review.

Karlsson, Gunnar. 2000. *The History of Iceland*. Minneapolis: University of Minnesota Press.
Magnússon, Sigurdur A. 1990. *The Icelanders*. Reykjavik: Forskot.
Nordal, Jóhannes, and Valdimar Kristinsson. 1996. *Iceland—The Republic*. Reykjavik: Central Bank of Iceland.
Rosenblad, Esbjörn, and Rakel Sigurdardóttir. 1993. *Iceland, from Past to Present*. Reykjavik: Mál og Menning.

On Icelandic Cinema and Directors

Åhlund, Jannike. 1994. "Sagoligt kreativ." *Chaplin* 1 (February–March): 31–35.
Bernhardsson, Eggert Thór. 1999. "Iceland: Saga af kvikmynd." In *Heimur kvikmyndanna*, ed. Gudni Elísson, 859–68. Reykjavik: Forlagid and ART.IS.
———. 1999. "Landnám lifandi mynda: Af kvikmyndum á Íslandi til 1930." In *Heimur kvikmyndanna*, ed. Gudni Elísson, 803–32. Reykjavik: Forlagid and ART.IS.
Bjarnadótttir, Birna. 1999. "Náttúra tilfinninga í íslenskum kvikmyndum." In *Heimur kvikmyndanna*, ed. Gudni Elísson, 937–50. Reykjavik: Forlagid and ART.IS.
Breidfjörd, Huldar. 1999. "Skrítna Ísland: Um íslenskar vegamyndir." In *Heimur kvikmyndanna*, ed. Gudni Elísson, 962–69. Reykjavik: Forlagid and ART.IS.
Elísson, Gudni, ed. 1999. *Heimur kvikmyndanna*. Reykjavik: Forlagid and ART.IS.
Fridrikson, Fridrik Thór. 1994. "Sänk det nordiska vikingaskepet!" *Chaplin* 1 (February–March): 30.
Fridriksson, Fridrik Thór, and Árni Óskarsson. 1994. *Vor í Dal*. Reykjavik: Mál og menning.
Heiddal, Hjálmtý. 1995. "Skemtanir fyrir fólkid." *Lesbók morgunbladsins*, March 25.
Helgadóttir, Hafdís. 1999. "Hlutverk landslags í kvikmyndum: Svo á jördu sem á himni, Hrafninn flýgur og Land og synir." In *Heimur kvikmyndanna*, ed. Gudni Elísson, 950–58. Reykjavik: Forlagid and ART.IS.
Icelandic Film Centre/Kvikmynamidstöd Íslands (formerly Icelandic Film Fund/Kvikmynasjódur Íslands)/ http://www.icelandicfilmcentre.is
Icelandic Film Corporation. http://www.icecorp.is
Icelandic Filmmakers Association (Félag Kvikmyndagerdarmanna). 1996. *Land og synir* 1 (January–February).
———. http://www.producers.is
Indridason, Arnaldur. 1999. "Stofnun og saga kvikmyndafyrirtækisins Edda-film." In *Heimur kvikmyndanna*, ed. Gudni Elísson, 886–94. Reykjavik: Forlagid and ART.IS.
Jónasson, Kristján B. 1999. "Íslenska hjardmyndin: Andstædur borgar og sveitar i 79 af stödinni og Land og synir." In *Heimur kvikmyndanna*, ed. Gudni Elísson, 905–17. Reykjavik: Forlagid and ART.IS.
Møller, Birgir Thor. 1997. "Djöflaeyjan Rís." *Dagur-Tíminn*, March 11, 19.
———. 2001. "Fridrik Thór Fridriksson." *Kosmorama* (- *Filmkunstnere i tiden*) 227–28: 84–88.
National Film Archive of Iceland. http://www.kvikmyndasafn.is
Pétursson, Bödvar Bjarki. 1996. "Útlend dömubindaauglýsing á Thingvöllum?" *Land og synir* 6 (November–December).
Sen, Oddný. 1999. "Sjónvarpsbyltingin á Íslandi—Og áhrif hennar á íslenska kvikmyn-

dagerd fram til 1979." In *Heimur kvikmyndanna,* ed. Gudni Elísson, 927–37. Reykjavik: Forlagid and ART.IS.

Statistics of Iceland. http://www.hagstofa.is

Sveinsson, Erlendur. 1981. *Kvikmyndir á Islandi 75 ára.* Reykjavik: Gamla Bíó, Nýja Bíó og Kvikmyndasafn Íslands (National Film Archive of Iceland).

———. 1999. "Árin tólf fyrir daga Sjónvarps og Kvikmyndasjóds." In *Heimur kvikmyndanna,* ed. Gudni Elísson, 868–74. Reykjavik: Forlagid and ART.IS.

———. 1999. "Landsýn—Heimsýn: Kynningarmáttur kvikmyndanna á fjórda áratugnum." In *Heimur kvikmyndanna,* ed. Gudni Elísson, 852–59. Reykjavik: Forlagid and ART.IS.

Thórarinsson, Árni. 1994. *Krummi—Hrafn Saga Gunnlaugssonar.* Reykjavik: Fródi hf.

CHAPTER 13

Hrafn Gunnlaugsson—The Viking Who Came in from the Cold?

Bjørn Sørenssen

In 1991 Icelandic director Hrafn Gunnlaugsson completed a trilogy of what have been jokingly referred to as cod westerns—movies drawing on material from the Nordic Viking sagas but also engaging the legacy of Akira Kurosawa and Sergio Leone. Gunnlaugsson openly acknowledged this connection in relation to the first film, *When the Raven Flies* (1984, *Hrafninn flygur*), and the sequel, *The Shadow of the Raven* (1988, *Í skugga hrafnsins*), also clearly followed the pattern. The final film in the trilogy, *The White Viking* (1991, *Den hvite Viking*), was a major Nordic coproduction and was distributed as both a feature film and a television serial.

When the Raven Flies is mainly a tale of personal revenge that bears a clear resemblance to Kurosawa's *Yojimbo* (1961) and Leone's *For a Fistful of Dollars* (1964, *Per un pugno di dollari*). A little boy in Iceland witnesses the Vikings Eirik and Thor kill his parents and abduct his sister. The boy is spared by Eirik and Thor's henchman, even though the two leaders have instructed him to kill the boy, "who is old enough to have seen too much." Twenty years later a stranger arrives in Iceland aboard a Norwegian trade ship. By that time Iceland is the home of Eirik and Thor, who have settled there after fleeing from King Harald in Norway. The trade ship's strange passenger introduces himself as Gestur (Guest). Upon meeting Eirik's men, he demands to be taken to Eirik, for whom he has some important news. The plot events that follow the meeting between Eirik and Gestur resemble closely those of *Yojimbo* and *For a Fistful of Dollars:* by killing off the retainers of the two Vikings, Gestur manages to pit the two men against each other, culminating in Eirik's massacre of Thor's entire household. During the melee, Gestur steals into Eirik's home and reveals to Eirik's wife that he is her brother and has returned to seek vengeance. Torn between loyalty to her long-lost brother and to her husband and little son, she nevertheless betrays Gestur. Gestur is captured and tortured by Eirik and his men. In a final turn, Gestur's sister changes her mind and helps him escape, setting up a climactic confrontation between Gestur and Eirik, echoing similar ultimate showdowns in *Yojimbo* and *A Fistful of Dollars*.

In *The Shadow of the Raven,* Gunnlaugsson has set the action at a later stage in Icelandic history, using the tension between Nordic paganism—the Asa belief—and the newly established Christian religion as the backdrop for a dramatic tale of fighting among clans and blood revenge. As in *When the Raven Flies,* the drama turns around the arrival of a strange young man in Iceland. This time it is the Icelander Trausti, returning home after conversion and religious study in Norway, intent on spreading the word of Christian forgiveness among his bellicose countrymen. His efforts are obstructed by a fight over the rights to butcher a stranded whale. Trausti finds himself in the middle of a bloody feud. He endeavors to resolve the conflict through peacemaking and forgiveness. As a consequence, his farm is burned to the ground and his young wife killed on their wedding night. Trausti refuses to turn the other cheek and wreaks havoc on his enemies, invoking the tradition and wrath of Odin, Thor, and the other Nordic gods.

The White Viking also explores the conflict between the old and the new belief. The third film of the trilogy uses historical characters and actual events related to the introduction of Christianity to Iceland. The chief protagonists are a young Norwegian couple, Ask and Embla. They become instruments for King Olaf Tryggvasson as he attempts to convert Iceland and in this way control the island, whose population includes independent farmers fleeing from royal centralization in Norway.[1]

This essay gives some background for the trilogy by focusing on the saga connection as well as pointing out some of the narrative structures that make the seemingly unlikely combination of samurai film, the Italian spaghetti western, and the old Norse sagas plausible and highly relevant.

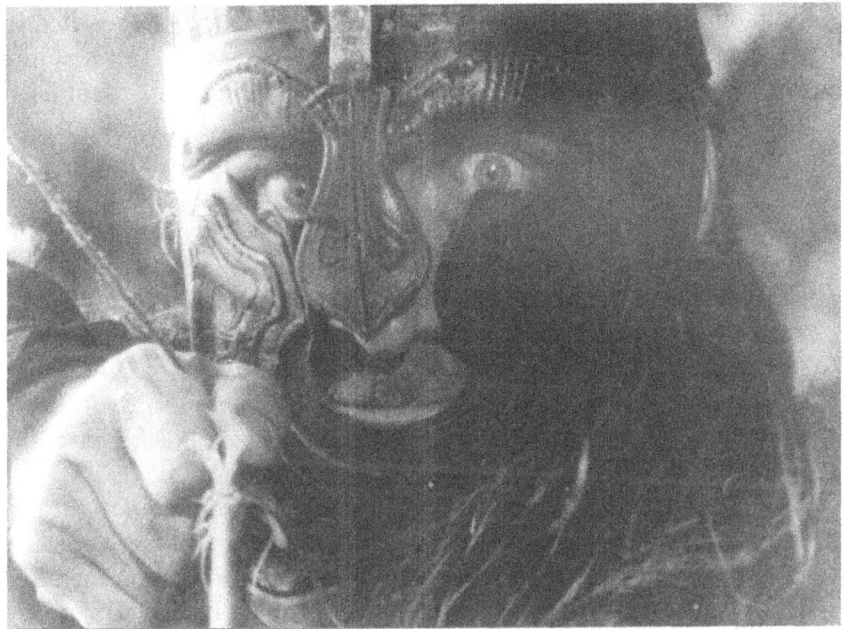

When the Raven Flies (1984) (courtesy of Norwegian Film Institute)

SAGA STYLE, SAMURAI FILM, AND ITALO-WESTERN:
WHEN THE RAVEN FLIES AND *IN THE SHADOW OF THE RAVEN*

A stranger arrives at the home of a widow, where he asks for and is granted a room for the night. He finds his hostess in tears and queries her about her unhappiness. She tells him that a notorious bandit has challenged her only son to a duel the next day. The stranger repays her hospitality by offering to take the place of her son. The following day he kills the bandit in the duel.

The place could have been the American West during the latter part of the nineteenth century, the woman a farmer's widow, and the bandit one of the henchmen of the local cattle baron. The scene could also easily be found in an Italo-western shot on the Andalusian plains, starring Clint Eastwood. Or we might envision Toshiro Mifune playing a samurai during the days of the Tokugawa shogunate, saving a hot-headed farmer's son from certain death by defeating a roaming *ronin* in a dazzling sword fight. However, this particular story is recounted in *Egil's Saga*. The place is Sunnmøre on the west coast of Norway more than one thousand years ago, the son's name is Fridgeir, the mother is called Gyda, the bandit is the berserker Ljot the Pale, and the hero is the protagonist of the saga, Egil Skallagrimsson from Iceland.

Ljot has challenged Fridgeir to a duel in order to kill him and acquire his farm. Egil accompanies Fridgeir to the islet where the duel is to take place. Ljot has already arrived: "Ljot was a very big man and strong. When he went forward to the dueling area in the field the berserk temper came on him so that he began to bellow violently, and to bite at his shield" (1975, 118). He accepts Egil's offer to fight him, a decision he soon rues. After Egil has chased him around the dueling ground with two swords, Ljot has to beg for a break, while Egil uses the time to mock his adversary in a poem. When they resume fighting the end comes quickly: "Egil told Ljot to get ready. 'I want us to fight this duel now.' Then Egil leapt at him and struck at him. He went so close to him that Ljot fell back and the shield was swept from him. Then Egil struck at Ljot and got him below the knee and took his leg off. Ljot fell then, and was lifeless. . . . Few men grieved for Ljot, since he had been the most ruthless of men" (118).

One does not need to read many pages of *Egil's Saga* or any other Icelandic saga in order to find similar action sequences, not unlike those we find in western and samurai movies. In Kurosawa's *Yojimbo* and Leone's *For a Fistful of Dollars* as well as in Gunnlaugsson's *When the Raven Flies,* we find scenes in which the hero—caught, beaten, and helpless—still manages to escape. These texts share a common feature, a defining character of the genre: action orientation. Thus, we find it quite natural to compare the sagas to the samurai and western movie. This is also one of the reasons why a movie like *When the Raven Flies* does not appear as a cheap pastiche of Kurosawa or Leone but as an appropriate way of transposing this specific literary material into cinematic form. With this set of connections in mind, it may be useful to review some of the traits shared by the sagas, the Italo-western (aka spaghetti western), and the samurai film tradition.

CHARACTERIZATION IN THE SAGA, SAMURAI FILM, AND ITALO-WESTERN

In his book about the sagas, Jorge Luis Borges draws attention to these narratives' remarkable "objectivity" in describing character and environment: "The characters of the sagas are neither wholly good or wholly evil. There are no monsters, neither of virtue or of vice. Nor does goodness triumph or evil meet with defeat. As in real life, there are coincidences illustrating the symmetric patterns of chance" (1969, 23). The remark also helps illustrate commonalities between the films of Kurosawa, Leone, and Gunnlaugsson. The nameless hero of Leone as well as Kurosawa's bodyguard in *Yojimbo* and *Sanjuro* appear as ambiguous characters, leaving the spectator uncertain about where to place them. This characteristic is emphasized more extensively in the later movies of Leone. The description given by Borges is as relevant to the characters in *The Good, the Bad, and the Ugly* as it is to the sagas.[2] The world of the saga, the Italo-western, and the samurai film is multifaceted, complex, and volatile. The character who appears to be a friend and an accomplice may become a dangerous and uncompromising enemy. Moreover, the restrained, descriptive mode makes it difficult to recognize immediately the functions of the dramatis personae.

An important element in this volatility is the indirect way these narratives deal with emotion: any overt display of emotion is made synonymous with weakness and is understood to be contrary to the mood of the narrative. Nevertheless, the reader and the audience are allowed glimpses into the emotional life of the protagonist. Kurosawa's hero shows an uncharacteristic care for the woman who is abducted in *Yojimbo*; he is instrumental in securing her own and her family's freedom. The fact that he apparently reacts with disgust and contempt toward their expressions of gratitude can be read as self-contempt for not being able to live up to his self-professed lack of emotions. Similar situations are also found in *For a Fistful of Dollars*. Gunnlaugsson, too, had originally planned a similar sequence for *Flight of the Raven* (Sjögren 1991).

Another trait the sagas, samurai films, and Italo-westerns share, which underscores the antiromantic character of the genre, is an amoral attitude toward the acquisition of wealth, apparent in the titles of the two first movies in the Leone trilogy and highlighted by the cynical greed expressed by Kurosawa's bodyguard in *Yojimbo*. In *For a Few Dollars More*, greed takes on a metaphorical character in the concluding sequence when the protagonist rides into town on a cart loaded with bodies to be delivered for cash. This unbridled materialism finds its match in *Egil's Saga*. Two chests of silver function as an important narrative impetus in Egil's story. Another example is found in an episode where

Egil returns to the court of the English king after having lost a brother in battle. He sits gloomily among the boisterously celebrating Vikings until the king, having heard about his misfortune, offers him a golden armband. The gift compensates him for the loss of his brother, and he brightens up and composes a poem in honor of the king. Soon enough, he is once again his old cheerful self.

THE REVENGE MOTIF IN *WHEN THE RAVEN FLIES*

Revenge is a central motif in the sagas, as in most strong clan societies. In this respect *When the Raven Flies* is markedly different from *Yojimbo* and *For a Fistful of Dollars,* for Gunlaugsson draws on the saga motif as a driving force in the narrative. The mystic stranger Gestur is motivated by his pursuit of personal revenge in his dealings with the Vikings Thor and Eirik, who have killed his parents and abducted his sister.

The revenge motif has a dominant position in the saga tradition, nowhere more than in *Njál's Saga,* where the climax of the story, the burning of Njál and is family, is the result of blood revenge getting out of control of the established wergild system (monetary compensation paid by a murderer to the relatives of the victim) practiced in medieval Iceland and regulated at the *Althing*.[3] The wise and cautious Njál has successfully navigated the intricate rules of wergild up to a point where this form of social contract is no longer able to prevent the spiral of violence. The fire at Bergthorskvál (Njál's home) is the climax of the saga, followed by the chilling epilogue in which Njál's friend Kári systematically tracks down and kills all but one of the raiders responsible for the massacre.

While the sequence of events in *When the Raven Flies* is roughly similar to *Yojimbo* and *For a Fistful of Dollars* (and in the last instance to Dashiell Hammett's *The Glass Key*) in the way Gestur sets up the foster brothers Thor and Eirik against each other in order to achieve his own aims, there remains a marked difference in the way this is treated in the three films. With Kurosawa and Leone this sequence is merely a proof of the protagonist's skill and cunning; with Gunnlaugsson it becomes an indication of the fanatical need for revenge driving Gestur. However, this apparent difference disappears when we compare the three movies on a larger scale. We find the revenge motif strongly represented in the movies of Sergio Leone, particularly in *Once upon a Time in the West* (1968, *C'era una Volta il West*), in which the mysterious harmonica-playing stranger is on a quest to avenge his father in a style worthy of a saga. And amid the obvious greed of the bounty hunters in *For a Few Dollars More* (1965, *Per qualche dollaro in più*), the cold-blooded Colonel Mortimer turns out to be motivated by personal revenge in his pursuit of the bandit. Even if it is not as strongly represented in Kurosawa's samurai films, the literature this film tradition springs from is deeply steeped in the honor code of Japanese clan society, where revenge plays an important role. The classic Japanese samurai narrative is that of the "forty ronin," the masterless samurai avenging their murdered master.

THE LACONIC: SAGA-STYLE NORTH, EAST, AND WEST

A prominent stylistic trait from classic saga literature is easily recognized in the movies of Leone, Kurosawa, and Gunnlaugsson—that of laconic expression. Grand feelings and gestures are constantly underplayed, as in the scene where the bodyguard or Noname (in *Yojimbo* or *For a Fistful of Dollars*), passes the coffin maker on the way to the showdown with a group of tough swordsmen/gunmen, and orders three coffins. After the showdown, the protagonist again passes the coffin maker, remarking, "Sorry, *four* coffins!"

We find the same terse narrative economy in *Njál's Saga,* when Gunnar from Lidarende receives unwanted company:

> When his enemies came up to the house they did not know whether Gunnar was at home; so they wanted someone to go up to the building and find out. Meanwhile they sat down outside. Thorgrim the Norwegian climbed up on the roof. Gunnar saw a red coat appear at the window and lunged at Thorgrim with his halberd and struck him in the middle. Thorgrim's feet slipped from under him, he dropped his shield and tumbled from the roof. He then walked over to Gizur and the rest of the group who were sitting on the ground. Gizur looked at him and asked: "Well, is Gunnar at home?"
>
> Thorgrim answered: "Find that out for yourselves! All I know is that his halberd is!" With that he fell dead to the ground (1955, 159).

This laconic form of expression is richly represented in one of the direct inspirational sources of the movies of Leone and Kurosawa: American "hard-boiled" crime novels, represented by authors like Raymond Chandler and Dashiell Hammett. Hammett's novel *The Glass Key* serves as the source for *Yojimbo* as well as *For a Fistful of Dollars*. The laconic element in this literary tradition is frequently related to the British tradition of understatement, as in this description from Chandler's *Farewell, My Lovely*: "He was a big man but not more then six feet five and not wider than a beer truck" (1949, 7). This technique of understatement frequently borders on the sarcastic, a vivid element in the contrapuntal commentaries of the sagas as well as in the "wisecracking" of the hard-boiled detective novel. We find frequent parallels to this in Japanese literary tradition, in Zen Buddhist philosophy, and in the related Haiku tradition. To draw this similarity even further, it is possible to point out a strong likeness between the short and rough-hewn stanzas of the Nordic bards in the sagas and the concise fifteen syllable verse of the Haiku.

On the whole, it is impossible to avoid the specific Japanese background when discussing the films of Leone and Gunnlaugsson. When Kurosawa made *Yojimbo* in 1961, this particular film hardly represented anything specifically new in Japanese cinema. What it did was to widen the scope of an already established genre known as *chambara* (literally, *sword theater*), in its turn a subgenre of the kind of historical drama known as *jidai-geki*. A common trait in this genre tradition is the orientation toward action, similar to that of the Nordic saga tradition, where the complicated and rigid rules and traditions connected with sword fighting figure prominently. This set of rules was also known as the *bushido code*, defining the way of the samurai in Japanese society during the Tokugawa shogunate, most explicitly expressed in the book *Hagakure*. The samurai, an unproductive caste of warriors, was in reality an economic liability to Japanese society for more than 250 years. Having originally been necessary in the battle for the power of the shogunate, they became increasingly superfluous in the peaceful years following the battle of Sekhigahara in 1600, having no outlet for their warrior skills other than local feuds. With the passing of time, there was also an increase in the number of samurai who had lost their masters without being able to find new employment, the so-called ronin, who eventually became a social problem. This is the background for the portrayal of the ronin appearing in the post–World War II chambara in movies like *Seven Samurai* (1954, *Shichinin no Samurai*), *Sanjuro* (1962, *Tsubahi sanjûrô*), and *Yojimbo*, and one of the consequences of this portrayal is a clear deromanticization of the samurai image.

Hrafn Gunnlaugsson

THE ANTIROMANTIC HERO: THE OUTSIDER
WHO DOES NOT WANT TO COME IN FROM THE COLD

At this point it is possible to sum up some of the arguments in favor of comparing the Italo-western and Kurosawa's samurai movies with the Nordic saga world rather than with the classic Hollywood western.

The Hollywood western tradition, as it evolved from its roots (for example, *The Virginian,* [Victor Fleming, 1929], *The Squaw Man,* [Cecil B. DeMille, 1931]), is largely about socializing and civilizing. The genre reflects a commonly shared view of American history as the history of the civilization of a continent. The events in the classic Hollywood western are continually played out on the borders of this civilization: the frontier. The protagonists of this tradition are inevitably agents of the civilization process, imposing civilization on nature, Native Americans, and lawless cattle barons. They may themselves feel ill at ease and lonely as they participate in the civilizing processes for which they've paved the way, but when they eventually ride into the sunset, they do so in the certainty that they have facilitated progress, whether it is Alan Ladd in *Shane* (George Stevens, 1953), Gary Cooper in *The Westerner* (William Wyler, 1940), or Henry Fonda in *My Darling Clementine* (John Ford, 1946). The hero in the classic Hollywood western is a romantic hero. He is driven, almost against his will, by the good forces that sustain the common good.

Egil Skallagrimsson would have felt uncomfortable in this company. His ideal society is one that appreciates the bold deed, where reward is mainly individual and material and one's debt to society is dependent on one's fellows. Should the hero happen to be alone, there is no society to speak of. The dominating conflict in *Egil's Saga,* his lifelong feud with King Eirik Bloodaxe of Norway, is more than a personal conflict; it is the fight of the individual against organized society, represented by the central political powers of the king. In his capacity as an outsider by principle, we find Egil Skallagrimsson in the company of the ronin Sanjuro Kuwatabake in *Yojimbo,* the nameless man with the poncho in *For a Fistful of Dollars,* and, of course, the avenging Gestur in Hrafn Gunnlaugsson's *When the Raven Flies.* They share a deep indifference to social progress: if progress should occur, and their actions contribute to the establishment of justice and order, it would be, to quote Borges again, "coincidences illustrating the symmetric patterns of chance."

The White Viking (1991) (courtesy of Norwegian Film Institute)

A GUEST WITH A MESSAGE: *THE WHITE VIKING*

Sam Goldwyn's apocryphal dictum, "If you want to send a message, use Western Union," was shared by many enthusiastic western fans when the first "problem" westerns appeared in the 1940s and 1950s, movies that used the western genre as a vehicle for treating various moral and/or political problems, represented by titles like *The Ox-Bow Incident* (William A. Wellman, 1943) (self-justice), *Shane* (violence as a problem), or *High Noon* (Fred Zimmerman, 1952) (the McCarthy processes—although the movie could also be read as a defense for the Korean War). This use of the western formula was characterized by André Bazin as "super westerns" (*sur-westerns*)—movies that went beyond the frame of the genre (1971, 150–51).

Some of the same skepticism toward "westerns with a message" was echoed in the reception of Gunnlaugsson's *White Viking*. Instead of a simple and timeless action-oriented plot, the viewer was presented with a historically inscribed problematic: that of the conflict between clan and feudal society, represented by the introduction of Christianity to the Nordic regions at the turn of the first millennium. In *The White Viking* Hrafn Gunnlaugsson is clearly inspired by the "great" family sagas of Nordic and Icelandic culture, like *Laxdala Saga, Njál's Saga*, and Snorri Sturlasson's monumental learned work, *Heimskringla—The Saga of the Norwegian Kings*, rather than the smaller clan sagas (for example, the Sturlunga Sagas) that had inspired his two *Raven* films. The pivotal point in the narrative is based on a historical event: the decision of the Icelandic Althing to make Christianity the official religion of the Icelandic people in the year 1000. The attempt made by the Norwegian king Olaf Tryggvason to Christianize the heathen Icelanders (and Norwegians) was a central subject in *Njál's Saga, Laxdala Saga*, and Snorri Sturlasson's saga of the Norwegian kings. The Saxon priest Thangbrand, who appears in all of these sagas, is used as a central character in *The White Viking*.

The manner in which Christianity was introduced to the island is of great importance for the Icelandic people. Unlike in Norway, where the Christian belief was forced on the populace by the king, the Icelanders made the conversion as a result of a decision at the Althing, proposed by the Asa priest Thorgeirr. And, also in opposition to the draconian measures taken by the Norwegian king against the hesitating and the renegades, the decree of the Althing stated specifically that any person who wanted to hold by the old gods might do so, as long as it was kept in private. According to the Icelandic scholar Einar Olgeirsson (1968, 105–8), Thorgeirr's proposal was a tactical decision intended to preempt the threat that Olaf Tryggvason would use conversion as a pretext to add Iceland to his Norwegian kingdom. In this way the introduction of the Christian religion was an important step forward that served to maintain and strengthen the Icelandic clan society against the threat of Norwegian central power.

However, in *The White Viking* Gunnlaugsson's main concern in this respect are the values represented in the old Norse Asa belief, understood in contrast with the values of the newly imported monotheistic religion. Gunnlaugsson himself characterizes pagan belief as something like "a Zen Buddhist religion" (Sjögren 1991), a worldview based on pleasure in life. According to him, its openness toward life stood little chance against a religion like Christianity, in which death plays such an important role.

THE CENTRAL CHARACTERS: OLAF AND THANGBRAND

The emphasis on this problematic is no doubt one of the reasons that the main protagonists and main romantic interest of *The White Viking*, the couple Ask and Embla (not coincidentally also the names of the first two human beings in Asa cosmology), evolve little in the film and remain "flat," largely uninteresting characters—at least when compared to the characters who represent the struggle between the new and the old belief in Iceland, King Olaf of Norway, his henchman Thangbrand, and the priest Thorgeirr (who in the context of the movie is made the father of Ask).

These latter characters are portrayed in a manner very different from the rather one-dimensional character portrayal of the *Raven* films—as complicated, troubled, and intriguing personalities. Of special interest is the portrayal of King Olaf Tryggvasson by Egill Ólafsson. Gunnlaugsson has made a dramatic departure from the way this most idolized of the Norwegian Viking kings appears in Snorri Sturlasson's sagas, where Snorri forcefully depicts him as a young, tall, fair-haired athlete. Gunnlaugsson's Olaf is a middle-aged, short, one-eyed, cruel person with a fanatical devotion to his newfound religion. This devotion is illustrated through the animated conversation Olaf conducts with a crucifix he always carries with him. This conversation takes on a tone of magical-realism, giving Olaf a more complex personality than mere evil antagonist. The portrayal of the Saxon priest Thangbrand is more faithful to the saga sources, but the character is given some additional psychopathic traits by Gunnlaugsson. Hints of a masochistic/homoerotic relationship with King Olaf are given, as Thangbrand is tortured by the thought that Christ speaks directly to Olaf but not to him, the king's spiritual guide. The cruelty and violence Thangbrand shows toward "the heathen" is not an invention of Gunnlaugsson; the source material furnishes ample evidence of such.

In *The White Viking* Hrafn Gunnlaugsson employs a life/death metaphor in his description of the relationship between Asa belief and Christianity. We meet the Asa belief through a fertility ritual in the opening sequences of the movie, when Ask and Embla are wed in a ritual consecrated to the fertility goddess, Freya. This ceremony suddenly develops into a blood wedding, becoming a festival of death, when Olaf, Thangbrand, and their men attack the temple, burning it and killing most of the guests in the name of Christ. In the convent where Embla is held as a hostage while Ask is sent out on his mission as a "white Viking" to convert the Icelanders to Christianity, death metaphors connected to Christianity dominate through images of the hysterical, morbid nuns worshipping a threatening crucifix in a ceremony at a dark pool.

The portrayal of the Iclandic Asa priest Thorgeirr is as multidimensional as the characters of Olaf and Thangbrand. Initially he is portrayed as lethargic, almost incapable of action. At a later stage it turns out that his apparent passivity is a ruse enabling him to solve the local intrigue set off by an ambitious second wife on behalf of her son. Later he is shown as motivated by personal ambition to manipulate the Icelanders into making decisions later generations would laud as wise and cunning.

In light of the complicated and intricate characters and historical intrigue that distinguish the film, it is little wonder that the fictional protagonists, Ask and Embla, are superficial and of little interest.

ICELAND AND NORWAY—REALISM AND ROMANTICISM

This fact may explain why the film as a whole is less satisfying than the two *Raven* films. Hrafn Gunnlaugsson has delivered a cod western with a message, violating the narrative tradition referred to above from which he draws his inspiration. Hence he comes into conflict with the spirit of the source material for the film—the world of the sagas. In addition to this, there is also an interesting conflict within the movie, between realism and romanticism.

The White Viking contains many of the qualities of the *Raven* films. This is especially true of the scenes shot in Iceland, in which the director, true to tradition, lets action function as an integral part of character and environmental description. This harmonizes with the narrative tradition of the sagas. The laconic character of these scenes is far more apparent than in the scenes shot in Norway. There is also a comic quality in the Icelandic scenes totally lacking in the Norwegian scenes. Take, for instance, the scene where the white Viking Ask arrives in Iceland equipped with sword and cross, ready to convert the people at the first farmstead to which he is welcomed. Instead of meeting with fear or awe, resistance or submission, he receives largely the same attention as that offered to persistent Jehovah's Witnesses in contemporary society. His zealous religious campaign is quickly smothered between the thighs of the buxom farmer's wife, and he leaves the farm in a definitely lower key.

There is in this respect a marked difference in the scene changes between Norway and Iceland. The portrayal of Iceland Hrafn Gunnlaugsson offers to the viewer, is, in visual terms, akin to the Iceland portrayed in the *Raven* films—a country where people were barely able to survive, portrayed with a kind of rough saga realism that in many ways corresponds with the way the West is portrayed in Leone's films—as the dirty outskirts of civilization.

The contrast to the scenes shot in Norway is formidable and interesting. They remind the viewer more of scenes belonging to a Hollywood production such as *The Vikings* (1958), with its fjords, forests, glaciers, and waterfalls shot under glittery sunshine and bearing all the marks of a romanticized interpretation of landscape and the historical past. The tendency toward a romanticized visual appearance in the Norwegian scenes contrasts with the grim realism of the Icelandic scenes, creating an uneasy split in the material of the film.

At the time of its premiere, some critics speculated on the external reasons for the apparent duality of *The White Viking*. They overwhelmingly ascribed it to a similar intervention by outside forces as those that Sergio Leone had to endure in the case of *Once upon a Time in the West*. There may well be practical reasons for the ambiguous way the saga material has been handled in *The White Viking*. But the twofold quality of the film seems primarily to result from a tear in the narrative fabric, represented by the split between the action-oriented saga tradition and the wish to convey values in the form of a critique of civilization. This split turns out to be too much for the chosen format. In *The White Viking* Hrafn Gunnlaugsson has done what Egil Skallagrimsson and Sergio Leone never allowed themselves to do—let his feelings get the better of him.

ACTION-DRIVEN NARRATIVE
TRANSCENDING TIME AND GEOGRAPHY

Hrafn Gunnlaugsson's trilogy, when viewed in the context of Kurosawa and Leone, is a reminder of the stability of certain narrative forms over time and across geographical boundaries. The emphasis on action, the predominance of certain motifs, and the stability and apparent predictability of the characters make an interesting parallel to Vladimir

Propp's structural studies of Russian folklore in the first half of the twentieth century.

Propp's key element was the study of actions—or *functions* in his terminology—of the main characters as described in the vast and apparently diverse world of folktales from all over Russia. He maintained that the functions of characters serve as stable, constant elements in a tale, thus making them perfect as "building blocks" for tales, making way for a useful comparative instrument in the study of folktales regardless of their historical or geographical provenance (1968, 21). Propp's main conclusion was that "all fairy tales are of one type in regard to their structure" (23). This kind of structural approach can easily be applied to the films of Hrafn Gunnlaugsson, Akira Kurosawa, and Sergio Leone discussed in this essay. Whether the fictional world is the historical world of medieval Iceland, the Japanese Tokugawa shogunate, or the frontier period in North American history, each is a world based on similar action sequences, supporting Propp's argument that in terms of typology, tales with identical functions should be regarded as one type (22). As shown, Gunnlaugsson's experiment in expanding the type of narration in *The White Viking* led to a hybrid form generally regarded by audiences and critics as a deplorable departure from the original formula of his "Viking films."

This is a reminder that the apparently close ties to the narrative world of the Icelandic sagas to a large extent is founded on narrative structure rather than on historical markers, making the similarities to narratives based on Japanese and North American culture far from coincidental. Referring to the life-worlds of geographically and historically different societies, they nevertheless share a fictional world built on the principle of heroic action.

NOTES

1. Gunnlaugsson's films are neither the only nor the first attempt to use the rich narrative material of the Icelandic sagas in cinema. In 1981 Águst Gudmundsson (who in the previous year had made the first Icelandic feature film, *Land and Sons* (*Land og synir*), made an adaptation of the action-filled *Saga of Gisle Sursson* with the title *Outlaw* (*Utlaginn*), a film that in many ways paved the way for *When the Raven Flies*.
2. As an aside, it may be worth mentioning that Hrafn Gunnlaugsson on one occasion served as a guide for the blind Argentine poet laureate during a visit to Thingvellir, the ancient parliament of the Icelanders (Sjögren 1991).

3. The Althing was the yearly assembly of Icelandic clansmen held to make, uphold, and execute law in Viking times. See Byock's *Viking Age Iceland* for a helpful discussion of the Althing and its social context (2001, especially 170–206). An account of the debate at the Althing about converting is included in the *Book of the Icelanders* (*Islandingarbók*), and also in *Njál's Saga* (1955, chapters 100–5.)

WORKS CITED

Bazin, André. 1971. *What Is Cinema?* Vol. 2. Trans. and selected Hugh Gray. Berkeley: University of California Press.
Borges, Jorge Luis. 1969. *Den norrøne litteratur.* Trans. Hans Erich Lampl and Niels Magnus Bugge. Oslo: Cappelen.
Byock, Jesse. 2001. *Viking Age Iceland.* New York: Penguin.
Chandler, Raymond. 1949. *Farewell, My Lovely.* Harmondsworth: Penguin.
Egil's Saga. 1975. Trans. and ed. Christine Fell. London: Dent.
Njál's Saga. 1955. Trans. Carl F. Bayerschmidt and Lee M. Hollander. New York: New York University Press.
Olgeirsson, Einar. 1968. *Fra ættesamfunn til klassestat.* Trans. Roar Bugge. Oslo: Ny Dag.
Propp, Vladimir. 1968. *Morphology of the Folktale.* Austin: University of Texas Press.
Sjögren, Olle. 1991. "De oklippte vikingen: Ett samtal om vårt nordiska våldsarv med Hrafn Gunnlaugsson." *Filmhäftet* 73–74 (June).

Contributors

Ib Bondebjerg is professor of cinema in the Department of Film and Media Studies, University of Copenhagen. Among publications he has coauthored and edited are *Media and Culture in a Changing Europe* (2002), *The Danish Directors: Dialogues on a Contemporary National Cinema* (2001), *Moving Images, Culture, and the Mind* (2000), *Intertextuality and Visual Media* (1999), and *Television in Scandinavia: History, Aesthetics, and Politics* (1996). Bondebjerg has served as director of the Center for Media and Democracy in the Network Society (2002–5) and, together with Peter Golding, as codirector of the European Science Foundation Research Project "Changing Media—Changing Europe" (2000–5). He was also chairman of the Danish Film Institute from 1997 to 2000.

Pil Gundelach Brandstrup is an independent scholar and TV journalist working in Copenhagen. She holds an M.A. degree in film studies from the Institute of Film and Media Studies, University of Copenhagen, where she has also taught on Danish cinema and globalization. She was a Fulbright Scholar at the University of Wisconsin–Madison in 1998–99. She is currently working in television production as a journalist and producer. She has authored or coauthored articles on Danish cinema for *Nationale spejlinger: Tendenser i ny dansk film* (2003), the Danish Film Institute magazine *FILM,* and other publications.

Thomas A. DuBois is professor of Finnish studies and folklore in the Department of Scandinavian Studies, University of Wisconsin–Madison. He has published extensively on Finnish and Nordic folklore and literature, including *Finnish Folk Poetry and the Kalevala* (1995), *Finnish Folklore* (2000), coauthored with Leea Virtanen, and *Nordic Religions in the Viking Age* (1999). His more than thirty published articles also include research on cinema and folklore, including "Folklore, Boundaries, and Audience in *The Pathfinder,*" *Sami Folkloristics* (2001).

CONTRIBUTORS

Trevor G. Elkington is assistant professor of English and cultural studies in the Department of English, University of Copenhagen. He is currently working on a study titled *Subworld: New Media and Underground Globalization*. His essays include "Crossing Over: New Queer Cinema, Independent Film, and the Anxiety of the Mainstream," *Kosmorama* (2002); "Costumes and Dogma: Danish Film in the United States," in *Nationale spejlinger: Tendenser i ny dansk film* (2003); and "Teknologi og virkelighed—I teori og praksis," *Kosmorama* (2002). He is also author of an article on Ebbe Kløvedal Reich, published in the *Dictionary of Literary Biography*, vol. 214.

Mette Hjort is senior lecturer in the Department of Intercultural Studies, University of Aalborg, and associate professor in the Department of Comparative Literature, University of Hong Kong. Previously, she was for many years director of cultural studies at McGill University. Hjort is the author of *The Strategy of Letters* (1993). She coauthored with Ib Bondebjerg *The Danish Directors: Dialogues on a Contemporary National Cinema* (2001). She is also editor or coeditor of *Purity and Provocation: Dogme 95* (2003), *The Postnational Self* (2002), *Cinema and Nation* (2000), *Emotion and the Arts* (1997), and *Rules and Conventions* (1992). A book on contemporary Danish cinema, focusing on small-nation issues in the context of globalization, is near completion.

Gunnar Iversen is professor of film studies in the Department of Drama, Film, and Media Studies at the Norwegian University of Science and Technology, Trondheim, where he teaches courses on European, North American, and Asian film history. His books include *Tancred Ibsen og den norske gullalderen* (1993) and *Den italienske neorealismen* (1987); coauthored volumes include *Virkelighetsbilder: Norsk dokumentarfilm gjennom hundre år* (2001) and *Nordic National Cinemas* (1998). He has also served as coeditor of a number of books, including *Nærbilder: Artikler om norsk filmhistorie* (1997).

Birgir Thor Møller is an independent scholar and freelance stage manager associated with Metronome Production, based in Copenhagen. Born in Iceland, Møller moved to Denmark in 1983. He holds an M.A. in film studies from the Institute of Film and Media Studies, University of Copenhagen. He has published articles and interviews related to Nordic and Icelandic film history in a variety of publications, including *Kosmorama*.

Andrew Nestingen is assistant professor in the Department of Scandinavian Studies, University of Washington, where he teaches Finnish studies, Scandinavian cinema, and cultural theory. He is currently completing a book titled *Criminal Scandinavia: Genre, Social Imaginaries, and the Welfare State*. Recent articles include "Nostalgias and Their Publics: The Finnish Film Boom" (2003), *Scandinavian Studies;* "Timely Subjects: Leena Krohn, Temporalities, and Gender" (2004), *Scandinavian Studies;* and "Leaving Home: Global Circulation and Kaurismäki's *Ariel*" (2002), *Journal of Finnish Studies.*

Mervi Pantti is research fellow in the Department of Communication at the University of Helsinki. She is currently completing a book titled *Media markkinoilla* (2004). Her book *"Kansallinen elokuva pelastettava"—Elokuvapoliittinen keskustelu kotimaisen elokuvan tukemisesta itsenäisyyden ajalla* (2000) is the first history of Finnish state support of cinema. She has published numerous scholarly articles on national cinema, media policy, and young people and popular television, in both English and Finnish. She also works as a television critic for *Helsingin Sanomat*, Finland's largest daily, and contributes regularly on cinema and television to several Finnish magazines and newspapers.

Eva Novrup Redvall is an independent scholar, curator, and journalist. She holds an M.A. degree in film studies from the Institute of Film and Media Studies, University of Copenhagen, where she has been teaching graduate courses on Nordic film and narrative strategies since 2001. She coedited the anthology *I billedet er alt muligt* (2000) and has contributed to other anthologies on Danish film, most recently *Nationale spejlinger: Tendenser i ny dansk film* (2003). She is a regular contributor on cinema to numerous Danish film magazines and has served as film critic for the newspaper *Information* since 1999.

Linda Haverty Rugg is associate professor of literature and cinema in the Department of Scandinavian, University of California–Berkeley. She is currently working on a book titled *The Auteur's Autograph: Cinematic Auteurism and Autobiography.* Her prizewinning *Picturing Ourselves: Photography and Autobiography* was published in 1997. Selected articles include "Herzog's Kinski and Bergman's Liv: Cinematic Auteurism and the Shadow of the Vampire," in *Comunicación y sociedad* (2001); "Writing on the Body: Scars as Metaphor for the Break between Analog and Digital Representation," in *Sensuality and Power in Visual Culture*

(2001); and "'Carefully I Touched the Faces of My Parents': Bergman's Autobiographical Image," in *Biography* (2001). Her work has also appeared in *Scandinavian Studies, Seminar,* and *Literature/Film Quarterly.*

Peter Schepelern is associate professor of cinema at the Institute for Film and Media Studies, University of Copenhagen. His single-author publications include *Lars von Triers film: Tvang og befrielse* (2000), *Lars von Triers elementer* (rev. ed., 1997), and *Den fortællende film* (1972). He is editor and coauthor of *100 års dansk film* (2001), *Filmleksikon* (1995), and *Tommen: Carl Th. Dreyers filmjournalistiske virksomhed* (1982). Since 1997 he has served as editor of the Danish film periodical *Kosmorama*. His has also taught in the United States as a visiting scholar at the University of Southern California (1983–84 and 1987–88).

Bjørn Sørenssen is professor of cinema in the Department of Art and Media Studies, Norwegian University of Science and Technology, Trondheim. His books include *"Gryr i norden": Norsk arbeiderfilm 1928–1940 i internasjonalt perspektiv* (1980), *Kinoens mørke, fjernsynets lys* (coauthor, 1996), and *Å fange virkeligheten: Dokumentarfilmens århundre* (2001). He has published articles on film history, documentaries, and new media technology in several Nordic and English-language anthologies as well as in *Filmavisen, Film History, The Velvet Light Trap, Z,* and other periodicals. He has taught and done research at the University of North Carolina–Chapel Hill (1983–84), the University of Texas (1994–95), and the University of California–Santa Barbara (1987–89 and 2000–1).

Rochelle Wright is professor of Scandinavian, cinema studies, comparative literature, and women's studies at the University of Illinois–Champaign-Urbana. Her most recent book is *The Visible Wall: Jews and Other Ethnic Outsiders in Swedish Film* (1998). Essays on Ingmar Bergman, Alf Sjöberg, and Swedish national cinema have appeared in books as well as in *Purdue Film Studies Annual, Filmhäftet,* and *Scandinavian Studies.* She has also published widely on literary topics.

Index

Aakeson, Kim Fupz, 96, 97, 98
Abish, Walter, 76
Abrahamsen, Svend, 84, 148
Abramson, Hans, *Benjamin*, 58
Abril, Victoria, 330
Academy Award, 36, 37, 38, 40, 42
ACE. *See* Atelier du Cinéma Européens
Action film, 39, 266–67, 344, 350, 354
Actors/cast: and Axel, 206, 310; and Bergman, 230; of Bornedal's *Dina*, 213; and Carlsen's *Wolf at the Door,* 204; and coproduction, 143, 151, 153, 154, 156–57, 197, 198, 199, 211, 212; and Danish film, 132, 133; director as, 228, 240; and Dogma 95, 83, 98; in Finnish film, 188; in Kaurismäki, 296; in Leigh and Cumming's *The Anniversary Party,* 49; in Swedish immigrant film, 60; of Troell's *Hamsun,* 3, 4–5; in Vinterberg, 87. *See also* Filmmaking
Aesthetics: and American independent film, 44; of auteur, 222; and Danish film, 122, 124; and Dogma 95, 73, 75, 84, 87, 101–2; of Pölönen, 252; sixties movements against, 81; in von Trier, 88, 89. *See also* Art
Ahokas, Harri, 181
Aitio, Tommi, 284
Alarcón, Norma, *Between Women and Nation,* 13
Albarn, Damon, 330
Albee, Edward, 87
Alfvén, Hugo, 199, 200
Alienation, 74, 322, 325
Allen, Woody, 233–39, 240; *Crimes and Misdemeanors,* 236–39; *Hollywood Ending,* 240; *Interiors,* 236; *Love and Death,* 235; *Radio Days,* 312; *Shadows and Fog,* 233; *Stardust Memories,* 240
Allende, Isabel, *House of Spirits,* 132
Allers, Roger, *The Lion King,* 7
Almodóvar, Pedro, 325, 330
Altman, Rick, *Film/Genre,* 287, 288, 289–90
Altman, Robert: *Nashville,* 43; *Short Cuts,* 43
American Zoetrope, 317
Amis, Martin, 76
Ancher, Anna, 199, 200
Ancher, Michael, 199, 200
Andersen, Jesper, 201, 206, 210
Anderson, Paul Thomas, *Magnolia,* 41
Anderson, Wes, *Rushmore,* 41
Andersson, Bibi, 229
Ang Lee, *Crouching Tiger, Hidden Dragon,* 40
Anselmo, Giovanni, 81
Anti-Semitism, in Swedish film, 56–57, 58–59, 59, 61
Arnfred, Morten, 89; *Johnny Larsen,* 90; *Me and Charly (Mig og Charly),* 90; *Night Vision (Spor i mørket),* 150; *The Russian Singer (Den russiske sangerinde),* 153
Art, 82; and auteur, 225; classical conceptions of, 81; collaborative, 239; and Danish film, 114, 118; and Dogma 95, 74, 93; Finnish film as, 165, 167, 169, 170, 172, 182, 183, 184, 187, 188, 189; and Norwegian film, 263; state investment in, 11. *See also* Aesthetics
Artaud, Antonin, 81
Arte povera, 81
Arteta, Miguel, *Chuck and Buck,* 48
Art film: and coproductions, 152; Danish, 118, 119, 120, 121, 122–23, 125, 128, 132; defined, 24n. 14; European, 118;

INDEX

Art film *(continued)*
and Finnish film, 181; and Icelandic film, 312; and Kaurismäki, 283, 286; market for, 34; and Norwegian film, 265, 267; rise of, 11; and von Trier, 133–34

Art film festival network, 136

Art film theater, 36, 51

Arthy, Natasha: *Mirakel (Miracle)*, 98; *Old, New, Borrowed, and Blue (Se til venstre, der er en svensker)*, 85, 94, 98

Artista Filmi, 177

ASA, 114–15, 117

Astala, Erkki, 165, 172, 177, 189

Astruc, Alexandre, "The Birth of a New Avant-Garde: La caméra-stylo," 79

Atelier du Cinéma Européens, 147

Audience: in Allen-Bergman relationship, 239; American, 33, 35, 37–38, 39–52; auteur's link with, 225; of Axel's *Prince of Jutland*, 206; and Bergman, 224–25, 231, 232, 240; of Bornedal's *Dina*, 214, 215; of Carlsen's *Wolf at the Door*, 204–5; of coproductions, 143, 153, 155, 158, 159, 195, 197, 199, 200–202, 203, 207–9, 212, 214, 215; and culture, 8; and Danish film, 122; and Dogma 95, 93; of European film, 185; of Fares, 66; and Finnish film, 166, 172, 173, 174–75, 178, 179, 181, 183, 185, 187, 188; of Fridriksson, 313, 318, 321, 326, 327; for Gaup's *Pathfinder*, 269, 272–73; Generation X as, 41; and genre, 286–87; and global marketing, 31–32; global vs. national, 203; and Godard, 240; of Grede's *Hip, Hip, Hurra!*, 201; of heritage film, 201–2; and Icelandic film, 310, 312; of independent films, 41; of Kaurismäki, 282–83, 288, 289, 292, 295; of Kragh-Jacobsen, 48; national, 208; and national cinema, 13, 282; national vs. transnational, 6–8; and Nordic Film and TV Fund, 194; and Norwegian film, 261, 263–64, 265, 267, 276; of Pölönen, 243, 244, 250, 252, 255, 256, 257, 258; research on, 22; of road movies, 291; of Soderbergh, 40; of Swedish film, 59, 60; and transnationalism, 2, 193, 212; of Troell's *Hamsun*, 4, 5; and Truffaut, 225–26, 226, 227. *See also* Market

August, Billie, 123, 133; *The Best Intentions (Den goda viljan)*, 38, 133, 150, 154, 158; and coproductions, 150, 152–53, 154, 211; as cross-over director, 8; *Honey Moon (Honning måne)*, 90; *House of Spirits (Åndernes hus)*, 7, 45, 132, 152; *Jerusalem*, 133, 154, 158, 213; *Les misérables*, 132; *Pelle the Conqueror (Pelle Erobreren)*, 5, 35–37, 38, 39, 42, 111, 131, 133, 141, 143, 195, 196; *Smilla's Sense of Snow (Frøken Smillas fornemmelse for sne)*, 45, 132, 152; *Twist and Shout (Tro, håb og kærlighed)*, 39; and von Trier, 133–34

Auteur: and Allen, 236; and assimilation, 240; and Bergman, 232; and Dogma 95, 74; and Finnish film, 176, 179, 186, 284; and globalization, 221; Kaurismäki as, 283, 284; and language, 234, 240; link with audience of, 225; and national culture, 221–22; politics of, 222–23; Soderbergh as, 40; and Truffaut, 222–23, 225, 228–29, 230. *See also* Director

Authenticity, and Kaurismäki, 296–97, 300, 301, 302

Autobiography: and Bergman, 229; and Truffaut, 226–28

Avant-garde, 81, 82, 102

Axel, Gabriel, 123, 142; *Babette's Feast (Babettes gæstebud)*, 5, 35–37, 38, 42, 111, 131, 133, 141, 142–43, 269; *The Prince of Jutland (Prinsen af Jylland)*, 153, 205–6, 207; *The Red Mantle (Den røde kappe)*, 310, 316

Bacon, Henry, 290, 295, 301

Bagh, Peter von, *Guide to the Cinema of Sweden and Finland*, 12

Bagher, Reza, *Wings of Glass (Vingar av glas)*, 55, 65–66, 68, 70

Balling, Eric, 114; *The Girl Gogo (79 af stödinni)*, 310, 322; *The Olsen Gang (Olsen-banden)*, 116; *The Olsen Gang (Olsen-banden)* series, 116, 117, 118; *The Olsen Gang Outta Sight (Olsen-banden deruda)*, 117; *The Olsen Gang Sees*

INDEX

Red (Olsen-banden ser rødt), 117
Barba, Eugenio, 82
Barr, Jean-Marc, *Lovers*, 99
Barsotti, Carlo, *A Paradise without Billiards (Ett paradis utan biljard)*, 60
Barth, John, 76
Barthes, Roland, 224
Bay, Michael, *Armageddon*, 9
Bazin, André, 84, 350
Belvaux, Remy, *Man Bites Dog (C'est arrivé près de chez vous)*, 102
Benediktsson, Einar Örn, 330
Bergenstråhle, Johan: *A Baltic Tragedy (Baltutlämningen)*, 59; *Foreigners (Jag heter Stelios)*, 60
Bergfelder, Tim, 191
Bergman, Ingmar, 133; and Allen, 233; and coproductions, 150; and French New Wave, 223; Godard on, 229; on Parsa, 69; reception of, 221; self exhibition in, 239–40; and Truffaut, 227–28, 239; WORKS: *Cries and Whispers*, 236; *Fanny and Alexander (Fanny och Alexander)*, 59; *Illicit Interlude (Sommarlek)*, 234; *Magic Lantern*, 233; *Persona*, 78, 229–32, 236, 240; *Summer with Monika (Sommaren med Monika)*, 227, 228, 233, 239; *The Magician (Ansiktet)*, 233; *The Naked Night (Gycklarnas afton)*, 234; *The Serpent's Egg*, 59; *The Seventh Seal (Det sjunde inseglet)*, 234, 235; *The Touch (Beröringen)*, 59; *Wild Strawberries (Smultronstället)*, 234, 236, 238, 239, 321; *Winter Light (Nattvardsgästerna)*, 78
Bertelsson, Thráinn, 337n. 4; *Deep Winter (Skammdegi)*, 313; *Magnús*, 315; *New Life (Nýt líf)*, 315; *Pastoral Life (Dalalíf)*, 315; *A Policeman's Life (Löggulíf)*, 315
Biancaniello, Matthew, *The Breadbasket*, 100–101
Bier, Susanne: and coproduction, 209–10, 212; *Credo*, 157; *Family Matters (Det blir i familien)*, 156, 210; *Freud Leaving Home (Freud flyttar hemifrån)*, 61, 158; *Like It Never Was Before (Pensionat Oskar)*, 150, 158; *once and a lifetime (Hånden på hjertet)*, 150; *The One and Only (Den eneste ene)*, 128; *Open Hearts (Elsker dig for evigt)*, 50, 85, 96, 97, 98, 210
Björk, 307, 313
Blixen, Karen (Isak Dinesen), 133
Bly, Robert, *Iron John*, 252–53, 254, 255, 256
Boncel, André, *Man Bites Dog (C'est arrivé près de chez vous)*, 102
Bonnevie, Marie, 213, 215
Boorman, John, *Deliverance*, 268
Bordwell, David, 24n. 14
Borges, Jorge Luis, 76, 344–45
Bornedal, Ole: *I Am Dina (Jeg er Dina)*, 134, 153, 196, 199, 209, 212–15, 216; *Nattevagten (Nightwatch)*, 8–9, 45, 136–37
Bostrup, Charlotte Sachs, 97
Brandstrup, Pil Gundelach, 194
Brecht, Bertolt, 80, 81
Bresson, Robert, *A Man Escaped (Un condamné à mort s'est échappé)*, 78
Bruñel, Luis, 223
Budget: and coproduction, 148, 151, 159; and Danish film, 120, 121–22, 131, 175; and Dogma 95, 84; of Finnish films, 175, 178; for Gaup's *Pathfinder*, 269; and Nordic Film and TV Fund, 194; of Nordic films, 6. *See also* Cost; Funding/finance; Profit
Buena Vista, 176, 266
Byun, Daniel H., *Interview (Intyebyo)*, 99

Cahiers du cinéma, 79, 222, 223
Calvino, Italo, 76
Camera: and Dogma 95, 73, 83, 87, 91, 99, 102; in Truffaut, 227; Ullmann on, 230–31; and Von Trier, 77. *See also* Filmmaking
Cameraman, and Bergman, 230, 231–32
Cameron, James, *Titanic*, 6, 126
Campbell, Martin, *Golden Eye*, 128
Camre, Henning, 145
Capitalism, 169, 293
Capra, Frank, *It's a Wonderful Life*, 286, 293
Carlsen, Henning, 142, 209; *A Happy Divorce (En lykkelig skilsmisse)*, 161n.1; *Hunger (Sult)*, 118, 143, 154;

363

Carlsen, Henning (*continued*)
  I Wonder Who's Kissing You Now, 157;
  Two Green Feathers (Pan), 38, 155, 195–96, 215–16; *We Are All Demons (Klabautermanden),* 143; *The Wolf at the Door (Oviri),* 142, 143, 195, 203–5, 206, 209, 215
Cassavetes, John, 80–81; *Husbands,* 80; *A Woman Under the Influence,* 80, 96
Cattaneo, Peter, *The Full Monty,* 257
Celant, Germano, 81
Censorship, 48
Chabrol, Claude, 79, 101; *The Cousins (Les cousins),* 88; *The Good Girls (Les bonnes femmes),* 88
Chandler, Raymond, 347; *Farewell, My Lovely,* 348
Children's film, 122, 312
Christensen, Benjamin, 10
Christensen, Bo, 162n.17
Christensen, Mads Egmont, "Dogma and Marketing," 50–51
Cinema sector, 36, 51; Danish, 119, 120, 121; Norwegian, 262, 263–64; and ticket cost, 263–64, 312
Cinema verité, 225
Circulation, homophilic, 210–11
Clark, Larry, *Kids,* 48, 99
Clausen, Erik, 137
Cocteau, Jean, *Beauty and the Beast (Belle et la Bête),* 43
Cofinancing. *See* Funding/finance
Cole, Tristan de vere, *The Dive (Dykket),* 266
Columbia TriStar Egmont, 176
Columbus, Chris, *Harry Potter,* 128
Comedy: and coproduction, 158; and Danish film, 115, 117; and Finnish film, 188; and Fridriksson, 324; and Icelandic film, 309, 312, 315
Coming-of-age film, 38–39, 40, 272
Commodification, 170, 293, 294, 296, 302
Communicative space, 199, 209, 211
Consultant system, 124–25
Coppola, Francis Ford, 317
Coproduction: actors in, 143, 151, 153, 154, 156–57, 197, 198, 199, 211, 212; audience of, 143, 153, 155, 158, 159, 195, 197, 199, 200–202, 203, 207–9, 212, 214, 215; and August, 196; Bier on, 209–10; Carlsen on, 209; and content, 197–99; creative control of, 149–50; crew of, 150; and culture, 144, 145, 149–50, 159–60, 198, 202, 208, 209, 210, 211; and Danish film, 131, 132, 194; and Denmark, 211; director of, 198, 199, 211, 212; distribution of, 198, 216n.1; and economy, 148–49, 196–97; European, 132; funding of, 142, 144, 148–49, 151–52, 155, 156, 159, 160, 198, 209; and globalization, 211; and Gunnlaugsson, 341; and heritage, 195, 197; history of, 191; and Icelandic film, 309, 310, 317; Kragh-Jacobsen on, 211; and language, 142, 150, 151, 152, 153, 154–55, 161, 162n.17, 195; and national culture, 202, 214; and nationality, 143, 214; natural, 196, 197, 198, 199, 201, 202, 203; and natural investment, 196–97; and Nordic Film and TV Fund, 196, 197, 198, 199; and Norway, 211; prevalence of Nordic, 192; and producer, 197, 198, 199, 211, 212; and production, 197, 216n.1; self-defeating, 199–209; and Sweden, 150, 151, 154, 160, 211; and television, 211; and transnationalism, 193
Corrigan, Timothy, *A Cinema without Walls,* 291, 292–93, 295, 300
Cost: for Finnish film, 166; of Finnish films, 175; and Norwegian film, 264, 267; and transnationalism, 193. *See also* Budget; Funding/finance; Profit
Costner, Kevin, *Dances with Wolves,* 7
Costume drama genre. *See* Historic film/costume drama genre
Country-city theme, 307, 308, 312–13, 314, 320, 322, 323, 329
Cove, George, *De Düva,* 235
Cowboy, 245, 249, 268
Cowie, Peter, 12, 272
Crime film, 115, 266–67, 268, 294
Crossroads, 287–88, 289, 290, 291, 292, 295, 300, 322
Cruz-Malave, Arnaldo, *Queer Globalizations,* 13
Cultural authenticity, 199

INDEX

Cultural ownership, 195, 199
Culture: in Allen-Bergman relationship, 238–39; ambiguity of national, 13; American, 33, 323; and audience, 8; and auteur, 221–22, 225, 240; and Axel's *Prince of Jutland,* 206; in Bagher, 66; and Carlsen's *Wolf at the Door,* 204; and coproductions, 144, 145, 149–50, 159–60, 195, 197, 198, 202, 208, 209, 210, 211; and Danish film, 112, 115, 116, 118, 120, 121, 131, 146; epiphanic, 192, 193, 198, 203, 209, 210, 211, 212; and European film, 128, 184, 185; and Fares's *Jalla! Jalla!,* 8; and Finland, 168, 169, 170, 171, 179–80, 181, 183, 186–87, 189, 281–82, 297, 300, 302; and Fridriksson, 318, 319, 320, 323, 324–25, 332; and Gaup's *Pathfinder,* 270–72, 273, 274; and genre, 287, 289; global, 276; and globalization, 33; and government funding, 31; and Grede's *Hip, Hip, Hurra!,* 201; and Gunnlaugsson, 341, 342, 350–55; and historic film, 8; homogeneity of, 13–14; hybrid, 191, 193, 209, 214, 215, 297; and Iceland, 307, 308, 311, 312–14, 318, 319, 320, 322, 323, 324–25, 329–31, 332; and Kaurismäki, 284, 285, 286, 288, 290, 292, 293, 294, 295, 297–98, 299, 300–301, 302; local, 276; and market, 7; and marketing, 31, 32; and migration, 15; and national cinema, 13; and nation-based categorization, 1; and Norwegian film, 276–77; popular, 248–49, 293, 295, 300, 314, 319, 323; in road movies, 293; state investment in, 11; and Sweden, 8, 59, 63, 64, 68, 70; and transnational production, 2; and Troell's *Hamsun,* 3. *See also* Heritage; History; Society
Cumming, Alan, *The Anniversary Party,* 49

Dale, Martin, *Europa, Europa,* 145, 184
Danish coproduction, 131, 132
Danish film, 111–38, 141–61, 180, 194, 263. *See also specific directors*
Danish Film Board, 112, 124
Danish Filmfond (Film Fund), 114, 119
Danish Film Institute, 84, 85, 112–13, 120, 122, 124, 125, 142, 145, 153–54, 162n.14, 193, 210
Danish Film Museum, 112
Danish Film School, 111, 112, 119
Danish Film Studio, 120
Danish Film Workshop (Danske Filmværksted), 120
Danish New Wave, 44, 111, 117, 118, 123
Danish Short Film Council, 119
Danish Short Film Fund (Dansk Novellefilm), 123, 125
Danish workshop system, 125
Dansk Kulturfilm (Danish Culture Films), 114
Davies, Terence, 81
DeMille, Cecil B., *The Squaw Man,* 349
Demy, Jacques, 76
Denationalization, 192, 195, 215
Denmark: and August, 196; and Axel's *Prince of Jutland,* 206; and Bornedal's *Dina,* 213, 214, 215; and coproductions, 150, 154, 211; Danish Media Desk, 146; domestic cinema of, 6; economy of, 14; and Europe, 147; and Finnish films, 175; and globalized market, 1; migration to, 15; Ministry of Cultural Affairs, 162n.14; and public film policy, 113; and public support, 118, 119, 121, 124–26; race/ethnicity in, 15; Statens Film Central (National Film Board), 114; Talent Film Fund (Talentudviklingspuljen), 125
Denmark's Radio (DR), 124, 125
De Sica, Vittorio, *Bicycle Thieves,* 286, 293
Diesen, Trygve Allister, *The Isle of Darkness (Mørkets øy),* 158, 268
Dinesen, Isak. *See* Blixen, Karen (Isak Dinesen)
Director: as actor, 228, 240; auteur as, 221; in Bergman, 230, 231–32; Bornedal as, 8; and coproduction, 198, 199, 211, 212; and Danish film, 132; and Dogma 95, 74, 77–78; and Finnish film, 176, 185–86, 188, 189; Norwegian, 276; von Trier as, 89. *See also* Auteur; Filmmaking
Distribution: of coproductions, 147, 198, 216n. 1; and Danish film, 113, 120, 121,

365

Distribution (*continued*)
126; of European film, 147; and Finnish film, 167, 172, 175–76, 177, 182, 185; and Gaup's *Pathfinder*, 269, 273–74; global, 31, 39; and Kaurismäki, 283; and Nordic Film and TV Fund, 211; of Norwegian film, 262; in United States, 31–52

Documentary, 83; Danish, 114, 119, 120, 122, 124, 125; and Finnish film, 171; by Fridriksson, 317

Dodd, Carley H., *Dynamics of Intercultural Communication*, 210

Dogma 95, 73–103, 111; and art house circuit, 51; and coproduction, 148, 159, 162n.13; and Danish film, 123, 126, 128; *D day (D dag)*, 91–92, 93; and festival circuit, 51; globalization of, 135–36; influence of, 9; international success of, 180; Manifesto of, 45, 84; transnational impact of, 45–52; Vow of Chastity of, 45, 48, 73–74, 75, 77, 78, 83, 87, 95. *See also specific directors*

Domenici, Antonia, *Diapason*, 100

Donner, Jörn, *Rooftree (Tvärbalk)*, 59

DR (Danish state television), 84–85, 86

Dreyer, Carl Th., 10, 114, 118; *The Passion of Joan of Arc (Le passion de Jeanne d'Arc)*, 43, 78; *They Reached the Ferry (De nåede færgen)*, 298

DuBois, Thomas A., 300–301

Duchamp, Marcel, 101

Duncan, Patrick, *84 Charlie Mopic*, 102

Dyer, Ricard, 212

Eastwood, Clint, *Pale Rider*, 274

EAVE. *See* European Audio-Visual Entrepreneurs

Ebert, Roger, 36, 43, 45–46, 50

Economy: American, 41; and coproduction, 148–49, 196–97; of Denmark, 14; and European film, 185; of Finland, 14, 167, 168, 169, 170, 171, 179–80, 186, 188, 189, 244, 245–46, 294, 297; and globalization, 14–15, 22; of Iceland, 14, 326, 328–29; in Kaurismäki, 294; and national cinema, 13, 282; of Norway, 14–15, 265; planned, 169; of Sweden, 14; and transnationalism, 193. *See also* Welfare state

Edda-film, 310

Edvardsson, Egill: *Agnes*, 316, 324; *The House (Húsid)*, 316

Egil's Saga, 344, 345–46, 349, 354

Einarson, Oddvar: *Blackout*, 267; *Karachi*, 267; *Turnaround*, 267

Elmer, Jonas, 137; *Let's Get Lost*, 43, 44, 102; *Mona's World (Monas verden)*, 103

Emmerich, Roland, *Independence Day*, 128, 327

Enquist, Per Olov, 155; *The Legionnaires (Legionärerna)*, 59

Erichsen, Bjørn, 85

Erlingsson, Gísli Snær: *Behind Schedule (Stuttur frakki)*, 315; *Benjamin dove (Benjamín dúfa)*, 315; *Ikingut*, 315

Eurimages program, 131, 142, 146–47, 148, 160, 205, 315

Europe: as context, 22; and coproductions, 146; and Danish film, 123, 126, 128, 131, 135, 147, 175; and Finnish film, 168, 169, 170, 171, 179, 183–86, 188; and Kaurismäki, 283; and Troell's *Hamsun*, 4; and United States, 144–45

European Audio-Visual Entrepreneurs, 147

European Council, 146–47

European film, 34, 37–38, 118, 135, 274

European New Wave, 116, 123

European Union: and Danish film, 121, 126, 128; of European film coproductions, 146; and Finnish film, 183–84; Media program of, 146–47, 183, 185

Excess, 294–95, 296, 300, 302

Fabro, Luciano, 81

Fagerström-Olsson, Agneta: *Hammarkullen, or See You in Kaliningrad (Hammarkullen eller Vi ses i Kalinengrad)*, 62; *Seppan*, 60

Faiman, Peter, *Crocodile Dundee*, 258

Family, 55, 65, 67–68, 97, 116, 133

Fares, Josef, *Jalla! Jalla!*, 7, 8, 55, 62–64, 66, 67, 68, 70, 71n.1

Far til fire series (Danish film series), 116

Fasbinder, Rainer Werner, 80

Faurschou, Jørn: *Body Switch (Farligt venskab)*, 157; *Night Vision, Albert*, 157

Faustman, Hampe, *Our Lord and the Tattare (Gud fader och tattaren)*, 58

Fellini, Federico, 228

INDEX

Fennada-Filmi, 10, 176
Feuerbach, Ludwig, 83
Figgis, Mike, 101; *Timecode,* 47, 92
Film: Bergman on illusory nature of, 224; commercial, 181, 183, 184; Danish, 111–38, 118, 141–61, 180; and Dogma 95, 74, 75, 83, 87; domestic, 10–11, 175–77; as entertainment, 114, 118, 169, 182, 183; European, 184; and fiction, 84; Finnish, 165–89, 243–58, 281–82; and history, 226; Icelandic, 307–32; Norwegian, 261–77; popular, 169, 172, 244, 248; Swedish, 55–70; and Truffaut, 225–26, 227; as universal language, 223. *See also specific directors*
Film City, 84
Film festivals, 34, 36, 51, 212, 311–12
Filmforderung Hamburg, 148
Filmhuset, 317
Film institute, 11
Film i Väst, 148, 163n.21
Filmmaking: and Bergman, 230–32, 233; collaboration in, 230, 232; and coproductions, 151; digital, 46–49; and Dogma 95, 73, 83, 85, 87, 91, 102; and Vinterberg, 87. *See also* Actors/cast; Camera; Director; Producer; Production; Setting
Film Museum, 119
Filmography, 11–12
Filmraadet (Film Council), 114
Film/TV fund, 123
Fincher, David, *Fight Club,* 41
Finland, 57, 58; and coproductions, 162n.15; domestic cinema of, 6; economy of, 14, 167, 168, 169, 170, 171, 179–80, 186, 188, 189, 244, 245–46, 294, 297; and globalized market, 1; men's studies movement in, 252; Ministry of Education, 170, 171–72; Ministry of Trade and Industry, 171; and national cinema, 281–86
Finney, Angus, 185, 186
Finnish Committee on Culture and Communication, 179
Finnish film, 165–89, 243–58, 281–82. *See also specific directors*
Finnish Film Foundation (Suomen elokuvasäätiö), 165, 166–67, 170, 171–72, 178, 179, 180, 181, 182, 183, 187, 188, 189, 282; *Objectives for the National Cinema,* 170, 177, 179, 182, 186
Finnish New Wave, 166, 187
Finnkino, 175
Flamholc, David, *Night Bus 807 (Nattbuss 807),* 61
Fleischer, Richard, *The Vikings,* 310, 354
Fleming, Victor, *The Virginian,* 349
Flinth, Peter, *Eye of the Eagle,* 162n.17
Fly, Per, *The Heritage (Arven),* 328
Folklustspel, 56
Ford, John, 223; *My Darling Clementine,* 349
Formalism, 76
Forman, Milos, *One Flew over the Cuckoo's Nest,* 318
Fredholm, Gert, *One-Hand Clapping (At klappe med en hånd),* 103
French cinema vérité, 83
French film, 128
French New Wave, 73, 79, 87–88, 223, 224
Fridell, Daniel, *Cry (30:e november),* 61
Fridriksson, Fridrik Thór, 279; *Angels of the Universe (Englar alheimsins),* 314, 317–19; biography of, 319; *Children of Nature (Börn náttúrunnar),* 308, 314, 320–23, 330; *Cold Fever (Á köldum klaka),* 23n. 6, 303n.10, 314, 320, 323–25, 332; and coproduction, 317; *Devil's Island (Djöflaeyjan),* 319–20, 321, 325–27, 328; *Falcons,* 330–32; *Icelandic Cowboys (Kúrekar Nordurins),* 314; influence of, 307, 308–9; and Jarmusch, 323; and Kristinsson, 316–17; *Movie Days (Bíódagar),* 319, 322, 323, 337n. 4; and Reykjavik film festival, 311, 312; *Rock in Reykjavik (Rokk í Reykjavík),* 313, 330; *The Saga of Burnt Njal (Brennu Njáls saga),* 313; *White Whales (Skytturnar),* 319, 328
Fromberg, Carsten, *Bad Seed (Ondt Blod),* 156
FS-Filmi, 176
Funding/finance: for Axel's *Prince of Jutland,* 205, 206; of coproductions, 142, 144, 148–49, 151–52, 155, 156, 159, 160, 198, 209; and culture, 11; and Danish film, 113, 118, 123, 124, 125–26, 263; and European film,

Funding/finance (*continued*)
146–48, 184; by Film i Väst, 163n.21; for Finnish film, 168, 169, 171–72, 175, 177, 181, 182, 183, 184, 185, 186–87, 188; and Fridriksson, 324; for Gaup's *Pathfinder,* 269; government, 31; and Icelandic film, 315–17; of Kaurismäki, 282; methods for, 24n. 16; multinational, 2; for national cinema, 10; by national film institutes, 11; and Nordic Film and TV Fund, 197, 211; and Norwegian film, 263–64, 265, 266, 276; pan-European sources of, 9; through cofinancing, 157–58, 209, 282, 324; of Troell's *Hamsun,* 2, 3, 4; of von Trier, 282. *See also* Budget; Cost; Profit

Gad, Mette, 203–4
Garbo, Greta, 10
Gardell, Jonas, 150
Gaugin, Paul, 203–4
Gaup, Nils: *Head above Water (Hodet over vannet),* 269; *Misery Harbour,* 38, 158, 270; *Nini,* 270; *Pathfinder (Veiviseren; Ofelas),* 39, 262, 267, 268–69, 270–76; *Shipwrecked (Håkon håonsen),* 269; *Tashunga (North Star),* 269
Gender, 55, 62, 63–64, 65–66, 243–44, 252–58. *See also* Sexuality; Women
Generation X, 41
Genre: and Danish film, 136; and Dogma 95, 74, 75, 95, 98; and Kaurismäki, 286–90, 293, 294–95, 300, 302; Norwegian, 261–77. *See also* Action film; Art film; Comedy; Coming-of-age film; Crime film; Documentary; Historic film/costume drama genre; Love story; Melodrama; Quest narrative; Road movie; Thriller genre; Western genre
Genz, Henrik Ruben, *Bror, min bror (Theis and Nico),* 94
German film, 128
Germany, 115, 160. *See also* Nazism
Gilardi, Piero, 81
Gilbert, Craig, *An American Family,* 83
Gillis, Andrew, *Security, Colorado,* 100
Gíslason, Óskar, *The Bakka Brothers in Reykjavik (Reykjavíkurævintýri Bakkabrœdra),* 309
Gislason, Tomas, *P.O.V.,* 102
Globalization: and American culture, 33; and auteur, 221; and coproductions, 146, 211; and Danish film, 122–38; and Denmark, 121; dynamics of, 191–216; and economy, 14–15, 22; and Finland, 281, 297; and Fridriksson, 325; and Hollywood, 9, 33, 193; in Kaurismäki, 294; kinds of, 192; and language, 16, 141; of market, 1–2; and national cinema, 15–16, 141; and Nordic cinema, 12; and Norwegian film, 276; research on, 12; and studio system, 8, 9; as threat, 8; transformation through, 14; and transnationalism, 192–93; and United States, 9. *See also* International orientation; Transnationalism
Godard, Jean-Luc, 76, 79; *Band of Outsiders (Band à part),* 88; on Bergman, 223, 224–25, 229; "Bergmanorama," 223; *Breathless (A bout de souffle),* 79, 88; *British Sounds,* 80; *La chinoise,* 80; and international cinema, 223; *The Joy of Knowledge (Le gai savoir),* 80; *Pierrot le fou,* 88; *Pravada,* 80; on time, 226, 227, 228; *Vent d'est,* 80; *A Woman Is a Woman (Un femme est une femme),* 88
Godzich, Wlad, 214
Goldcrest, 266
Gorin, Jean-Piere, 80
Göteborg Film Festival, 212
Government/state: and Danish film, 111–12, 114; and Dogma 95, 84; and Finnish film, 165–66, 167–68, 169, 170, 171, 175, 177, 179, 186, 188; funding from, 31; and Norwegian film, 263–64, 265. *See also* Law; Politics; Tax; Welfare state
Gowariker, Ashutosh, *Lagaan,* 40
Gråbøl, Sofie, 158, 204
Grede, Kjell: *Good Evening, Mr. Wallenberg (God afton, herr Wallenberg),* 38, 61; *Hip, Hip, Hurra!,* 195, 199–202, 203, 206, 209, 215
Greenaway, Peter: *The Draughtsman's Contract,* 76; *Drowning by Numbers,* 77
Grønlykke, Jakob: *Heart of Light (Lysets*

INDEX

hjerte), 156
Grønlykke, Lene, 117, 118
Grønlykke, Sven, 117, 118
Grotowski, Jerry, *Towards a Poor Theatre*, 81–82
Groupe Dziga Vertov, 80
Gudmundsson, Ágúst, 337n. 4; *Land and Sons (Land og synir)*, 308, 312, 315, 322, 328; *Outlaw, the Saga of Gísli (Útlaginn)*, 316, 355n. 1
Gudmundsson, Loftur, *Between Mountain and Shore (Milli fjalls og fjöru)*, 309
Gudmundsson, Már, 320; *Angels of the Universe (Englar alheimsins)*, 317
Gullestad, Marianne, 15
Gunnarson, Gunnar, *The Story of the Borg Family (Borgslægtens historie)*, 329
Gunnlaugsson, Hrafn, 348; *Father's Estate (Óðal feðranna)*, 312, 313, 322; *Flight of the Raven (Sjögren)*, 345; *Inter Nos (Okkar á Milli—Í hita og þunga dagsins)*, 314, 337n. 4; *Lilja*, 311; *Raven films*, 352, 353, 354; *The Sacred Mound (Hin helgu Vé)*, 312; *The Shadow of the Raven (Í skugga hrafnsins)*, 341, 342; *When the Raven Flies (Hrafninn flýgur)*, 311, 316, 341–42, 344, 346, 349; *The White Viking (Den hvite Viking)*, 341, 342, 350–54, 355
Gustavson, Eric: *Blackout*, 266; *Weekend*, 268
Gyorski, Vladimir, *Resin*, 100

Halldórsdóttir, Gudný: *Honour of the House (Ungfrúin góða og húsið)*, 315; *Men's Choir (Karlakórinn hekla)*, 315; *Stella í Orlofi (The Icelandic Shock Station)*, 337n. 4
Halle, Randall, *Camera Obscura*, 13
Hallström, Lasse, 8; *My Life as a Dog (Mitt liv som hund)*, 39, 312
Hamer, Bent, *Eggs*, 43, 267
Hamlerich, Rumle, *Sort Lucia (Black Lucia)*, 158
Hammett, Dashiell, *The Glass Key*, 346, 347
Hamsun, Knut, 3–4, 154, 155; *Hunger (Sult)*, 143, 203; *På gjengrodde stier (On Overgrown Paths)*, 4

Hannula, Mika, 284
Hansen, Bo hr., 87
Hansen, Thorkild, *Processen mod Hamsun*, 3
Harlin, Reny, 8; *Cliffhanger*, 9; *Die Hard 2*, 9
Hartley, Hal, 81, 317; *No Such Thing (Monsters)*, 303n.10, 317; *Trust*, 43; *The Unbelievable Truth*, 43
Hawks, Howard, 223
Hedegaard, Tom, *The Olsen Gang—Final Mission (Olsen Bandens sidste stik)*, 157
Heinämaa, Sara, 285, 290
Helgason, Hallgrímur, *101 Reykjavík*, 330
Helgeland, Axel, 213
Helismaa, Reino: *The Brother of the Logger of the West (Lännen lokarin veli)*, 248; *Rovaniemen markinoilla (At the Rovaniemi Market)*, 247–48
Hellström, Gunnar, *Simon the Sinner (Simon Syndaren)*, 58
Henning-Jensen, Astrid, 114
Henning-Jensen, Bjarne, 114, 116; *Ditte, Child of Man (Ditte Menneskebarn)*, 39
Henriksen, Morten: *De nøgne træer*, 8; *The Magnetist's Fifth Winter (Magnetisørens femte vinter)*, 38, 134, 150, 154, 155, 158
Henrikson, Anders, *Dangerous ways (Farliga vägar)*, 58
Heritage, 195, 197, 201, 206, 208. *See also* Culture; History; National culture
Heritage film. *See* Historic film/costume drama genre
Herzog, Werner, 80, 99
Hesselegoldt, Lars, *Katja's Adventure (Falkehjerte)*, 156
Hewitt, Peter, *Bill and Ted's Bogus Journey*, 235
Higson, Andrew, 13; "Re-presenting the National Past," 37; *Waving the Flag*, 23n. 1, 282
Hildebrand, Weyler, *Shanty Town (Söderkåkar)*, 57
Hilden, Jytte, 84
Hilmarsson, Hilmar Örn, 314
Hirschbiegel, Oliver, *Entscheidung (Murderous Decisions)*, 92
Historic film/costume drama genre: and American audience, 35, 37–38, 39–40;

369

INDEX

Historic film/costume drama genre (*continued*)
audience of, 201–2; and Bornedal's *Dina*, 215; and coproductions, 154–56; as culturally specific, 8; Danish, 114–15; Finnish, 181, 188; and Gaup's *Pathfinder*, 273; and Grede's *Hip, Hip, Hurra!*, 200; and Gunnlaugsson, 341; Troell's *Hamsun* as, 2, 5

History: and August, 196; and auteur, 225; Danish, 116; and film, 226; and Gunnlaugsson, 350–53; and Kaurismäki, 290, 297–98. *See also* Culture

Hitchcock, Alfred, 223, 228; *Rope*, 76

Hjort, Mette, 135, 282

Høegh, Peter, *Smilla's Sense of Snow (Frøken Smillas fornemmelse for sne)*, 45, 132

Hoel, Mona J., *Cabin Fever (Når nettene blir lange)*, 100

Höglund, Gunnar, *Obsession (Kungsleden)*, 59

Holden, Stephen, 42, 50

Hollywood: and Danish film, 111, 123, 131, 134–35; and Dogma 95, 74; and European costume drama, 5; and Finnish film, 169, 175; and globalization, 9, 33, 193; and independent films, 41, 42; and Italian neorealism, 78; and market, 5–6; and marketing, 31, 33; as model, 184, 185; and Nordic domestic markets, 7; and Nordic Film and TV Fund, 194; and Norwegian film, 262, 264, 267, 268; post–World War I, 10; and road movies, 291; and western genre, 274–75, 276. *See also* United States

Holmberg, Sten, 200

Holst, Maurus, *Cross My Heart and Hope to Die (Ti kniver i hjertet)*, 312

Holst, Per, 213

Homophily, 210–11

Hopper, Dennis, *Easy Rider*, 268, 280, 294, 295, 298, 320

Horror film, 268

Hudson, Hugh, *Revolution 1776*, 266

Hugo, Victor, 132

Iceland, 1, 14, 162n.15, 311, 317, 326, 328–29

Icelandic film, 307–32. *See also* specific directors

Icelandic Film Corporation (IFC), 317

Icelandic Film Fund, 308, 309, 312, 317

Identity, 65, 169, 293, 296, 297

Illusion, 74, 232, 233

Image: in Allen, 234, 235; and Bergman, 229–30, 231, 232; in French New Wave, 224; in Fridriksson, 321; of Iceland, 322; and Kaurismäki, 290, 293, 295, 296, 300, 302; in road movies, 291, 293; in Truffaut, 227; in Truffaut-Bergman relationship, 227–28, 239

Immigrant film, 55, 56, 59–70. *See also* Migration

Independent film, 40–45

Indridason, Andrés, *The Fishing Trip (Veidiferdin)*, 312

Industry: European film as, 184, 185, 188; Finnish film as, 165, 167, 168, 169, 170, 177, 183, 184, 186, 187, 188, 189

International orientation: and Finnish film, 167, 179; and Gaup's *Pathfinder*, 273–74; and Icelandic film, 314–17; and Norwegian film, 265, 266, 267, 276. *See also* Globalization; Transnationalism

Ipsen, Bodil, 116

Irony, 290, 295, 301

Irvine, Don, 44–45

Isaksen, Eva, *Cellophane (Cellofan)*, 268

Italian neorealism, 78–79, 116

Italo-western, 343, 344, 349

Iversen, Ebbe, 216n.6

Iversen, Gunnar, *Nordic National Cinemas*, 12, 180

Ivory, James: *The Bostonians*, 37; *Maurice*, 37; *The Remains of the Day*, 37; *A Room with a View*, 37

Jacobsen, Johan, 114, 116

Jacobsen, John M., 269

Jargil, Jesper: *De lutrede (The Purified)*, 75, 86; *The Exhibited (De udstillede)*, 89, 92; *The Humiliated (De ydmygede)*, 89

Jarmusch, Jim, 101, 319, 325; *Mystery*

370

INDEX

Train, 303n.10, 312; *Stranger Than Paradise*, 43
Jensen, Anders Thomas, 90, 97; *Blinkende lygter (Flickering Lights)*, 7, 43
Jensen, Knut Erik, *Cool and Crazy (Heftig og begeistret)*, 264
Jensen, Peter Aalbæk, 150, 317
Jensen, Torben Skjødt: *The Man Who Would Live Forever (Manden som ikke ville dø)*, 157
Jessen, Lisbeth, *After "The Celebration,"* 86
Jews, 56–57, 58–59, 61, 238–39
Jóhannesdóttir, Kristín, *Rainbow's End (Á hjara veraldar)*, 314
Jónasson, Óskar, *Remote Control (Sódóma Reykjavík)*, 322
Jonsson, Bo, 316, 317
Jónsson, Thorsteinn, 325; *Atomic Station (Atómstödin)*, 313, 316, 322, 328, 337n. 4; *Dot, Dot, Comma, Dash (Punktur, punktur, komma, strik)*, 316, 337n. 4; *The Sky Palace (Skýjahöllin)*, 316
Jonze, Spike, *Being John Malkovich*, 41
Jorgensen, Geir Hansteen, *The New Country (Det nya landet)*, 62, 279
Josephson, Erland, *Benjamin*, 58
Joyce, James, 76
Juergensmeyer, Mark, 193
Julsrud, Karin, *1732 Bloody Angels (Høtten)*, 268

Kallifatides, Theodor, 60
Kalmar, Are, *Scared to Death (Livredd)*, 268
Kaplan, Caren, *Between Women and Nation*, 13
Karabuda, Barbara, *Black-skull (Svartskallen)*, 60
Karabuda, Günes, 60
Kárason, Einar, 320
Kári, Dagur: *Lost Weekend*, 96–97; *Noi, the Albino*, 212
Kasdan, Lawrence: *The Big Chill*, 100; *Silverado*, 274
Kastoryano, Riva, 212
Kaurismäki, Aki, 187–88, 279; *Ariel*, 279, 287–88, 289, 293–94, 319; *Drifting Clouds (Kauas pilvet karkaavat)*, 283, 286, 297; and Fridriksson, 319; *Juha*, 283; *Leningrad Cowboys* films, 292; *Leningrad Cowboys Go America*, 279, 280–81, 283, 285, 294–97, 298; *Leningrad Cowboys Meet Moses*, 279; *The Man without a Past (Mies vailla menneisyyttä)*, 180, 212, 297, 301; road movies of, 291, 292, 293; *Take Care of Your Scarf, Tatiana (Pidä huivista kiinni, Tatjana)*, 279, 280–81, 283, 285
Kaurismäki, Mika: *The Clan (Klaani—tarina sammakoiden suvusta)*, 279; *Rosso*, 279
Kemp, Július, 325; *Wallpaper (Veggfódur)*, 322, 328
Kempley, Rita, 36
Kerouac, Jack, *On the Road*, 291, 295
Kier, Udo, *Broken Cookies*, 99
Kiønig, Carl Jørgen, *Blessed Are Those Who Thirst (Salige er de som tørster)*, 267
Kirzanc, John, *Tamara*, 92
Kivi, Aleksis, *Seven Brothers (Seitsemän veljestä)*, 292
Kjærulff-Schmidt, Palle, 118
Kleiser, Randal, *Flight of the Navigator*, 266
Kluge, Alexander, 80
Koivusalo, Timo, *The Swan and the Wanderer (Kulkuri ja joutsen)*, 175
Kokkonen, Ere, *A Charming Mass Suicide (Hurmaava joukkoitsemurha)*, 188
Kopple, Barbara, 240
Korch, Morten, 90–91, 114–15, 116
Korine, Harmony: *Gummo*, 48, 99; *Julien Donkey-Boy*, 48, 99
Korkala, Veikko, 181–82
Kormákur, Baltasar: *101 Reykjavik*, 43, 308, 330, 331; *The Sea (Hafid)*, 308, 327–28, 331
Kounellis, Jannis, 81
Kracauer, Siegfried, 84
Kragh-Jacobsen, Søren, 44, 84; *The Boys from St. Petri (Drengene fra Sankt Petri)*, 90; on coproduction, 211; *D day (D dag)*, 92; and Dogma 95, 47; *Emma's Shadow (Skyggen af Emma)*, 37, 90; international success of, 180; *Isfugle (Kingfishers)*, 90; *The Island on Bird Street (Øen i Fuglegaden)*, 153; *Mifune (Mifunes sidste sang)*, 48, 50–51, 85, 90, 91, 103, 136, 211;

INDEX

Kragh-Jacobsen, Søren (*continued*)
  Rubber Tarzan (*Gummi Tarzan*), 90;
  Skagerrak, 153, 196
Kristensen, Hans, *The Twopenny Dance*
  (*Klinkevals*), 134, 157
Kristinsson, Ari, *Flames of Paradise*
  (*Myrkrahöfdinginn*), 316
Krøyer, Peder Severin, 199, 200, 201; *Hip,
  Hip, Hurra!*, 200
Kurosawa, Akira, 354, 355; *Sanjuro*, 345;
  Yojimbo, 341, 344, 345, 346, 347,
  348, 349
Kusturica, Emir, *Underground*, 137
Kvikmyndasjódur Íslands. *See* Icelandic
  Film Fund
Kyösola, Satu, 303n.6

Laderman, David, *Driving Visions*, 292
Lakness, Halldór, *Salka Valka*, 310, 328
Lakoff, George, 207
Lampelam Jarmo, *The River* (*Joki*), 43
Lang, Fritz, 223
Language: and auteur, 234, 240; and Axel,
  206, 310; and Bergman, 229, 233–35;
  and Bornedal's *Dina*, 214–15; in
  Carlsen's *Wolf at the Door*, 204–5; and
  coproduction, 142, 150, 151, 152, 153,
  154–55, 161, 162n.17, 195; and Danish
  film, 132; and Dogma 95, 75; film as
  universal, 223; and Finnish film, 169;
  and Gaup's *Pathfinder*, 267, 273; and
  Global English, 214–15; and globaliza-
  tion, 16, 141; Iversen on, 216n. 6; in
  Kaurismäki, 299–300; and market, 7;
  and marketing, 31, 32, 233–34; and
  national cinema, 10, 282; and Solum's
  Turnaround, 266; in Troell's *Hamsun*, 3,
  5, 23n. 3
Lannoo, Vincent, *Strass*, 100
Lapine, James, *Impromptu*, 37
Larsen, Birger, *The Big Dipper*
  (*Karlsvognen*), 156
Larsen, Peter Gren, *Baby Doom*, 157
Lauritzen, Lau, 114
Law: and Danish film, 111–12, 119–20,
  121, 122, 123–24, 146. *See also*
  Government/state
Laxdala Saga, 351
Laxness, Halldór, 311, 313
Lee, Spike, 49–50; *Bamboozled*, 50

Leigh, Jennifer Jason, *The Anniversary
  Party*, 49
Leigh, Mike, 81, 97, 137, 325
Lejeune, Philippe, 226
Lemmeke, Ole, 155
Lense-Møller, Lise, 150
Leone, Sergio, 348, 355; *For a Few Dollars
  More*, 345, 347; *For a Fistful of Dollars*,
  341, 344, 345, 346, 347, 349; *The
  Good, the Bad, and the Ugly*, 345; *Once
  Upon a Time in the West*, 346–47, 354
Leth, Jørgen: *The Five Obstructions*, (*De fem
  benspænd*), 77; *Life in Denmark* (*Livet i
  Danmark*), 77; *The Perfect Human* (*Det
  pefekte menneske*), 77
Levring, Kristian: *D day* (*D dag*), 92; and
  Dogma 95, 84; *Et skud fra hjertet* (*A
  Shot from the Heart*), 94; *The King Is
  Alive*, 49, 51, 78, 85, 91, 94
Lindblad, Helena, 70
Lindman, Åke, *Gold Fever in Lapland*
  (*Lapin kullan kimallus*), 188
Lindmark, Peter, *9 millimeter*, 61–62
Linklater, Richard, *Slacker*, 41, 52n. 4
Linnankoski, Johannes, *Laulu tulipunais-
  esta kukasta* (*The Song of the Blood-Red
  Flower*), 246, 247
Literary heritage film, 115, 132–33,
  134, 135
Ljungdalh, Jøergen, 192
Loach, Ken, 81
Logger/lumberjack, 243–58, 301
Love story, 293, 294, 310, 321
Lucas, George, *American Graffiti*, 265
Lumière, Auguste and Louis, 83
Lynch, David, 325
Lyytikäinen, Pirjo, 284

Madsen, Kenneth, *A Day in October* (*En
  dag i oktober*), 153
Madsen, Ole Christian: *Edderkoppen* (The
  Spider), 96; *Kira's Reason: A Love Story*
  (*En kærlighedshistorie*), 50, 85, 87, 94,
  96, 136; *Pizza King*, 7, 43, 96
Madsen, Svend Åge, 76
Mainstream film, 112; and Danish film,
  119, 120, 121, 122, 123, 128, 131, 136
Mainstream film theater, 34, 36
Makavejev, Dusan, *Montenegro*, 60–61
Mäkelä, Aleksi, *Wild Ones* (*Häjyt*), 175,

INDEX

180–81
Malmros, Nils, 136; *Barbara*, 38, 42, 134, 154, 155, 158; *The Tree of Knowledge (Kundskabens træ)*, 90, 312
Manalansan, Martin F., *Queer Globalizations*, 13
Manzoni, Piero, *Merda d'artista*, 81
Market: complexity of global, 34; and coproduction, 143, 145, 148–49, 152, 155; and culture, 7; and Danish film, 119, 121, 122, 126, 128, 146; domestic, 6–7; and film culture, 112; and Finnish film, 166, 168, 169, 170, 174, 180, 185, 188, 189; globalized, 1–2; and Hollywood, 5–6; and language, 7; for national cinema, 10; for Norwegian film, 262; of Troell's *Hamsun*, 4; for western genre, 274–75. *See also* Audience
Marketing: and culture, 31, 32; and Danish film, 113, 126; and Finnish film, 172, 181, 182; and Hollywood, 31, 33; of Kaurismäki, 283; and language, 31, 32, 233–34; and national cinema, 282; transnational, 31–32
Marques, José Luis, *Fuckland*, 99–100
Marshall, Garry, *Pretty Woman*, 7
Martini, Rich, *Camera*, 100
Maslin, Janet, 46
Matila and Röhr Productions, 177
Mattsson, Arne, *Salka Valka*, 310
McGuigan, Jim, 169
Media program. *See* European Union
Melodrama, 57, 115, 294
Mendes, Sam, *American Beauty*, 41
Merchant, Ismail: *The Bostonians*, 37; *Maurice*, 37; *The Remains of the Day*, 37; *A Room with a View*, 37
Merchant-Ivory films, 5, 37
Merendino, James, *Amerikana*, 101
Merikanto, Oskar, 247
Merry Film, 117
Merz, Mario, 81
Mesmer, Franz Anton, 155
Metacinema, 295
Migration, 14, 15, 196, 280. *See also* Immigrant film
Miller, George, *Mad Max*, 280
Miller, Toby, *Global Hollywood*, 5–6, 31, 193
Minkoff, Rob, *The Lion King*, 7

Miramax, 36
Moallem, Minoo, *Between Women and Nation*, 13
Modernity, 116, 320, 321, 322, 323, 328
Moland, Hans Petter, *Zero Kelvin (Kjærlighetens kjøtere)*, 38
Molander, Gustaf: *Dear Relatives (Kära släkten)*, 57; *The Invisible Wall (Den osynliga muren)*, 58
Møller, Birgir Thor, 279
Möller, Marianne, 171, 183, 185, 186
Monson, Shaun, *Bad Actors*, 100
Montgomery, Robert, *Lady in the Lake*, 76
Moodysson, Lukas: *Show Me Love (Fucking Åmål)*, 39, 158, 180, 280; *Together (Tillsammans)*, 43, 280
Morality/ethics, 69, 271, 272, 297, 345
Morgan Kane series, 275
MTV3 (Finnish commercial television company), 172
Music: and Dogma 95, 73; and Fridriksson, 313–14; and Icelandic film, 307; in Kaurismäki, 299, 300; and Kormákur, 330; in Pölönen, 250
Mykkänen, Jouni, 177, 188
Myrick, Daniel, *The Blair Witch Project*, 49, 102

Nabokov, Vladimir, 76
Nagase, Masatoshi, 323, 324
Næss, Petter, *Elling*, 7, 264
National categorization, 1–23
National cinema, 9–11, 13, 15–16, 141, 187–88, 191, 281–86
National culture: and auteur, 221–22; and coproductions, 202, 210; and Danish film, 112, 115, 116, 118, 120, 121, 131; and European film culture, 128; and Finnish film, 166, 167, 168, 169, 281–82, 297, 300, 302; and Fridriksson, 318, 324–25, 332; and Gaup's *Pathfinder*, 274; and government funding, 31; homogeneity of, 13–14; and Icelandic film, 311, 313–14, 319, 322, 324–25, 332; and Kaurismäki, 285, 286, 288, 292, 293, 294, 297–98, 300–301, 302; and Norwegian film, 276–77; and Troell's *Hamsun*, 3
National Film Board, 119
Nationalism, 208, 282, 285

Nationality, 143, 214
Nazism, 3–4, 58, 61. *See also* Germany
Neal, Steve, "Westerns and Gangster Films since the 1970s," 275
Neorealism, 84
Newell, Mike, *Enchanted April*, 37
New German cinema, 295
New Wave, 76
Nexø, Martin Andersen, 143, 196
Nielsen, Asta, 10
Nielsen, Elsebeth Gerner, 145
Nielsen, Jesper W., *Okay*, 97, 103
Niemi, Raimo, *Tommy and the Wildcat (Poika ja ilves)*, 175, 180
Nimbus Film, 84, 97, 99
Niskanen, Mikko, *Eight Fatal Shots (Kahdeksan surmanluotia)*, 249
Njál's Saga, 346, 347, 351
Nolan, Christopher, 267; *Memento*, 43
Nørby, Ghita, 3, 4–5, 154, 204–5
Nordic Council, 147, 194, 212
Nordic film, 31–52, 34, 43–44, 114
Nordic Film and TV Fund, 131, 142, 146, 147, 160, 163n.20, 192, 193–94, 196, 197, 198, 211, 315
Nordic Film Award, 212
Nordic film institutes, 147, 194
Nordisk Film, 3, 10, 213
Nordisk Film Kompagni, 142
Norén, Lars, 87
Norway: Audiovisual Production Fund, 263; and Bornedal's *Dina*, 213, 214, 215; and coproductions, 151, 211; domestic cinema of, 6; economy of, 14–15, 265; and globalized market, 1; and Hamsun, 4; New Norwegian Film Policy, 263, 276; race/ethnicity in, 15; State Production Committee, 265–66; in Troell's *Hamsun*, 2
Norwegian film, 261–77. *See also specific directors*
Norwegian Film, Ltd., 263
Norwegian Film Fund, 263
Norwegian Film Institute Production Support, 263
Norwegian Ministry for Cultural Affairs, 263
Nutley, Colin, *Under the Sun (Under solen)*, 8
Nykvist, Sven, 230, 231–32, 236, 239, 310

Oberhausen Manifesto, 80
October Films, 46
Oddsson, Hilmar, *Tears of Stone (Tár úr steini)*, 324
O'Fredericks, Alice, 114; *Father of Four (Far til fire)*, 116; *The Red Horses (De røode heste)*, 116
Øie, Pål, *Wilderness (Villmark)*, 261, 276
Olesen, Annette K.: *Forbrydelser (In Your Hands)*, 96; *Minor Mishaps (Små ulykker)*, 97, 103
Olgeirsson, Einar, 351
Olsen, Lasse Spang, *In China They Eat Dogs (I Kina spiser de hunde)*, 43
Olsson, Stellan, *The Great Day on the Beach (Den store badedag)*, 157
O'Neill, Eugene, 87
Oplev, Niels Arden, *Portland*, 42, 44
Orion Classics, 36
Oskarsdóttir, Valdís, *D dag—den færdige film (D Day—Completed Film)*, 93
Osten, Suzanne: *Just You and Me (Bara du och jag)*, 61; *Speak! It's So Dark (Tala! det är så mörkt)*, 61
Østgård-Lund, Harald, *Halfway to Haugesund (Halveis till Haugesund)*, 280
Ottarsdóttir, Katrin, *Bye-Bye Bluebird*, 43, 156, 279
OuLiPo, 76

Päätalo, Kalle, 249
Pakkala, Teuvo, *Tukkijoella (On the Logging River)*, 246–47
Palladium, 114, 117
Palsbo, Ole, 114, 116
Pálsdóttir, Kristín B., 337n. 4
Pantii, Mervi, 283–84; "Kansallinen elokuva pelastettava," 284
Parikka, Pekka, *The Winter War (Talvisota)*, 180
Parker, Andrew, *Nationalisms and Sexualities*, 13
Parody, 235, 247–48, 249–51, 257
Parsa, Reza: *The Limit (Gränsen)*, 70; *Before the Storm (Före stormen)*, 55, 68–69, 70
Pasanen, Spede, 182
Pascali, Pino, 81
Passer, Dirch, 115
Payne, Alexander, *Election*, 41

INDEX

Peltonen, Matti, 297, 301
Penn, Arthur, *Bonnie and Clyde*, 295
Perec, Georges, *La disparition (A Void)*, 76
Peter Rommel Productions, 317
Pilsnerfilm, 56
Pink, Sydney, *Reptilicus*, 161n.1
Pinzás, Juan: *Días de voda*, 100; *Once upon another Time (Era outra vez)*, 100
Pistoletto, Michelangelo, 81
Polanski, Roman, 101
Politics: and coproduction, 144–48; and Finnish film, 166, 167, 171. *See also* Government/state
Politique des auteurs, 222–24
Pollack, Sidney, *Out of Africa*, 7, 24n. 9
Pölönen, Markku: *Badding*, 181; *Land of Happiness (Onnen maa)*, 243; *A Summer by the River (Kuningasjätkä)*, 188, 243–44, 245, 247, 249–58
Pooelvoorde, Benoit, *Man Bites Dog (C'est arrivé près de chez vous)*, 102
Poppe, Erik, *Schpaa*, 267
Popular culture. *See* Culture
Pornography, 93, 117, 161n. 1
Possible Films, 317
Postmodernism, 281, 292, 325
Poststructuralism, 292
Powers, Ed, 83
Pöysä, Jyrki, 245
Pred, Allan, 15
Prédal, René, 284
Prison film, 294
Producer: and coproduction, 197, 198, 199, 211, 212; and Danish film, 132; of Finnish film, 185–86, 188. *See also* Filmmaking
Production: of coproductions, 216n. 1; and Danish film, 113, 114, 120, 122, 125, 126; and digital filmmaking, 46–49; and Dogma 95, 85, 103; of European film, 184; and Finnish film, 166, 167, 169, 172, 175, 180, 181, 182; and Icelandic film, 309, 312, 315–17; and national cinema, 282; and Nordic Film and TV Fund, 194, 197; and Norwegian film, 262–64, 265, 267; transnational, 2; of Troell's *Hamsun*, 3, 4. *See also* Coproduction; Filmmaking
Production companies, 121, 175, 176–77, 177, 182–83, 185
Profit: of August's *Pelle the Conqueror*, 36; of Axel's *Babette's Feast*, 36; from Norwegian film, 263, 264, 265. *See also* Budget; Cost; Funding/finance
Propp, Vladimir, 354–55
Psychoanalysis, 292

Queneau, Raymond, *Exercices de style (Exercises in Style)*, 76
Quest narrative, 291, 293
Qvist, Per Olov, *Guide to the Cinema of Sweden and Finland*, 12

Race/ethnicity, 14, 15, 55–70
Realism, 84, 115, 116, 132, 133–34, 243, 276, 320. *See also* Social realism
Reality, 82, 83, 87, 230, 231. *See also* Truth
Reception, 22, 221, 222, 240. *See also* Audience
Redvall, Eva Novrup, 194
Refn, Nicolas Winding, 52n. 6, 137; *Bleeder*, 43, 136; *Fear X*, 136, 153, 196; *Pusher*, 43, 102, 136
Reitz, Edgar, 80
Rengel, Martin, *Joy Ride*, 100
Renoir, Jean, 223
Resn, Anders, *Black Harvest (Sort høst)*, 134
Resnais, Alain, 76
Reunala, Aarne, 244
Reykjavik, 309, 310, 312–13, 320, 322, 328, 329, 330, 331
Rillumarei films, 247
Ringgaard, Peter, *A Scent of Paradise (Et hjørne af paradis)*, 153
Risan, Leidulv, *Etter Rubicon (Rubicon)*, 266
Rivette, Jacques, 79
Road movie: and Fridriksson, 319, 320, 321, 324, 325, 331; and Kaurismäki, 279–81, 286, 288, 289, 291–94, 295, 299, 300
Robsahm, Thomas, *The Greatest Thing (Det Største i verden)*, 8
Rohmer, Eric, 79, 223
Romney, Jonathan, 285, 290
Rønnow-Klarlund, Anders, *The Eighteens (Den attende)*, 44
Rósinkranz, Gudlaugur, 310
Rossellini, Roberto, 223, 228

Rostrup, Kaspar, *Waltzing Regitze (Dansen med regitze)*, 37
Roussel, Raymond, 76
Rukov, Mogens, 90, 96
Russell, David O., *Three Kings*, 41
Russian film, 78
Russo, Mary, *Nationalisms and Sexualities*, 13

Saarela, Olli: *Ambush (Rukajärven tie)*, 8, 175, 180, 188; *Bad Luck Love*, 43
Saga, 115, 117, 342, 344–46, 348, 353, 354, 355n. 1
Sahindal, Fadime, 68
Salles, Walter, *Central Station (Central do Brasil)*, 280
Sami, 57–58, 270–71, 275
Samurai film, 343, 344, 347, 348
Sànchez, Eduardo, *The Blair Witch Project*, 49, 102
Sandemose, Aksel, 143
Sandgren, Åke, 211–12; *Beyond (Dykkerne)*, 95; *Johannes' Hemmelighed (Johannes's Secret)*, 95; *The Miracle in Valby (Miraklet i Valby)*, 95; *The Slingshot (Kådisbellan)*, 61; *Truly Human (Et rigtigt menneske)*, 51, 85, 94, 95–96, 136, 212
Sandrew Metronome, 176
Sarris, Andrew, 222
Scherfig, Lone: *Italian for Beginners (Italiensk for begyndere)*, 50, 85, 87, 94–95, 98, 103, 128, 136; *Morten Korch*, 94; *On Our Own (Når mor kommer hjem)*, 157; *Wilbur Wants to Kill Himself (Wilbur begår selvemord)*, 132, 153, 196
Schlesinger, Philip, 191
Schlöndorff, Volker, *Voyager*, 94
Schmidt, Arno, 76
Schmidt, Rick, *Chetzemoka Curse*, 100
Schrøder, Peter: *Just a Girl (Kun en pige)*, 134; *Lost Spring (Det Forsømte forår)*, 134
Schumacher, Joel, *Tigerland*, 102
Scola, Ettore, *Ugly, Dirty and Mean (Brutti, sporchi e cattivi)*, 327
Scorsese, Martin: *The Age of Innocence*, 37; *Mean Streets*, 7, 43
Scott, Ridley, *Thelma and Louise*, 280

Self, 227, 228, 229–30, 239, 296, 297. *See also* Subjectivity
Setting: and coproductions, 151; and Dogma 95, 83, 102; in Fridriksson, 321–22; and Kaurismäki, 296, 301; and nation-based categorization, 1. *See also* Filmmaking
Sexuality: in Bergman, 230–31; and Finnish film, 247; in Pölönen, 251, 256; in Swedish film, 63–64, 64; in Taslimi, 67; in Truffaut, 228. *See also* Gender; Women
Sicas, Vittorio de: *The Bicycle Thief (Ladri di biciclette)*, 79; *Umberto D*, 79
Sigurdsson, Jóhann, 309
Sigur Rós, 313–14
Silent film, 10, 34, 115, 142
Sjöström, Victor, *The Outlaw and His Wife (Berg-Ejvind och hans hustru)*, 309
Skagen artists, 199–200, 201
Skjoldbjærg, Erik, 8; *Insomnia*, 8, 43, 267
Skou-Hansen, Tage, 8
Sletaune, Pål, *Junk Mail (Budbringeren)*, 158, 267
Smith, Kevin, *Clerks*, 41, 52n. 4, 102
Snellman, Hanna, 244, 245
Social realism, 265, 266, 273, 276, 310, 312. *See also* Realism
Society: and August, 133; Danish, 116; and Dogma 95, 88; Finnish, 244–46, 247, 297; and Fridriksson, 320, 321, 326–27; in Hollywood western vs. saga, 349; Icelandic, 320, 326–27, 329–31; in Kaurismäki, 294, 295, 299; in Kormákur, 328; in road movies, 291, 292; Sorlin on, 325–26, 327; Swedish, 55–56, 59, 63, 68, 70, 280; in von Trier, 88, 89. *See also* Culture
Soderbergh, Steven: *Full Frontal*, 102; *sex, lies, and videotape*, 40
Softley, Iain, *The Wings of the Dove*, 37
Soila, Tytti, 247; *Nordic National Cinemas*, 12, 180
Soinio, Olli, 172
Solar Films, 177
Solum, Ola: *Orion's Belt (Orions belte)*, 265–66, 267, 274; *Turnaround*, 266
Sommer, Doris, *Nationalisms and Sexualities*, 13
Sommerfeldt, Gunnar, *The Story of the Borg*

376

INDEX

Family (Borgslægtens historie), 329
Sorenson, Michael, *Converging with Angels*, 100
Sorlin, Pierre, 325–26, 327
Soysal, Yasemin, 212
Spanish film, 128
Spielberg, Stephen, 101
Staho, Simon, *Wildside (Vildspor)*, 156
Stanilavsky, Constantin, 81
Star, 114, 118, 123, 212
Stark, Jim, 23n. 6, 323, 324
Steene, Brigitta, "The Transpositions of a Filmmaker," 221, 222, 240
Stevens, George, *Shane*, 349, 350
Stöd 2 (Icelandic television), 315
Stone, Oliver, *Natural Born Killers*, 294
Stravinsky, Igor, 76
Strindberg, August, 87
Studio system, 8, 9, 10, 41, 114, 168
Sturlasson, Snorri, *Heimskringla*, 351, 352
Sturlunga Sagas, 351
Subjectivity, 230, 232, 293, 294, 296–97. *See also* Self
Sundance Film Festival, 40
Sundvall, Kjell, *Jägerna (The Hunters)*, 7
Suomen Elokuvateollisuus, 176
Suomi-Filmi, 176
Survivor (television series), 84
Sutherland, Donald, 143, 204
Svendsen, Lotte, 137; *Gone with the Fish (Bornholms stemme)*, 157
Svensk Filmindustri, 10, 177
Sweden, 148, 244, 246; and August, 196; and Bornedal's *Dina*, 214, 215; and coproductions, 150, 151, 154, 160, 211; culture of, 8, 59, 63, 64, 68, 70; domestic cinema of, 6; economy of, 14; and Finnish film, 177; and globalized market, 1; immigrant film in, 55, 56, 59–70; international success of, 180; migration to, 15; population of, 56; race/ethnicity in, 15; society in, 55–56, 59, 63, 68, 70, 280
Swedish film, 55–70. *See also specific directors*
Swedish Film Institute, 316
Sydow, Max von, 143, 154

Tarantino, Quentin, *Pulp Fiction*, 42
Tarkovsky, Andrei, 226

Taslimi, Susan, *All Hell Let Loose (Hus i helvete)*, 55, 67–68, 70
Tax, 114, 119, 169, 265, 266, 267. *See also* Government/state
Taylor, Charles, 205, 297; *Ethics of Authenticity*, 296; *Sources of the Self*, 296
Television, 62, 92, 97, 117, 118, 124, 125, 147, 168, 172, 211, 283
Thomas, Anders, *The King Is Alive*, 94
Thomas, Kevin, 4
Thompson, Kristin, 294
Thórleifsdóttir, Thórnhildur, 337n. 4
Thorodssen, Ásdís, *Ingaló*, 328
Thorsteinsson, Indridi G., 312; *The Girl Gogo (79 af stödinni)*, 310
Thriller genre, 115, 158, 266–67, 268, 312
Tilden, Leif, *Reunion*, 100
Time, 224, 226, 227, 228, 237, 238
Toiviainen, Sakari, 301, 303n.6; *Levottomat sukupolvet*, 284
Tornatore, Giuseppe, *Cinema Paradiso (Nuovo cinema paradiso)*, 312
Toronto International Film Festival, 44–45
Toubiana, Serge, 222–23
Transnationalism, 1–23, 31–32, 191, 192–93, 195, 209, 212. *See also* Globalization; International orientation
Triepcke, Marie, 200
Troell, Jan: *Hamsun*, 2–3, 4–5, 6, 9, 23n. 3, 38, 42, 44, 154–55, 158; *As White as in Snow (Så vit som en snö)*, 38
Truffaut, François: "A Certain Tendency in French Cinema," 79; as actor, 240; and auteur, 222–23, 225, 228–29, 230; and Bergman, 227–28, 239; *The 400 Blows (Les quatre cents coups)*, 88, 225, 226–28; *Day for Night (La nuit américaine)*, 228, 240; and international cinema, 223; *Jules and Jim (Jules et Jim)*, 88; *Les mistons*, 88
Truth, 74, 82, 83, 84, 87, 224. *See also* Reality
Tuhus, Oddvar Bull: *Blücher*, 266; *Fifty-Fifty*, 265; *Hockeyfeber (Hockeyfever)*, 265
Turan, Kenneth, 43, 46
Turk, John, 47
Turunen, Heikki, *The Last Wedding (Kivenpyörittäjän)*, 243
TV2 (Danish television), 124, 125

INDEX

UIP, 176
Ullmann, Liv, 229, 230–31; *Kristin Lavransdatter*, 38; *Sophie (Sofie)*, 38, 156–57
United States: and coproduction, 144–45; culture of, 33, 323; and Danish film, 116, 126; distribution in, 31–52; and Finnish film, 166, 174; and Gaup's *Pathfinder*, 269, 272, 273; and globalization, 9; and independent film, 40–45; as model, 184, 185; in Pölönen, 250–51; studio system of, 114. *See also* Hollywood

Van Sant, Gus, 101; *Drugstore Cowboy*, 42
Vertov, Dziga, 83; *Kino-Pravda*, 78; *The Man with the Movie Camera (Tjelovek s kinoaparatom)*, 78
Vestergaard, Jørgen, 158
Viking film, 310–11, 312
Viking Film Ab, 316, 317
Vilhunen, Jukka, 182, 183, 184
Villealfa Film Productions, 177
Vinterberg, Thomas: *The Celebration (Festen)*, 46–47, 48, 49, 50, 85, 86, 87, 90, 93, 96, 102, 135–36, 159, 327; and Danish film, 123; *D day (D dag)*, 91; *De største helte (The Greatest Heroes)*, 86; and Dogma 95, 75, 84, 88; *Drengen der gik baglæens (The Boy Who Walked Bachwards)*, 86; *The Greatest Heroes (De største helte)*, 156, 280; international success of, 180; *It's All about Love*, 132, 153, 196; *Koplevs Krydsfelt*, 86; *Sidste ongang (Last Round)*, 86
Visconti, Luchino, *Rocco and His Brothers (Rocco e i suoi fratelli)*, 327
Von Bagh, Peter, 284, 292, 302n. 4
Von Sydow, Max, 3, 239
Von Trier, Lars: and August, 133–34; and coproduction, 148, 150, 152, 153, 159, 162n. 12, 317; as cross-over director, 8; and Danish film, 121, 123; and Dogma 95, 45, 73, 83, 84, 87–88; and financing, 282; international success of, 180; and Kaurismäki, 302n. 3; and Korch novels, 116; on Kragh-Jacobsen, 90; and transnational film, 23n. 6; WORKS: *Breaking the Waves*, 9, 45–46, 77, 78, 89, 97, 99, 103, 111, 132, 148–49, 152, 317; *Dancer in the Dark*, 49, 89, 99, 132, 152; *D day (D dag)*, 91–92, 93; *Dimension*, 77, 99; *Dogumentary*, 84; *Dogville*, 99, 196; *Epidemic*, 75, 77, 89, 132; *Europa (Zentropa)*, 45, 89, 99, 132, 152, 162n.9; *Livet i Danmark (Life in Denmark)*, 77; *Morten Korch*, 91; "Preliminary Instructions to the Kinoglaz Circle," 78; *The Element of Crime (Forbrydelsens element)*, 45, 89, 121, 132; *The Five Obstructions, (De fem benspænd)*, 77; *The Idiots (Idioterne)*, 48, 50, 82, 83, 85, 87, 88–89, 90, 94, 102, 136, 159, 162n.12; *The Kingdom (Riget)*, 75, 77, 103, 148, 157; *The Purified*, 77, 89; *Verdensuret* (The World Clock), 77, 89, 92
Vørsel, Niels, 76

Wachowski, Andy, *The Matrix Reloaded*, 24n. 8
Wachowski, Larry, *The Matrix Reloaded*, 24n. 8
Waldau, Nicolaj Coster, 158
Warhol, Andy, 101
Wassmo, Herbørg, 134, 215; *Dina's Book*, 196, 213
Watzlawick, Paul, *Pragmatics of Human Communication*, 207
Weinstein, Bob, 40
Weinstein, Harvey, 40
Welfare state, 11, 14, 118, 169, 170, 184, 297. *See also* Economy; Government/state
Wellman, William A., *The Ox-Bow Incident*, 350
Wenders, Wim, 80, 101, 312, 319; *Kings of the Road (Im Lauf der Zeit)*, 295; *Paris, Texas*, 296, 303n. 10; *Wings of Desire (Der Himmel Über Berlin)*, 320
Western genre, 267, 269, 273, 274–76, 341, 343, 344, 349, 350
West Germany, 80
Widding, Astrid Söderbergh, *Nordic National Cinemas*, 12, 180
Widerberg, Bo, *All Things Fair (Lærerinden)*, 154
Wied, Gustav, 134
Willis, Gordon, 236
Willis, Sharon, *Camera Obscura*, 13

Wincer, Simon, *Lonesome Dove,* 274–75
Windeløv, Vibeke, 150
Wiseman, Frederick, 83
Women, 65–66, 67–68, 89, 253, 254, 255. *See also* Gender; Sexuality
Wyler, William, *The Westerner,* 349

Yaeger, Patricia, *Nationalisms and Sexualities,* 13
YLE (Finnish public service broadcasting company), 172

Zavattinis, Cesare, "Some Ideas on the Cinema," 79
Zdravkovic, Vladan, *Babylon,* 101
Zentropa, 94, 97, 150, 162n. 9, 317
Zhang Yimou, *Hero,* 40
Zinnemann, Fred, *High Noon,* 350
Zwart, Harald, 8; *Agent Cody Banks,* 9; *One Night at McCools,* 9

www.ingramcontent.com/pod-product-compliance
Lightning Source LLC
Chambersburg PA
CBHW070258240426
43661CB00057B/2585